W9-BCB-479

Gastro Obscura

A FOOD ADVENTURER'S GUIDE

★ ★ ★ ★

CECILY WONG • DYLAN THURAS

with additional writing by Rachel Rummel, Anne Ewbank, and Sam O'Brien

WORKMAN PUBLISHING • NEW YORK

An Important Note to Readers

Not everything in *Gastro Obscura* should be eaten. Some of the foods in this
book are a wonder to learn about, but do harm to partake in.
As for the rest, we encourage you to try them.

....

Copyright © 2021 by Atlas Obscura, Inc.
Cover collage © 2021 by Martin O'Neill

Library of Congress Cataloging-in-Publication Data is available.

ISBN: 978-1-5235-0219-6

Art direction and design by Janet Vicario
Illustrations by Alan Berry Rhys
Photo research by Sophia Rieth and Aaron Clendening
Photo credits listed on page 414

Workman books are available at special discounts when purchased in bulk for
premiums and sales promotions as well as for fundraising or educational use.
Special editions or book excerpts also can be created to specification.
For details, contact the Special Sales Director at specialmarkets@workman.com.

Workman Publishing Co., Inc.
225 Varick Street
New York, NY 10014-4381
workman.com

Printed in South Korea
First printing September 2021

10 9 8 7 6 5 4 3 2 1

CONTENTS

INTRODUCTION

Eating may be the most immersive, visceral travel experience. It requires an engagement of every sense, from the sound of dishes clattering in an alleyway kitchen, to the smell of garlic hitting hot oil, to the joy of seeing a plate of food before you as you sit, utensil in hand, about to taste. Humans around the world are bound by the necessity and pleasure of eating, and there is no faster way to glimpse the heart of a place than by experiencing its food.

A guiding mantra at Atlas Obscura is that wonder can be found around every corner—not just in uncharted and far-flung locales but down the street, down some stairs, into the Victorian-era public toilet that now houses a London coffee bar. While travel is a beautiful way of seeking wonder, you'll find within these pages that adventures don't always require a plane ticket. From the award-winning smokehouse in an Arkansas living room, to the Thai food stalls in a California parking lot, to the Mexican auto body shop that transforms into a taqueria every night—wondrous food is everywhere.

Gastro Obscura is a book that scratches the surface of a mind-bending world of eating. We love tasty food, but we aim to be explorers rather than gourmands. Seekers rather than epicureans. This book is more than a menu of foods worth tasting—it's a collection of forgotten histories and endangered traditions, obscure experiences, culinary ingenuity, and edible wonders. It's a noisy, delicious, action-packed feast that spans seven continents, and over 120 countries and, as often as possible, tells you exactly where and how to experience things for yourself.

Most of the entries in this book came from the Atlas Obscura community—over half a million incredible users who share tips with us every day—and our remarkable team of editors who scour the earth to find even more wonders. What you hold in your hands is a massive, collaborative effort made possible by every person who pointed us to a surprising restaurant, a charming fruit, or a Canadian hockey arena above the Arctic Circle that locals have turned into a thriving greenhouse.

We have always believed that wonder can be found wherever you are open to searching for it. Well, here it is, sitting right in front of you, waiting to be eaten. Dig in.

Cecily Wong and Dylan Thuras

Every morning, dabbawalas throughout Mumbai transport homemade lunches to office workers, using codes on the packages to indicate their destination.

Europe

GREAT BRITAIN AND IRELAND
WESTERN EUROPE • EASTERN EUROPE
SCANDINAVIA

GREAT BRITAIN AND IRELAND

FRIDAY NIGHT PUDDING FEAST

THE PUDDING CLUB AT THE THREE WAYS HOUSE HOTEL • ENGLAND

How to try it

Interested parties must call the hotel and book in advance. After gorging on pudding, you can sleep in one of the hotel's seven dessert-themed rooms.

From the outside, the Three Ways House Hotel is a typical 19th-century British bed-and-breakfast, made out of golden stone and engulfed in ivy. On Friday nights, however, the hotel plays host to the Pudding Club—an institution with a self-proclaimed mission of preserving the "great British pudding."

Since 1985, dozens of dessert-lovers from around the world have gathered weekly to gorge on a banquet of British puddings, presented with pomp by the hotel's resident Pudding Master—the mastermind who curates the menu. Traditionally, British pudding is a cake-like dish made with suet, or hardened animal fat, that's steamed for hours and can be sweet or savory. But the word can also apply to desserts in general, and at the Pudding Club, the Friday feast includes traditional puddings like jam roly-poly, spotted dick, and sticky toffee pudding, as well as non-steamed puddings like rice pudding, sliced-bread-and-fruit summer pudding, apple crumble, passion fruit roulade, and syrup sponge cake.

The seven-course pudding extravaganza is a feat of endurance, and those who make it through the evening are awarded a certificate. According to Pudding Master Lucy Williams, the club is not just about indulgence, but celebrating dishes that have fallen out of modern favor.

The Three Ways House Hotel was originally a doctor's house.

BRAWNY LIQUID BEEF

BOVRIL • ENGLAND

How to try it

Beloved Bovril is widely available in British supermarkets. If you're interested in how the beef extract has been marketed over the decades, visit the Museum of Brands in Notting Hill, London. It has a bunch of old Bovril posters and vintage-style merchandise.

In 1870, as Napoleon III led his troops into the Franco-Prussian War, he ordered one million cans of beef to feed his men. The request went to a Scottish butcher living in Canada named John Lawson Johnston, who tweaked a recipe for meat glaze to make "beef fluid," a thick, glossy paste that tastes exactly as you might guess: very salty and very beefy. The result was Bovril, England's iconic concentrated beef paste.

Bovril was touted as a constitution-boosting, meaty superfood that could be spread on buttered toast or diluted and drunk as a restorative tea. Marketing claims (some endorsed by real scientists) declared the paste could make the infirm well, the elderly strong, and the young healthy. One advertisement even claimed that "Bovril fortifies the system against influenza."

Victorians loved the beef-in-a-jar. From breakfast tables to hospitals to football stadiums, a hot thermos of Bovril tea became the preferred way to warm up and gain strength. The foodstuff was considered patriotic—it fed British soldiers during the Boer War—and it was celebrity approved.

Ernest Shackleton ate Bovril during his 1902 Antarctic expedition. Famous Victorian strongman Eugen Sandow claimed Bovril gave him strength. Even Pope Leo XIII was depicted in a Bovril ad (albeit without his permission) drinking a mug of beef broth above the slogan: "Two Infallible Powers: The Pope and Bovril."

Fluid beef made Johnston a very wealthy man. In 1896, he sold Bovril for £2 million and died four years later, in Cannes, on a yacht.

Early 20th-century ads for England's favorite liquid-beef-in-a-can.

A KINGLY LIQUOR TO DRINK WHILE DRIVING

THE KING'S GINGER • ENGLAND

King Edward VII was 62 when he took the throne from his mother, Queen Victoria, in 1901. Elderly and overweight, he still partied hard. His joyrides around the English countryside in his topless Daimler exposed him to the very British elements (chilly and damp) and concerned the royal physician.

In 1903, the doctor commissioned an established London merchant, Berry Bros., to formulate a warming, fortifying beverage to put in the aging monarch's driving flask. The result was The King's Ginger, a brandy-based elixir with ginger, honey, and lemon, designed specifically "to stimulate and revivify His Majesty during morning rides."

The king loved his new zesty liqueur. Not only did he drink it in his "horseless carriage," he brought it along while hunting and generously passed around the bottle. By the time Edward died in 1910, the royal family was hooked. Berry Bros. continued to make and sell The King's Ginger exclusively to nobility, who purchased hundreds of cases of it every year in unlabeled bottles.

In recent years, a bartender asked the maker, now Berry Bros. & Rudd, for a standardized version of the elusive drink, and the company enlisted a Dutch distiller to make the beverage for the masses. A modern version debuted in 2011, using a base of neutral grain spirits instead of brandy, along with ginger, lemon oil, Glenrothes single malt scotch, and sugar. At 82 proof, it takes just a few sips to get your engine revving.

How to try it
Find The King's Ginger (for the masses) online and at retailers across the UK, USA, Australia, and New Zealand.

NOTTINGHAM'S SUBTERRANEAN DRINKING DEN

THE LOST CAVES • ENGLAND

How to try it

The access to the Lost Caves is somewhere in the vicinity of the Mecure Hotel and the Lost Property Bar. Dress warmly. Any more information would spoil the fun.

Damp, dimly lit, and decorated with skulls, chandeliers, and stuffed animals, this secret drinking establishment is part of the extensive cave system that's cut into the soft sandstone below the city of Nottingham.

Accessed via a dark and uninviting alley, through a heavily disguised door with a brass skull handle, you'll find a staircase to the basement beneath a 200-year-old building. In this basement, a further series of rock-cut steps leads into the cavernous void beneath the city. The final descent into the Lost Caves is by escort, as there is a strict maximum occupancy. Inside, 26 feet (8 m) below the venerable George Hotel (now the Mecure), which has accommodated guests as diverse as Charles Dickens and Elizabeth Taylor, is a most unlikely cocktail palace.

When, why, and by whom these deep grottoes were excavated is unknown; however, they appear to have been adapted for the purpose of storing and brewing ale on rock-cut ledges. Today, instead of barrels of beer, the cushion-padded rock ledges are used as seating for the bar's subterranean drinkers.

Beneath the streets of Hockley is one of Nottingham's best-kept secrets.

OUTLAWED ICE-CREAM WARE

PENNY LICK • ENGLAND

How to try it

Penny licks are a rare collectible these days. Wash well before using.

Penny licks were England's most nefarious ice-cream paraphernalia. As the name suggests, a few licks of ice cream cost just a penny. Included in that price was the sizable risk of contracting tuberculosis.

In the mid-1800s, ice cream had become a beloved and affordable treat, sold all over the streets of England. Ice-cream vendors called Jacks served tiny scoops in glass cups called penny licks, which came in three sizes: the standard and most popular penny lick, the wee ha'penny (halfpenny) lick, and the larger tu'penny (two penny) lick.

These small glasses were designed especially for ice cream—or more specifically, for an ice-cream optical illusion. As Jacks paddled the dessert into the cup, the conical shape and thick glass magnified its contents so that even the tiniest serving appeared bountiful.

After finishing their ice cream, customers licked their glasses clean and handed them back to the Jack, who would serve the next customers from the unwashed cups.

When tuberculosis swept the nation, the medical establishment pointed to the penny licks. An 1879 English medical report blamed a cholera outbreak on the reuse of glassware, and fear of tuberculosis led the city of London to ban penny licks in 1899. Some vendors continued to use the illicit ice-cream cups through the 1920s and 1930s, until a breakthrough in ice-cream technology eradicated the need for their glassware for good. The mighty waffle cone emerged as the new single-use vessel of choice, knocking out the penny lick with its portability, edibility, and complete absence of infectious disease.

"THE NOTED EEL-AND-PIE HOUSES"

M. MANZE • ENGLAND

The M. Manze Eel and Pie House at 87 Tower Bridge Road is the oldest eel-and-pie shop still standing in London. Open three or four hours a day, Manze's serves only lunch, and their lunch menu consists of just two things: eels and pies.

Throughout the 1700s, eels were so plentiful in the River Thames that a net cast at any spot would pull up a hearty catch of cheap protein. Working-class East Londoners, or Cockneys, grew to love them, and eels became the go-to meal for the city's workhands. Capitalizing on the eel craze, pie shops (which generally trafficked in mutton and potatoes) started serving them up how their clients liked them: naturally jellied.

How to try it

M. Manze has three locations in London—the Tower Bridge location is the oldest. The second oldest, on Peckman High Street, was built in 1927.

Thanks to a huge amount of collagen, eels are gelatinous by nature. With skin and bones intact, round chunks of eel are boiled in water flavored with vinegar, bay leaves, peppercorns, and onion, then left to cool in the liquid, which gently congeals into a translucent jelly. These quivering hunks of cold, tender meat are considered Britain's first fast-food takeaway, commonly scooped into cups, doused with hot chili vinegar, and eaten on the go.

By the end of World War II, London boasted more than 100 eel-and-pie shops—but as the Thames grew polluted, supply decreased and the city's interest in eel eating waned.

At Manze's, eels are still king. They can be ordered cold and jellied or hot and stewed, or served with mash and slathered in "liquor"—an alcohol-free parsley sauce that also goes on pies. The small, no-frills shop is operated by the grandson of the original owner, Michele Manze, who came to London in 1878 from the Italian village of Ravello. The decor, with its green-and-white tiles and long communal tables, hearkens back to Victorian days, when eels reigned supreme.

A server at Manze's adds parsley sauce to a plate of mash and pie.

TABLE ETIQUETTE IN THE *Victorian Age*

Nineteenth-century England was rife with highly specialized eating utensils, serving devices, and table decor—especially extravagant in well-to-do homes. Designed in the spirit of gentility over essential function, Victorian kitchen gadgetry served a higher purpose, which was impressing dinner guests, brandishing status, and proving just how fabulous a fussy table could be.

ICE-CREAM FORKS

The first recorded owner of a table fork was an 11th-century Byzantine princess who died of plague. Some said this was an apt punishment for using a fork, which looked suspiciously like the devil's pitchfork. The Victorians had no such concerns, and forks were used with abandon. A spoon could be used when eating a bowl of ice cream but the ice-cream fork—a shallow, three-tined protospork—was used exclusively for eating ice cream served on a plate.

MUSTACHE CUPS

Impressively shaped mustaches of the era looked stately and dignified until confronted with a hot cup of tea. The heat melted the mustache wax, causing the corners to droop.

In the 1870s, British potter Harvey Adams invented the mustache cup, featuring a patented, wing-shaped ledge that created a handy barrier between facial hair and tea.

The cups came in many shapes and sizes, from the large pint-size "farmers' cups" to small porcelain pieces sculpted like conch shells or embossed with the name of the owner.

CELERY VASES

Wild celery, native to the Mediterranean, wasn't cultivated in England until the early 1800s, and it didn't grow easily. Those who succeeded in obtaining some celery needed a way to flaunt it. Glass-blown celery vases—featuring embellishments like fluted edges and the owners' name engraved on the bottom—were used as centerpieces on fashionable tables.

PICKLE CASTORS

These jewel-toned, pressed-glass jars were a mainstay on posh Victorian tables. The castors were fitted in a silver holder, accompanied by small silver tongs, and were embellished with anything from personal messages to gargoyles.

Beyond their role as ritzy table decor, pickle castors signaled that a home employed enough servants to prepare pickles, and display the produce.

PIE BIRDS

Placed in the middle of a pie, the small, hollow ceramic birds released steam from the hot filling, while appearing to blow huge gusts of air through their upturned mouths.

The idea was that this bird chimney would vent the pie and keep any juices from bubbling over, but as any baker knows, a few cuts with a knife would perform the same trick, albeit without the avian whimsy.

MEAD-MAKING PARADISE

THE HOLY ISLAND OF LINDISFARNE

In the 7th century, at the request of King Oswald of Northumbria, Irish monk Saint Aidan established a monastery on the isolated tidal island of Lindisfarne. The monastery, which survives in ruins, would become the base for spreading Christianity throughout Anglo-Saxon England. Many also believe that the Lindisfarne monks were excellent mead-makers, who crafted the golden liquid in the name of spirituality. Mead is one of the oldest tipples in the world, appearing in ancient Greek texts, Hindu scriptures, and Norse mythology, in which drinking certain meads was a pathway to scholarly intelligence.

Often called the elixir of the gods, it's fitting that some of the finest mead is produced on "Holy Island." While monks no longer helm the operation, mead-maker J. Michael Hackett was drawn to the history of Lindisfarne. In the early 1960s, he opened St. Aidan's Winery on the island and set about making a modern version of the ancient brew, which he called Lindisfarne Mead. Drawing cues from the ancient Romans, who included grape juice in their meads, the team at St. Aidan's starts with a base of fermented honey, adding aromatic herbs, fermented wine grapes, and water drawn from a local well. A neutral spirit fortifies the holy mixture, which tasters describe as light, silky, and dry. The medieval mead from the tiny island (population 180) is now distributed internationally.

How to try it

St. Aidan's Winery is open to the public during Lindisfarne Island's "open tide" times, when the island is safely reachable by causeway. About twice a day, during high tide, the island becomes inaccessible.

Indian Curry IN BRITAIN

During their 200-year occupation of India, the British developed a fondness for the country's complex, pungently spiced cuisine. Curry, especially, made a big splash in the 19th-century English diet: Housewives worked hard to re-create Indian flavors with domestic ingredients while Queen Victoria, credited with making curry fashionable in England, employed an Indian staff who prepared food for the royal family.

To make the dish more accessible, Brits invented curry powder in the 18th century. The spice blend, with its base of turmeric, garlic, cumin, and fenugreek, was a far cry from Indian cooking, where different dishes were spiced uniquely and the catch-all word *curry* did not exist. (The word *curry* is likely a bastardization of the Tamil word *kari*, which, depending on how it's pronounced, can mean "to blacken" or "to bite." Fifteenth-century Portuguese colonists took it as an all-purpose word for Indian food: curry.) As British influence spread around the globe, so did curry powder, which was introduced as a British food to countless cuisines in places like Japan, Thailand, and the Caribbean. Even Indians, working abroad as indentured laborers, were given rations of curry powder with their pay.

In the mid-20th century, Bangladeshi immigrants arrived in London, mostly jumping ship at the port after toiling in the engine room on long steamship voyages from India. The new arrivals bought up small cafés and "chippies" (fish and chips shops) that had been damaged by the bombings in World

A chef tends to trays of yellow curry in a stall at the Southbank Centre food market in London.

War II and could be had for a bargain. Alongside the English standards, these new shops sold curry and rice for the growing South Asian community. They also stayed open late— a strategic move to attract the English drinking crowd, who began to order curry as their post-pub meal, sometimes with rice, sometimes with chips.

The influx of Indian immigrants throughout the 20th century kept curry pumping through the country. Chicken tikka masala, the creamy tomato curry found on every Indian restaurant menu, is perhaps the dish that best represents the

British Indian palate. Most food historians believe the dish was created in the UK by an accommodating Indian chef. When his Indian chicken preparation was too dry for gravy-loving English tastes, the chef drowned the tandoori meat in sauce, creating a curry that sells tens of millions of servings every year. As of 2015, one of every five restaurants in the UK serves curry, and the most popular among them is chicken tikka masala.

What was once a cheap option for takeout has become a point of pride for Britain. Michelin stars and international honors now decorate the walls of

many Indian restaurants in the UK. The British Curry Awards, modeled after the American Academy Awards, is a televised black-tie affair that holds a distinguished place on the British social calendar (former prime minister David Cameron called them the "Curry Oscars"). Culinary luminaries, along with celebrities, come together to honor the best Indian restaurants in the UK. The neon-lit venue holds 2,000 esteemed guests, and the ceremony is syndicated around the world, from Europe to Australia, the Middle East to South Africa, where it's enjoyed by millions of curry fans.

A FABLED FISH HEAD PIE

STARGAZY PIE

Tom Bawcock's Eve, a Christmastime festival held in the Cornish seaside village of Mousehole, celebrates the night that Tom Bawcock, a 16th-century Mousehole folk hero, sailed out to fish despite dangerous storms. As the story goes, he returned with enough catch to end a local famine. In some versions of the tale, Bawcock brought along his cat, who helped calm the storm.

To honor the brave fisherman, revelers tuck into stargazy pie, a classic savory fish pie of potatoes, eggs, and white sauce, with the added flourish of intact fish heads (and sometimes tails) craning their necks through the crust, as though looking up at the stars. An anchovy-like fish called a pilchard is typically used, but really any small fish will do—so long as it has a head.

How to try it
Tom Bawcock's Eve is held annually on December 23. The Ship Inn, a historic pub perched on the edge of the harbor's wall, gives out free stargazy pie to celebrate the holiday, often doled out by a local fisherman dressed as Tom Bawcock.

A COFFEE BAR IN A VICTORIAN-ERA URINAL

THE ATTENDANT, FITZROVIA • ENGLAND

How to try it

The Attendant has other shops in London, but only the Fitzrovia location (27A Foley Street, London) has the urinals.

These ornate, underground urinals once served the Victorian gentlemen of London. Now they serve diners espresso, flat whites, and avocado toast. Walk down the stairs to take your seat at one of the full-size, porcelain urinals and sip your coffee among the most elite, historical toilets in Fitzrovia.

Originally built in the 1890s, these public toilets were closed in the 1960s. They sat boarded up for more than 50 years before being reimagined as an upscale coffee bar.

HEALTH MILK ON A BUDGET

ARTIFICIAL ASSES' MILK • ENGLAND

How to try it

Making artificial asses' milk has fallen out of fashion, but if you must, snail season starts in the summer.

Since antiquity, donkey milk has been used as a cure-all and cosmetic—by those who could afford it. Cleopatra was said to bathe in tubs full of asses' milk to preserve her skin. Hippocrates recommended donkey milk for a range of conditions, including liver problems and fever, and from the 1700s to the early 1900s, Europeans considered donkey milk a superfood that cured lung problems, blood problems, and even hysteria. Poet Alexander Pope drank donkey milk for his many health issues, writing in a 1717 letter, "I also drink asses' milk, upon which I will make no jokes tho' it be a fertile subject." The composition of asses' milk closely resembles human breast milk, and so orphanages and new parents found it a helpful supplement.

But asses' milk was not cheap, and those looking for an affordable alternative attempted to replicate the natural product. An 18th-century recipe for "Mock Asses Milk" begins with boiling barley in water, adding hartshorn (ground-up deer antlers), enrigo root (a thistle-like plant believed to soothe coughs), and a handful of snail shells, and then diluting the brew with cow's milk.

Snails show up in almost all the renditions of ersatz donkey milk—often tossed in whole. The "Mock Asses Milk" author included a finger-wagging note at the end of his recipe, saying, "You may leave out the snails if you don't like them, but it is best to use them."

The Knights Templar Longevity Diet

Graybeards were a rare sight in the 13th century. Male life expectancy—even for the wealthy— was just 31 years. For those who made it to their twenties, that number jumped to 48 years. The Knights Templar, then, were an extraordinary exception: Many members of the Catholic military order lived long past 60, and even then, they usually died at the hands of their enemies rather than from illness. While many believed the knights' longevity was bestowed upon them from above, modern research suggests the order's strict dietary rules could have been the vital force behind their health.

The knights, an order of renowned fighters, warriors, and jousters, are believed to have lived genuinely humble lives. Early in the 12th century, a long and complex rulebook called the Primitive Rule of the Templars established the knights' vows of poverty, chastity, and obedience. Knights were ordered to eat together silently, and table items were to be passed "quietly and privately . . . with all humility and submission." The men also ate in a kind of buddy system. Due to an alleged "shortage of bowls," two knights shared one eating vessel, and each man was ordered to monitor his eating partner, making sure he wasn't taking more than his share or eating too little. (As the order was notoriously rich, this bowl sharing was likely a demonstration of abstinence.)

Balancing the fasting demands of the devout and the nutritional requirements of active, military lives, the knights alternated days of meat eating and vegetarianism. Three days a week, the knights ate meat—usually beef, ham, or bacon— which was especially abundant on Sundays. Meatless days brought bread, milk, eggs, cheese, grains, and vegetable stews to the table. On Fridays the knights fasted, which meant land animals were replaced by fish. Their varied diet was supplemented with wine, served in moderate and diluted rations. By medieval standards, these practices put the knights at the apex of clean and sensible living, which extended their lifetimes well beyond what was considered, at the time, possible without divine intervention.

Jacques de Molay (ca. 1243–1314), last Grand Master of the Knights Templar.

DORMANT UNDERGROUND DAIRY

BOG BUTTER · IRELAND

How to try it
If you have a bog nearby, wrap some butter in a cheesecloth and towel, bury it, and leave it there for at least a few months. Remember to make a note of your burial site.

When digging up peat in rural Ireland, it's not uncommon to bump into a huge block of butter. Wrapped in animal skins or packed into a wooden or earthenware container, chances are the butter has been buried for hundreds of years, and while it might be too funky to actually be tasty, it's likely still safe to eat.

Bog butter is exactly what it sounds like: cow's milk butter buried in peat bogs. (It can also refer to underground beef tallow, but that's less common.) Bog butters are typically several hundred years old, but some have been around for multiple millennia: A 3,000-year-old bog butter was recently taste-tested and described as having an extremely moldy aftertaste.

The butter, of course, was not intended to be eaten centuries later. Bogs are cool, low in oxygen, and high in acidity, and therefore excellent places for preserving perishable items (also evidenced by the remarkably well-preserved human remains extracted from bogs). The bog was likely used as a refrigerator, and the owners of the butter never came to get it—or simply forgot where they left it. Other theories suggest that the butter was an offering to the gods or was being hidden from thieves and invaders. Whatever the reason, a lot of butter was abandoned in the bogs around Ireland and the UK and is still being found today. The older the butter, the funkier the flavor. Recently, there have been experiments that intentionally age

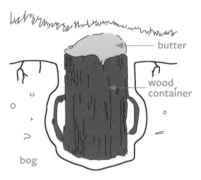

butter in bogs. They found that if you let the butter bog age for just a few months, the taste can be pleasantly earthy, like good Parmesan cheese.

HONEYCOMB TOFFEE AND PURPLE SEAWEED

DULSE AND YELLOWMAN · NORTHERN IRELAND

How to try it
The Ould Lammas Fair typically occurs on the last Monday and Tuesday of August. The dulse and yellowman are sold separately and can be combined.

Before there was salted caramel popcorn or chocolate-covered pretzels, there was dulse and yellowman, an old-school sweet-and-salty treat sold at the Ould Lammas Fair in Ballycastle, the oldest fair in Northern Ireland, with roots in the 17th century.

Yellowman, the sweet half, is a golden, toffee-like honeycomb made from brown sugar, golden syrup, butter, vinegar, and baking soda. The last two ingredients create a carbon dioxide reaction, which gives the candy a unique crunchy and bubbly consistency. Smashed with a hammer, yellowman is usually sold in uneven shards.

Dulse, the salty counterpart, is a type of seaweed harvested at low tide along the coasts of Northern Ireland. Irish monks began harvesting this seaweed (an activity known as "dulsing") some 1,400 years ago. It can be eaten raw or tossed into soups, but most often dulse is dried in the sun and turned into chewy, reddish-purple seaweed chips.

Why these two became a classic combination is open to debate, but dulse and yellowman have been sold alongside each other for hundreds of years. A local shopkeeper and bog-oak carver named John Henry MacAuley memorialized their partnership in a ballad about the fair, which included the lines, "Did you treat your Mary Ann to some dulse and yellowman/At the Ould Lammas Fair in Ballycastle-O?"

A vendor sells yellowman at Lammas Fair.

AN EDIFICE TO AN ELITE FRUIT

DUNMORE PINEAPPLE HOUSE ∘ SCOTLAND

On Christopher Columbus's second voyage to the Caribbean, in 1493, he and his men stumbled upon a deserted village on the island now known as Guadaloupe. They found a pile of fresh produce, among them the strange, impossibly sweet fruit that Columbus described as resembling a pinecone, with the sweet interior of an apple. Smitten, he brought the pineapple back to Spain, where Europeans quickly developed a passion for the tropical fruit.

Sugary foods and fresh fruits were a rarity in 16th-century England, and the pineapple became a highly sought-after item, not just for eating but for showing off. Only the richest and best connected had access to the exotic fruit, which had to be transported on long, blistering journeys across the ocean, and often spoiled before reaching port. By the 17th century, pineapples were in such demand that a thriving rental market emerged: A pineapple could be hired for a party, used as a centerpiece, then returned so it could be bought and eaten by someone wealthier. (An 18th-century pineapple cost about $8,000 in today's currency.) Ship captains also used the fruit as status symbols, displaying them outside their homes as a way to announce their return from exotic travels abroad.

The Pineapple House in Airth, Scotland, is perhaps the world's most extravagant proclamation of wealth and homecoming. John Murray, the fourth Earl of Dunmore, left his ancestral home in Scotland for the wilds of the colony of Virginia, where he became the last English governor of the region. When he returned to Scotland in 1776 (with a reputation for terrible diplomacy), he constructed a behemoth 45-foot (13.7 m) pineapple atop his mansion, announcing to his neighbors that he was home, and he was wealthy. The house may be a symbol of colonial excess but the masonry work is exceptional, full of artistic detail and technical merits, and in 1973 the house was restored by the National Trust for Scotland.

How to try it
The Dunmore Pineapple House is open to the public and available to rent for holidays. It sleeps four.

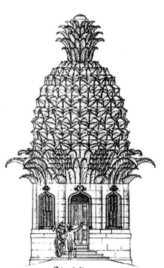

North Elevation

THE LEADING IRON SOFT DRINK

IRN-BRU • SCOTLAND

How to try it

Irn-Bru is available everywhere in Scotland. For a very Scottish cocktail, order the Irn-Bru Spritz at Bertie's fish-'n'-chip restaurant in Edinburgh. It combines Irn-Bru with Prosecco and Angostura bitters.

Originally called Iron Brew, the bright orange soda of Scotland was forced to change its name after World War II, when British legislation cracked down on food labeling. Suddenly, the words on packaging had to reflect what was actually inside, and the problem wasn't iron: The soda, which has a light but discernible taste of rust, contains .002% ammonium ferric citrate. The issue was that Iron Brew wasn't actually brewed, and so it became Irn-Bru. The sweet, creamy soda remains the most popular soft drink in Scotland, outselling even Coca-Cola.

That Irn-Bru contains iron is a point of pride for the drink. Advertisements, which have attracted controversy over the years, feature drinkers gaining muscleman strength and women shaving their newly grown beards. The blatantly false phrase "Made in Scotland from Girders" was used for years (the iron in Irn-Bru is a food additive). The drink has been compared to liquid bubble gum with a spicy aftertaste similar to ginger, although many devotees contend the flavor is impossible to describe faithfully. It's often called Scotland's other national drink because the beloved soda falls second only to whisky.

The equivalent of 20 cans of Irn-Bru is sold every second.

HAGGIS HURLING

THE WORLD HAGGIS HURLING CHAMPIONSHIP • SCOTLAND

How to try it

Scotland holds the world championships around the birthday of noted poet and haggis lover Robert Burns on January 25. The prize for breaking the haggis hurling record is a year's supply of haggis.

A stuffed sheep's stomach soars through the air, spinning rapidly before thudding to the ground. The boiled exterior, free from any tears, still holds the contents crammed inside. It is a well-thrown haggis.

Haggis hurling is one of Scotland's stranger sports. Contestants climb atop a platform, usually an overturned whisky barrel, and lob a boiled sheep's stomach stuffed with sheep pluck (a sheep's heart, liver, and lungs), onion, oatmeal, suet, and spices. The goal is to throw the haggis, Scotland's national dish, as far as possible. Each haggis is inspected prior to hurling to ensure the food hasn't been enhanced with firming agents.

Haggis hurling as we know it today began when Robin Dunseath, an Irishman, placed a newspaper ad about reviving the "ancient sport" at the 1977 Gathering of the Clans (a two-week gathering of descendants from Scotland's various clans).

Dunseath alleged that the game arose from a 17th-century custom where women tossed haggis to their husbands while they worked in the bogs and the men caught the airborne puddings in their kilts.

Dunseath eventually became the president of the World Haggis Hurling Association and wrote an entire book, *The Complete Haggis Hurler*, about the sport's history. Decades later, he revealed the whole thing was a hoax—he originally placed the advertisement to gauge the gullibility of the Scots.

But his revelation didn't end the fun. Haggis hurling is still popular at Highland games and festivals throughout Scotland and countries with suitable numbers of Scots. The World Haggis Hurling Championship is held annually. The current world record belongs to Lorne Coltart, who managed a 217-foot (66 m) throw at the Milngavie Highland Games in 2011. Dunseath, meanwhile, has distanced himself from the sport he invented and has said that he finds it surreal that people—gullible or not—still hurl haggis.

A competitor at the 2015 World Haggis Hurling Championship.

The Village Sin Eater:
The Worst Freelance Gig in History

When a loved one died in parts of England, Scotland, or Wales in the 18th and 19th centuries, decorum required that the family place bread on the chest of the deceased, then call upon a paid professional to absolve the departed of all worldly transgressions. This professional was not a priest, but the local sin eater, whose job it was to eat the chest bread and, with it, all the misdeeds of the deceased.

This was not a metaphorical service. The family who hired the sin eater believed that the bread literally soaked up their loved one's sins, and once it had been eaten, all the misdeeds were passed to the hired hand. The sin eater's soul was considered sullied with the depravities of countless men and women, and although the service was distasteful, it was also an essential step in getting loved ones to heaven.

The literal price of absorbing a lifetime of sin wasn't much better. For each service, the sin eater made a mere four English pence, the equivalent of a few US dollars today. Those who were willing to risk their souls were very poor, but perhaps they were on to something else: The bread and ale they were required to consume, while technically representative of sin, was still a free meal of bread and ale.

The origins of sin eating are murky, but the practice likely grew from older religious traditions. Historically, scholars believed it came from pagan rituals, but some academics now think it developed from a medieval custom: Before a funeral, nobles once gave food to the poor in exchange for prayers on behalf of the deceased. Symbolic breads like the ones eaten on All Souls' Day, which represent the dead and are eaten by the living, may also connect to sin eating.

The last known sin eater in the United Kingdom was Richard Munslow, who took on the role after losing his three children to whooping cough. He died in 1906. Nearly 100 years later, he was commemorated with a churchyard ceremony and a proper funeral of his own.

WELSHMAN'S CAVIAR

BARA LAWR • WALES

How to try it

Try laverbread toast as part of a Full Welsh breakfast at the Pettigrew Tea Rooms in Cardiff. (The rest of the Full Welsh: sausage, bacon, egg, mushrooms, tomatoes, baked beans, and black pudding.)

Laverbread, or bara lawr in Welsh, might be the only "bread" you can spread on toast.

The thick, sticky, and nutritious goop is made by boiling laver, a green-black seaweed that grows along the Welsh coastline. Packed with protein and minerals, especially iron and iodine, the seaweed has a briny flavor akin to oysters or olives. You can eat the seaweed raw, but most prefer the taste after it's been boiled for about six hours and then kneaded into a paste (the kneading may be the reason it's called laverbread). The resulting spread tastes of the sea, salty and crisp.

Whether fried in bacon fat, mixed with oatmeal into laverbread cakes, or simply spread on a slice of toast, bara lawr is an essential part of a full Welsh breakfast.

This former food of last resort for early Welshmen is now a point of pride. Welsh actor Richard Burton called this local delicacy "Welshman's caviar." In 2017, the European Commission bestowed the humble laverbread with a protected-food designation, which it shares with iconic food and drink like Parma ham and champagne.

Wild laver growing at Freshwater West, a beach in Pembrokeshire, Wales.

WESTERN EUROPE

THE CASTLE BEER SPA

STARKENBERGER BEER POOLS · AUSTRIA

Inside the 700-year-old castle owned by Austrian brewer Starkenberger, you can enjoy a complete beer-centric experience with beer trivia, beer history, beer drinking, and the natural extension of these activities: bathing in beer.

The seven 13-foot-deep pools each contain some 42,000 pints of warm beer (and some water). Bathers can sit and relax, fully immersed in ale, which is rich in vitamins and calcium—said to soothe the skin and help cure open wounds and psoriasis.

The pools opened in 2005 when the old fermentation cellar of the 700-year-old castle became obsolete. The beer pool is kept quite hot, so order a cold one while you soak. Drinking from the pool is ill-advised.

How to try it

Starkenberger Castle is located in Tarrenz, in western Austria, perched at the top of a hill. At about $300 for a two-hour session, bathing in beer isn't exactly affordable, but it's considerably cheaper than the 42,000-pint DIY option.

The walls of the spa feature painted murals.

INTERNATIONAL COLLECTION OF SOURDOUGH STARTERS

SOURDOUGH LIBRARY · BELGIUM

Hidden inside a Belgian baking corporation's research center is a sourdough library: 107 sourdough starters kept alive and fed to preserve the biodiversity of bread. Glass-door fridges line the walls, the Mason jar samples displayed almost jewel-like, two to a shelf. Karl De Smedt, who has run the library since 2013, knows the story behind each starter. His quest is to find and identify as many sourdough starters as possible. And according to Mr. De Smedt, he is the world's only sourdough librarian.

The starters on the shelves are leavened naturally, with living yeasts and bacteria from their home environments. When part of the starter is added to flour and water and baked, it results in a loaf of sourdough bread. Before the rise of commercial yeasts some 160 years ago, most of the world's bread was made with starters. Depending on the microbes in the ingredients, the air, and even on the baker's hands, each starter has the potential to produce a uniquely flavored loaf.

De Smedt regularly travels to add starters to the collection, which currently contains samples from approximately 20 countries including Japan, Hungary, China, and Italy. Each was made by different people and with different ingredients, from juice to holy water. Every few months, the starters are fed with flour from their home bakeries so that their microbial makeups don't change too much. Regular feedings can keep bacteria colonies alive indefinitely, so some starters have illustrious histories that can be traced back decades. In De Smedt's library, for example, there are starters sourced from the descendants of Yukon gold miners, who used the bubbling mix to make bread and flapjacks for hungry miners.

How to try it

The Sourdough Library, located in St. Vith, Belgium, is not open to the public. However, if you reach out to Karl De Smedt on social media (his Instagram is @the_sourdough_librarian), he's known to give tours.

A HEDONISTIC GAUNTLET

MARATHON DU MÉDOC • FRANCE

How to try it

You can register for the Marathon du Médoc on their official website. Book your accommodations well in advance, because the hedonistic race is extremely popular.

Runners competing in the annual Marathon du Médoc must complete a 26.2-mile (42.2 km) run in the September heat, while wearing a costume not intended for racing, and stopping along the way to drink 23 glasses of wine and nibble on local specialties like foie gras, oysters, steak, and ice cream. Many of the runners even begin the race hungover: The night before, it's tradition to partake in a "pasta party" that features copious amounts of local wine.

The 10,000 or so participants dressed as Smurfs, adult babies, grapes, and hula dancers traverse a stunning landscape of vineyards, stopping at designated chateaus to eat and imbibe. Along the route there are bands and orchestras playing music where runners can pause for a dance break and lakes to jump in for cooling off. During breaks, racers drink water and pop Imodium to stabilize their weakening constitutions, which doesn't always do the trick. All that bouncing shellfish and bordeaux leads to frequent sightings of cartoon characters vomiting along the side of the road, then starting up again.

The idea is to finish, not to win. The race lasts for six and a half hours and a common technique is to use the full amount of time to enjoy the journey as much as possible. Still, running 26 miles is never an easy feat. Even when emboldened by liquid courage, it's best to channel the wisdom found on a sign once seen along the course: "Pain is just the French word for bread."

The costumed, culinary marathon runs through the Médoc wine region before the grape harvest.

THE INSCRUTABLE LIQUEUR OF LIFE

GREEN CHARTREUSE • FRANCE

How to try it

Green Chartreuse is sold at liquor stores worldwide. To learn all about how it's made, visit the Chartreuse Cellar in Voiron, France. It happens to be the longest "liqueur cellar" in the world, and the tour ends with a tasting.

In 1084 CE, St. Bruno of Cologne formed an order of silent monks called the Carthusians. They resided in a valley of the Chartreuse Mountains, a region of the French Alps near Voiron. By 1605, they were a large, well-respected order, and King Henri IV's Marshal of Artillery presented the Carthusians with an ancient alchemical manuscript for an elixir that would prolong life.

After looking over the document, even the most learned of monks were at a loss. The concoction called for 130 different plants. It required advanced distillation, infusion, and maceration techniques. No one attempted the recipe until 1737, and even then, it's assumed the monastery's apothecary took creative liberties.

A lone monk delivered the first bottles of the potent herbal tonic (which was 69 percent alcohol) to surrounding villages by mule. In 1764, the Carthusians adapted the recipe into a milder liqueur called Green Chartreuse. The update, which was still potent at 55 percent alcohol, is the version we consume today: herbaceous and sweet with sinus-clearing heat. The monks themselves recommend serving it cold, either chilled or on the rocks.

Despite increasing demand, the order has continued the tradition of having just two monks handle the entire process, passing down the recipe through the generations. Today, only Dom Benoît and Brother Jean-Jacques know all the ingredients and how to turn them into the beloved vegetal liqueur. Once they've readied a batch, they age it in huge oak casks inside the world's longest liqueur cellar. Several years later, the same men test the product and decide if it's ready for bottling.

Champagne Was Once an Energy Drink

On July 24, 1908, the London Olympic marathon went down in history as one hell of a race: Fifty-five runners started off from Windsor Castle, but only 27 made it to the finish line. The majority of runners quit before the halfway mark, and a number of them were drunk.

Before the mid-20th century, brandy, champagne, and strychnine (best known now as rat poison) were thought to be performance enhancers, a tradition with roots in ancient Greece and imperial China. The drinks were doled out to endurance athletes by trainers, who often followed behind in cars or on bicycles, as a midrace boost. Alcohol was commonly accompanied by drugs, such as heroin and cocaine, to dull pain and increase aggressiveness. Stimulant drugs ran unchecked until the 1920s, while alcohol was used all the way into the '80s. (Champagne was especially revered for its rejuvenating effervescence.)

Irish-American Olympian Johnny Hayes crossing the finish line to de facto victory.

At the 1908 Olympic marathon, however, the potent draughts proved unreliable. Twenty-year-old Canadian runner Tom Longboat, the favorite to win, fell victim to the brutal summer heat and, at mile 17, turned to champagne. Two miles later, he collapsed and was out of the race. Meanwhile South African Charles Hefferon took

a massive four-minute lead, but two miles from the finish line he also accepted champagne, which caused such intense stomach pain he let two runners pass and finished third.

At the finish line, 80,000 spectators watched as the front-runner, Italian pastry chef Dorando Pietri, reeled toward the end. In the last quarter mile alone, an exhausted and dazed Pietri had collapsed five times, had run in the wrong direction, and had his heart massaged by concerned medics. Worry for Pietri's life resulted in a doctor supporting him across the finish line, causing his eventual disqualification and a redistribution of the race's medals. Some say Pietri was simply drunk, while others believe both he and Longboat were suffering from strychnine poisoning.

But not all the boozed runners fared poorly. De facto gold medalist Johnny Hayes admitted to an energizing gargle of brandy during the race, and bronze medalist Joseph Forshaw also turned to brandy in order to treat a stubborn side stitch. At the time, trainers believed that dehydration was better treated with wine than water (the 1924 Paris Games stocked its rehydration stations with glasses of wine), which is a theory that has since been dismantled by science, along with a mess of soused runners.

24-HOUR MOLLUSKS

OYSTER VENDING MACHINE • FRANCE

How to try it

The oyster vending machine is located at La Maison Neuve on Ars-en-Ré. It accepts credit cards.

There are a wide variety of oyster shops on France's Île de Ré, but none stay open throughout the night. Oyster farmers Brigitte and Tony Berthelot, whose shop L'Huitrière de Ré is open six days a week, make their mollusks available at all hours with a vending machine that dispenses fresh oysters 24/7 next to their shop.

The vending machine was specially fitted for oysters, which are available in packages of two to five dozen. A dozen oysters runs about $8, which is the same price as next door at their store. (For safety and health reasons, all oysters are sold closed.) Customers who order ahead of time can text their request to the store and have their order placed in the vending machine, where it can be retrieved with a personalized code. With this option, they can add on other grocery items like pâté and sea asparagus, which will be waiting beside their oysters.

COCAINE-LACED WINE

VIN MARIANI • FRANCE

How to try it

The days of cocaine-laced bordeaux are over, but try regular bordeaux—it's very good.

In 1859, Italian scientist Paolo Mantegazza published a paper on the potential benefits of a little-studied South American plant called *coca*. Inspired by the findings, a French chemist named Angelo Mariani invented a potent tonic—bordeaux wine spiked with 6 milligrams of coca leaf per ounce.

Vin Mariani became a smash hit in Paris, then spread throughout Europe and the United States. This was due in part to Mariani's aggressive marketing campaign, which involved commissioning famous artists to design advertisements. An endorsement from the pope didn't hurt, either. The pontiff praised the fortifying effects of the tonic wine "when prayer was insufficient." Throngs of celebrities—from Ulysses S. Grant and Thomas Edison to Queen Victoria, Henrik Ibsen, and Jules Verne, sang the praises of Vin Mariani. And a volume of *Medical News* from 1890 confirms that "no recognized medical preparation has received stronger endorsement at the hands of the medical profession."

Vin Mariani was potent stuff. When cocaine and alcohol are imbibed together, a third chemical compound, called cocaethylene, forms as the intoxicants are metabolized in the liver. This intense psychoactive is more euphoric, powerful, and toxic than cocaine or alcohol alone.

In this 1899 advertisement, Pope Leo XIII endorsed the popular cocaine wine.

Mariani, hailed as the world's first cocaine millionaire, didn't stop with wine. He made coke-laced teas, throat lozenges, cigarettes, and even a signature spread called Mariani margarine.

But all parties must come to an end. In 1906, the United States began enforcing labeling regulations, and the dangers of cocaine became more widely known. A coca-less version of Vin Mariani was produced in the United States, but it lost sales to a competing beverage that was also originally based on coca: Coca-Cola.

THE WORLD'S LARGEST FRESH FOOD MARKET

RUNGIS MARKET • FRANCE

Five miles south of Paris, in a suburb called Rungis, lies a little-known epicenter of international gastronomy. Occupying about 578 acres, Rungis Market has a seafood section the size of a soccer field, a fromage pavilion with hundreds of different cheeses, ceiling-high towers of lettuce and oranges, and a department specifically for game meat. Beyond the onslaught of groceries, there are also 19 restaurants, a bank, a post office, a hotel, gas stations, and the market's own police force.

It takes about 13,000 workers to run Rungis Market, many of whom are second- or third-generation vendors. Work begins around midnight, with the various departments opening their doors beginning at 2 a.m. (Seafood opens first, fruits and vegetables last at 5 a.m.)

A version of this market has existed since the 5th century, but the location has changed throughout time. In 1135, Louis VI moved it from the banks of the Seine to Paris's city center, where it became the famed Les Halles. It remained in Les Halles until 1969, when it moved to its current location in Rungis.

How to try it
To visit the market you'll need to book a tour, which often includes breakfast at Rungis. Shopping requires a buyer's card, which costs an annual fee.

More than one million tons of fruits and vegetables pass through the Rungis Market each year.

HAND CHEESE WITH MUSIC

HANDKÄSE MIT MUSIK • GERMANY

How to try it
Try the Frankfurt restaurant Lohrberg-Schänke, which serves hand cheese along with other Hessian specialties.

Handkäse mit Musik is a specialty of the southern Hesse region, where slices of the handmade rounds (hence the name "hand cheese") are paired with tart Apfelwein, or apple cider. Buttered bread is a popular vehicle for the translucent, smelly cheese, along with a smear of onion and a sprinkle of caraway seeds.

Locals say that after eating this cheese, the music comes later—a nod to the flatulence that accompanies eating raw onions.

Beyond stinky-cheese lovers and fart-joke enthusiasts, Handkäse mit Musik has gained a strong following of dieters, bodybuilders, and runners. The cheese is high in protein, low in fat, and really gets digestion moving.

SPAGHETTI ICE-CREAM SUNDAE

SPAGHETTIEIS • GERMANY

How to try it
Dario Fontanella's family ice-cream parlor is still going strong. You can eat the original Spaghettieis at Eis Fontanella in Mannheim.

Telling a kid they're getting ice cream and giving them a plate of dinner food instead will likely result in outrage and despair. Unless the plate is Spaghettieis—an ice-cream replica of Italy's national dish and a ubiquitous German treat.

Dario Fontanella, the man responsible for this ice-cream artifice, was the son of a northern Italian immigrant who arrived in Mannheim, Germany, in the 1930s and eventually opened an ice-cream parlor. In 1969, Fontanella decided to honor his family's homeland with dessert.

Fontanella re-created an iconic bowl of spaghetti, tomato sauce, and parmesan cheese by feeding vanilla gelato through a chilled spaetzle press. This device extruded thin strands of ice cream shaped just like the egg noodles it was designed to produce. Fontanella placed his ice-cream "spaetzle" on a bed of whipped cream and topped it with strawberry "tomato" sauce and white chocolate "parmesan" shavings. A wafer or cookie on the side mimicked a piece of Italian bread.

Today, the dessert is so well-known that no German child would think twice before diving into a bowl of the faux-spaghetti. And even though Fontanella was awarded the Bloomaulorden—the highest citizen's award in Mannheim—he never patented the creation. As a result, just about every German ice-cream parlor makes some version of the frozen delight. Outside the country, the sundae that masquerades as dinner remains relatively unknown and can still trick children.

A SHRINE TO VOLCANIC TOMATO PASTE

TOMATO INDUSTRIAL MUSEUM • GREECE

When the Vlychada tomato-paste factory opened in 1945, Santorini was still a sleepy island. There was no electricity; coal powered the machinery, and seawater was pumped in to wash and steam the tomatoes. Farmers reached the factory on foot, leading mules carrying woven baskets full of tomatoes. The factory was a gathering place for islanders, who took immense pride in the singular tomatoes produced from their soil.

Domati Santorini may look like standard cherry tomatoes, but they are uniquely marked by the island's climate and geology. Santorini sits on an active volcano, which erupted in 1646 BCE and covered the island in rich volcanic ash. The local tomato's sweet flavor, intense aroma, and thin skin come from these ancient nutrients, along with its ability to thrive with minimal water. (Like many crops on the dry island, they pull the moisture they need from the morning mist and require no irrigation.) The already concentrated flavor makes exceptional paste, or pelte, and tomato factories flourished from the 1920s to 1970s. The tomato business has since declined, but the iconic crop is still a pillar of Santorini cuisine and its heyday has been memorialized at the Tomato Industrial Museum.

Despite the dreary name, the museum's exhibits give insight into a lost side of the island, before tourism became the main industry. Beyond processing equipment and historical materials, the museum shows interviews of elderly former factory workers telling stories about a bygone era, which you can watch while eating bruschetta and sipping a glass of local wine.

How to try it

Guided tours run every 30 minutes and are included with the €5 admission. Also included is entrance to the contemporary art gallery next door.

A RARE AND NAMELESS SEAFOOD

FRIED OCTOPUS INK SACS • GREECE

The small, mountainous island of Kalymnos has some of the best, most obscure seafood in all of Greece, and fried octopus ink sacs might be the most unknowable of them all. Not only is this dish difficult to find, it has no official name.

The key to a good fried ink sac is to avoid puncturing it so that it holds its delicate shape and retains most of the ink inside. After briefly boiling it to harden the skin, chefs carefully cover the nugget in flour and lightly fry it in olive oil. Typically seasoned with just salt and pepper, the texture is like thick oatmeal, while the flavor has the rich gaminess of chicken liver.

The ink sacs are a part of Kalymnos's long history of embracing offal. When sea-sponge harvesting was the island's main industry, divers would be at sea for months and subsisted on every part of the fish they captured. Although the industry has been greatly diminished by sponge disease outbreaks, the divers' food philosophy has left its mark on local cuisine. A search through the island's fish markets and tavernas will reveal the likes of two-pound octopus roe, parrotfish intestines, and sea squirts preserved in saltwater.

How to try it

Sink your teeth into some ink sacs at O Sfouggaras, a beachfront restaurant in the southern Kalymnos village of Vlichadia.

..... FOOD PIONEER .....

TOM CARVEL

(1906–1990)

When listing the innovations of the Greeks—among them philosophy, geometry, alarm clocks, and the Olympics—soft-serve ice cream doesn't come readily to mind. But Tom Carvel, born in Athens as Thomas Karvelas, is the man behind this iconic invention.

An immigrant, Carvel lived on New York City's Lower East Side and scraped together a frugal living shining shoes, fixing cars, and drumming in a Dixieland band. At the age of 26, a doctor found a tubercular spot on his lung and gave him three months to live. In search of fresh air, Carvel borrowed $15 from his future wife, Agnes, and fled to upstate New York to live out his few remaining days selling ice cream from the back of a truck.

On Memorial Day weekend in 1934, two years after his diagnosis, a flat tire forced Carvel to pull off to the side of the road, derailing his plans to sell cold treats on one of the busiest ice-cream days of the season. But passing cars mistook him for a roadside stand and stopped for ice cream, delighted by the unique texture of his melting desserts. Business was better than usual, and so Carvel decided to stay put, striking an agreement with the pottery store next door for use of their electricity. In 1936, Carvel was still alive and still selling his (slightly melted) ice cream, so he expanded into the pottery store, which remained a Carvel shop for 72 years.

Taking hold of his second chance at life, Carvel went to work. Distilling knowledge he gained while working in Army post exchanges during World War II, Carvel built his own machinery. He engineered a system that used a short icy barrel, where cream would freeze instantly along the wall, with sharp blades that would scrape the cold cream into soft ribbons. And although ice cream was his medium, he is perhaps best known as the "father of franchising." He began peddling fully built stores, which included training, equipment, recipes, and his trademark.

Carvel became the unlikely mascot of his growing ice-cream empire. He was known for a deep, gravelly, attention-grabbing voice, described as "terrible, but mouthwatering," which he broadcast widely through the radio commercials he famously performed live and unscripted. For decades, Carvel was one of the best-known voices in advertising, doling out ad-libbed commentary on achieving the American Dream. He is credited with the invention of not just soft-serve, but also the ice-cream cake, the "buy one get one" coupon, and a College of Ice Cream Knowledge. He held more than 300 patents, copyrights, and trademarks.

When Carvel died in 1990, there were approximately 800 ice-cream stores operating under his name, and by most accounts, he'd made a triumphant exit (he'd recently sold his business for $80 million). But scandal surrounds the octogenarian's passing. Carvel's niece, Pamela, and his widow, Agnes, spent two decades in court battles against the president and vice president of Carvel's foundation and trust—whom Pamela accused of murdering her uncle with poison. Although much of the proceedings ended inconclusively (Pamela's request for the body to be exhumed was denied), Carvel's legacy remains formidable—his ice-cream powerhouse is still thriving in his adopted country.

LSD NIGHTMARE FISH

SALEMA PORGY • CYPRUS

I n Arabic, it is known as "the fish that makes dreams," which is a mild way of describing the visions the salema porgy is capable of inducing. Certain porgies contain a toxin known to trigger several days of vivid, sometimes frightening hallucinations, which scientists equate with the effects of taking LSD.

The potent silvery sea bream lives off Africa's east coast and throughout the Mediterranean. Ancient Romans supposedly used the fish as a recreational drug, while Polynesians employed its psychedelic powers during ceremonies. The effects can last for days and can include dark, demonic hallucinations. A 2006 study published in *Clinical Toxology* examined two cases of men who ate salema porgy on the French Riviera. One man had auditory hallucinations of "human screams and bird squealing." The other "was not able to drive anymore as he was seeing giant arthropods around his car."

Scientists understand very little about the forces at work behind the fish's hallucinogenic side effect, which is officially known as ichthyoallyeinotoxism. One theory is that it's the result of something in the phytoplankton they eat. There might also be seasonal influences at play: The 2006 study reports that levels of the trip-inducing toxin are highest during autumn, but most poisonings happen in late spring and summer. Further complicating things is that most salema porgy aren't hallucinogenic at all, and those that are lack uniform poison distribution. The head is a common psychedelic source, but some sections are toxin-free, and unfortunately you won't know for sure until you're chasing enormous spiders from your car.

How to try it
Salema porgy is available throughout the Mediterranean, particularly around the French Riviera.

From the outside, you can't tell which of these porgies will give you nightmares.

Unicorn Horns

The Whimsical Way to Test for Poison

For centuries the great minds of Europe, from Aristotle to Leonardo da Vinci, believed unicorns were real. So did physicians, who claimed the pure white horn of the unicorn could detect poison—a valuable tool at a time when illnesses and ailments were often chalked up to poisoning. The theory went that the horn, when dipped in food or wine, would smoke or sweat if it came in contact with poison.

By the Middle Ages, the unicorn horn was the must-have item among the royal and the royally rich (especially those with enemies). But how did they get a unicorn horn in a world without unicorns?

For years, the Vikings held the secret: Out sailing in Arctic waters, they hunted narwhal whales for their single ivory tooth, which grew up to nine feet in length and swirled, tapering to a point. Back ashore, the Vikings sold the tusks as unicorn horns, and by the 12th century, the twisted shape of the narwhal tusk was the accepted image of a unicorn's magical extremity.

Rare and irrationally expensive, "unicorn horns" became both status symbol and mystical tool. Lorenzo de Medici owned a narwhal tusk that was worth 6,000 gold coins, while Queen Elizabeth I reportedly received one worth £10,000 (the price of an entire castle). Danish rulers were once crowned on a "unicorn horn" throne, which is still on display at Copenhagen's Rosenborg Castle. Remarkably, there was not a single case of a horn smoking, sweating, or detecting poison, which did not deter the booming, centuries-long unicorn horn trade.

RENAISSANCE WINE WINDOWS

BUCHETTE DEL VINO • ITALY

Around the city of Florence, be on the lookout for small windows along the street level, most of them plastered over and painted. Called "buchette del vino" in Italian, these sealed-up portals were once used for the easy distribution of Italy's favorite beverage, and hence their name: wine windows.

In 1559, Cosimo de' Medici decreed that noble families could sell wine from their vineyards directly from their palaces. Anyone on the street could knock on the windows built into the facades of the Renaissance palaces, asking for wine service. A servant would take the customer's empty bottle and their payment, refill the bottle in the cellar, and pass it back to the street.

When bubonic plague swept through the city in the 17th century, the system became even more valuable. The windows allowed vendors to sell wine without hazardous hand-to-hand or face-to-face contact. At a time when drinking water was often contaminated with disease, wine was prized for being both sanitary and medicinal.

By the 20th century, the buchette del vino had fallen from favor, but several windows have recently reopened in a new era of social distancing. Babae, for example, a restaurant in Florence's Santo Spirito neighborhood, revived its centuries-old wine window and safely dispenses glasses of red.

The Wine Window Association has placed plaques beneath some of Florence's prominent buchette del vino.

MAGGOT PECORINO

CASU MARZU • ITALY

You slice into a wheel of perfectly aged pecorino, peel back the top, and find a wriggling mass of maggots. If it's casu marzu, all is going according to plan.

"Rotting cheese" in Sardinian, casu marzu is the product of larvae-driven fermentation. Cheese makers initiate the process by cutting a small hole in a wheel of sheep's milk cheese and leaving it outside. Flies—*Piophila casei*, to be exact—slip in through the opening and lay eggs. After the larvae hatch, their excretions break down the cheese's fats and proteins, creating a soft, creamy texture.

When the gooey liquid known as lagrimas ("tears") leaks through the rind, the cheese is ready to eat. It is pungent and sharp, a bit like ripe gorgonzola, with a mild acidity left in the larvae's wake.

Even though the creamy hunk of cheese might look harmless, approach with caution. As *The Science of Cheese* points out, "Cheese skippers [maggots] are able to jump a few inches, so consumers are advised to protect their eyes" when unsealing the wheel.

Sure, a maggot to the eye would be unfortunate, but the larvae can do far more damage to your insides if they're alive when eaten—including pain, nausea, and vomiting. But you can't just buy cheese with the maggots already dead; that's a sign it's gone bad. The solution? Plenty of people take the risk and eat the live maggots. Alternatively, they mash them to death and smear the cheese on pane carasau, a type of flatbread. Or they seal a piece of cheese in a zipped plastic bag. When the sound of pattering maggots stops, it's snack time.

Although casu marzu is the most famous maggot-infused cheese, it's not the only one. Elsewhere in Italy, there's marcetto in Abruzzo, casu du quagghiu in Calabria, saltarello friulano in Friuli, and cacie' punt in Molise.

How to try it
Due to health risks, casu marzu's legal status is murky (it's banned in the EU), so you've got to do some sleuthing to find it. A simple inquiry at a Sardinian cheese shop will usually point you in the right direction.

The Gladiator Diet

What epitomizes the Western ideal male physique more than the Roman gladiator? Lean and rippling with muscle, gladiators are portrayed in classical art and contemporary pop culture as specimens of corporeal perfection—when in reality their abdominals and pectorals were likely covered in a quivering layer of subcutaneous fat.

The excavation of a 2,000-year-old gladiator grave, which housed the bones of 67 fighters, showed that gladiators carb-loaded. Using a technique called isotopic analysis, Viennese researchers tested the gladiators' skeletal remains for elements such as calcium and zinc and found the fighters ate little meat, but plenty of carbohydrates and calcium. Their findings were confirmed by Pliny's *Natural History*, where gladiators are referred to by the nickname *hordearii* ("barley eaters").

According to the researchers, the largely vegetarian diet was not the result of poverty, but a way to improve gladiators' performance on the battlefield. Weight-adding foods such as carbohydrates provided a layer of bodily protection, which meant nerve endings would be less exposed and bleeding cuts less perilous. As an added benefit, the extra protective layer of fat created a more satisfying spectacle: Flesh wounds would gush blood, but the gladiator could keep on fighting.

Like modern athletes, gladiators also took calcium supplements. They drank potent brews made of charred plant or bone ash; the calcium level in their bones was exorbitant compared with the bones of average citizens.

Before a big gladiator game, fighters were sometimes invited to a celebratory banquet, where they had the rare opportunity to eat more decadent foods, such as meat. But attending these banquets was also a risk, as drunk and disorderly hosts and guests were liable to start the bloodshed early, and in the pursuit of entertainment, some gladiators lost their lives before the competition officially began.

THREADS OF GOD

SU FILINDEU • ITALY

How to try it

Book a trip to Sardinia during the Feast of San Francisco in May and October. Don't forget your walking shoes.

Twice a year, pilgrims in Sardinia trek from the city of Nuoro to the village of Lula under cover of night. They walk in solidarity, forgoing sleep and shelter—sometimes by the hundreds, sometimes by the thousands. Twenty miles later, at the entrance of Santuario di San Francisco, they reach their destination.

These seekers persist not to find the sanctuary itself, but to eat what may be the rarest pasta in the world. Su filindeu—literally "threads of God" in Sardinian—is unfathomably intricate. It's made by only three women on Earth, all from the same Sardinian family, who work every day to produce and stock enough pasta to feed the pilgrims who arrive, just twice a year, for the Feast of San Francesco. In Nuoro, this tradition has been passed down through the women of the Abraini family for nearly 300 years.

The ingredients are simple: semolina wheat, water, and salt. The serving preparation is similarly uncomplicated: gamy mutton broth and a helping of tangy pecorino cheese. Making the pasta, however, is nearly impossible. Engineers from the Barilla pasta company attempted, unsuccessfully, to build a machine that could reproduce the technique. Celebrity chef Jamie Oliver also visited Sardinia in hopes of mastering the elusive noodle. After two hours, he gave up.

Paola Abraini, the current matriarch of the su filindeu tradition, says the hardest

part is "understanding the dough with your hands." She kneads the mixture until it feels like modeling clay, then separates it into smaller pieces and works them into cylinders. If the semolina lacks elasticity, she dips her fingers in a bowl of salt water. If it feels dry, unsalted water does the trick. The balance, says Abraini, can take years to understand. She should know, because she's been at it for more than 40.

When the consistency reaches perfection, Abraini stretches the dough in the air like an accordion, then doubles it and pulls again. With each pull the strands multiply, growing increasingly thin. After eight pulls, she's left with 256 wispy threads. She gingerly stretches the fine pasta across a circular wooden frame, crisscrossing three layers of noodles to form an intricate "woven" pattern. After the su filindeu dries in the sun, it's broken into square pieces and put aside for the pilgrims.

Paola Abraini, matriarch of the only family that can make su filindeu, displays her mastery.

SMUGGLER'S SALAMI

CACIOCAVALLO DELL'EMIGRANTE • ITALY

Imagine it's the early 20th century. You're leaving your hometown in southern Italy, about to board a ship that will take you thousands of miles across the Atlantic to build a new life in the United States. Naturally, you begin to think about comfort foods. In the New Country, you'll want your beloved cheese and cured pork. The cheese is easy, permitted to freely cross into America. But how will you bring the soppressata, when meat is banned from entering the country? A group of migrants from Vallo di Diano in Salerno managed to solve the riddle: You hide the pork inside the cheese.

Caciocavallo dell'emigrante, literally the "caciocavallo of the migrant," is the ingenious method of concealing one illegal delicious thing (spicy pork soppressata) inside a second—legal—delicious thing (a ball of caciocavallo cheese). The name of the cheese, which refers to a cavallo ("horse"), derives from the traditional cheese-making technique of hanging it in pairs, linked by a rope that resembles reins.

Today, there are only a handful of cheese makers who still create this contraband cheese-salami ball, following a recipe that has been handed down, mostly orally, across generations.

How to try it
Depending on your country's meat-import regulations, you might be able to order caciocavallo of the migrant from Italian retailers online. But for the real thing, you'll need to go to Salerno.

SICILY'S MANNA BAKERY

FIASCONARO • ITALY

How to try it

Fiasconaro is located in Castelbuono's Piazza Margherita. It ships its panettone all over the world, but those able to visit the bakery are rewarded generously with samples.

For centuries, scholars have debated the origins of manna, the mysterious substance that, according to the Bible, God provided as food for the Israelites while they traveled through the desert. But in Pollina, a region in the Madonie mountains of Sicily, there's no debate: Manna is the dried sap of *Fraxinus angustifolia*, the narrow-leaf ash tree. A substance with ancient roots, manna has been cultivated in Sicily since around the ninth century, when Arabs introduced the practice of collecting the ash tree's resin. Today, manna is collected by a small handful of producers, many of them over the age of 70, during a fleeting harvest window at the end of summer. With the advent of cheap sugar and modernization, it's a tradition in decline, but a local sweet shop is working to put manna back on the map.

Fiasconaro is an artisan bakery in the town of Castelbuono. Among its specialties is a panettone—Italy's traditional Christmas bread—drenched in manna icing. Sicilian manna has a delicate, natural sweetness some describe as a cross between honey and maple syrup. The biblical substance, all sourced by hand from the region's harvest, also flavors the bakery's gelato and a thick, spreadable cream that's well worth a culinary pilgrimage.

Manna drips from incisions on a narrow-leaf ash tree.

A VERY DISTRACTING EASTER CAKE

CASSATA SICILIANA • ITALY

How to try it

Pasticceria Oscar in Palermo makes an excellent traditional Cassata Siciliana.

Sicilians have a proverb: *Tintu è cu nun mancia a cassata a matina ri Pasqua*, or "Sad is the one who does not eat cassata on Easter morning." Cassata Siciliana is the superstar of Sicilian Easter, an elegant, baroque-style confection with a liqueur-soaked sponge cake, layers of sweetened ricotta, pistachio-tinted marzipan, white glaze, and colorful candied fruit. Traditionally served at Easter, the cake is a decadent way to break the Lenten fast.

Nuns, who began the tradition of making cassata for Easter, were the first to experience the beguiling power of the delicious cake. In 1574, nuns at a convent in the Sicilian village of Mazara del Vallo liked making and eating the cake so much that they neglected their prayers, and the local diocese banned cassata making during Holy Week.

The version enjoyed today was invented by Salvatore Guli, a 19th-century Palermo baker who added marzipan and colorful decorative swirls to the cake's exterior—taking inspiration from the nuns of Palermo's Martorana convent, who famously made marzipan that resembled fruits. The flavors that make cassata Siciliana so uniquely delicious showcase the island's multicultural history. Sugar, almonds, lemons, and oranges came from ancient Arab influence. The sponge cake came from Spanish rule and the white fondant icing from the French conquest.

CURED TUNA HEART

CUORE DI TONNO • ITALY

Every year between May and June, bluefin tuna migrate through the Mediterranean Sea. They travel through Gibraltar, up to Corsica, and down to Sardinia, where fishermen set up nets during the fleeting season. The short window of time, coupled with increased regulation around this prized and increasingly rare fish, means that Sardinian chefs make use of every possible part of the bluefin, including the heart.

To prepare cuore di tonno, a fresh tuna heart is salted and pressed under weights for about three weeks. After the organ has been drained of its moisture, it's left to dry in the open air until the black, briny mass is rock hard. The ocean-heavy odor might recall the bilge of a ship, or another Sardinian specialty, bottarga (cured tuna roe). The practice harks back to a time before refrigeration, when the abundant summer catch had to be cleverly preserved and rationed throughout winter.

Like bottarga, cuore di tonno is a powerhouse of flavor, and a few shavings off the block will impart a salty, savory, metallic tang to a dish. A shower of grated tuna heart over fresh ribbons of pasta topped with an egg yolk is a classic application, but the delicacy can also be added to soups and sauces or sliced thinly, doused with olive oil, and eaten as an antipasto.

How to try it
The menu at Al Tonno di Corsa in Carloforte, Sardinia, revolves around tuna and includes both tuna heart salad and bottarga.

The tuna hearts are left out to air-dry until they are rock hard.

Fish Sauce Factories

Fish sauce was a wildly popular Roman condiment. Called garum, it was made by salting fish entrails and allowing them to ferment into golden, pungent, umami-laden liquid.

Archaeologists have excavated an immense, sprawling trail of fish sauce factories across the ancient Roman Empire, dotting the coastlines from the western Mediterranean to the northern reaches of the Black Sea.

The factories, which date between the 2nd century BCE and the 6th century CE, featured a central patio, rooms to clean the fish and store the product, and an array of sunken rectangular basins for fermenting the garum, typically built from cement and lined with a paving material called opus signinum that kept precious liquid from seeping out. Finished fish sauce was poured into amphorae (slim ceramic jars) and distributed throughout the empire in what was a booming, sophisticated network of production and transport.

Garum factories made use of every fishy morsel: The flesh of large fish was salted and dried, while the entrails, along with less desirable small fish, were used to make garum. Like other fermented products (think wine), garum varied hugely in quality. The purest sauce, distilled from tuna parts, could fetch $500 a bottle in today's currency, while cheap baitfish-and-viscera varieties were the fish sauce of commoners and enslaved people. For everything in between, mackerel was the fish of choice.

The densest concentration of factories was found along

OF THE ROMAN EMPIRE

fish migration routes, enabling fishermen to bring their catch ashore and directly to the processing sites. The Strait of Gibraltar, which every spring still plays host to schools of traveling bluefin tuna, was surrounded by factories that would process the massive annual catch. Shoals of sardines around the western tip of France made the region of Brittany another fish factory hot spot, home to an enormous site called Les Plomarc'h, which cranked out cheap garum for the Roman army. Away from the migratory fairways, the salting sites were modest; this is especially true closer to Rome, where there was a demand for fresh fish at market.

Garum was used as something of a mother sauce: By adding honey, vinegar, herbs, or oil, Romans created dozens of derivative condiments. In the famed first-century Roman cookbook *Apicius*, more than 75 percent of the 465 recipes call for garum. Excavations of Pompeii revealed that Romans of all social classes had easy access to fish sauce and used it daily: The city's signature garum container, the urceus, was found everywhere throughout Pompeii's ruins, in shabby shops and wealthy homes, even kosher versions in Jewish kitchens. Across the empire, garum amphorae have been recovered underwater, lost in ancient shipwrecks, and on land from Britain to Africa, showcasing the expansive, formidable reach of Rome's fallen condiment.

Delicious Diaspora

DUTCH INDONESIANS IN THE NETHERLANDS

Until the very end of the 16th century, the Portuguese ruled the spice trade world, sailing between Indonesia and Portugal on a nautical route they fiercely guarded. That all changed in 1592, when a Dutch cartographer published a chart with detailed instructions on how to sail to Indonesia, known then as the East Indies.

Shortly after, three Amsterdam merchants began plotting an expedition in secret: A spy was sent to Lisbon, posing as a merchant, to confirm the cartographer's charts, which were also cross-referenced with intelligence from other knowledgeable Dutch travelers. With this information, the men raised enough capital to build four ships, hire 248 crew members, and set sail in 1592.

By most accounts, the voyage was a catastrophe. The roundtrip journey took more than two years, during which they lost 154 men, killed one Javanese

prince, were stranded six months on Madagascar, and held for ransom, raided, and generally disgraced. But they did return with pepper, nutmeg, and mace, all of which were so valuable at the time that the expedition was still deemed a profitable success. In 1602, the Dutch set up a trading post in Java, eventually taking forcible control of the entire country and remaining there until Indonesia gained independence in 1949.

Three hundred years of colonial rule and intermarriage led to a braiding of cultures and a mixed-race community known as "Indos." Today, roughly 10 percent of the Dutch population has some Indonesian blood. And Indonesian cuisine—spice-heavy, sweet, sour, and spicy—has found its place among traditional Dutch fare, sometimes evolving into new Indo dishes unique to the Netherlands.

Rijsttafel is the ultimate example of Netherlands-specific Indonesian cuisine. Dutch for "rice table," rijsttafel was created in Indonesia for the Dutch colonists as a way to indulge in a large assortment of dishes from the numerous islands. Rijsttafel consists of many small plates, typically a dozen or more curries, stir-fried vegetables, satays, fritters, and stews, served with rice in various preparations, together on the same table. Not only was this meal indulgent for the colonists, it was also

meant to impress visiting dignitaries with its breadth and magnitude. Since Indonesia's independence, rijsttafel is not easily found on the islands—Indonesians are less interested in excess and find that mild Javanese dishes, for example, don't necessarily go well with the heavily spiced food of Sumatra. But the rice table is alive and well in the Netherlands, where the meal is loved on land and—even today—by seafaring Dutch: A Dutch naval tradition is to eat rijsttafel every Wednesday afternoon.

Spekkoek (or "lapis legit" in Indonesian) is a riff on a German multilayered spit cake, called Baumkuchen, where batter is brushed onto a rotating spit, layer by layer. When Dutch traders arrived with this recipe, Indonesians added spices (cinnamon, clove, nutmeg, mace) to the batter and built the layers in a pan, using a broiler to cook each delicate stratum before carefully adding a dozen more. This labor-intensive preparation required butter from the Netherlands and spices from Indonesia, resulting

in a special-occasion cake that's still expensive today (in Amsterdam, spekkoek goes for about €20 a kilo, about 2.2 lb).

Friet saté pairs the ubiquitous Dutch french fry with a generous topping of peanut sauce (called saté sauce because it's typically used for meat skewers).

Split pea soup with rice and sambal (spicy chili sauce), **macaroni and cheese packed with lunch meat** (hot dogs, Spam, or corned beef), and **steamed meatloaf with sweet soy sauce** are all classic Indo comfort foods.

THE WORLD'S FIRST FLOATING FARM

FLOATING FARM • NETHERLANDS

How to try it

Floating Farm is located in the Merwehaven, a harbor within Rotterdam's port. It's currently open to the public on Fridays and Saturdays from 11 a.m.–4 p.m.

n 2019, a new farm opened in one of Europe's largest and busiest ports—not in the area, but literally floating in the port of Rotterdam. Called Floating Farm, it's the first of its kind, though hopefully not the last.

The idea came to CEO and founder Peter van Wingerden while in New York City during Hurricane Sandy. In the wake of the flooding, he watched the largely imported produce disappear from city markets and realized the world of tomorrow would need to produce food closer to consumers—and it might need to float. His solution for the future is now realized in the three-story concrete platform that's home to 35 cows producing 700 liters of milk every day.

The farm is unparalleled in its sustainability. Half the farm's energy comes from 50 solar panels floating beside it in the shape of a milk bottle. On the farm's top level, cows graze from a mixture of hay and grass clippings from local parks and golf courses, and drink purified rainwater collected from the roof. Their manure is converted into fertilizer, which is used to regrow the very fields from which they'll later eat.

Only two humans are needed to operate the farm. Most of the work is performed by robots, using AI to milk, feed, and clean up after the cows. The milk itself is processed on the farm's second floor, and the pasteurized milk and yogurt are sold on-site and in grocery stores throughout the city.

This three-story floating farm is home to 35 lactating cows.

BLOOD-SUCKING SEA MONSTER

LAMPREY ∘ PORTUGAL

If you're a species that has spent millions of years sucking blood, getting cooked in a vat of your own is due punishment. Such is the plight of the parasitic sea lamprey, which gets boiled in a bloodbath as part of traditional Portuguese cuisine.

At first glance, lampreys might seem more like monsters than meals. These parasites resemble wormy eels with sharp, winding rows of teeth. In the North American Great Lakes, they're not seen as dinner, but as parasites that kill other species and accumulate mercury.

But one man's horrific, prehistoric pest has been another man's delicacy for thousands of years. Roman servants prepared lamprey at Julius Caesar's banquets. During the Middle Ages, only members of the upper class had access to its hearty, prized meat. Across southwestern Europe, Christians were drawn to lamprey's texture, akin to slow-cooked steak, and its lack of fishy aftertaste. Demand was especially high during Lent, when eating land animals was forbidden.

In Portugal, stewed lamprey is still a suitable beef replacement. From January through April, you'll find this creature marinated in its own blood and served with rice all over the country. Every March, 30,000 gourmets flood the small village of Montemor-o-Velho for the annual Lamprey and Rice Festival. During the Christmas season, nuns, bakers, and families celebrate by fashioning sea monsters out of sweet egg yolk. This treat, known as lampreia de ovos, features a lamprey replica covered in icing—a more kid-friendly version than the blood-coated dish.

How to try it
Fresh lamprey is seasonally available in restaurants across Portugal, as well as in Spain and France. In Finland, lamprey is served pickled year-round.

DECOY SAUSAGE

ALHEIRA ∘ PORTUGAL

After the Spanish Inquisition spread to Portugal in the 16th century, Jews had to tread very carefully. The ruthlessly pro-Christian era was deeply anti-Semitic, and those practicing Judaism were persecuted, exiled from the country, or burned at the stake in Lisbon's Rossio Square.

Even practicing Judaism in secret was a dangerous game. Informants were everywhere, pouncing at the opportunity to report an overheard Hebrew prayer or, equally incriminating, a lack of hanging sausages. To protect themselves, the Jews of Mirandela created alheira, a decoy sausage that looked just like the porcine variety but was made with kosher-friendly poultry and bread. Hanging in their homes and gracing their dinner tables, the sneaky sausage likely saved hundreds of lives.

Today, not all alheira is kosher, and pork fat is often mixed into the filling, which can contain anything from veal to duck to salt cod. The garlicky smoked tube meat (alheira gets its name from the Portuguese word for garlic, *alho*), typically served with fries and a runny egg, has earned a near universal place on Portuguese menus, beloved now for its taste rather than its life-saving abilities.

How to try it
Head to the northeastern city of Mirandela, where the alheira is protected by a PGI (Protected Geographic Indication) certification. All sausages are produced according to strict regulation and are considered the best in Portugal.

BACON FAT PUDDING

PUDIM ABADE DE PRISCOS · PORTUGAL

How to try it

Casa dos Ovos Moles in Lisbon makes traditional, Braga-style bacon pudding they sell by the kilo (the equivalent of 2.2 lb), the half kilo, or in individual servings.

In the northern Portuguese city of Braga, in the parish of Priscos, there once lived a man named Manuel Joaquim Machado Rebelo. Known as the Abbot of Priscos, Rebelo became one of the country's most lauded chefs during the 19th century, preparing elaborate banquets for the royal family and Portugal's elite. The abbot was notoriously close-lipped about his recipes, but he did let one slip, and his formula for pork fat and wine pudding became his legacy.

Pudim Abade de Priscos begins with a golden liquid caramel slathered around a pudding mold. Poured into the caramel skin is a classic custard of sugar, egg yolks, and cinnamon, amped up by two regional ingredients: port wine and pork fat. The effect is a smooth, velvety bite with the subtle unctuousness of lard, cut by the wine's sweet acidity. Two hundred years later, the Abbot's bacon fat pudding is still considered a first-class recipe and a Portuguese classic. It's often described as a magic trick of gastronomy because the custard is so ethereal it vanishes in your mouth.

THE SAUCIEST SANDWICH IN PORTO

FRANCESINHA · PORTUGAL

How to try it

Porto is the hotbed of francesinhas; try Lado B Café for a saucy version, or Café Santiago F for a cheese-centric rendering surrounded by fries.

Your typical francesinha, or "little French woman," is a sandwich only by definition. Indeed there is bread, and between that bread is meat, but the word *sandwich* does not do justice to the magnitude of the meat, which is a trio of cured ham, steak, and linguiça sausage. Nor does it suggest that the meat and bread are covered in gooey melted cheese, then slathered in a secret sauce that contains beer, tomato, chilies, and, allegedly, even more meat. A runny egg adds surplus lubrication, which means there is typically a side of french fries for dipping in the "sandwich."

Residents of Porto, where the behemoth was born, suggest limiting yourself to two francesinhas a month, both for general health and safety as well as to ration your delight throughout the year. Delight rationing has been an ongoing issue for this dish: Originally a popular food for bachelors, the sandwich was once considered so decadent, it was inappropriate for a woman to order one.

A HOME FOR MACANESE CUISINE

CASA DE MACAU • PORTUGAL

For more than four centuries, Portugal controlled the small island of Macau, just off the coast of southern China. When Portuguese traders first landed in the 16th century, Macau was under the control of the Ming dynasty, who used it as a commercial port until around 1550. After a rocky start, relations improved when the Portuguese helped rid the coastline of pirates, and the Chinese allowed the Portuguese to settle. By the mid-19th century, the Portuguese had colonized the island. They erected Portuguese-style buildings, controlled the port, and enslaved Macanese women—and women from other Portuguese colonies—as wives.

Tasked with cooking for their European husbands, the wives from Macau, Goa, and Malacca (all former Portuguese colonies) improvised the dishes they'd never tasted. Bacalhau, the Portuguese dried codfish, was braised in soy sauce and tamarind. Coconut milk replaced cow's milk and sweet-and-savory Chinese sausage, called lap cheong, was used in place of chouriço. Wives learned to bake pastéis de nata, the predecessors to the Chinese egg tarts known as dan tat. They made samosas that tasted more like egg rolls and Portuguese-style fried rice.

In Lisbon, the Casa de Macau helps preserve this historic gastronomy. The private association, according to its president, was founded to unite the Macanese diaspora: Portuguese raised in Macau who have returned to Europe and those with mixed Portuguese and Macanese blood. (The term *Macanese* is still complicated because it describes natives of Macau, both with and without Portuguese heritage.) At special events throughout the year, the Casa de Macau serves a Macanese meal in a Macanese-style dining room, decorated with East Asian art and pictures of the founders on the wall.

How to try it

Casa de Macau is located outside Lisbon's city center, at Avenida Almirante Gago Coutinho, 142.

Pastéis de nata.

Macau's inner harbor, ca. 1880.

VERMOUTH HOUR

LA HORA DEL VERMUT • SPAIN

Every afternoon in Madrid, when the sun is at its highest, internal clocks chime and locals begin to fill the neighborhood bars, gathering for the singular, essential purpose of preparing their appetites for lunch.

Known as vermouth hour ("la hora del vermut" in Spanish), this daily ritual is fundamental to the routines of many Spaniards, occurring just before the big daytime meal. The objective is to tease open your hunger with an aperitif (an alcoholic drink meant to stimulate the appetite), and in Spain, the daytime standard is vermouth—so popular

A Sip Before Dinner

Aperitifs are a glorious facet of the European lifestyle. Like a slow seduction before a meal, aperitifs open the palate and arouse the appetite before you settle into the main event. A pre-meal glass of liqueur or fortified wine—enlivened with a mix of fruits, roots, and spices—is a tradition that extends across the continent, because when it comes to extracting maximum pleasure from everyday eating, no one does it like the Europeans.

LILLET
A key ingredient in James Bond's favorite martini, Lillet is 85 percent white bordeaux wine, 15 percent macerated-citrus liquor. (France, 17% ABV*)

OUZO 12
Fiery and sweet, anise-flavored ouzo turns from clear to cloudy when poured on ice. (Greece, 38% ABV)

GINJA SEM RIVAL
Ginja, the local sour cherry, steeped in aguardente ("fire water") is the most traditional drink of Lisbon, served as a thick, sweet shot—with or without the cherries. (Portugal, 23.5% ABV)

*alcohol by volume

it's usually available on tap, in at least a few varieties. The classic Spanish vermouth is red, sweet, and herbaceous, made from a white wine that's been fortified with brandy and left to steep with a combination of warm spices, bitter herbs, and fruits such as orange, cherry, or grapefruit. Straight from the tap, served over ice or straight up, Spanish vermouth is notoriously smooth and easy to drink—much less sweet than the traditional Italian variety. Snacks are also a major component of la hora del vermut. Mussels, anchovies, and the ubiquitous jamón (ham) all make for excellent accompaniments; olives are pretty much obligatory. Spaniards are known for their late schedules—lunches in the early evening and dinners at 11 p.m. are commonplace here—and so a glass of vermouth and a hearty snack is a welcome early-afternoon repast.

How to try it

Every bar in Spain will have a selection of vermouths, often on tap, most of which are produced within the country. In Barcelona, Quimet & Quimet has been pouring vermouth for more than a century in a quintessentially old-school joint. At Bar Electricitat, they leave a bottle of vermouth on your table and you tell them how many glasses you've had.

Becherovka kiosk in Karlovy Vary, the liqueur's hometown.

MAURIN QUINA
A fortified wine laced with cherries, quinine (bark extract), and bitter almonds. (France, 16% ABV)

YANHELIVKA
With hints of dill, ginger, mesquite, and lemon, this Ukrainian blend is also touted as an aphrodisiac. (Ukraine, 33% ABV)

MANDARINE NAPOLÉON
The recipe for this cognac flavored with mandarin peel was inspired by Napoleon, who liked his cognac with a touch of orange. (Belgium, 38.5% ABV)

RABARBARO ZUCCA
Chinese rhubarb, bitter orange peel, and cardamom make a sweet, botanical tipple. (Italy, 16% ABV)

BECHEROVKA
A closely guarded, medicinal synthesis of cinnamon, clove, chamomile, and ginger. Technically a digestif meant for after-dinner sipping. (Czech Republic, 38% ABV)

FRIED LEMON LEAF CHALLENGE

PAPARAJOTES • SPAIN

How to try it

Paparajotes are available only within Murcia, typically during the spring, when you can find them at festivals such as Bando de la Huerta. During the off-season, the paparajotes at Rincón de Pepe and La Parranda Taberna are very tasty.

No matter how well you speak castellano or tolerate the blazing summer sun, Murcianos of southeastern Spain can always tell whether you're a local by how you eat a paparajote—the traditional treat of the citrus town—made by battering a lemon leaf, deep-frying it, and dusting it with cinnamon and sugar. Take a bite of the paparajote and your cover is blown. The lemon leaf, which is unpalatably bitter, is not for eating. Its purpose is to give the paparajote shape and a slight citrus tang. To pass the test, pick up the leaf by its stem, pull the batter off, and eat the crispy, sugary, donut-like shell. Discard the lemon leaf, and you've passed a cultural test as well as enjoyed the delightful, hyper-regional sweet that leaves most tourists cringing from lemon peel mouth.

MONASTERY FOOD CAFÉ

CAELUM • SPAIN

How to try it

Caelum is open from 10 a.m. to 8:30 p.m. every day, including Sundays.

Within Barcelona's medieval Jewish quarter, Caelum ("heaven" in Latin) provides a treasure trove of delicacies made in monasteries all around Spain. The café specializes in sweets, such as the nun-made egg yolk candy Yemas de San Leandro from Seville, and Tocinillo de Cielo, a custard invented by 14th-century nuns in Jerez de la Frontera.

The ground floor holds the cozy café, complete with an elaborate window display of heavenly cakes and pastries, where visitors can enjoy their chosen treat along with coffee and tea. Afterward, a trip to the building's basement offers a surprising piece of medieval history. Below the café are the remains of the quarter's public baths, whose stone walls and vaulted ceilings are right at home among the centuries-old monastic delights.

AN ENCHANTING PARTY PUNCH

QUEIMADA • SPAIN

At every good Galician punch party, the host recites an incantation, then sets the bowl of punch on fire. Like any proper host, she wants to ward off the evil spirits and invite good fortune for her guests. After the alcohol burns in a brilliant blue flame, she ladles the queimada into cordial glasses.

The taste of the caramelized sugar and lemon peel, the earthy coffee beans, and the heat of orujo brandy swirl magically together in the glass. The first sip banishes evil spirits, the second clears your mind of hate, and the third fills your soul with passion.

Queimada is a traditional punch of Galicia, and the ritual surrounding its consumption is known as conxuro da queimada ("the spell of queimada"). Although the drink's origin is unknown, it draws from the cultures of Celtic Druids, the Moors, and Spanish colonies in South America. Galicians perform the ritual at events such as weddings or dinner parties. If you can't get an invite to either, visit Galicia in June or October: There are queimada performances on Halloween, which is derived from the Celtic holiday of Samhain, and St. John's Night (also known as Witches' Night) on June 23.

How to try it

Instructions on how to conduct your own conxuro da queimada can be found online, but if you try this at home, make sure to use a clay pot or earthenware bowl, which best contains the fire.

WAFFLE ROULETTE VENDORS

BARQUILLEROS DE MADRID • SPAIN

Barquillos are simple treats: waffle dough pressed into a checkered pattern, then rolled into tubes, cones, or other shapes. But to get one (or ten), you'll have to play for it. Waffle vendors, called barquilleros, will remove the outer metal canister and begin a game of roulette using a wheel on its top. You can pay once to spin for either one or two barquillos, or pay more and spin as many times as you want, racking up waffles until you stop or the ticker lands on one of the four golden markers, at which point you lose everything.

How to try it

Barquilleros de Madrid, the shop run by the Cañas family, is located at Calle de Amparo 25.

Barquilleros at Madrid's Las Fiestas de la Paloma in 2015.

The traditional barquillo nearly vanished during the food shortages under Francisco Franco's dictatorship. Luckily, the Cañas family of Madrid persisted in carrying on the barquilleros' legacy, and today Julián Cañas, a third-generation barquillero, maintains a shop in the city's Embajadores neighborhood. On weekends, Cañas and his sons also roam Madrid's plazas and parks with baskets of waffles under their arms and roulette tins on their backs.

Barquillos can also be found in pastry shops, but for the most authentic experience, look for a barquillero in public spaces such as the Plaza Mayor, El Rastro market, or El Retiro park. The roaming, gambling members of the Cañas family also make appearances at fiestas such as the San Isidro Festival.

THE ART OF TABLE-SIDE FROTHING

ASTURIAN CIDER POURING • SPAIN

How to try it

In Asturias, you don't order a glass of cider. The drink comes by the bottle, which includes the tableside pouring and frothing service.

A long-distance pour at a sidería in the Spanish town of Ribodesella.

In Spain's northern region of Asturias, cider pouring is more performance art than table service. At local cider bars, known as sidrerías, servers pop the cork and hoist the open bottle high into the air. From this altitude, the elevated hand tips the bottle while a lowered hand catches the cloudy liquid in a glass until it's roughly a quarter full.

The servers aren't just capitalizing on an opportunity for theatrics, they're enhancing the taste of the beverage. Asturian cider, made from fermenting five kinds of apples into a funky medley of barnyard flavors, contains approximately 6 percent alcohol and is almost entirely flat. The long-distance cascade into the glass creates a splash that supplies effervescence and foam while also releasing the cider's aromas. Because bartenders might spill a few drops in the process (perhaps due to all their no-look pours), some establishments litter the floor with sawdust to absorb the constant splashing and spills.

Rather than sipping and savoring the tart drink, patrons shoot their small pour back in one swift go. The drinker then shakes out any last dregs of cider onto the floor to freshen the cup for the next drinker, and the entire pouring ritual begins again.

EASTERN EUROPE

PICKLED BAR CHEESE

NAKLÁDANÝ HERMELÍN • CZECH REPUBLIC

U Fleků, the oldest barhouse in Prague, serves the quintessential Czech bar snack: a soft, round cheese called hermelín, with a creamy white interior. Sliced in half lengthwise, the cheese is layered in a jar with spice-and-herb-infused oil that typically includes onion, garlic, bay leaves, black peppercorn, and, for a spicy variety, red pepper. Left to marinate for about ten days, the cheese picks up all the pungent flavors of the oil, which mingles with the mushroom notes of the cheese, growing increasingly powerful as the mixture ages. The cheese retains its gooey texture, which is why a few slices of deep-fried brown Czech bread, called topinki, are always within reach.

Despite it's name, the cheese isn't actually pickled—it's marinated. But less ambiguous is the proper way to eat this herbaceous delicacy: with a fork in one hand and a cold Czech beer in the other.

How to try it

At U Fleků, you can eat pickled hermelín at communal tables while waiters roam for business, carrying big trays of housemade dark lager, which is the only beer served here.

HOW TO ENJOY A FLUFFY BEER

MLÍKO • CZECH REPUBLIC

The Czechs, inventors of the pilsner, drink the most beer per capita of any nation on Earth. With a beer culture this pervasive, it's only natural that they'd create a philosophy around how to pour and enjoy their favorite drink. At a bar in Prague, beer drinkers not only choose their favorite brew—they also select their preferred pouring method. Mlíko, or milk beer, which renders a whole beer white and foamy, resembling a tall glass of milk, might be the most misunderstood style.

How to try it

The traditional pilsner pub Lokál Hamburk in Prague is especially adept at transforming beer into beer fluff. Mlíko should cost half the price of a standard pour.

Outside the Czech Republic, too much foamy head on a beer is considered an amateur move, a watery nuisance that takes up valuable space in the glass. But the foam in mlíko is a different substance entirely, made by opening the tap just slightly and finessing a thick, creamy lather into the mug. The mlíko foam has a cloudy, velvety body and sweet taste—nothing like the sensation of gulping air that comes from a poorly pulled draft. Because the foamy milk beer is less alcoholic than a regular pour, mlíko makes a great nightcap, an easy lunchtime beer, or the beverage of choice when in a rush because the foamy drink is easy to down quickly.

A bartender pours a milk beer in Pilsen, home of Pilsner Urquell.

Mlíko is the lightest of the Czech pouring styles, with just a sliver of amber liquid on the bottom. The standard pour, called hladinka, is three parts beer to one part foam. Another pour, called a šnyt, contains about two parts of beer, three parts of foam, and a couple of inches of empty glass—a style that comes to the rescue when drinkers need to start slowing down but can't bear the embarrassment of ordering a small beer.

TINY-HOUSE WINE STORAGE

VRBICE WINE CELLARS • CZECH REPUBLIC

Vrbice is a town of about 1,000 people, located in the winemaking district of Břeclav. The village stands like an island surrounded by a sea of vineyards, which produce some of the best wine in eastern Europe. The village is known for its picturesque wine cellars.

The most famous of the cellars, the Stráž cellars, were built in the 18th and 19th centuries. Cut into the village's sandstone hillside and adorned with elegant Gothic arches, the cellars look like tiny houses from a fairy tale. Inside, the long corridors are stocked with wine. The interior walls are dusted with mold that, together with the stable temperature and humidity belowground, help to create an ideal environment for maturing wine. In certain cases, the original builders kept digging, stacking multiple layers of cellars, one above the other: The largest of Vrbice's cellars, called U Jezírka, goes seven stories deep.

How to try it

Vrbice is located in the southeast Czech Republic. Many of the cellars are available for visits and will offer tastings of the region's wine.

FERMENTED-BREAD SODA

KALI • ESTONIA

Dense, sweet Estonian black rye—so sacred that old folklore demands that a loaf fallen to the ground should be picked up immediately and kissed before returning it to its proper place—is a mainstay on every Estonian table. Locals have also found a way to drink their favorite carbohydrate, parlaying their rye into a fizzy drink that's become the country's most popular soda.

The rye bread, already made from a fermented batter, is fermented again to make kali. Rye slices are boiled until soft, then mixed with yeast, sugar, and maltose. After the mixture has fermented for a day, it's sieved through a cheesecloth, sweetened with additions such as lemon and raisins, and ready to drink. The slightly alcoholic drink tastes like a cross between dark beer and kombucha—malted, sour, and effervescent. It's an easy-drinking refreshment that's far more nutritious than the average cola: Rye bread provides vitamin B and magnesium, and the lactic acid from the fermentation can aid digestion.

How to try it

Ochakovsky is a Russian commercial brand of kvass (their equivalent of kali) available in Eastern European grocery stores and online. In Estonia, you'll find home-brewed kali everywhere.

Street vendors once pushed carts around Tallinn's cobbled streets selling kali by the glass, but today you can find bottled versions of what many call "Estonian Coca-Cola" on supermarket shelves. But Estonians swear the supermarket brands are just not the same as traditional kali, and they'd be correct: Many commercial brands of kali are not fermented, which makes the taste more soda than soda beer.

Other Fortified Sodas

These are sodas made with ingredients that claim to aid everything from digestion to arthritis to diabetes.

CARIBBEAN	VIETNAM	SWITZERLAND	SOUTH KOREA	USA
Mauby Fizz	Tribeco	Rivella	Tamla Village Co.	Dr. Brown's Cel-Ray
made with tree bark, anise, vanilla	made with white fungus, swiftlet bird's nests	made with milk whey, minerals	made with Jeju onions	made with celery seed

When the Soviet Union Paid Pepsi in Warships

In the summer of 1959, many Russians got their first taste of Pepsi. Accustomed to carbonated mineral water and bread-based sodas, many Russians' first impression of Pepsi was that it smelled like shoe wax and tasted too sweet. But the American brand was determined to enter the untapped market—even if the communist government couldn't compensate them in the traditional manner.

It all began with a rare exchange of culture at the American National Exhibition in Moscow, which was meant to showcase Americana through exhibits sponsored by US brands. Pepsi executive Donald M. Kendall went to Moscow with the mission of getting a Pepsi in the hands of Soviet leader Nikita Khrushchev. The night before the exhibition, Kendall approached then Vice President Richard Nixon at the American embassy, and he agreed to lead Khrushchev to the Pepsi booth. The next day, Nixon delivered as promised, and a photographer snapped a picture of the two world leaders sipping cups of Pepsi.

Vice President Richard Nixon watches Kliment Voroshilov and Nikita Khrushchev sample Pepsi for the first time.

For Kendall—who catapulted up the ranks of Pepsi, eventually becoming CEO—the USSR was the land of opportunity. In 1972, he negotiated a cola monopoly that locked out Coca-Cola until 1985. Cola syrup began flowing through the Soviet Union, becoming what the *New York Times* named "the first capitalistic product" available in the USSR. But it wasn't business as usual.

Soviet rubles were worthless internationally and prohibited from being taken abroad, so the USSR and Pepsi had to barter. Cola was traded for Stolichnaya vodka, which Pepsi sold in the US. But when an American boycott banned Stolichnaya, they had to trade for something else: In the spring of 1989, Pepsi became the middleman for 17 used submarines, a frigate, cruiser, and destroyer, which a Norwegian company bought for scrap. In return, Pepsi was allowed to double the number of soda plants in the USSR.

In 1990, a new $3 billion deal was signed. Pepsi agreed to sell Soviet-built ships abroad in order to finance their expanding Russian enterprises, which now included another American institution: Pizza Hut.

But a year later, the Soviet Union fell, taking with it Pepsi's monopoly and business deals. Suddenly, their long balancing act turned into a scramble to protect their assets in a free-for-all made more complex by redrawn borders, inflation, and privatization. The new Pizza Huts were hobbled—their mozzarella was sourced from Lithuania. Plastic soda bottles were located in Belarus and Pepsi's new ship business was stranded in now-independent Ukraine.

Kendall, who had since retired, lamented that the Soviet Union had essentially gone out of business. Over several months, Pepsi pieced parts of the deal back together as Coca-Cola aggressively entered the former Soviet Union. Despite a huge marketing push from Pepsi (they launched a giant replica Pepsi can to the Mir space station and erected two billboards over Pushkin Square), Coke beat out Pepsi as Russia's most popular cola in 2013, ushering in a new era where soft drinks, vodka, and destroyers had to be bought with legal currency.

Pepsi advertisement above Pushkin Square in 1998.

ANCIENT GEORGIAN WINE VESSELS

QVEVRI • GEORGIA

I n 2017, archaeological excavations in southern Georgia unearthed terra-cotta jars from the 6th century BCE, which meant Georgians have been making wine for 8,000 years, predating even the Greeks and the Romans. Called qvevri, the oversize, lemon-shaped jars are used for fermentation and storage and belong exclusively to the Georgian winemaking tradition.

Producing a qvevri, which is always made by hand, requires considerable craftsmanship. A slight imbalance of weight or thickness can make a qvevri crack or wobble. Selecting the right clay, which imparts essential minerals to the wine, is also critical. There are only a small number of remaining craftsmen, who likely learned the trade from their parents. It can take months to make a single qvevri—but once it's done, it can last for centuries.

To make traditional Georgian wine, pressed grapes, along with their skins, stalks, and pips, are loaded into a beeswax-coated qvevri that's buried beneath the ground. The qvevri is sealed shut, and the mixture is left to ferment for about half a year. The distinctive shape of the qvevri allows the grape seeds and skins to sink to the bottom, while the juice stays on top to mature. Winemakers say using the qvevri makes their wine naturally stable, eliminating the need for chemical preservatives.

Between vintages, qvevris are rigorously cleaned with lime, water, and a special brush made from cherry bark, then relined with beeswax. Cleaning a qvevri can be almost as taxing as making one, especially when it's already set in the ground. Although qvevri vary greatly in size, the largest can hold approximately 2,600 gallons (10,000 liters) and are big enough for a person to roam around inside.

How to try it
Visit the cellar and taste the wine at the Alaverdi Monastery in eastern Georgia, where they've been following tradition for more than a thousand years.

An ancient monastery's winemaking room, containing rows of subterranean qvevri.

THE ELOQUENT, EXISTENTIAL TOASTMASTER

TAMADA • GEORGIA

How to try it
Supras are generally invite-only affairs.

A Georgian feast is called a supra, and presiding over every supra is a tamada, or toastmaster, who leads the diners on a long and winding existential journey throughout the meal. A few times an hour, the tamada will rise and speak to the guests, who may consist of a casual gathering of friends or an elaborate wedding celebration. He doesn't shy away from the difficult topics: A good toastmaster will address matters of the mind and soul, themes of life, death, God, and humanity, and will speak of them with honed finesse. There will be metaphors and historical references, all bound by a rhythm that's nearly poetic. He will raise his glass to his fellow diners and sit until it's time to toast again.

Hospitality is deeply rooted in Georgian culture and to be a tamada is a significant honor, typically bestowed upon the eldest and most well-spoken man at the table. (Women tamadas are a recent development and still rare.) If a tamada is especially skilled, he'll be asked to officiate the ceremonies and meals of those beyond his circle, often becoming locally famous. Respected as men of stature and ideas, tamadas are almost never paid. They provide a service to the community, and their community venerates them with deep gratitude.

A traditional Georgian feast in the town of Mestia.

The younger generation has openly embraced the tradition, and though they may conduct their supras a little differently (less food, more women as tamadas), they still prize the discourse around the big questions of existence and the fellowship that happens around a table.

CAMPFIRE BACON FAT

SÜLT SZALONNA • HUNGARY

How to try it
A slab of smoked fatback from your butcher, cut into chunks and skewered, will work perfectly. Rye bread is the preferred accompaniment.

Imagine a block of pure pork fat—no muscle, no skin—lightly smoked and cut into cubes. When slid onto a wooden skewer (preferably cut fresh from a fruit tree) and melted over an open fire, this becomes the beloved Hungarian campfire treat known as sült szalonna. As the cube sizzles and begins to drip salty, liquid pork, a thick slice of bread catches the fat and soaks up the flavor. After a few cycles of plunging the skewer into the flames and dangling it over the bread, the slice should be entirely saturated in fat and ready to be decorated with bits of red onion, tomato, cucumber, or—in classic Hungarian style—with paprika.

SPIT-ROASTED CAKE

SAKOTIS • LITHUANIA

Most cakes are created in about the same way: You mix a batter, pour it into a pan, and bake it in an oven. Spit cakes, in dramatic contrast, are cooked by flinging batter onto a rotating dowel over an open flame.

Variations of spit cakes are popular across Europe. In Hungary, Slovakia, and the Czech Republic, spit cakes tend to be tubular; in Germany, Baumkuchen looks like donuts stacked one on top of the other.

One of the most dramatic spit cakes, though, is the Lithuanian version, sakotis. In the final stages of the cooking process, bakers increase the speed at which the spit rotates, which causes spikes to form as batter is flung toward the fire. The result is a cake that resembles a Christmas tree. Sakotis, after all, means "branchy tree."

Making sakotis can easily take five hours. Bakers ladle batter along the spit in regular stages, and the skill comes from knowing just how much batter to add—and just how long to wait—so all the batter stays on the cake. By piling more batter in the middle, and then cutting the final product in two, bakers can achieve a treelike appearance. For fancy affairs, like weddings, they may decorate enormous sakotis that stand taller than some guests, with sugary flowers, nuts, and drizzles of chocolate. The cake itself is spongy and moist yet firm with a slight chew. It smells pleasantly of vanilla but tastes like a classic, eggy yellow cake.

In 2015, to inaugurate a tree cake museum, the company Romnesa organized the baking of a record-holding, 12-foot-long (3.7m) spit cake.

How to try it

You can buy sakotis all over Lithuania. In Vilnius, Lithuania's capital, you'll find towers in the windows of bakeries, slices served in cafés, and packaged trees on supermarket shelves.

A slotted spoon helps with even batter distribution.

ORNAMENTAL SMOKED CHEESE

OSCYPEK • POLAND

How to try it

Counterfeit oscypek is a problem in Poland, with many forgers swapping in cow's milk and using dyes to mimic the smoked color. Ensure it's the real deal by going straight to the source: U Jancoka, a highland guesthouse, is operated by cheese-making shepherds.

Fewer than 150 people are qualified to produce the Polish highland cheese oscypek. Shepherds, known as bacas, are typically at the helm of this traditional operation. They care for the sheep that graze in the Tatra mountain range of southern Poland and use their milk to create beautiful spindles of golden, smoked cheese.

A Balkan tribe called the Vlachs introduced shepherding and cheese making to the mountain's meadows nearly 1,000 years ago, and modern bacas continue to operate in ancient fashion. They work in small huts, using only wooden tools, often retaining their traditional dialect and dress. Fresh batches of cheese are cast in sycamore molds, which are carved with intricate decorations. Historically, the molds depicted imagery related to the cheese's function (often as currency or gifts), but today the designs are purely ornamental. The molds can be ovals, barrels, hearts, or animals, but only the spindle-shaped variety has earned protected status from the European Union, and those spindles must weigh between 21 and 28 ounces (600 and 800 grams), measure between 7 and 9 inches (17 and 23 centimeters) in length, and be produced between April and October, during the sheep's grazing season.

When the cheese has taken on its form, bacas soak it in saltwater, hang it from a beam, and smoke it using pine or spruce wood. This gives the exterior a slick golden hue while preserving the creamy white interior. The finished product has the texture of firm mozzarella, but the flavor is briny, smoky, and sharp, with notes of toasted chestnut. Grilled until soft and stretchy and topped with fruit preserves, oscypek might taste even better than it looks.

Transylvania

Transylvania is home to a slow-paced pastoral lifestyle. Villages have been slow to modernize: Especially in the 12th-century Saxon villages, many people don't have cell phones and still prefer horse-drawn carriages to cars. Locals often live off their land and their animals, producing small batches of old-world, artisanal food. The farm-to-table lifestyle means things taste better, but little travels beyond the region's borders—so to taste their land, you'll have to go. Here's the best of Transylvania:

Magiun of Topoloveni is a fruit spread made from four (or more) Romanian plum varieties, cooked for ten hours until it becomes a sticky, dark brown paste. The plums here are so sweet that the recipe never uses sugar.

Inima de Bou ("heart of ox") tomatoes were the favored variety of the Saxons—intensely sweet, pulpy, and thin-skinned. They are disappearing in most of Romania, but still grow in their native Transylvania, albeit in much smaller quantities.

Şuncă (ham) is a point of pride in Transylvania, where pigs are raised and processed without machinery—just as they were centuries ago—and have a naturally complex and meaty flavor lost in commercial operations.

A shepherd in the Hăşmaş Mountains making cheese in a hut.

Brânză de burduf is a soft sheep's milk cheese produced on the slopes of the Bucegi Mountains and aged in the bark of a fir tree, which produces a uniquely spicy and verdant taste.

Kürtöskalács (chimney cake) is made by wrapping dough around a wooden spit that rotates over hot cinders. As it barbecues, the dough turns into a chewy, peelable cake while a coating of sugar becomes a sticky caramel coating.

MAGICAL CHEESE-RIPENING CAVE

GROTTO OF TAGA • ROMANIA

How to try it
Due to the very limited production of the cave, Năsal cheese is difficult to find outside of Transylvania.

According to Transylvanian legend, the commune of Taga was once controlled by a cruel and wealthy count. The people were starving and, to feed themselves, were forced to steal the count's cheese, which they hid in the town cave. When they came to retrieve the contraband cheese, they discovered it had changed color, from white to reddish-yellow, and had acquired a funky smell. To their surprise, the transformed cheese was delicious. When the count discovered what they'd done, he took the cheese—and the cave—for himself.

Although the story is legend, the cave is very real, and it remains the only place in the world that can produce this hyper-regional, soft cow's milk cheese called Năsal, after the small village where the cave is located. Năsal is a smear-ripened cheese, which means bacteria or fungi grow on the rind. The cave in Năsal contains naturally occurring *Brevibacterium linens*, a bacteria present on the human skin that causes foot odor, which—in tandem with a stable temperature and humidity—gives the cheese a deep and earthy flavor impossible to re-create elsewhere.

Wheels of Năsal cheese age in the grotto.

Since the 19th century, when a Romanian architect and his son began producing the cave cheese, Năsal has been steadily gaining a devout following, even winning a gold medal at the Paris World Expo. A commercial operation began in 1954, which tried to expand the facility beyond the cave, but the cheese suffered, the price increased, consumption waned, and so the cave was closed in 2013. After enormous public outcry, the cave reopened less than a year later. Today, the cheese of Năsal lives on, feeding off that dank, delicious foot bacteria that makes it uniquely Transylvanian.

BLOOD CANDY NUTRITIONAL SUPPLEMENT

GEMATOGEN • RUSSIA

How to try it
Gematogen is widely available in Russia, typically at the pharmacy, and in Russian grocery stores worldwide.

Gematogen has all the hallmarks of candy: the dark appearance of chocolate, the sticky chewiness of caramel, and plenty of sweetness. These features do an impressive job of masking all the cow's blood, which is the main ingredient in this Soviet-era treat.

The packaging, which features smiling cartoon children and animals, also does wonders for marketing the bloody contents. In fact, many young Russians grew up eating the treat without realizing what it contained. Sold at pharmacies and drugstores, gematogen was dispensed more like medicine than candy. Adults were prescribed daily doses of about 1.75 ounces (50 g), children under the age of 13 needed an adult's consent, and pregnant women and breastfeeding mothers required a consultation before eating it. These days fresh cow's blood is often swapped out for powdered stuff, but it remains the leading candy bar for anemia, malnutrition, and fatigue.

THE HIGH-TECH WAY TO FEED COSMONAUTS

MIR SPACE STATION DINING TABLE · RUSSIA

The Mir station was the world's first experiment with long-term space habitation, orbiting Earth from 1986 to 2001, with the capacity to support three crew members (among them cosmonaut Valeri Polyakov, who still holds the record for longest continuous space sojourn at 437 days). To feed these space workers in the compact microgravity station, the Russians designed a high-tech table for communal dining.

Located in the station's core module, the multicolored space table had slots where cosmonauts could heat up tins and tubes of food such as liver stroganoff and chicken in white sauce. Other cans, such as caviar and cheese, were eaten at space temperature. About 65 percent of each meal was composed of freeze-dried food, which could be reconstituted from a spigot in the table that dispensed hot and cold water. A built-in vacuum system sucked up any stray crumbs, but the meals were designed with easy cleanup in mind: Crumbly things were prebroken into bite-size pieces and flaky items were coated with an edible film that kept everything together. (According to American astronaut Andy Thomas, the space food in general was surprisingly delicious, especially the soups and fruit juices.) The table itself could be folded against the wall to create room when not in use, but that rarely happened because the cosmonauts found they could simply float over it.

The Mir station was in service for 15 years, three times longer than expected, and it had the battle scars to prove it: There were mold breakouts, a fire, and a collision with a cargo spacecraft. After being decommissioned, the body of the space station was mostly broken up, but the table was brought back to Earth and currently resides at the Memorial Museum of Cosmonautics in Moscow.

How to try it
The Memorial Museum of Cosmonautics is open seven days a week and costs 250 rubles, or about $4.

Soviet cosmonauts Sergei Krikalev and Aleksandr Volkov eating lunch aboard the Mir station in 1988.

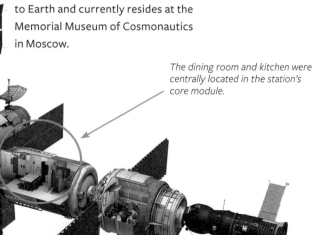

The dining room and kitchen were centrally located in the station's core module.

THE BRIEF, HIGH-FLYING ERA OF

From 1928 to 1937, when the *Hindenburg* disaster incinerated the future of zeppelin travel, the German-owned airships offered a dining experience to rival a modern luxury cruise ship. The menus leaned heavily toward the German palate, with an emphasis on cream and meat, modeled after the cuisine of traditional, high-end European hotels.

Zeppelins, which were the size of buildings, flew significantly lower than modern planes do and therefore avoided the dry, pressurized air that dulls taste and smell on today's commercial flights. Food tasted like itself, which helped passengers enjoy the 7.5 pounds (3.5 kg) of lavish victuals they were allotted each day, including fattened duckling, champagne-braised cabbage, lobster, and caviar.

The emphasis on German cuisine was a strategic choice. Although there was hope that these commercial zeppelin flights would one day be profitable, they were primarily a way to demonstrate a kind of German cultural strength. After being trounced in World War I, the Germans used zeppelins to show the world they were at the cutting edge of luxury and transport, sparing no expense to make their point. Tables were laid with vases of fresh flowers and blue-and-white china. Plates and teapots were inlaid with real gold. The dining room of the *Hindenburg* was furnished with lightweight, state-of-the-art aluminum Bauhaus furniture. (Napkins, oddly, were seriously regulated: Passengers were given a single white cloth napkin, in a personalized envelope which they had to keep and reuse for the entire journey.)

Drinking was perhaps the most popular activity aboard a zeppelin. The well-stocked bar had as many as 15 varieties of wine, as well as mixed drinks divided into "Sours," "Flips," "Fizzes," "Cobblers," and "Cocktails." Prairie oysters, a hangover cure made with hot sauce and a whole raw egg, were listed on the bar menu below the libations.

Zeppelin Dining

Europe's largest market is housed in giant zeppelin hangars.

At the turn of the 20th century, five giant neoclassical and art deco style hangars were built in the center of Riga, Latvia, to house zeppelins. When the German-made airships fell from favor, the hangars were turned into Riga's Central Market, the largest market bazaar in Europe. The market spans 778,000 square feet and houses 3,000 trade stands. During the Nazi occupation, the space was used to house troops and army supplies, but the market was reinvigorated under the Soviets.

Each of the five hangars in Riga's Central Market has a theme: meat, fish, dairy, produce, and general gastronomy.

Russians Once Preserved Their Milk with Frogs

Before the boon of refrigeration, Russian tradition held that a live frog dropped in a pitcher of milk would prolong its freshness.

There are Russian fables about frogs in milk. One proverb tells of two frogs who have fallen into a jug of milk, one who gives in to despair and drowns, and the other who stays afloat by swimming furiously. By morning, the sprightly frog has churned the milk into solid butter and escapes. Another story describes Babushka-Lyagushka-Shakusha, the magical, sentient "Grandmother Hopping Frog," swimming around in a bath of milk.

So was the preservation trick simply based on an old wives' tale? In 2012, these wives of yore were vindicated: A team of Moscow scientists proved that the secretions from certain frogs have antibacterial and antifungal properties, which may have helped in the preservation of milk. Inspired by a childhood

of drinking frog milk, lead scientist Dr. Albert Lebedev discovered 76 antimicrobial peptides in the Russian brown frog, many of which had antibiotic compounds that protect against bacteria in their wet habitats. Some of these compounds were as effective at killing salmonella and staph bacteria as modern prescription antibiotics.

Still, it's not recommended to drop any random frog into your milk because they can also spread harmful pathogens. The scientific pursuit of amphibian-inspired medicine is an ever-expanding and exciting world (a different frog, the North American mink frog, secretes a chemical effective against the drug-resistant bacterium *Acinetobacter baumannii*), but when it comes to milk, the refrigerator—along with the expiration date—is undeniably the best line of defense.

MILK VODKA

ARAGA • RUSSIA

How to try it

Araga is primarily made at home in the countryside, so you likely won't find it in stores. In Tuva, your best shot at tasting it is to get an invitation to a local family's yurt.

For centuries the nomadic people of Tuva, a remote region of Russia just north of the Mongolian border, have turned the milk from their yaks, cows, and goats into a bevy of useful food products stable enough to withstand long journeys. Among them is araga, the Tuvan moonshine distilled from fermented sour milk.

Araga is produced in a homemade still called a shuuruun, crafted from the hollowed-out trunk of a poplar tree. The wooden cylinder is set inside a large pot over the stove and sealed off at the top with a container of cold water. As the fermented milk, or khoitpak, heats up at the bottom of the pot, the steam trapped inside produces condensation, which slowly trickles out of the shuuruun's long spout. The result is a clear, sour liquor of 5 to 20 percent alcohol that tastes milder when warm. Considered a special drink, araga is reserved for celebrations and rituals and is mostly served to the community elders: An old Tuvan custom states that a man must be married before his first taste.

STURGEON SPINAL CORD

VYAZIGA • RUSSIA

Sturgeon—famous producers of the ultimate luxury food, caviar—are prized in Russia for another delicacy: vyaziga. Made from the fish's spinal cord, vyaziga is used in Russian cooking to impart a rich, intense flavor that comes from the sturgeon's marrow. The decadent ingredient was famously served in a second-course consommé in the last, fateful meal for first-class passengers aboard the *Titanic*.

Because sturgeon lack vertebrae, the spinal cord can be pulled from the body in one very long piece (the stretchy, gelatinous cord can be multiple feet long). Once harvested, the cord is dried and then crushed into powder, which is typically reconstituted in water to make to make a thick, sticky paste.

In Russia, the dish most often associated with vyaziga is the kulebyaka: a pie so complicated, time-consuming, and expensive to make that most Russians have only read about it in stories by Nikolai Gogol and Anton Chekhov (who referred to it as a "temptation to sin"). The intricate kulebyaka is an oblong construction of many layers, each layer separated from the next by a "pancake" made from dough rolled out very thin. Fish, such as salmon or sturgeon, makes up the base layer, which supports a balancing act of rice, creamed mushrooms, onions, eggs, and boiled cabbage, all held together by a paste of vyaziga. Wrapped in pastry, the pie is often decorated with little fish, leaves, or flowers made of dough.

Although still used, vyaziga is less common in Russian cooking today. This decline in popularity is mostly due to the overfishing of sturgeon, but the ingredient has also suffered from its association with the downfall of some of history's most opulent eaters.

How to try it

Vyaziga is still available in Russian grocery stores and is considered essential to making a true kulebyaka.

SIBERIAN SASHIMI COMPETITION

FESTIVAL STROGANINA • RUSSIA

How to try it

Festival Stroganina takes place in early December. Although there's no easy way to get to Yakutsk, the most reliable method is to fly: It has a small airport with a single runway.

The Russian city of Yakutsk is located fewer than 300 miles (483 km) from the Arctic Circle. Many of Yakutsk's residents are descended from the Yakut people, who have lived in the region since the 7th century and are famous across Russia for their hunting and fishing prowess. Despite experiencing the coldest temperatures of any major city on Earth, Yakutsk's locals like to be outdoors hunting, ice fishing, and in December (when lows average about –40°F) throwing an open-air celebration for their culinary specialty, stroganina—thin slices of sashimi stripped from the flank of a frozen whitefish.

The festival's opening ceremony is a judged presentation of these curls in elaborate stroganina sculptures, ranging from friendly snowmen to towering mammoths. The main event is a partnered trial: Men hold the frozen fish vertically by its tail and slide a sharp Yakutian knife (a 4-to-7-inch asymmetrical blade specially designed for long slices) along the fish's abdomen, producing elegant, diaphanous curls of sashimi. Their female partners dash back and forth between fish and plate, collecting stroganina and arranging it as artfully as possible. During judging, time is weighed against beauty, and a winner is chosen by a panel of fishermen, government officials, and sashimi enthusiasts. Knife vendors, fish salesmen, and merchants of fish-skin clothing and gloves round out the stroganina-themed celebration.

The Siberian sashimi is served simply, with salt and pepper, and should melt with the heat of your mouth. The bite-size blast of protein also makes an ideal chaser. As one saying goes, only sled dogs eat stroganina without vodka, and at the Festival Stroganina, there is plenty of vodka and champagne flowing into glasses carved from ice.

A Yakut woman in national clothing holding frozen ribbons of stroganina.

CHERNOBYL'S EXCLUSION ZONE CAFETERIA

CANTEEN 19 • UKRAINE

On April 26, 1986, a reactor at the Chernobyl nuclear power plant exploded, causing the world's biggest nuclear power disaster. The explosion killed dozens of workers and first responders, and scientists still dispute how many people have since died from radiation-related cancers. Today, forestry workers, biologists, and construction crews continue efforts to dismantle the reactor and remove waste in the 1,000-square-mile (2,600 km^2) Exclusion Zone. When they're ready to take a break and eat, many of them head to Canteen 19.

Canteen 19, the Exclusion Zone's most popular dining hall, serves hearty Eastern European fare, including borscht, schnitzel, kompot, and sweet, cream-filled crepes. In addition to Chernobyl workers, the canteen feeds tour groups on Ukrainian government–sanctioned trips. (To enter the Exclusion Zone, guests must sign up for a tour or hire a private licensed guide, have their passports checked by the Ukrainian government, and pass through a military checkpoint.)

Diners must pass through a radiation detector before entering the austere canteen, which looks like an institutional lunch line, with white-uniformed workers scooping up meals from a line of prepared foods. The cafeteria offers a glimpse into contemporary Chernobyl life, as well as the opportunity to eat alongside the people still cleaning up after the disaster.

How to try it
Canteen 19 is open from 9 a.m. to 6 p.m. Many tour operators will make a stop here for lunch, which, if not included in the tour, costs about $10.

PORK LARD PLAYGROUND

SALO ART MUSEUM • UKRAINE

No trip to the city of Lviv is complete without a little pork fat art. Called salo in Ukraine, the salt-cured fat is usually eaten raw, often on bread, with just black pepper and paprika to counter its rich fattiness. The shelf-stable fat (which, thanks to salt-curing, is safe to eat for up to two years) also makes a great medium for sculpture, as evidenced by the Salo Art Museum.

Although a museum in name, the space is more like a contemporary art gallery housed in a restaurant that becomes a nightclub on the weekends. Human busts,

How to try it
The Salo Art Museum is open 7 days a week.

body parts, aliens, and animals are all whittled from the creamy, butter-textured fat, and line the walls of the industrial space. A giant replica of a human heart—which set the record for largest heart made out of lard—is proudly preserved behind glass. Rounding out the lard experience is the museum restaurant, which doubles down on the art theme. Most meals are served with small salo statues carved into strikingly realistic lions, pigs, soldier heads, and Elvis Presleys. There's also salo sushi, salo chocolate, and a vast supply of booze to cut through any lingering feelings about having eaten a pig constructed of pig fat.

After hours, the white couches and neon lighting transform the space to a nightclub with a live DJ, because when it comes to salo, it's never too far.

The works on display are among the world's most caloric figurines.

BUTTER WEEK

MASLENITSA • UKRAINE

How to try it
Maslenitsa is celebrated all over Ukraine the week before Lent, with particularly large parties (and publicly burning effigies) in Kyiv.

Before it was named Maslenitsa (literally "of butter"), this week-long celebration was a pagan festival to cast off winter and welcome spring. But when Christians joined the festivities, the party gradually evolved into a pre-Lenten feast that heavily featured the most decadent food permitted during fast days: dairy.

Also known as "Pancake Week," Ukrainian Maslenitsa is now a jubilant time for reconnecting with family and loved ones, particularly over pancakes. Each day brings a different theme, and a different person with whom to eat pancakes. Monday is for women, with men making the pancakes. On Wednesday, mothers-in-law traditionally invite sons-in-law for pancakes. Friday, the roles reverse and the son-in-law plays host. Saturday is for sisters-in-law. On Sunday, everyone eats pancakes together. Called mlyntsi, the pancakes are typically crepe-thin, made from a loose, dairy-heavy batter. As they're served all day long, mlyntsi can be sweet or savory, eaten with cottage cheese, fruit preserves, mushrooms, or caviar.

Revelers burn an effigy of "Lady Maslenitsa."

To accompany the pancake binge, Maslenitsa brings a revival of folk customs: Dancing and singing in traditional dress, ice skating, competitions, and snowball fights are loud and vivacious, meant to break the stillness of the cold months. On the final day, an effigy is burned that symbolizes death and resurrection—a ritual surviving from pagan times. The pancakes, too, are often considered a nod to the old tradition. Pagans worshipped the returning sun, and pancakes, being round and hot and yellow-hued, are their culinary representation.

WEDDING BREAD

KOROVAI • UKRAINE

On the Saturday preceding a Ukrainian wedding, seven married women gather to make korovai, a wedding bread that symbolizes the community's blessing of a new union. These women, who knead the dough and sing folk songs, must be happily in their first marriage, infusing the bread with their good fortune. When it's time to bake the dough, a happily married man must place the bread in the oven. Then everyone prays for the best. A cracked or malformed korovai is a bad sign for the marriage, but the higher it rises and the more decorations or layers it contains, the better the marriage will be.

Though wedding breads are a part of ceremonies across much of eastern Europe, Ukrainian korovai tends to be the most ornate. Each flourish crafted from dough has a specific meaning: Roses symbolize beauty, ears of wheat mean future prosperity, and a wreath of periwinkle represents the strong connection that binds the couple. Two birds often grace the top of the bread, one baked with its wings outstretched to represent the groom, the other with wings furled to symbolize the bride.

During the wedding, the korovai is displayed prominently beside the altar. Afterward, every guest must eat a piece. In some versions of the tradition, the bride and groom both break off a bit of bread, and whoever comes away with the bigger slice will be the head of the household.

How to try it
A few Ukrainian bakeries online will ship their korovai internationally. Prices start at about $100 and increase as the bread becomes more elaborate. It all depends on how happy you'd like your marriage to be.

SCANDINAVIA

SPICY BIRTHDAY RITUAL

PEBERSVEND · DENMARK

Hundreds of years ago, traveling spice salesmen were notorious bachelors. They never stayed in one place for long enough to settle down, and a man who remained single was called a pebersvend—literally, a "pepper companion." Today, Danes still refer to unmarried adults as spice salesmen. (A single woman is a pebermø, or "pepper maiden.") To celebrate an unwed person's birthday, Danes like to douse them in spices.

A 25th birthday calls for getting "cinnamon-ed." Often, friends attack the birthday pebersvend or pebermø by tying them to a post, making them don goggles, and then pelting them with handfuls of ground spice. At age 30, the cinnamon attack is upgraded to pepper, and the birthday victim is likely to receive at least one pepper grinder as a gift.

SAUNA SAUSAGE

SAUNA MAKKARA · FINLAND

In Finland, the sauna is a cultural institution. Finns once gave birth and washed their dead in the heated rooms because they were the cleanest spaces in the home. Now there are 3.3 million saunas for a population of 5.5 million, meaning just about every household has one.

As with any treasured national pastime, there are rules. First, you must strip and shower. When you enter, lay a towel on your seat and prepare to get hot: The temperature should be 158–212°F (70–100°C). It's good to work up a healthy sweat, but if you start to feel dry, simply ladle some water onto the hot stones to create steam, known as löyly. When you've had enough, go outside and cool off by jumping in a lake or rolling in snow.

With all that sweating and jumping, you're probably hungry, which means it's time for sauna sausage. While you were sizzling inside the steam room, so was your meal. Makkara, a traditional Finnish sausage, is often heated over the hot stones of a sauna stove, known as a kiuas. For a crispy exterior, the bare sausage goes directly on the kiuas. For tender sausage and easy cleanup, wrap them in foil or get yourself a special holder made of Finnish soapstone and used exclusively for the cooking of sausage in saunas.

The sausages, which typically come plain or with cheese inside, pair perfectly with the sweet-hot zing of mustard. Called sinnapi, Finnish mustard is often made on the stovetop at home, using mustard powder, sugar, lemon juice, vinegar, and the special ingredient: a big glug of cream. Cooked down to a thick, amber spread, sinnapi is a crucial sausage condiment that cannot be swapped out for any old supermarket mustard.

Sausages cooked in special holders are extra tender.

Finnish Mustard

5 tablespoons hot dry mustard (such as Colman's)

½ cup sugar

1 teaspoon salt

1 cup cream

1 tablespoon olive oil

2 tablespoons apple cider vinegar

1 tablespoon lemon juice

1. Mix together the mustard, sugar, and salt, making sure to remove all lumps. (Use a sieve if necessary.)

2. Transfer the dry mixture to a small saucepan and add the cream one tablespoon at a time, incorporating each spoonful before adding another.

3. Add the olive oil, vinegar, and lemon juice and stir.

4. Bring the mustard to a boil over medium heat, then lower the heat and simmer for 7 to 8 minutes, stirring constantly.

5. Let cool, transfer to a sealable jar, and keep in the refrigerator.

MUSTARD

Before mustard was a condiment, it was a poultice for bronchitis and toothaches, an ointment for skin inflammation, and a powdered additive to a soothing, sleep-inducing bath. As early as the 5th century BCE, the Greeks prized the easy-to-grow plant for its antiseptic properties and ability to stimulate blood circulation. Scientist Pythagoras found that the essential oils, when applied to a wound, pulled toxins from the body, which led him to use mustard as a treatment for scorpion stings. Physician Hippocrates applied mustard plasters to chests and let the heat from the dressing loosen phlegm and ease breathing.

Around the 4th century CE, the Romans had a new idea. They mixed young wine with the crushed seeds of the medicinal plant, tasted the paste, and named the new flavor sensation "flaming hot must." Long before the Silk Road opened to Europe, mustard (mustum being the Romans' unfermented grape juice, and ardens the Latin for "fiery") was one of the continent's first breakout spices, and it soon spread to the rest of the world.

Because of its antibiotic properties, an unopened jar of mustard will rarely spoil. It doesn't require refrigeration, will not develop mold or bacteria, and will never become unsafe to eat. Coupled with the distinctive zing that flatters everything from Indian curries to American hot dogs, dim sum to barbecue sauce, nearly every region in the world has developed their own application for the spicy, versatile, and medicinal plant.

Dijon

In the French city now synonymous with the condiment, they made their mustard with verjus, the tart juice of unripe grapes, which made a sharper, more sophisticated variety soon coveted around the country. The Duke of Burgundy, an avid 14th-century mustard lover, held a gala where guests reportedly consumed 85 gallons of Dijon in a single sitting. Pope John XII of Avignon declared a new Vatican position called Grand Moutardier du Pape, or Grand Mustard Maker to the Pope, and appointed his nephew, believed

to be a dilettante living near Dijon, to mix all his mustards. (The idiom "the pope's mustard maker," which refers to a pompous person in an insignificant role, came from this appointment.) By 1855, a man named Maurice Grey was winning awards for his Dijon-mustard-making machine, the first of its kind to automate the process. He sought out a financial backer and found Auguste Poupon. Together, combining their last names to form the Grey Poupon brand, they rolled out their signature Dijon, prepared with white wine and manufactured at high speed.

Colman's

Jeremiah Colman, an English miller, pioneered the technique of grinding mustard seeds into a fine powder without allowing the oils to evaporate, which preserved the spicy, intense flavor. In 1866, Colman became the official mustard maker to Queen Victoria and later, during World War II, his mustard was one of the few foods that wasn't rationed because it was essential to flavoring bland wartime food.

Kasundi

Traditionally, Bengalis had elaborate rituals surrounding the harvest and washing of mustard seeds to make the traditional mustard relish, kasundi. On a spring day called Akshaya Tritiya, groups of married women bathed in odd numbers, then washed the mustard seeds facing east, chanting in wet saris. Over the next week, the seeds were ground into a pulp, spiced, and mixed with water, salt, and green mango, before fermenting in a clay pot. Originally, only Brahmins (the highest Indian caste) were allowed to make the mustard sauce, but it's now open season for kasundi making. The spicy chutney is the preferred dipping sauce for fried foods, especially the beloved Bengali vegetable fritter, called a chop.

Chinese Mustard

This thick, pungent paste inflames the nasal passages like horseradish or wasabi. There is no special ingredient to the mixture, just ground brown mustard seeds (*Brassica juncea*, or Chinese mustard) mixed with water. After about 15 minutes, the paste reaches peak potency, then slowly declines. A good swap for Chinese mustard powder is Colman's, which is a blend of *Brassica juncea* and the slightly milder white mustard, *Sinapis alba*.

Mostarda di Frutta

The 14th-century dukes of Milan were trendsetters in mixing sweet and spicy. Chunks of fruit such as apples, quince, or cherries were preserved in sweet and hot mustard syrup, then served atop their ducal roasts. In Italy today, the term *mostarda* refers to the hot and fruity condiment.

HELSINKI'S POP-UP RESTAURANT PARTY

RESTAURANT DAY • FINLAND

How to try it

To be fed by the residents of Helsinki, time your trip for the third Saturday of February, May, August, or November.

On Restaurant Day in Helsinki—which occurs on the third Saturday of February, May, August, and November—anyone can open a restaurant, anywhere. All around the Finnish capital, citizens sell ceviche from pop-up stands, muffins from jewelry stores, and homemade food from old train depots, borrowed kitchens, bus stops, stairwells, and the occasional boat. Anything goes: Restaurants are erected for babies, currywursts are slung from dark basements. In a city where residents don't engage in much small talk, Restaurant Day has altered Helsinki's social fabric. It's a day for people to talk to one another, to approach strangers and chat about what they're cooking.

Restaurant Day got its start in 2011, when Helsinki resident Timo Santala wanted to start a mobile bicycle bar, selling drinks and tapas, and was frustrated by the city's red tape. Santala imagined a day where a restaurant could open with no licenses and no limitations, and inaugurated Restaurant Day in May 2011. Since then, the free-for-all food carnival has become so beloved that the city government decided to support the festivities. (It helps that there have been no known cases of Restaurant Day food poisoning.)

The rogue entrepreneurial holiday has spread to other countries, too, from Iceland to islands in the South Pacific—where communities are connecting over shared food and conversation. In Russia, a Restaurant Day chef cooked chicken in the seam of an old Soviet car motor. In Nicaragua, one restaurant owner took payment in the form of a poem or a song.

SNOWMOBILE COFFEE IN THE HUGGING TREE FOREST

HALIPUU'S CAMPFIRE BARISTA • FINLAND

How to try it

HaliPuu forest is a 25-minute drive from Kittilä Airport (KTT). You can adopt a tree for five years, during which time you can visit it freely, while sipping on a smoky latte.

The Campfire Barista, Steffan Wunderink's one-of-a-kind café, offers up exceptional drinks prepared over an open fire that he drags behind a snowmobile through a forest in the far northern reaches of Finland.

The forest, which belongs to his wife's grandfather, was a gift from the Finnish state after the family lost their home during World War II. Instead of using the forest as timber, the family decided to put the trees up for adoption and invite tourists to come spend time with them. It was while working as a guide on this land—now known as HaliPuu (Hugging Tree) Forest—that Wunderink became the Campfire Barista.

Using an open fire as his stove, Wunderink gained a reputation for his wondrously smoky, espresso-based drinks, as well as a chai latte made from an antioxidant-rich native mushroom called chaga. When a local complained about having to trek into the forest for her daily caffeine fix, the C.F.B. went mobile.

Wunderink bought a snowmobile and built a sled that could safely hold a wood-fired grill. Then, in a windfall of upgrades, he partnered with a friend with ties to a single-estate, biodynamic coffee farm in India, who also happened to operate a solar-powered coffee roaster out of a converted sea container in town.

During winter months, you can catch Wunderink's café in front of the tourism office in the center of town, in his family's forest, or at a number of public events. In the warmer months, without a snowpack to ride on, he's restricted to stationary events and festivals. His menu has expanded beyond espresso-based drinks and chaga chai to organic teas, warm black currant juice, and lingonberry marshmallows you can roast over his fire.

FERMENTED BIRDS IN A SEAL SKIN

KIVIAK • GREENLAND

This Inuit tradition begins with a hunt: Using just sight and feel, a skilled hunter casts a long-handled net high into the air to catch small auks mid-flight, netting hundreds of birds over the course of a single day. The summer months, when the weather is moderate and the birds plentiful, are the time to make kiviak so it will be ready by winter, when hunting sites are perilously icy and sustenance scarce.

Auks are small Arctic birds, about half the size of puffins, little enough to be held in a palm. Up to 500 auks are needed for a kiviak, which takes the birds—left whole with feathers intact—and stuffs them into the cleaned skin of a seal. Once packed with auks, any excess air is removed from the seal sack, often by jumping on it, then the opening is sewn shut and the seam is rubbed with seal fat, which repels flies. The massive bird-and-seal package is buried under a heap of stones and left to ferment for a minimum of three months (but will keep for up to 18). The seal skin retains a thick layer of blubber, and the fat allows the tiny birds to slowly soften as they age, bones included. Save for the feathers, every part of the bird will be eaten.

Come winter, when the Greenland days are long and dark, kiviak provides a celebration. The fermented auks are considered special-occasion food, saved for birthdays and weddings, and unearthing the bundle means a long-awaited feast. The birds remain mostly intact, but the meat and innards are almost creamy, with a taste often compared to the ripest of gorgonzola cheese crossed with the anise flavor of licorice. Kiviak is always eaten outdoors because the smell is as pungent as the taste. It is also imperative that the birds be auks: In 2013, several people in the town of Siorapaluk died from eating kiviak made from eider birds, which don't ferment as well as auks.

How to try it
Kiviak is hard-won food, but if you're willing to trek to eastern, western, or polar Greenland, you can try to wrangle an invitation to a local birthday party.

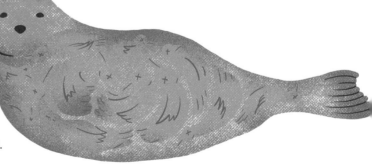

Engastration

The centuries-old culinary technique of stuffing one animal inside another animal, sometimes beyond sense or recognition.

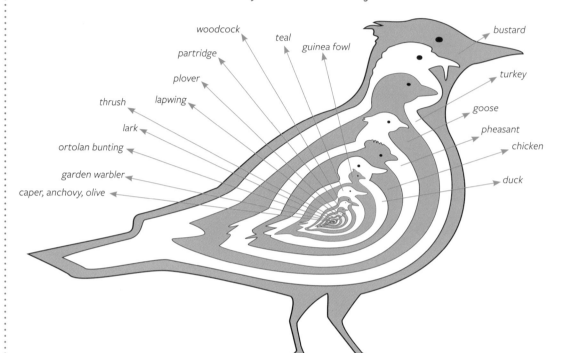

woodcock · teal · guinea fowl · bustard · partridge · plover · turkey · thrush · lapwing · goose · lark · pheasant · ortolan bunting · chicken · garden warbler · duck · caper, anchovy, olive

RÔTI SANS PAREIL ("UNPARALLELED ROAST")

A French recipe from 1807 instructs the cook to stuff a caper into an anchovy, which is then placed into the cavity of an olive, which can be stuffed easily into a garden warbler, which fits nicely into an ortolan bunting, and then, with some finesse, into a lark, which is fitted inside a thrush, then pushed into a lapwing and shoved into a plover, which slides into a partridge just before being rammed into a woodcock, muscled into a teal, shunted into a guinea fowl and crammed into a duck, then a chicken, then a pheasant, before

the final, large-bird sprint, which shoves the menagerie into a goose, which should fit into a turkey and, if all goes well, slides snugly into a bustard. Slow-cooked in a hermetically sealed pot of broth, your 17 birds will be ready to eat in 24 hours.

TROJAN BOAR

This ancient Roman recipe begins with a gutted 1,000-pound (454 kg) hog, washed twice in wine and rolled in musk and pepper. Half the enormous cavity was filled with a collection of thrushes, sow's udders, gnat snappers, and eggs,

while the other half was plugged up with polenta. Oysters and scallops were inserted in the mouth and pushed down into the belly, then the whole hog was sewn up, washed in liquor, and roasted. Aptly nicknamed after the Trojan horse, this engorged boar was served up at brawny events like gladiatorial contests, chariot races, and the inaugurations of emperors.

BEDOUIN STUFFED CAMEL

The whole stuffed camel is a gastronomic legend— or is it? Fish, stuffed with hardboiled eggs and rice, are packed into chickens that are stitched into a

couple of lambs, maybe a goat, and loaded into the body of a camel, which is boiled then roasted on a spit. This camel, allegedly prepared at prominent wedding feasts in Saudi Arabia and the United Arab Emirates, appears in culinary memoirs and many cookbooks, but firsthand accounts are still rare. *Guinness World Records* claims the camel is "the largest item on any menu in the world," and pictures of the desert delicacy do exist; still, the skeptics remain convinced that the Saudis are pulling off an elaborate, impressively executed camel joke.

FERMENTED SHARK

HÁKARL • ICELAND

Pieces of fermented shark hang in an open warehouse.

When trying hákarl—the dried and fermented shark of Iceland—it's common to gag. Even a bite-size cube has an extraordinarily high ammonia content, which smells (and some say tastes) like urine. But Vikings would advise you to pinch your nose and be thankful for their innovation. Had the shark not been fermented per their specifications, you might not even live to be repulsed because the meat would have been chock-full of poison.

When fresh, Greenland sharks contain large amounts of trimethylamine oxide, which can cause powerful, uncontrollable intoxication when eaten. The Vikings, when confronted with a meaty creature that grew up to 24 feet long, devised a method for draining the poison from its flesh. They buried a cleaned shark in a shallow pit of gravelly sand, placed rocks on top of the sand to weigh the shark down and press the liquid from its body, and left it to seep and ferment for 6 to 12 weeks. After digging the shark up, they cut it into strips and hung the pieces to dry for several months. The finished product lasted practically forever, making for perfect Viking food.

But what's great for a Viking is not always great for a modern palate. Putrid pee aroma aside, hákarl is a hardcore piece of meat. Soft, white bits from the body are often described as a gruesome cross between fish and blue cheese, and the reddish belly meat is unapologetically chewy. Even Icelanders are polarized by this food; many, in fact, have never tried it themselves.

In recent years, hákarl has become popular with tourists, who keep the traditional industry alive and don't mind that modern curing methods involve more plastic containers than dirt and rocks.

How to try it
Most of the country's hákarl is produced at the Bjarnarhöfn Shark Museum, where you can sample a piece. The midwinter Þorrablót festival, which celebrates Icelandic heritage, is another place you'll be sure to find it.

VOLCANIC SPRINGS BANANA PLANTATION

GARÐYRKJUSKÓLI RÍKISINS • ICELAND

How to try it

The plantation is not a traditional tourist site, but visitors can call ahead to see the fruit. The school is located at Reykjumörk Street, whose name translates to smokefield, with several fumaroles along the way making the air hazy and warm.

Less than 200 miles (322 km) from the Arctic Circle, the plantation at the Icelandic National Gardening School is a tropical oasis. Surrounded by volcanic hot springs, the plantation's easy access to geothermal energy and an unusually warm climate allow them to grow warm-weather crops like bananas as well as avocados, cocoa, and coffee. Many Icelanders will tell you it's the largest banana plantation in all of Europe—and it might be, depending on who's measuring.

The Icelandic banana-growing experiment began in the 1940s, when import taxes on produce were high and geothermal energy was cheap. For nearly a decade, Icelanders ate local bananas grown in geothermal-heated greenhouses that held at a steady 70°F (21°C). But in 1960, the government removed the import duties on fruit, and Iceland's greenhouse bananas could no longer compete against the international market. Today, most bananas sold in Iceland are shipped into the country from tropical climates, but the plantation in Reykir still manages several hundred trees that produce 1,000 to 4,400 pounds (500 to 2,000 kg) of bananas annually.

Whether the plantation can be called the largest in Europe is up for debate. Technically, Spain and France control larger plantations, but they're located in their respective warm-weather colonies on the Canary Islands, Martinique, and Guadeloupe. The plantation in Iceland, which is completely isolated from the outside banana world, may end up serving a different purpose: A fungal pathogen called Panama disease has been wreaking havoc on banana plantations and many fear it could wipe out the world's most widely consumed banana, the Cavendish. (This has happened before: The Cavendish's predecessor, the Big Mike, was lost in the 1950s.) Quarantined in the far north, the Icelandic bananas might end up being the last bananas standing.

Bananas thrive in a steamy greenhouse—even in chilly Iceland.

Showboating Royals

During the Middle Ages, showing off often went too far—especially at banquets, where royals loved to flaunt how rich, creative, and hilarious they were. Among nobility, throwing the most elaborate feast became such competitive sport that a new term was coined for their preferred method of showboating. Sotelties, or entremets in French (literally "between courses"), were dishes meant not to eat, but to entertain: Fish suspended in jelly appeared to be swimming, dough castles were plastered in gold leaf, slivers of almonds mimicked the spikes of a hedgehog, and meatballs were made to look like oranges. Cute at first, by the 14th century the practice was getting out of hand. Frantic for ways to remain on top, royal kitchens in England and France began reaching for more ostentatious farces. Animals became the medium of choice (another flashy move, as vegetables were considered food for the poor), and although some did laugh, chances are those people were megalomaniacs.

Redressed birds were a classic banquet centerpiece. Swans and peacocks, with their elegant plumage, were meticulously skinned to get their feathers off in one neat piece. After the birds were roasted, cooks redressed them in their skins. To keep things interesting, sometimes a bird was sewn inside the feathers of a different bird because the only thing droller than a roasted peacock sewn back into its skin was a goose replacing that peacock.

The **cockentrice** was allegedly created for King Henry VIII to impress the visiting king of France. The recipe, written like a surgical guide, instructs the chef to procure a capon and a pig, then to scald and clean them both before cutting each animal in half at the waist. Using a needle and thread, the front half of the pig is stitched to the back half of the capon, creating a new hybrid animal guaranteed to dazzle. (The order could also be reversed: chicken top, pig bottom.)

Singing chickens were made by sewing shut the bottom of a bird's neck, filling the cavity with mercury and ground sulfur, and sewing the neck again at the top. When reheated, the chemicals pushed air through the restricted passage of the neck and produced a sound akin to singing. This technique was used to prank chefs, too: Chickens were known to wail and jump from pots in what may have been the creepiest kitchen of all time.

Regular pigs became **fire-breathing pigs** when their mouths were stuffed with alcohol-soaked cotton, then lit on fire to create the optical illusion. For extra-special occasions, many animals were assembled and made to sing and breathe fire in religious and allegorical spectacles.

Chickens were the primary victims in the gruesome movement to make living food that looked dead. Submerged in hot water, they were plucked alive and glazed, then put to sleep by tucking the bird's head beneath its wing. When awakened at the table, the chicken would flee down the table, knocking over glasses and jugs and making women shriek in what royals considered a top-notch joke. Lobsters also made good fodder: After being doused in extra-strong brandy, live lobsters turned red and could be easily mixed in with the platter of cooked lobsters.

The top half of a pig sewn into the bottom half of a capon was a dish meant to impress the king of France.

HOT SPRING RYE BREAD

HVERABRAUÐ • ICELAND

How to try it
Laugarvatn Fontana is a hot spring spa that leads tours of its on-site geothermal bakery twice daily. A tour includes a tasting of the bread hot from the ground, served with butter.

Every day, a small but devoted group of Icelandic bakers trudges out to the nearest geothermal spring, digs a hole in the hot black sand, and deposits a box full of just-mixed bread dough. About a day later, they go back out and dig up the box. Inside they find a hot loaf of rye bread, gently steamed by the heat of the spring, that's dense, chewy, nutty, and just a little bit sweet.

Iceland comprises a labyrinthine network of underground volcanic hot springs, and more than 50 percent of the country's energy comes from geothermal sources. The bread must also absorb some of this power, because after a few bites of this hearty loaf, you might feel ready to climb a mountain or ford an icy river. Hverabrauð means, literally, "hot spring bread," but one of the food's nicknames—þrumari, or thunder bread—hints at another powerful side effect. All that fiber, after all, can wreak havoc at the other end of your digestive system.

Of course most Icelanders bake their rye bread (rúgbrauð) in modern ovens, but those who opt for geothermal heat swear the taste and texture is vastly superior.

A baker digs up geothermal bread on the shore of Lake Laugarvatn.

BEER ON HORSEBACK COMPETITION

BEER TÖLT • ICELAND

Icelandic horses are famous for their tölt—a smooth, lateral gait unique to the northern breed. The steady, four-beat stride can pick up velocity while remaining comfortable for riders, letting them remain fairly still in the saddle while their steeds zip around the track. To prove just how steady their horse can be, there is the beer tölt, a game in which the rider holds a full mug of beer while putting his mount through its paces. The objective is to spill as little beer as possible because the rider who loses the least gets to drink the most.

The beer tölt is a reliable feature at Icelandic horse shows. Competitors ride at various speeds, in forward and lateral directions, holding the mug with a single hand. Sometimes there is music. The sight of a dozen equestrians, each holding a beer with intense concentration as their horses bounce jauntily beneath them, is as impressive as it is ridiculous—and is an ideal way to show off your steady horse, your quirky personality, and your respect for beer.

How to try it
Friðheimar Farm in Selfoss, southern Iceland, features various horse shows including the beer tölt.

ICELANDIC HOT DOGS

PYLSUR • ICELAND

Compared with more intimidating Icelandic specialties like sour rams' testicles and fermented shark, the Icelandic hot dog known as pylsa is a comparatively accessible, and notoriously delicious, national dish.

Pylsur (just one hot dog is a pylsa) are built from a triumvirate of meats: lamb, pork, and beef. They also feature two kinds of onions, crispy-fried and raw, and a selection of condiments including ketchup sweetened with apples and a special sauce known as remolaði. The latter condiment is the Icelandic cousin to France's remoulade, a mayonnaise-based sauce spiked with pickles, vinegar, and onions.

The subtle blend of meats is the key to the pylsa's complex flavor. Beef provides the fat, pork the texture, and lamb a subtle gaminess. Icelandic lambs have a very nice life—they roam freely around the island, feasting on berries and vegetation, which make their meat abundantly flavorful. Icelanders also cook their hot dogs in a mixture of water and beer. The country's most famous supplier, Bæjarins Beztu Pylsur (literally "The Best Hot Dogs in Town"), is a contender for the title of world's greatest hot dog stand. The historic chain, which has been serving hot dogs since 1937, is a national institution with a perpetual line that's included celebrity chefs from around the world and former US president Bill Clinton.

How to try it

Bæjarins Beztu Pylsur has five locations in Reykjavík, the oldest being in Tryggvagata, near the harbor. Try ordering "one with everything" (eina með öllu).

Other Famous Hot Dogs

NEW JERSEY, USA

Italian

Fried hot dog, fried potatoes, bell peppers, onions in pizza bread

MEXICO

Sonora

Bacon-wrapped hot dog with beans, onions, tomato, chilies

SWEDEN

Tunnbrödsrulle

Hot dog with fresh onions, mashed potatoes, lettuce, shrimp salad, in a flatbread

KOREA

Potato Dog

Hot dog on a stick dipped in batter with crinkle-cut french fries, deep fried, drizzled with ketchup

COLOMBIA

Perro Caliente

Boiled hot dog with pineapple salsa, coleslaw, potato chips, Costeño cheese, salsa rosada (ketchup and mayo), quail egg

A NORWEGIAN LOVE STORY

FROZEN PIZZA • NORWAY

How to try it

A classic Norwegian way to eat frozen pizza is adding extra cheese before baking, then drizzling it with ketchup.

The average grocery store needs two aisles to house their frozen pies.

Norwegians eat more pizza (per capita) than any nation on Earth. And of the 50 million pizzas consumed each year, 47 million of them are pulled from the freezer and baked at home.

Pizza arrived in Norway in the 1970s and was the first foreign food to burst onto the local scene. An American named Louis Jordan, who learned to make pizza from a Neapolitan living in New Haven, Connecticut, opened a small pizzeria in Oslo called Peppes with the help of his Norwegian wife, Anne. Peppes boasted nine varieties of American- and Italian-style pies, which were a thrilling culinary departure from the traditional meat-and-potatoes fare of the time. Peppes, which remains one of the most popular pizza chains in Norway, quickly expanded.

The frozen pizza movement came a decade later, when the brand Grandiosa set out to make a pie large enough for a family to share. The cheesy baked good was still new to the general population, and according to Norwegian pizza lore, the factory manager who agreed to produce the frozen pies did so without actually knowing what a pizza was. The company placed their bets on tomato sauce, Jarlsberg cheese, and paprika, and never looked back: This signature recipe still sells nine million pies every year.

THE GREAT CARAMEL CHEESE ACCIDENT

BRUNOST TRUCK FIRE • NORWAY

How to try it

Stock up on varieties of brunost at Fenaknoken, an Oslo delicatessen. While there, you can also pick up some reindeer sausage and cloudberry jam.

In 2013, a truck carrying 60,000 pounds (about 27,000 kg) of brunost—Norway's favorite caramelized cheese—was barreling through a tunnel in Tysfjord when it caught fire. The blaze spread to the truck's cargo, whose fats and sugars fueled the flames and kept the fire raging for five days, emitting so much toxic gas that firefighters could not approach until the cheese had burned through. The tunnel was ravaged and closed for weeks, but the biggest national tragedy was the loss of all that good brunost—the decadent "brown cheese" loved by Norwegians. One member of the Norwegian Roads Administrations lamented, "I didn't know that brown cheese burns so well."

Brunost is not technically a cheese, but a by-product of cheese making. Leftover whey is simmered with milk or cream into a sweet, caramelized paste with a fudge-like texture and salty-sweet, almost tangy flavor. The only acceptable tool for cutting a brown cheese is an ostehøvel—the great Norwegian invention that we know simply as a cheese slicer. Eating brunost has fewer rules and the sweet cheese can find its way into almost any meal. Rye toast, waffles, and sandwiches (strawberry jam plus brunost makes a Norwegian version of a peanut butter and jelly) are all perfect vessels for brown cheese. Brunost, in all its beautiful versatility, can also be melted into stews, mixed into meatballs, and used to sustain weeklong fires that ruin tunnels and make international news.

Weaponized Food

Food has long been a dependable vessel for murder. Typically paired with poison, edibles are widely regarded as a neat, quick, and (relatively) civilized way to slay an enemy. During the Joseon dynasty in Korea, a ceremonial cocktail called sayak was used exclusively to execute the very elite (regular people were decapitated or hanged). Mathematician Alan Turing died from a bite of a cyanide-laced apple (whether it was intentional or an accident is still a matter of debate). Although poison is the obvious choice, history proves there are many ways to off a person with groceries.

CHOCOLATE BOMBS: The Nazis were known to put bombs in so many things—thermos flasks, mess tins, motor oil cans, watches—that the British intelligence service hired an artist to draw 25 detailed mock-ups of Nazi booby-trap bombs as a manual for agents who might need to defuse them. Among these drawings was one of an exploding chocolate bar intended to kill Winston Churchill, along with anyone within several yards. Dark chocolate (nearly impossible to find at the time) concealed the explosive steel-and-canvas device, which was wrapped in black-and-gold paper and earmarked for Churchill's living room. Fortunately for the prime minister, the Nazis' plan was intercepted before he could be tempted by the candy.

CHEESE CANNONBALLS: In 1841, Uruguayan Navy Commodore John H. Coe ran out of cannonballs in the middle of battle. He and his opponent, Admiral William Brown of Argentina, had been engaged in close combat, their iron cannonballs shot from the decks of their ships, about 33 yards (30 m) across the water. Cannonballs gone, Commodore Coe remembered a stock of cheese that hadn't aged well—it was so hard, a lieutenant had broken a knife trying to cut it. Coe loaded the cannon with the compacted Edam

and fired away. Cheese cannonballs struck the main mast, tore holes through the sails, and flew through a porthole, killing two men. The Argentinians retreated, unwilling to lose more men to defective dairy, and the battle was won.

MAD HONEY: Made from a rare species of rhododendron that contains a natural neurotoxin called grayanotoxin, mad honey is produced around the Black Sea region of eastern Turkey, where the locals call it deli bal. Overconsumption can lead to nausea, numbness, and hallucinations, which is exactly what happened in 67 BCE, when the army of King Mithridates left chunks of mad honeycomb along the road used by the invading Romans. Unable to resist, the Romans gorged themselves on the sweet snack, and when they began to lose physical and mental capacity, the Persian army came back and finished the job.

POISON MILKSHAKE: Fidel Castro is said to have survived some 600 assassination attempts during his rule as prime minister and president of Cuba. Playing into his weakness for ice cream (he famously concluded a large lunch with Gabriel García Márquez by eating 18 scoops), the CIA planned to slip a capsule of poison into his chocolate milkshake. But when the assassin went to retrieve the pill from the freezer it was stuck, and it tore open when he tried to get it out. "This moment was the closest the CIA got to assassinating Fidel," said Fabian Escalante, former head of the Cuban secret service, which makes sense if you consider the other attempts: a bacteria-filled wetsuit, LSD cigars, an exploding conch shell, and thallium salt intended to make his beard fall out and thus cause him to lose the respect of his people.

The subaquatic dining room can seat up to 40 guests.

THE WORLD'S LARGEST UNDERWATER RESTAURANT

UNDER • NORWAY

How to try it
There is a long waiting list to dine at Under, and the tasting menu isn't cheap. You can check availability and make reservations on the restaurant's website.

Under, submerged off the coast of Lindesnes on the southern tip of Norway, is the first underwater restaurant in Europe and the biggest in the world. Sixteen feet below sea level, visitors dine on local delicacies while watching fish glide across the submerged panoramic window. In Norwegian, the word *under* means both "below" and "wonder."

The architecture firm behind Under, Snøhetta, has designed other wondrous structures (including the iconic Oslo Opera House) but constructing a subaquatic restaurant posed unique challenges. They needed to ensure the building could withstand a harsh ocean environment of waves, storms, and constant water pressure. Beyond sound construction, the architects designed the restaurant to slowly integrate into its surroundings, eventually functioning as an artificial reef where underwater life can grow.

From the outside, Under looks like a container that fell off a truck and slid into the water. But after walking inside and descending the stairs, visitors enter a whole new world. The minimalist dining room, with dark silhouetted tables and chairs, is bathed in the soft aquamarine glow of the sea. In addition to the underwater entertainment, the fixed seasonal tasting menu features hyperlocal foods intended to take diners outside their comfort zone, including shellfish, seabirds, wild sheep, sea kale, and arrowgrass.

THE VIKINGS' SOLUTION FOR SCURVY

SPRUCE BEER • SWEDEN

Sailors and scurvy once went hand in hand. Long sea voyages required foods that could keep for long periods of time, which meant fresh produce, along with the vitamin C it contained, was an impractical luxury. Especially in

Scandinavia and the Great White North, the Vikings endured some bleak, barren winters—but what they lacked in produce, they made up for in pine trees.

For several centuries, maritime explorers boiled the tips of evergreens into a drink called spruce beer, which contained enough vitamin C to keep them relatively scurvy-free. Before the disease had a medical name, the Vikings believed the liquid spruce kept them healthy, boosted strength in battle, and enhanced fertility.

By the 16th century, European explorers in North America were recording the use of spruce to fight scurvy. In Newfoundland, it became one of the most popular, readily available drinks around. Even Captain James Cook, in his 1784 book *Voyage to the Pacific Ocean*, describes two of his men brewing the fragrant beer for the crew's daily consumption. The elixir was carried on British navy ships and drunk by British and colonial American armies, until the end of the 1800s, when the practice died out in favor of other vitamin sources.

Spruce beer tastes a lot like drinking a Christmas tree. Fans describe it as crisp and refreshing, while detractors equate the strong flavor to pine-based cleaning products.

How to try it

Today, Canada is the leading market for spruce beer, which can be shipped globally, but anyone can make a home brew following 18th-century recipes available online.

THE NOBEL PRIZE BANQUET HALL

STADSHUSKÄLLAREN • SWEDEN

The Stadshuskällaren, or the City Hall Cellars, is the venue for the Nobel banquet, which takes place each December 10 and is attended by geniuses, humanitarians, and Swedish nobility. On all other days of the year, however, you can visit the restaurant as a regular person and eat a banquet from ceremonies past.

Every banquet, from every year, is available to order. The 2017 Nobel banquet, for example, with its crispy saddle of lamb and frosty bilberry bavarois, is available to order, plated on the bespoke green-and-gold Nobel china used at the actual banquets each year. For a unique historical experience, visitors can have a banquet from a Nobel year that fêted one of their cultural heroes. Fans of Gabriel García Márquez can have the banquet from 1982 (with Arctic char in dill cream sauce and Nobel ice cream), and Marie Curie devotees can toast her 1911 chemistry prize by dining on fonds d´artichauts duchesse and poularde fermière (artichoke bottoms "duchess style" and farm chicken).

Unfortunately, Nobel banquets don't come cheap. The price of the previous year's banquet is currently 1,865 SEK ($200) per person. Vintage menus (anything earlier than the previous year) have varying prices, require a party of 10 or more, and need to be booked at least a week in advance. If that sounds too lavish, you can always stop into the restaurant for lunch and gawk at the Stadshuskällaren's vaulted ceilings and lush decor.

How to try it

The Stadshuskällaren is located at Hantverkargatan 1 in Stockholm, and is open for lunch Monday to Friday (11:30 a.m. to 2:30 p.m.) and for dinner Wednesday to Saturday (5 p.m. to 11 p.m.).

The restaurant, open since 1922, still retains some original furnishings.

EUROPE'S DELIGHTFUL
Food Museums

THE HERRING ERA MUSEUM

Siglufjörður, Iceland

Iceland's largest maritime museum re-creates the boom days of the herring rush in the country's northernmost town. From the early 1900s to 1969, the tiny village exploded with thousands of herring workers who came to salt and process the summer catch. The museum is housed in an old salting station and brings to life the work and living quarters of the period and place, which Icelanders call "the Atlantic Klondike."

THE FOOD ADDITIVES MUSEUM

Hamburg, Germany

Tucked away in a wholesale market, this museum shines a light on the mysterious world of emulsifiers, stabilizers, dyes, thickeners, sweeteners, preservatives, and flavorings. Learn why we eat so much sawdust and how the world slowly legislated against the use of poisonous additives, such as arsenic.

THE DISGUSTING FOOD MUSEUM

Malmö, Sweden

A collection of 80 polarizing foods from around the world, including guinea pig, durian, and maggot-infested cheese, the museum highlights the subjectivity of disgust. Showcasing foods beloved in one country and loathed in another, there are plenty of opportunities for smelling and tasting, encouraging visitors to challenge their notions of disgust.

Above: Goat's rennet cheese (sallu sardu); Left: Fresh durian fruit

THE BAKED BEAN MUSEUM OF EXCELLENCE

Port Talbot, Wales

Previously an IT worker for British Petroleum, in 1986 the man once known as Barry Kirk sat naked in a bathtub of baked beans for 100 hours, setting a world record. The event led him to change his name to Captain Beany and open a bean-centric museum in his two-bedroom apartment. The tiny museum is packed with baked-bean tins and memorabilia from around the world, a "Branston Bathroom," and a "Heinz Kitchen."

Asia

THE MIDDLE EAST · SOUTH AND CENTRAL ASIA
EAST ASIA · SOUTHEAST ASIA

THE MIDDLE EAST

THE ORIGINAL FRUIT LEATHER

T'TU LAVASH • ARMENIA

Sun-dried fruit leather has added color to Armenian markets for centuries.

How to try it

Vendors sell t'tu lavash along the path to Geghard Monastery, a medieval site named after the spear that stabbed Christ at the crucifixion.

Armenia is a country blessed with fruit. Each year, the small landlocked nation is blanketed in grapes, pomegranates, figs, apples, and apricots. With such incredible seasonal bounty, Armenians make t'tu lavash, a dried, rolled fruit leather that, when unwound, can be as large as a tablecloth. The technique hails from ancient times, when the dried fruit sheets made for practical food storage. The sweet, tart snacks are still popular today. T'tu lavash means "sour lavash," and lavash refers to the ubiquitous flatbread served around the country. The fruit leather is eaten plain, wrapped around nuts, or melted into a soup with fried onions called t'ghit, which is served with a side of regular lavash.

HAND-PULLED COTTON CANDY

PASHMAK • IRAN

How to try it

Haj Khalifeh Ali Rahbar is a sweetshop in the city of Yazd that sells pashmak, along with nearly every kind of Persian sweet imaginable.

Iran's cotton candy, called pashmak, requires both man and machine to achieve its soft and fuzzy, melt-in-your-mouth strands. (In Persian, pashmak means "like wool.") Compared to Western cotton candy, where hot sugar syrup is pushed through the tiny holes of a spinning drum before quickly solidifying into wispy candy, pashmak is old school. It's made by caramelizing water and sugar in a massive vat, then stretching and kneading the mixture on a large work surface as it cools, until it acquires the texture of taffy. Rolled by hand into a dense, sticky ring, the caramel is then placed atop a mass of flattened dough made from toasting flour in butter. The two substances slowly combine with the help of skilled hands and a special machine with octopus-like appendages. The mechanized arms start in a tight cluster, then expand, stretching the candy and dough outward.

The human hands push the mixture back to the center, then the pashmak octopus expands and stretches the candy again. This slow, laborious process happens over and over, until the delicate strands begin to emerge and the mixture takes on the fluffy, frayed appearance of wool.

The finished product—which comes in flavors from sesame to cardamom—is cut up, boxed, and sold in the country's sweetshops. In Iran, pashmak is often a topping for ice cream or a garnish for cake. Its light, ethereal texture gives away none of the candy's dense beginnings, but the flavor is notably complex. While pashmak is sweet, it's also nutty and buttery from the toasted flour, making it a sophisticated version of the colorful fairground variety.

What Iranian cotton candy lacks in color and fluff, it makes up for in buttery, toasted flavor.

Other Sweets from Iran

Frozen Treats

FALOODEH

One of the world's oldest frozen desserts, dating back to the days of yakhchals. The 2,500-year-old treat is a kind of sweet noodle slush, made by combining cooked vermicelli with crushed, rose water–flavored ice. The crushed ice is soft, refreshing, and lightly floral, while the noodles give a chewy texture. Topped with a squeeze of lime, faloodeh is still one of Iran's most popular treats.

BASTANI-E NOONI

Flavored with the traditional blend of saffron and rose water, this Persian ice-cream sandwich is encased between two thin crispy wafers and rolled in pistachios. Although bastani-e nooni are available year-round, they become especially popular during Nowruz, the Persian New Year.

The Single Iranian Seed
That Launched America's Pistachio Industry

In 1979, a group of Iranian college students stormed the American Embassy in Tehran, taking dozens of hostages. The crisis dominated relations between the two countries, influencing politics for generations—and proved beneficial for American pistachio production. When the American government slapped a retaliatory embargo on Iranian pistachios, California's nascent pistachio industry exploded. Today, Iran and the United States are neck and neck for the accolade of the world's top producer.

From a botanical perspective, this was a remarkable turnaround. Pistachios are notoriously difficult to cultivate. They like hot, dry climates, but they also need cold winters to fruit. Pistachio trees also take about a decade to mature, and even then many trees produce nuts only in alternate years.

Iran's climate, especially the high-altitude desert town of Rafsanjan, is uniquely suited to the finicky crop. The nut was brought to the United States in the late 19th century by Middle Eastern immigrants, hungry for a taste of home. These pistachios were "non-fertile," good for snacking but not for planting.

In 1929, California's Chico New Plant Introduction Station sent William E. Whitehouse, a deciduous tree researcher and "plant explorer,"

to Iran with a singular mission: to collect pistachio seeds for planting. For six months, he searched for pistachios and returned to Chico with 20 pounds of different varieties. The station planted and evaluated 3,000 trees, and one pistachio rose above the others—the round, unblemished, crisp-tasting Kerman, from a prominent orchard in Rafsanjan. A female mother tree planted around 1931 at the Chico research station is the source of all pistachios commercially grown in California.

For decades, pistachio planting stayed small-scale and demand was still fulfilled by Iranian imports. The fledgling American industry didn't have its first commercial harvest until 1976.

Then came the 1979 hostage crisis and the sanctions that followed. The American pistachio industry took the opportunity to organize; even after the sanctions were lifted, there was still a 300 percent tariff on importing the Iranian nuts.

The pistachio is heralded as "the single most successful plant introduction to the United States in the 20th century." The hard-to-grow plant is now a $1.6 billion industry in California alone, where Whitehouse's single, all-important seed has family members spread across 200,000 acres.

In Zarandieh, Iran, a man hauls fresh pistachios to be dried in the sun.

ANCIENT PERSIAN ICE HOUSES

YAKHCHALS • IRAN

Standing tall and majestic like giant clay beehives, yakhchals are a feat of ancient Persian ingenuity. Long before electricity or refrigeration, these conical structures made eating ice cream in the desert possible as early as 400 BCE. Constructed from a special mixture of sand, clay, egg whites, lime, goat hair, and ash called sarooj, the visible portion of the yakhchal sits atop a vast underground chamber where ice was made and stored. In an incredible act of engineering, the chamber was fed by a series of underground channels called qanats, which flowed from an aqueduct. Using a combination of wind towers, strategic venting, and shade from the outer walls, water typically froze overnight. Additional ice was often brought from the mountains and stored in the yakhchals to facilitate the cooling process. The ice was then cut into blocks that could be transformed into frozen treats. With all that pent-up cold air, yakhchals also functioned as early refrigerators, storing perishables such as meat and dairy that would otherwise spoil in the heat of the desert.

How to try it

Many yakhchals still stand in Iran today. One of the easiest to find is near the Narin Castle in Meybod, but there are also some in Yazd and Kerman.

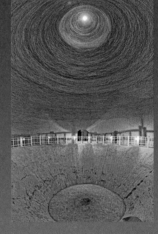

The advanced technology of this majestic ice house, one of four in the city of Abarkuh, dates back more than 2,000 years.

How Bootleg Fast Food Conquered Iran

Before the 1979 revolution, when religious clerics took control of the country, Iran's capital, Tehran, was a cosmopolitan city full of Western influences: secularism, miniskirts, and fast-food chains such as McDonald's and Kentucky Fried Chicken. But when Ayatollah Ruhollah Khomeini came to power, he pushed a return to traditional Islamic values. Everything Western became contraband, including American-style fast food.

When Khomeini died in 1989, citizens grew gutsier about flouting the ban on Western culture. Many Iranians maintained contact with the West through satellite television and relatives abroad. Others traveled to places such as Dubai, where they saw the far-reaching success of fast food. Iranian entrepreneurs wanted to bring these food options to Iran, but sanctions, tariffs, and a fraught relationship between Iran and the United States made it impossible to get the real thing. Instead, they opened imitations: Mash Donald's, Subways, Sheak Shack, and Pizza Hot.

Menu item names, such as Dahbel Dahn (KFC Double Down) and Wooper, were adjusted to fit the Persian vernacular's rich vowels. In other cases, traditional ingredients met Western formats to create one-of-a-kind dishes, such as

Tehran's ZFC (above) and Pizza Hot (below)

lavash-wrapped burritos stuffed with jujeh (chicken) kebab, grilled vegetables, saffron rice, and yellow raisins.

In most countries, these eateries would have to worry about lawsuits from Pizza Hut, Shake Shack, and KFC. But Iran's murky relationship with the United States gives these entrepreneurs some leverage. Although legal institutions in Iran exist for McDonald's lawyers to shut down Mash Donalds (in 2010, Baskin-Robbins managed to close five bootleg ice-cream shops), the dysfunctional political relationship between the two countries makes enforcing intellectual property rights frustrating at best. Most companies with little or no legitimate presence in Iran are inclined to devote their resources to enforcing trademarks in bigger markets.

The larger concern for the enterpreneurs behind Sheak Shack and Subways is the Iranian government. Even imitations are considered symbols of American imperialism, and authorities can—and will—shut them down for promoting gharbzadeghi, a Persian term for "westoxification." The restaurant owners must strike a balance: imitating Western chains enough to draw Iranians who want to try those brands, but not so closely that the government accuses them of corrupting and Westernizing the country.

DESERT IN BLOOM

KASHAN ROSE WATER FESTIVAL • IRAN

How to try it

The city of Qamsar, located 134 miles south of Tehran, becomes a rose-scented festival hub every May.

Most of the year, Kashan County is a monochromatic landscape of arched, khaki-colored buildings spread on dusty, windswept hills. But each spring, this desert region bursts into bloom and the land fills with roses, in soft pastels and electric pink, scattered across a bed of green. From May to June, local workers carefully wade through the thorny bushes of the region's gol Mohammadi, or Mohammadi rose, picking thousands of pounds of the flower to distill into rose water.

Visitors from across Iran and the world pour into the otherwise sleepy city of Qamsar to celebrate the fragrant harvest. Modern rose water production is often industrial, but some Kashan County producers still distill the liquid using a centuries-old process called golab-giri. This technique involves slowly boiling the petals in sealed copper pots and letting the steam rise and slowly collect in tubes—much like distilling hard liquor. The tubes lead outside of the pot and into

Roses in Kashan are gathered into large vats before being distilled into rose water.

a pitcher where, over the course of a few hours, the condensed liquid is collected. This potent distillate yields both rose oil, a highly concentrated liquid prized for its fragrance, and rose water, which is less expensive and used in traditional medicine and Persian cooking.

During festival time, rose water is available everywhere, fresh from the manufacturer or bottled at the central bazaar. Iranian rose water is widely considered the best in the world because the country's producers take great pride in getting the petals swiftly from the fields to the copper pots to preserve the roses' natural aroma and flavor.

MARSH TAFFY

KHIRRET ∘ IRAQ

n midsummer every year, the souks of southern Iraq are tinged with the gold dust of khirret (pronounced "khar-ee-at"), a crunchy candy made from the pollen of an aquatic plant that grows in the region's marshes. The delicately sweetened confection is bright yellow and tightly compressed, like a chunk of chalk or a solid clump of mustard powder.

The Ma'dan people who live in the marshes of al-Ahwar, a UNESCO World Heritage Site, eat every part of the bardi plant (*Typha domingensis pers*), which also goes by the name "cattail." During the springtime, the male flowers release pollen, which is stripped off the plant to make khirret (khirret means "the stripped"). The canary-colored pollen is set out to dry in the sun, filtered to remove impurities, then mixed with sugar, wrapped in cheesecloth or a bag, and steamed. The steam binds everything together, and the solidified khirret is ready to be sold at market.

Khirret is considered a festival food for Iraqi Jews. One theory is that the marsh reeds became sacred for the Jewish community because baby Moses was kept hidden and safe among the Egyptian papyrus reeds, which resembled the ones found in Iraq. Baghdadi Jews traditionally served khirret during Purim until around the mid-20th century, when the group started a mass migration to Israel. Although khirret didn't make the trip with them, it remains a seasonal delicacy in southern Iraq.

How to try it
During the summer, check markets in Basra and Nasiriyah for the compressed pollen candy.

A THORNY SYMBOL OF CONFLICT

SABRA • ISRAEL

How to try it

The prickly fruits are available during the summer and are sold in Israeli and Palestinian markets, often peeled or with their thorns removed. The cactus makes excellent jam, juice, and syrup, but is commonly eaten ripe and raw, regardless of who is doing the eating.

For the Israelis and Palestinians living in one of the most disputed regions in modern history, the prickly pear cactus is political. The small oblong fruit with thick, spiny skin and sweet, acidic flesh grows abundantly in the area and is eaten with zeal in both countries. Called sabra in Hebrew and sabr in Arabic, the fruit has become a core but contentious symbol of Israeli and Palestinian national identities.

On one side of the conflict, the sabra is the symbol of an Israeli ideal: tough on the outside, yet soft and sweet on the inside. It also connotes a person with roots in the soil, namely a Jew born and raised in Israel. The tall prickly pear bushes, which

grow in flat paddle shapes and yield both fruits and flowers during the summer months, are often used in landscaping around Israeli homes and buildings.

Across the border, the symbolism of the fruit is more of perseverance than of strength. Sabr, which is also the Arabic word for "patience," grows in the most inhospitable of environments. It takes root in sand and rocks, resists droughts, and still manages to produce a sweet, delicate fruit. In many of the Palestinian villages now occupied by Israel, all that remains are the bushes of sabr, and so the cactus has become an emblem of Palestinian dispossession. Although eating is the main use of sabr, one West Bank artist, Ahmad Yasin, uses the cactus as a canvas, transforming the plants in his backyard into a gallery of political scenes he uses as a form of cultural resistance.

DESERT TRUFFLE MARKET

FAGGA SOUK • KUWAIT

How to try it

The truffle souk is located in Al Rai, where truffles are flown in daily during the season.

In the early spring, the truffle souk in Al Rai, just northwest of Kuwait City, bustles with connoisseurs sniffing for white-and-beige culinary gold. The demand for desert truffles, called fagga in Kuwait, is so high that more than 500 vendors apply each year for the 120-odd available stalls.

The deserts of the Middle East and North Africa are prime ground for desert truffles, which are lighter in color, less pungent, and cheaper than their European counterparts. Though they hail from the fungi kingdom, desert truffles look more like potatoes. Spongy with an earthy taste, the mushrooms act as a flavor enhancer for meats, stews, and sauces. They can also be eaten on their own, with a little olive oil and cilantro, or added to kabsa, a spiced meat-and-rice one-pot dish popular in the Gulf countries.

Since the Iraqi invasion in 1990, nearly all the truffles that make it to the souk come from neighboring countries such as Iran, Saudi Arabia, Libya, Morocco, and Tunisia. Kuwaiti foragers who once roamed the desert for the fancy fungus are now rightfully afraid of unexploded landmines left behind by the Iraqi army. Kuwait's changing landscape and climate are also to blame. Growing truffles requires rain,

which can be irregular, and space, which is being diminished by urban encroachment. Foraging in other countries, especially war-torn regions such as Syria and Iraq, can be just as dangerous, with reports of truffle hunters captured and killed by suspected Islamic State militants.

When rain and lightning fall on the desert midwinter, Bedouins rejoice. Although not fully understood, lightning seems to encourage truffle growth underground. Once the fungi mature, they begin to crack the soil, which shows harvesters where to dig for the desert delicacy. At market, a kilo fetches about $25–$65.

Competition is fierce to become one of the lucky hundred-plus vendors of desert truffles in Kuwait.

LAMB TAIL CONFIT

AWARMA • LEBANON

In Lebanon, awarma is a dish with roots invented before the advent of refrigeration. After butchering sheep during the warmer months, villagers would cook the meat slowly in its own fat—a technique called confit, which was traditionally a method of preservation. Sealed tightly, awarma could last for several months in the pantry and provide meat throughout the winter.

Awarma is made by rendering cubes of fat from the tail of a sheep (fat-tailed sheep, whose fat accumulates in massive baggy deposits, are common in the Middle East), then adding minced sheep's meat, salt, and cooking it until softened and brown. The versatile, unctuous dish is commonly cooked with eggs and eaten for breakfast, but it can also be added to kibbeh (a spiced meat and grain mixture), sprinkled atop hummus, or used to add meaty oomph in soups, stews, and pilafs.

How to try it
Al Soussi restaurant in Beirut is beloved for their traditional breakfasts, including a fluffy plate of eggs and awarma.

Fat-Tailed Sheep
ARE BOTH REAL AND DELICIOUS

According to Herodotus, the 5th-century Greek "father of history," travelers passing through Arabia would encounter flying snakes, birds building nests out of cinnamon, and sheep with tails so massive they dragged on the ground or were supported by custom-made wheeled carts. While Herodotus was notorious for peppering his histories with fantasy, the fat-tailed sheep are very much real.

For millennia, people have bred sheep with huge, fat-heavy tails. (About 25 percent of the world's sheep are still fat-tailed varieties, mainly found in the Middle East, Central Asia, and Africa.) Some breeds have bulbous, curled tails, while others have flat, wide tails like paddles. The broad tails of the Awassi sheep, a nomadic breed prized for milk production, can weigh about 26 pounds (12 kg)—which is modest compared to an 80-pound (36 kg) tail described by 16th-century chronicler Leo Africanus.

For sheep, extra tail fat provides energy reserves in harsh climates. In the desert, sheep must traverse extreme distances for grassland and water and so, like camels' humps, they store calorie reserves in their tails. For humans, the tail fat makes an excellent preservative and cooking grease. Located near the surface of the animal's skin, rather than close to the heat of the body, the tail fat is exposed to colder temperatures. Because of this, it has a lower melting point and a texture that's buttery and soft, rather than waxy, with a subtle lamb flavor.

Butchers often sell the sheep's tail separately. Bits of tail fat are commonly mixed into meats for kebabs, to give it extra juiciness and meaty flavor. The crackling rendered from pieces of tail fat can be served as an appetizer, while the liquefied fat might be brushed on baklava.

Artists from Israel to India immortalized fat-tailed sheep with rock paintings, mosaics, and glorious golden canvases. (There's even a mention of fat-tailed sheep in the Bible.) For Europeans and Americans, however, who were used to thin-tailed sheep, the creatures were a jaw-dropping concept. Up until the 20th century, travel accounts and farmer's almanacs described fat-tailed sheep with the whimsical wonder of Herodotus, complete with the attached cart. The fanciful nature of these depictions led skeptics to question whether sheep with tail carts were mythical (photographic evidence remains scarce), but scholars still argue the carts are real, citing 19th- and 20th-century references to sheep-tail carts in Afghanistan.

Many a traveler has written of woolly mythology that just might be true: sheep with tails so fat, they pulled them on carts.

Black nigella seed paste, when sweetened, makes for a striking pie that can only be found in Palestine.

BLACK TAHINI

QIZHA • PALESTINE

To love qizha, first you must know about it. The region's ongoing border dispute, which keeps many Palestinian products from leaving their home, means that few outside of Palestine know about the dark, tahini-adjacent paste. Made by roasting and grinding black nigella seeds, along with black sesame seeds for fat, qizha is shiny and viscous, the color of tar. It's bitter yet sweet, with an herbal undertone of mint. When visitors do discover qizha, many develop an addiction, and when they leave the country, they can't find it again.

The Palestinian city of Nablus is known as the culinary capital of the West Bank, and qizha is among their specialties. Qizha is typically sweetened and made into dessert. Qizha halwa and qizha semolina pie are customary, as is taking doses of the paste like medicine. In Arabic, nigella seeds are called hubbat al-baraka, or "seeds of blessing," for their range of purported health benefits. Especially among the older generation, Palestinians are known to eat it daily for its anti-inflammatory and anti-bacterial properties.

How to try it
In Nablus you can find top-notch qizha at Breik Roasting, which also sells local spices, coffee, and soap.

SWEET NOODLE OMELET

BALALEET • QATAR

How to try it

Balaleet is an affordable, often homemade dish. Shay Al Shoomoos is a restaurant owned and operated by a Qatari mother of five, Shams Al Qassabi, who is a rarity in the male-dominated business scene of Qatar. Located in the Souk Waqif, she makes an excellent sweet noodle omelet.

Eid al-Fitr marks the end of the monthlong Ramadan fast with a feast of special foods. For Qataris and their Gulf neighbors, that means food like balaleet. It's a noodle dish, but it's also an omelet. It's sweet but also savory. Soft but crispy. Almost always breakfast, but sometimes lunch or dinner.

Balaleet begins with rice noodles, which are parboiled, then fried in a pan with butter, sugar, cardamom, and saffron. (To get fancier, add curry, turmeric, or ginger.) The noodles should brown a bit, making some parts soft and others crunchy, before being finished with a sprinkling of rose water. Next, there's the

omelet, which should be cooked in hot oil very quickly so it forms a nice crust. With the omelet draped over the noodles, and then a handful of pistachios sprinkled over the top, each bite should be aromatic, salty, sweet, crunchy, and extremely delicious.

SILK ROAD CHILI POWDER

ALEPPO PEPPER • SYRIA

How to try it

The Syrian war has all but ended Aleppo pepper exports from the country. Turkish growers have picked up the production, using Syrian seeds to grow the plants.

Spices have flowed in and out of Aleppo for millennia. The city was a central trading point along the Silk Road, and its souks were collectively one of the great wonders of the ancient world. Heaped into great piles alongside goods from across the world, these spices were mixed with ingredients and recipes brought from Asia, Anatolia, and beyond, making for new dishes found nowhere else. (Supposedly, the sultans of the Ottoman Empire sent their chefs to Aleppo to spy.) Today, the world still covets Syria's spices, especially the Aleppo pepper.

A variety of *Capsicum annuum*, the Aleppo pepper was brought back from South America and introduced to Europe in the 1400s. Soon the peppers were growing across the Middle East, including the fertile ground of Syria, where the chilies took on a new flavor. The peppers became so connected to Syria that their name in Arabic, baladi, means "my country."

Traditionally, the spice was made by local families who processed the fresh peppers by hand—cleaning them with a dry cloth, gutting them, and drying them on rooftops around the country. Once dried, the peppers were ground with salt and olive oil and dried again to produce bright red, salty flakes with a sweetness like raisins or sundried tomatoes and a mildly spicy, earthy flavor.

In the late 20th century, chefs around the world began falling for the Aleppo pepper. Their discovery coincided with the loosening of Syrian state rules and international interest in the country's culinary scene. But when the Syrian Civil War broke out in 2012, the authentic Aleppo pepper became nearly impossible to get, which created a market for fake Aleppo pepper. Seeds were carried out by refugees and planted in Turkey, which now grows most of the "Aleppo pepper."

Aleppo is now in the difficult process of restoring life as it was before the conflict. Aleppo is considered by many to be the culinary capital of the region, and there is hope that the centuries-old, now world-famous, pepper will flourish in the city again.

In the covered souks of the ancient city of Aleppo, shoppers can get everything they need, from peppers to soap to rugs.

Dallah
THE WORLD'S MOST WELCOMING COFFEEPOT

The Arabic coffeepot, called a dallah, is the region's universal symbol of hospitality. Tall and elegant with a dramatic, arched spout and a slim, tapered waist, the dallah is the first thing used to welcome friends, visitors, and business associates. Upon entering a home or celebration, coffee preparation begins. In the United Arab Emirates, this involves a ceremony called gahwa, in which coffee beans are freshly roasted in a skillet, ground with cardamom using a pestle, brewed in a dallah, often filtered into a succession of smaller dallahs, then served to guests little by little, filling their cup just part of the way. The pouring process repeats for each guest until they shake their cup, indicating they've had enough.

The gahwa speaks to the core significance of coffee in the UAE, and the Arabian Peninsula in general—its power to gather people together and facilitate relationships, conversation, and ideas. The ritual of drinking together creates regular opportunities to exchange hospitality and sustain the region's oral traditions. Coffee is also a sign of wealth and generosity, which is why the dallah is featured on the one dirham coin in the UAE and has been used as a watermark on the country's banknotes. The dallah has become an emblem of warmth, strength, and welcome—and the coffeepot now stands all over Arabia in the form of statues, fountains, and entryways.

Dallah Fountain in Fujairah, United Arab Emirates

Dallah Fountain in Jeddah, Saudi Arabia

Dallah roundabout in Al Khor, Qatar

Dallah Sculpture in Abu Dhabi, United Arab Emirates

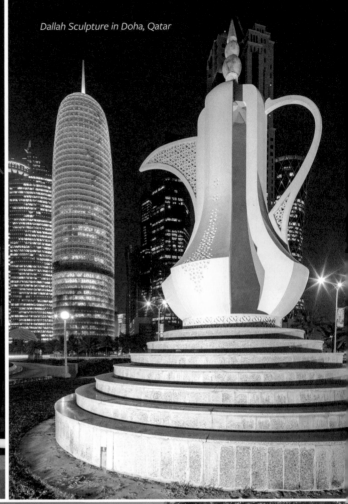

Dallah Sculpture in Doha, Qatar

Entrance to Capital Park in Abu Dhabi, United Arab Emirates

SOUTH AND CENTRAL ASIA

MENDED TEAPOT SOUP

CHAINAKI • AFGHANISTAN

How to try it

Bacha Broot, in the Old City near the bird market, is Kabul's oldest restaurant. Per tradition, men and women sit in separate rooms to eat their chainaki.

The tea shops of Afghanistan, called chaikhanas, have long been a refuge for locals in need of a break. Ranging from small rooms with mud floors to more luxurious guest houses, chaikhanas dot any well-traveled road, offering liquid Afghan hospitality: black or green tea, often sweetened and spiced with cardamom. In some shops, tea is dispensed into short glasses from a samovar. In others, the whole teapot is given to the guest to pour themselves.

With limited space and specialized equipment, chaikhana owners came to the handy realization that teapots could be used for more than just tea. Chainaki is a lamb or goat soup cooked slowly in a teapot. In the morning, a collection of teapots is filled with simple ingredients: a few pieces of meat, some chopped onion, a spoonful of split peas, salt, and a glug of water. Topped with the lid, the ceramic vessels are placed on a stove or tucked into hot embers where the meat slowly softens and the water transforms into a deeply savory broth. When a chainaki is ordered, a teapot is removed and served. The traditional way to enjoy teapot soup is by tearing naan into a bowl, pouring the hot soup over it, then eating it with your hand—always just one hand, always the right.

The teapots used for soup are often salvaged, which gives the dish a well-loved, eclectic presentation. In Afghanistan, broken teapots are taken to a professional mender called a patragar, who repairs them by drilling tiny holes in the pieces, stitching them together with thin metal wire, then closing up the gaps with a paste of egg whites and gypsum.

Broken teapots are given new life at chainakis, where they are used to pour soup over torn pieces of bread.

THE ALL-IMPORTANT MULBERRY

TOOT • AFGHANISTAN

Tall, bushy mulberry trees, many with centuries-old root systems, grow all across Afghanistan. In the summer, when they bear fruit, farmers spread out sheets beneath the branches and shake the trees, letting the ripe berries fall. In a country teeming with fruit, mulberries are among the most abundant and play a central role in the Afghan diet.

During the summer, fruit stands line the roads, selling mounds of fleshy mulberries. Although locals do eat them fresh, most mulberries are bought for drying, which also happens during the hot season. Roofs and yards are filled with berries shriveling in the sun. Dried mulberries are an Afghani pantry staple, stashed away for the winter when fresh produce becomes scarce. They're used as a condiment for bread, or as a self-contained tea bag when dropped in hot water. In a practice that originated with caravanning nomads, the dried berries were mixed with nuts and pressed into nutrient-packed blocks called chakidar, which were tied into the end of a traveler's turban and eaten as a snack. In the north of the country, where mulberries are especially plentiful, ground berries stand in for flour in a mulberry bread called talkhun.

How to try it

From June to September, mulberries blanket Afghanistan. The best berries are said to grow in the north, along the route from Kabul to Balkh.

Mulberry Bread

Makes 16 bars

½ pound dried mulberries

½ pound shelled walnuts

¼ teaspoon kosher salt

2 tablespoons water

16 walnut halves for topping

Fresh mulberries

Dried mulberries

1. Put all of the ingredients except the walnut halves in a food processor fitted with a metal blade and puree for 1 to 2 minutes until they form a thick, smooth, sticky paste.

2. Line an 8 x 8-inch baking pan with parchment or wax paper with the paper draping over two sides of the pan, to make removing the bars easier.

3. Press the mulberry–walnut mixture into the pan, making an even layer all over the bottom of the pan. Distribute the walnut halves evenly, making 4 rows of 4 walnuts, then gently press them halfway into the mixture.

4. Refrigerate for an hour to firm up the bars. Using the edges of the wax paper, lift the mixture out of the pan and set it on a cutting

surface. With a sharp knife, cut it into 16 squares with a walnut in the center of each square. Store in a sealed container at room temperature, or the refrigerator if you prefer them cold.

A VERDANT 19TH-CENTURY TEA GARDEN

LAKKATURA • BANGLADESH

How to try it

The easiest way to get to the estate is by CNG (a kind of auto-rickshaw used all over Bangladesh) from Sylhet city center. Upon arrival, you can report to the main office and hire a guide or simply wander around the garden by yourself. For seven color tea, head to Nilkantha Tea Cabin, about two hours south of Lakkatura.

In the northeastern city of Sylhet, an area renowned for the beauty of its tea gardens, Lakkatura is often considered the most picturesque. It is also one of the largest tea gardens in the country, covering a total of 3,200 acres. Officially established in 1875, the estate now produces an astounding 550 tons of tea each year. Tea has a long history here. Long before the region started producing it, Bengal was the terminus for the Tea Horse Road, the ancient caravan path that brought Chinese goods, most important, tea, to South Asian buyers.

The Lakkatura estate is a lush, quiet expanse intersected by a number of dirt roads. Some roads are used to transport tea and take visitors on rides through the carpeted hills of neatly manicured tea plants. Others are thoroughfares, part of a larger network that connects the garden to rural villages around the estate. During the harvest, makeshift villages pop up around the plantation to house the workers who come to pick and process the tea.

The British East India Company first introduced tea cultivation to Bengal in 1840, but it wasn't until 1857 that tea became a commercial occupation. In 2018, Bangladesh produced more than 80,000 tons of tea, making it the tenth-largest tea producer in the world. In Sylhet, tea is so plentiful a local teashop owner invented "seven color tea," or saat rong in Bengali. Using a secret recipe, he makes seven distinct tea mixes with spices and milk and layers them based on their densities to create a striking, stratified glass that has attracted the prime minister of Bangladesh, as well as a Qatari ambassador who reportedly enjoyed it so much, he paid 7,000 taka, or about $83, for his glass.

Tea Horse Road

Many boti blades can fold down flat for safe storage.

THE KNIFE THAT REQUIRES FEET

BOTI • BANGLADESH

How to try it

The largest botis are used specifically for fish, while blades with a round, serrated tip are used for grating coconuts.

Peer into most Bengali kitchens and you'll find women sitting on the floor, cutting up fish and vegetables in a swift rhythmic motion that requires both hands and feet. Unlike most knives, which are wielded over the food, the boti flips the script. Women maneuver an ingredient around the boti's blade, which stays completely stationary, and use its sharp edge to whittle the skin off potatoes or slice cucumbers.

A boti has two main features: a long, flat wooden board and a curved, upright blade. One foot is used to weigh down the board, either by squatting on it or sitting with a leg folded on top. The blade—which rises from the board, sharp side facing the cook—can shave a piece of garlic as well as it can dismember an entire pumpkin.

Watching a woman skillfully work a boti is mesmerizing. Her fingers boldly evade the blade, busting open heads of cabbages and broccoli with force, then carving out uniform, practiced shapes with the velocity and precision of machinery. For the biggest celebrations, Bengali women gather with their botis and sit together on the floor, in a colorful mess of peels and produce. For many Bengalis, the boti makes handheld knives irrelevant. Perhaps the only disadvantage, as women get older, is sitting on the floor—but there is a boti for that: Newer models are made to be screwed into a table, so cooks can sit in a chair while whittling.

THE LOST SUPERIOR PEPPER

LONG PEPPER • INDIA

How to try it

Long pepper is easy to find on Khari Baoli Road in New Delhi. The spice market there is not only the largest in India, but all of Asia.

India is the birthplace of two important peppercorns: one black, one long. Black pepper, now ubiquitous on tables around the world, is native to Kerala, on the southeastern coast, while long pepper grows in the north of India. Long pepper, with its tight and conical shape, was the first pepper to make its way from India to the Mediterranean and into the kitchens of ancient Greece and Rome. At the time, around the 6th century BCE, the piquant flavor was unlike anything Westerners had tasted before. Mustard and horseradish grew natively, but they'd never tried a spice that attacked their mouth like the blunt, earthy long pepper.

By the 4th century CE, black pepper entered the market. Unlike long pepper, the new pepper could grow outside its native home and as a result was significantly cheaper. Black pepper rose to prominence, usurping what many believe to be the superior-tasting long pepper.

Black and long pepper are closely related. They share an active compound called piperine, which activates the human body's heat-sensing pathways. But while black pepper delivers its flavor boldly and at once, long pepper is more complex. At first, long pepper's spice is more subtle, lingering, then growing in power and eventually tingling the way black pepper does. Long pepper also has a fruity mellowness, a citrusy bite similar to Sichuan peppercorns.

Today, as the Western world eats black pepper, long pepper is still popular in its native India. The floral, more understated pepper is used in the spicy soup rasam, lentil curries, and Indian pickle and is an essential ingredient in the mutton stew nihari.

ROCK STAR FRUIT

BASTARD OLEASTER • INDIA

Bastard oleaster doesn't just sound like a rock star, it looks like one, too. The small red fruit, which resembles a cherry tomato, appears to be dusted in silver glitter. Cut one open and you'll find an equally dramatic interior: an elongated seed with a striped pattern, kind of like a lightning bolt.

This fruity bastard tastes sour and a bit astringent. It has a slight tomato taste, which isn't surprising given that these fruits are packed with lycopene, a compound found in tomatoes. In northeast India, where they grow, bastard oleasters are a popular street snack. Vendors sell small bags of whole, sparkling fruits along with salt, which helps cut the astringency and sourness. The seeds are edible, but they have a fibrous hull that's difficult to chew. Those willing to work can split open the seeds to eat the kernel inside, but more often they're discarded.

How to try it
You're unlikely to find bastard oleasters outside of northern India. They occasionally show up at street markets in the city of Guwahati, but a better bet is to travel to the city of Shillong, where the fruits are sold as a snack outside bus stations.

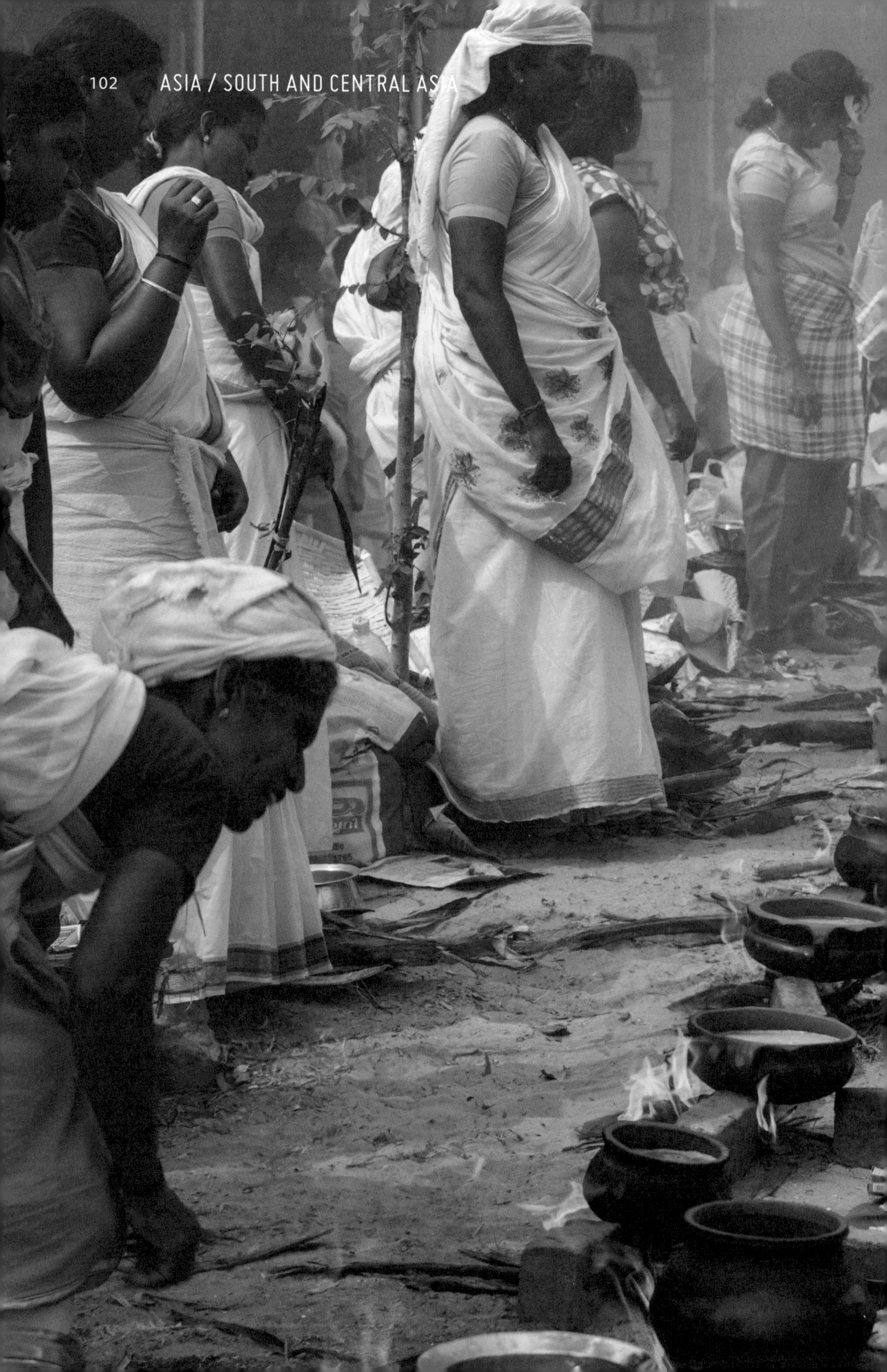

Women from all walks of life gather at the annual Pongala Festival, huddling around brick stoves to create rice pudding worthy of a goddess.

FOUR MILLION WOMEN MAKING RICE PUDDING

PONGALA · INDIA

On the ninth day of Attukal Pongala, a festival dedicated to the Hindu goddess Bhadrakali, Indian women find refuge in numbers. Considered the largest spiritual gathering of females in the world, four million women from all over India descend upon the city of Thiruvananthapuram in Kerala each year. They spread out over 15 miles (24 km), washing rice, grating coconuts, and gathering bricks for small makeshift fires. The sari-clad pilgrims have come to make an offering to the goddess. To do this, they cook a staggering amount of rice pudding called pongala.

The basic ingredients of pongala—clarified butter, coconut, rice, and cane sugar—are simple and affordable, which makes the ceremony accessible to any woman who wants to participate. (In fact, it was women from the "untouchable" Dalit caste who pioneered the event.) For each new ceremony, the women use a new cooking vessel, which they carefully select from the mountains of pots on offer throughout the city. For 24 hours, Thiruvananthapuram transforms into a sacred kitchen. The millions of women place their brick stoves side by side, forming a concentric circle around the Attukal Bhagavathy Temple. Devotees claim all available public space, setting up temporary hearths on streets, sidewalks, courtyards, bus stations, and railway platforms. At the sounding cue of a loudspeaker, the women strike matches, light their fires, and prepare their pongala offerings.

The goddess Bhadrakali is a fierce incarnation of Devi, who annihilates evil and brings prosperity to her followers. In this form, she is black or blue, wields a sword and sickle, and wears a necklace of skulls and a belt of severed heads. The ferocious deity is believed to embody fury as well as benevolent protection and is often worshipped as a universal mother figure. She is perhaps best known by her more affectionate name: Attukal Amma, or Mother.

When the pongala pot overflows, erupting in white foam, the goddess has accepted the offering. The atmosphere is highly emotional, with celebrants crying and chanting, sharing rice pudding, and basking in the strength of female solidarity.

How to try it
The pongala offering takes place as part of a ten-day festival that typically falls in February or March. Contact the Attukal Bhagavathy Temple for exact dates.

How to try it

The Golden Temple is in Atta Mandi in Amritsar's south. Shuttle buses run from the city's bus terminal.

Volunteers prep thousands of vegetables for the temple's 24-hour kitchen.

A HOLY KITCHEN FEEDING THOUSANDS FOR FREE

LANGAR AT THE GOLDEN TEMPLE • INDIA

Everyone who arrives at Shri Harmandir Sahib, also known as the Golden Temple, eats for free. The gilded Sikh structure is the main attraction in the city of Amritsar, which means the temple's kitchen serves about 75,000 free meals every day. On special occasions, the number can reach 100,000 or more.

This ritual, which is run almost entirely by volunteers, is part of a centuries-old practice known as langar, started by the first Sikh Guru, Guru Nanak. Langar is a display of humility and equality. Regardless of class, caste, or gender, everyone must

sit on the floor of a Sikh temple, side by side, and eat the same simple vegetarian meal, without the exchange of money.

Serving the thousands of visitors and pilgrims who come to the Golden Temple is a monumental task. The kitchen comprises multiple buildings, filled with rooms dedicated to specific preparations. In one room, volunteers sit in circles and chop vegetables for the sabzi, a vegetarian stew. In another room, a team cooks the sabzi, stirring giant wood-fired vats with wooden spoons the size of oars. The making of dal, the all-important lentil curry, requires its own building, a water hose, and about 28,660 pounds (13,000 kg) of lentils every day.

In recent years, rising demand has led the temple to supplement volunteers with machinery, including a device that can churn out 25,000 rotis in an hour. Each piece of bread, hot from the oven, is hand painted with ghee (clarified butter), before being sent out to the dining room.

At mealtime, thousands of people file into two large dining halls. They pick up a metal cafeteria tray, a cup for water, and cutlery, then take their place on the floor in rows. The volunteers walk down the row, holding steaming buckets of dal, sabzi, and rice pudding that they ladle into the compartments of the tray. When the rotis come, diners hold out their hands in a sign of respect, and the bread is placed in their open palms.

The meals are filling, nutritious, and simple. And although the food is indeed tasty, many visitors come as much for the ritual, for the exercise of eating together in equality and harmony, as they do for the meal.

Early 19th-century Sikh leader Ranjit Singh donated the gold for the temple's exterior.

FEEDING ANCESTORS BY FEEDING CROWS

SHRADH • INDIA

In the Hindu faith, it is said the dead visit the living on Earth every year on the anniversary of their passing. They come as crows, and it is the responsibility of the living to feed their ancestors their favorite foods, as part of a ritual known as shradh.

On these death anniversaries, called the tithi, relatives cook a feast that might contain half a dozen dishes of rice and dal, savory vadai fritters, and sweet vermicelli pudding—all tailored to the tastes of the deceased. The relatives spread out a banana leaf and take turns ladling the dishes onto it, which they will then carefully wrap and take outside to present to a crow. Sometimes, finding the crow can be the hardest part. If there is no crow outside, a relative might caw, trying to call a bird to where they are. If that doesn't work, the family will pack up the banana leaf and go roving for crows, getting into the car and driving slowly, scanning trees and rooftops. When they find the crow, they spread out the banana leaf and invite it to feast. The bird must eat the food in order to conclude the shradh, which signifies to the living that the soul of the loved one is sated and at peace.

How to try it

Shradh is especially important when honoring dead parents. It is typically performed by the eldest son, but daughters perform the ritual in the absence of sons.

SPICED CANNABIS MILK

BHANG • INDIA

How to try it

In the Rajasthani city of Jaisalmer, a government-authorized bhang shop can be found on Khejer Para Fort Road. During the festival of Holi, bhang is sold throughout the state.

Nicknamed the "Festival of Love and Colors," Holi is a joyous spring festival when revelers run through the streets, dousing one another in bright pigments and colored water. It's also the one time of the year when more conservative members of the family, such as grandmothers or uncles, might cut a little loose by getting loopy on bhang.

Bhang is an edible preparation of cannabis, most popularly incorporated into spiced, milk-based drinks. There's bhang thandai, flavored with almonds, fennel, rose water, saffron, and more, and bhang laasi, which brings yogurt to the party. Like other types of ingested cannabis, the effects of bhang are often hallucinogenic, leading to heightened physical and mental sensations that can be mild or severe, depending on the dosage, and can last an entire day.

MUMBAI'S EXTRAORDINARY

Dabbawala is a term for a "lunch box person," one of the 5,000 deliverymen (and a small handful of deliverywomen) who transport 200,000 homemade, multicourse meals to office workers, students, and other hungry people across Mumbai each day.

Starting at about 8 a.m., dabbas (lunch boxes) are picked up from apartment buildings across the city. A dabba contains three or four stackable cylindrical compartments. One compartment will typically contain rice or rotis. Another might hold dal or a curry, then vegetables, yogurt, or dessert. Although these meals are typically cooked at the recipient's home (generally by family members or domestic help), most workers commute during the morning rush hour, when there's no space on the train to carry their lunches. Instead of bringing the food themselves, dabbawalas—who are all

employed by the Nutan Mumbai Tiffin Box Suppliers Trust—trail behind them.

The dabba system, as we know it today, started in the late 19th century, when Mumbai was still known as Bombay and India was under rule of the British Raj. Indians from all over the country flocked to work in the city, and by 1891, Bombay's population had reached nearly 820,000. Parsis, Hindus, Muslims, Christians, Jews, and Jains worked side by side, bringing food from their homes to their new city.

Legend has it that the system arose when a Parsi banker hired a Maratha worker to pick up a homemade lunch from the banker's house, then deliver it to his office four miles away. Mahadeo Havaji Bacche, the deliveryman, was one of the many men parked at a nearby intersection, waiting for odd jobs. Bacche saw an untapped opportunity to deliver home-cooked meals

Indian law forbids the possession of hashish (resin) and ganja (buds)—but not industrial hemp, and not bhang. Regulation is up to each of the country's states, many of which explicitly allow its consumption. In Rajasthan, for instance, there are government-authorized bhang shops selling cookies and chocolates alongside drinks.

Bhang's roots go back some 3,000 years, to the Vedic period, and the substance (and cannabis in general) plays a prominent role in the mythology of the powerful ascetic-monk god Shiva. Holi is perhaps the best time to drink the ancient elixir, when there are enough sounds and sights to match the happy-go-lucky sensation of bhang.

Lunch Box Delivery System

to office workers, and in 1890, he hired a hundred Maratha workers to make it happen.

In the early days, dabbas were made at home by either a wife or a housekeeper, but today dabbas are sourced from many places. In addition to foods cooked at home, dabbawalas also have connections with kitchens that specialize in home cooking, many of which employ women-driven workforces as a way to encourage financial independence.

The modern dabbawala system is a relay between workers on bicycles, workers riding trains, and workers pushing carts and carrying crates. The lunch boxes change hands multiple times before reaching their destination, and each leg is guided by the series of numbers and letters on the label. Take B 5 W 6N2, for example. The B and the W stand for the lunch box's origin, Borivali West. The 6N2 denotes the

delivery destination: The 6 is the locality, the N is the building, and the 2 is the floor. The 5 refers to the destination train station. (In congested Mumbai, the dabbawallas rely on the rails.) This coded system yields a startlingly consistent and on-time delivery rate. It is so reliable: it bears a 99.9999 percent accuracy rate, or about one mistake for every 16 million deliveries.

Once lunch is over, the same relay is carried out in reverse. The empty dabbas are picked up, sorted, transported, and dropped back home. This round trip service costs 1,200 rupees (about $15) per month. The dabbawalas make about 15,000 rupees a month, or about $200.

Each day, thousands of deliverymen perform a complex relay across Mumbai with 200,000 lunch boxes.

THE LAST WILD APPLE FORESTS

ILE-ALATAU NATIONAL PARK • KAZAKHSTAN

How to try it

The apple forests now exist only in patches. There are various protected sections in the Ile-Alatau National Park, but hiring a guide to take you there is recommended as they are difficult to find.

I n the early 20th century, biologist Nikolai Vavilov first traced the apple genome to a small Kazakh town called Almaty. The apples he found there were strikingly similar to the American classic Golden Delicious. Even more incredible, the apples in Almaty were growing wild, dangling from a thicket of unevenly spaced trees, a phenomenon that existed nowhere else in the world.

Long before human cultivation, scientists believe birds, bears, and horses transported apple seeds from their native Kazakhstan into places like Syria, where the Romans found the fruit and carried it farther around the world. As the apple spread, it became increasingly difficult to pin down its true birthplace, until modern gene sequencing proved that the wild Kazak apple, known as *Malus sieversii*, was indeed the progenitor of the domestic apple. Almaty and its surrounding land was recognized as the origin of almost all apples. (Almaty means "father of apples.")

The Zailiyskiy Alatau mountain range surrounds Almaty, Kazakhstan.

What remains of Kazakhstan's wild apple forests can be found along the Tian Shan mountain range, where the trees are protected and growing safely. Pomologists report that the wild apples have a variety of flavors depending on how the bees pollinate the blossoms. There are honey- and berry-flavored apples, sour crabapples, apples that taste like licorice, and a few strains that would be sweet enough for the modern supermarket.

FERMENTED POCKET CHEESE

KURT • KYRGYZSTAN

Kurt is the invention of nomadic herders. Around Central Asia, where shepherds have roved with their animals for millennia, the dried cheese ball is a dietary staple, made slightly differently depending on where you are and what's available. In Kyrgyzstan, kurt is made by fermenting milk—which can come from a cow, sheep, goat, camel, or mare—then draining the whey from the curds. The soft, soured curds are rolled into balls (some traditions prefer discs, strips, or chunks) and dried in the sun until they are so hard, they must be gnawed. A well-made ball of kurt will keep for years.

These caloric dairy bombs are put to endless use. Kurt makes a ready-to-eat snack, but it's also a kind of creamy bouillon, dissolved into soups and stews, or melted into water for a hot drink. Kurt is also crumbled and used as salt, or dissolved into soda, or tossed into salad.

Sundried, fermented cheese has been around for thousands of years. In 2006, archaeologists in Xinjiang, China, unearthed a coffin containing a woman with chunks of kurt around her neck and chest. The archaeologists determined that the woman (nicknamed the "Beauty of Xiaohe") was buried around 2000 BCE, making the kurt approximately 4,000 years old. In 2017, this preserved kurt was considered the second oldest piece of cheese in the world, trailing behind a 7,000-year-old remnant found in Croatia. The nomadic people who occupy the Tian Shan Mountain area, where the Beauty of Xiaohe was found, still make cheese almost exactly the same way.

How to try it

Kurt balls are sold in markets around Kyrgyzstan, and its many derivatives can be found around the larger Central Asia region.

BOTTOMLESS MILLET BEER

TONGBA • NEPAL

On the narrow trails of the Himalayas, where travelers must carry their meals on their backs, multiuse ingredients are essential. Tongba, a brew-it-yourself millet libation, is one such staple. As long as there's a steady supply of hot water, one cup of the cooked, fermented millet can be easily stretched into several rounds of warming, yeasty beer.

Tongba provides near-instant gratification. Simply pour hot water over the millet, let the grains steep until the liquid turns cloudy, then stick in a straw and enjoy. A tongba straw is closed at the submerged end but perforated on the sides, which lets in liquid while filtering out the grains. When the mug runs dry, the process can be repeated four or five times without losing much flavor or potency. Depending on the millet, the alcohol content will vary, but it's usually lower than regular beer and provides a slow, mellow buzz. The taste is yeasty and earthy, with hints of bread and mushrooms.

The incredible refillable brew is especially important to the Limbu people of eastern Nepal, who use the drink for ceremonies, celebrations, and religious offerings. Today, the practice has caught on in the surrounding mountainous regions of Tibet, Bhutan, and India, as well as in restaurants across Nepal, where pitchers of hot water are placed on the table. The traditional drinking vessel is a cask-like mug, which is also called a tongba.

How to try it

Small Star in Kathmandu is a loud (and relatively expensive) local eatery known for traditional meals and exceptional tongba.

Several salt replicas of monuments have been built inside the Khewra mines, like this rendering of Minar-e-Pakistan, a national landmark in Lahore.

SALT MINE METROPOLIS

KHEWRA SALT MINES • PAKISTAN

The Khewra salt mines are the second largest in the world—behind the Sifto Canada, Inc., salt mine in Goderich, Ontario—turning out 325,000 tons of salt per year, and an estimated 220 million tons over its lifetime.

The massive mine, which covers an area of 1,184 square feet (110 square m) and runs 11 stories (748 feet, or 228 m) deep, has a tunnel system of 25 miles (40 km). To keep the huge space from collapsing in on itself, only 50 percent of the salt is mined, while the other half serves as structural support. Over the years, workers have constructed some incredible structures within the mine, including a miniature Badshahi Mosque—the famous Mughal-era masjid in Lahore—complete with a small salt minaret, as well as small salt versions of the Great Wall of China, the Mall Road of Murree, and Pakistan's national poet Allama Iqbal. All the miniatures are built from salt bricks, which vary from red to pink to white. Beyond the sculptures, there is a 20-bed clinic that treats asthmatic patents with salt therapy, and its own fully functioning post office, for use by the workers, which is the world's only post office built from salt.

Although a popular tourist destination today, the salt mines were the scene of brutal oppression and forced work by the British in the 1800s. Miners were locked in and not allowed to leave until they fulfilled their quotas. This policy included pregnant women, and a number of children were born within the mine. Strikes were met with violence, which is on display in the mines: The graves of 12 miners shot and killed in 1876 can be seen at the middle gate.

How to try it

An electric railway, in place since the 1930s, now brings tourists into the mine, but you can choose to walk the tunnels. It's easy to taste the output of Khewra, which is known as Himalayan salt and sold in many grocery stores.

Other Salty Wonders

DANIEL CAMPOS, BOLIVIA
Salar de Uyuni

The largest salt flat in the world is spread over 4,247 square miles (11,000 square km) in an endless sheet of hexagonal tiles. Generations of saleros historically harvested the flats, but their way of life is disappearing in a modernizing Bolivia. Today, the flats are mostly scenic. During the wet season, the expanse transforms into an enormous salt lake that perfectly mirrors the sky.

MOUNT ELGON, KENYA
Kitum Cave

This salt-rich cavity extends some 600 feet (183 m) into an extinct shield volcano and functions as a salt lick for animals in the Kenyan wild. When the cave was first discovered, the marks and scratches on its walls were assumed to be the work of ancient people, but they were actually left by elephants, who used their tusks to pull chunks off the wall and eat the salt, slowly excavating the cave over hundreds of years.

GRAND SALINE, TEXAS
The Salt Palace

This town's salt-mining history dates back to 1845. The Salt Palace is constructed entirely of salt, erected next to a salt deposit that's an estimated 16,000 feet (4,877 m) deep and contains a supply to last about 20,000 years. In Grand Saline, salt is everything. A museum for Morton Salt, North America's largest producer, the palace boasts a wall that visitors like to lick.

Salar de Uyuni in Bolivia stretches over 4,000 miles.

MAD HONEY

DELI BAL • TURKEY

When bees feed on the pollen of rhododendron flowers, their honey can pack a psychotropic punch. Depending on how much a person consumes, reactions can range from hallucinations and a slower heartbeat to temporary paralysis and unconsciousness. There are hundreds of types of rhododendrons, but only a few contain grayanotoxin, the compound that makes honey psychedelic. These special rhododendrons grow in the high Turkish mountains that line the Black Sea, where locals have been cultivating deli bal, or mad honey, for millennia and using it with strategic aplomb.

Mad honey was deployed in 67 BCE as a trap for invading Roman soldiers. Loyalists to King Mithridates placed honey along their path, which the Romans were unable to resist. When paralysis settled in, Mithridates's men came back to kill them.

By the 18th century, Europeans had developed a taste for the honey, which they imported by the ton and mixed into their drinks for a psychedelic tipple.

In smaller doses, mad honey is used in Turkey as folk medicine. About a teaspoon of the potent, red-hued nectar is believed to relieve hypertension, diabetes, and gastric pain among other things. More than a tablespoon is when poisoning symptoms generally kick in, but the potency can vary greatly from batch to batch.

How to try it

The mountain towns along the Black Sea are where to find the purest mad honey, but shopkeepers may be reluctant to sell it to outsiders.

Sea bass biryan

SULTAN CUISINE FROM THE OTTOMAN EMPIRE

ASITANE RESTAURANT • TURKEY

On a quiet side street in Istanbul, Asitane Restaurant prides on itself re-creating Ottoman cuisine. It's harder than it sounds. During the Ottoman period (1299–1922), secretive guilds prohibited chefs from writing down recipes. Complicating things further, any records of classical Ottoman preparations are in Ottoman Turkish, written in Arabic script, instead of modern-day Turkish, which

How to try it

Asitane is located at 6 Kariye Cami Sokake, in the Fatih district west of Istanbul's city center. They are open every day, 12 p.m.–11:30 p.m.

is written in the Latin alphabet. Undaunted, Asitane hired a team of academics and researchers to search for menus detailing historic feasts held by sultans, records of foods purchased for palace kitchens, and written accounts by foreign travelers. Slowly, the culinary detectives built a repertoire of hundreds of recipes, including many that are tied to specific dates. Historical specialties at Asitane include almond soup from 1539 served with pomegranate and nutmeg, 17th-century fried liver rissoles dunked in sweet-and-sour molasses, and slow-cooked goose atop almond pilaf. A perennial favorite is baked fruit (quince in the winter, melon in the summer) stuffed with lamb and beef. The hard-won, centuries-old dishes painstakingly re-created in the Asitane kitchen are perfect for anyone hungry for a literal taste of history.

MAGIC ORCHID THICKENER

SALEP • TURKEY

Consider the glamorous orchid: Most know the plant for its long stems, elegant blossoms, and hard-to-grow reputation. But in Turkey, the orchid is best loved for a hidden talent. Dried up and ground, the tubers of wild orchids make a flour called salep, which locals use as a special thickener in two essential Turkish foods.

When combined with hot milk, sugar, and spices, salep becomes a drink, also called salep, that dates back to the Ottoman Empire. The texture is viscous and smooth, coating the throat and mouth in a soothing way that's especially desirable during cold winter days. Salep is also traditionally considered a medicinal drink, with the power to heal respiratory and gastrointestinal problems.

A dondurma vendor pulls the ice cream high in the air.

The incredible flower is also what gives Turkish ice cream its signature texture. Called dondurma, Turkish ice cream is equal parts dessert and performance art. Vendors use a long metal rod to beat and knead the ice cream in a metal drum, which they then pull high into the air, creating a vertical trail of thick, elastic ice cream. Twirled onto the rod, vendors deposit a blob of ice cream onto a cone and hand it to a customer. Salep powder makes the ice cream thick and stable (dondurma is sometimes served like shawarma, sliced from a large mass with a knife), while also making it less prone to melting. As for the sticky elasticity, that comes from a pine resin called mastic sap, which also makes it chewy.

Salep has become such a popular product that Turkey's wild orchid population is being destroyed. It is now illegal to export real salep, and more and more shops are substituting rice flour or guar gum. Although the ancient flour performs some excellent tricks, as with everything, it's best in moderation.

How to try it

In Turkey, it's getting increasingly hard to find the real thing. Ali Usta in Istanbul serves both the hot drink and the ice cream.

SOVIET-ERA CARROT KIMCHI

MORKOVCHA • UZBEKISTAN

How To Try It

Look for morkovcha in big, bustling Uzbek bazaars, such as Chorsu Bazaar in Tashkent and Central Bazaar in Samarkand.

To those who don't know its history, morkovcha is a simple carrot salad. Julienned carrots are pickled in white vinegar and oil and seasoned with coriander, red pepper, and fresh garlic. Its name, which means "Korean carrots," hints at a deeper significance.

In the 1860s, faced with drought and famine, thousands of Koreans from the province of Hamgyong crossed the border into Russia. At first their new country embraced them, but there was soon pressure to assimilate to Russian culture and the Orthodox Christian faith. As the Russian czars tried to convert the first wave of immigrants, more arrived, many escaping the Japanese occupation. By the 1930s, nearly 200,000 Koreans, known as Koryo-saram, had settled in what was then the Soviet Union. Many Koreans assimilated, accepting Russian values, eating European food, and enlisting in the imperial army. But some Koreans remained in enclaves, preserving their culture and traditional cuisine.

In 1937, as tensions rose between the USSR and Japan, Joseph Stalin decided the Koryo-saram were an "unreliable people" and forcibly and violently relocated the population to remote parts of Uzbekistan and Kazakhstan. Many Koryo-saram died on the monthlong journey. Those who survived were forced to start over with nothing in an unknown land.

Morkovcha is an example of the cuisine that emerged from this brutal diaspora. Koryo-saram food is shaped both by early Russian influence and by the crops they found in Central Asia. When common Korean ingredients such as napa cabbage weren't available for kimchi, carrots were a handy substitute. Coriander seeds and fresh cilantro, both staples of Uzbek cuisine, made their way in, too.

As Soviet Koreans moved around the USSR to study and work in the 1960s, their cuisine spread and morkovcha became a staple outside the diaspora. The crunchy, garlicky, sweet-and-sour salad is so well loved that many Uzbek grocery stores sell packaged spice mixes so customers can make it at home.

BREAD STAMPS

CHEKICH • UZBEKISTAN

Uzbekistan's non is a round, flat bread that's light, chewy, and treated with such respect that every loaf is decorated with a stamp especially made for bread beautification. Called chekich, these stamps have fine, needle-like points that make tiny perforations into the dough. After they've been poked, the non is slapped against the blistering walls of a tandyr, or tandoor oven, where the bread will rise around the tiny holes, leaving an elegant, intricate design.

Besides being attractive, the designs affect the bread's texture, giving a unique blend of chewy, crunchy, and soft, depending on how much of the dough has been stamped. In Uzbekistan, the care given to bread borders on worship. Their non is ancient (the *Epic of Gilgamesh*, one of the earliest surviving works of literature, references Uzbek-style non), and there is a bread tradition for every occasion. Engaged couples are given pink and yellow non. Those leaving on a trip take a bite from a piece of non, then leave the rest behind for their safe return. If non is dropped on the ground, it is picked up and placed on a ledge or tree branch for birds to eat, while saying "*aysh Allah*" or "God's bread."

Though the bread is eaten every day, at nearly every meal, bakers take the time to lovingly stamp each loaf. As a common Uzbek proverb goes: "Respect for non is respect for country."

How to try it
Conveniently, chekich can be found at the same bazaars that have morkovcha (p. 114). Make a day of it!

Though the intricate designs may suggest otherwise, loaves of non are an everyday food in Uzbekistan.

EAST ASIA

FERMENTED TEA GOLD RUSH

PU'ER TEA • CHINA

How to try it

For full immersion, taste tea varieties at the Pu'er Tea Institute, south of Pu'er City in the autonomous Xishuangbanna prefecture.

The mountainous region of Yunnan, China, is an ideal place to grow pu'er tea, as its rolling slopes allow even rainfall distribution to plants at every level.

Winding through the southwestern mountains of China, east of Tibet, is an ancient caravan trail once used by traders to transport tea. The Tea Horse Road begins in Yunnan Province, which many believe to be the birthplace of tea. Around the 8th century, to make transportation easier, sellers compressed their tea into discs and wrapped them in bamboo leaves, which could be bundled and strapped to their animals. On the journey, the goods were exposed to sunshine, heat, and rain, causing the tea cakes to ferment. The region's famous specialty tea, pu'er, was born.

Like wine grapes, tea leaves are affected by terroir, cultivation, processing, aging, and storage. The very best pu'er grows wild in the rain forests of Yunnan Province, where hundred-year-old trees with deep root systems produce rich, complexly flavored leaves. (Bordered by Vietnam, Myanmar, and Laos, these forests look more like Southeast Asia than mainland China.) The picked leaves are fired in a wok, a process that removes moisture and breaks them down slightly, and then kneaded by hand and left to dry in the sun. After extensive tasting, the tea is blended with other tea leaves, pressed into discs, and left to ferment.

In the late 1990s, wealthy tea drinkers from Hong Kong to Taiwan became fascinated with pu'er, then fixated, then absolutely loony for it. The pu'er market exploded. The Chinese middle class invested like it was gold. Speculators bought all the tea they could, with little regard for quality. There were forgeries. Tea was shipped into Yunnan, stamped as pu'er, and sold as if it had come from the province. Labels were intentionally made to mirror the packaging of popular luxury brands. A decade before the boom, a kilo of pu'er sold for pennies. In 2006, right before the bubble burst, the same kilo went for hundreds of dollars.

Among aficionados, pu'er is treated like wine or cheese—as a living product that will change and develop for the duration of its life. Microbes are important—the Yunnan forests are rich with unique bacteria—as is the location where the tea was aged, how long it was aged, and by whom. In 2005, 500 grams of a 64-year-old "vintage" sold for $150,000.

While the pu'er frenzy has quieted, pu'er drinkers still make up a robust, devoted community. In China, pu'er is a popular gift, and the most sought-after tea (grown in places such as Lao Banzhang) gets bought before it can leave the country. Those who source for foreign demand have to make strategic partnerships with farmers, who keep their harvesting sites secret.

To drink pu'er, a small chunk of tea is broken from the cake and "rinsed" with an application of hot water, which is discarded. The second brew is good to drink, and many people brew their pu'er many times after that, enjoying the way the flavor changes. The finest pu'er is measured in both flavor and how it feels in the body. Many describe drug-like highs, both the calm, muscle-relaxing variety and the sweaty, panicked kind. The taste is almost impossible to describe—some dark, some earthy, some sweet, some harsh—as every brick tastes different.

Pu'er tea is one of the few teas protected by the Chinese government and must come from the Yunnan Province.

BOUNCY MEATBALL SHOP

FEI XIA LAO ER • CHINA

Every day at 3:30 p.m., the staff at Fei Xia Lao Er start breaking down fresh, still-warm slabs of beef and transforming them into meatballs that, when thrown against a table, will bounce a foot in the air. Along the windows of the small shop, a row of young workers sit on stools, ready to perform the 4 p.m. show that's taken place every day for 30 years. In each hand, they hold a metal baton. Before them is a solid hunk of beef. In 25 minutes, it will be paste.

If you didn't see the beef, you might think the employees were beating a drum. But with each rhythmic rise and fall of the metal batons, the quivering block of meat slowly loosens. The workers strike the meat, fold it, then strike again. According to owner Liping Hong, the pounding motion is not about strength, but posture. With the correct form—picked up from the elders in Hong's hometown—the pounding should be "easy."

The beef paste is ready when it's a light pink color, jiggly, and almost fluffy. Seasoning and starch are added, then the mixture is squeezed between the thumb and forefinger into little balls that are plopped directly into a vat of boiling water. The staff at Fei Xia Lao Er make 3,200 meatballs every day, which are usually gone within 24 hours.

The texture of the meatballs is light, refreshing, and springy. This is all thanks to the hand-pounding. Machinery destroys the muscle fiber in beef, whereas the slow beating keeps the fiber intact and gives the meatball its signature bounce.

How to try it

Fei Xia Lao Er is located on Feixia N Road in Shantou, but bouncy meatballs are a traditional specialty all over the Chaoshan region.

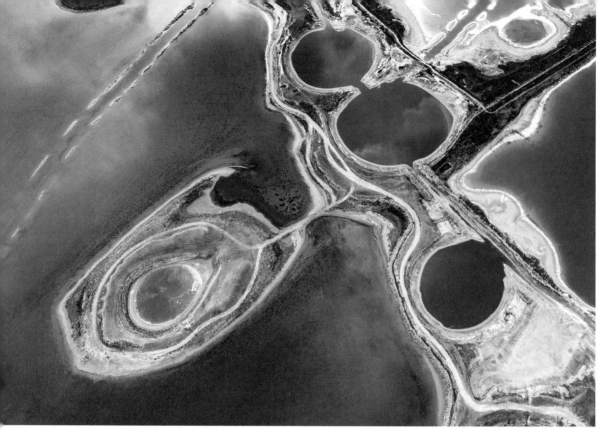

CHINA'S DEAD SEA

YUNCHENG SALT LAKE • CHINA

How to try it

There are several buses that run from downtown Yuncheng to the lake. Other salt lakes in China have suffered extreme pollution due to tourist attention. Help keep Yuncheng from the same fate by carrying your trash out with you.

When summer comes, the glassy water of Yuncheng Salt Lake in China's Shanxi Province turns a shocking rainbow. From above, the lake looks like a painter's palette, with dabbles of magenta, green, and aquamarine across the landscape.

Known as "China's Dead Sea" for its salinity, the vast lake has long been the focal point of Yuncheng's culture and economy. Chinese historians estimate that locals have harvested salt from the lake for more than 4,000 years. By the sixth century, Yuncheng Lake was responsible for a quarter of China's overall salt production. Local lore reports wars fought over possession of the lake, and nearby temples are dedicated to salt gods.

Today, most travelers come to the lake not to worship the salt gods, but to marvel at the landscape's surreal charm. As opposed to the Dead Sea, which is filled with chloride and is hostile to life, Yuncheng Lake is filled with sulfate, which supports a lush ecosystem. In the summer, algal blooms turn the water technicolor thanks to *Dunaliella salina*, an algae species that changes color when it reacts with salt. In winter, when the temperature dips below 23°Fahrenheit (-5°C), the salt forms crystals of mirabilite, also known as Glauber's Salt, transforming the landscape into a twinkling winter fantasy.

Yuncheng salt was traditionally harvested for culinary use through a five-step process that the Shanxi Province has officially recognized as a piece of the region's intangible heritage. Since the 1980s, however, producers have abandoned this process and pivoted toward industrial harvesting. Locals hope that the influx of visitors interested in marveling at the lake can also help inspire the preservation of local salt-harvesting traditions and the rich ecosystem that has given rise to an extraordinary natural beauty.

NAKED BOY TEA PET

PEE-PEE BOY • CHINA

In recent years, "tea pets" have made their way into the contemporary Chinese tea ceremony. The small figurines, shaped like animals, plants, or mythical creatures, are meant to be cared for by their owners, who "bathe" their little companions by pouring hot water over their bodies. Among China's favorite pets is "pee-pee boy," a hollowed-out child with a large head and a small penis.

Pee-pee boy is more useful than he first appears because his body functions—via bodily function—as a thermometer. When preparing tea, pee-pee boy takes a dip in room-temperature water, which he draws in through the hole in his member until he is half full. To check the temperature of your tea water, simply pour it over pee-pee boy's head, and if the water is hot enough, your tea pet will emit a long, arching liquid stream. If the water's too cold, pee-pee boy will lose his nerve.

Although the origins of pee-pee boy are unclear, the physics behind his steady stream are scientifically sound. A 2016 study exploring the thermodynamics of several pee-pee boys found that hot water poured over the noggin makes the air within the body expand, causing pressure to build and release a jet of "pee" seconds later. The correlation was simple: the hotter the water, the farther the stream. Additional factors affecting whizzing distance included head size (pee-pee boy's cranium is disproportionately large), ceramic thickness, penis size, and hole diameter.

Hollow ceramic figurines date back to the Tang dynasty (618–906 CE). If they were used like tea pets, researchers speculate that they could be the world's first thermometers, preceding Galileo Galilei's late-16th-century invention of the thermoscope.

How to try it
Pee-pee boys can be purchased online.

This small urinating boy may look like trouble, but he is one of China's favorite "tea pets."

A WORKING REPLICA OF THE *FRIENDS* COFFEE SHOP

CENTRAL PERK BEIJING • CHINA

Tucked away on the sixth floor of Beijing's Chaowai, SOHO Building A, is a shockingly good replica of Central Perk, the coffee shop hangout on the American sitcom *Friends*. Not only is it fitted with identical brick walls, tables, and the ever-present orange couch, it's also a fully functional coffee shop where customers can sip java, relax, and pretend they're in the show. There is even a resident Smelly Cat.

Created by owner Du Xin, who describes the show as his religion, Beijing's Central Perk is a mecca for Chinese fans of *Friends*, as well as those who simply want to practice their English. A TV plays episodes of *Friends* on loop with Chinese subtitles, which students say is a great way to pick up colloquialisms and mannerisms that aren't taught in the classroom. In the space next door, Du has also constructed a replica of the character Joey Tribbiani's apartment, complete with foosball table, dartboard, Etch A Sketch, and oversize TV console.

How to try it
Central Perk Beijing is located at 0616 Chaowai SOHO Building. According to visitors, the sixth floor of the building is vast, with many vacancies, so you may not find it right away.

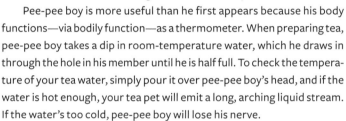

DOUBLE-YOLK EGG CITY

GAOYOU • CHINA

How to try it

Gaoyou holds an annual China Double-Yolk Duck Egg Festival, typically in April. Year round, salted double-yolked eggs are served in the region's teahouses, generally as a component of zaocha, or morning tea.

Two-yolked eggs are usually a rare, statistically random occurrence. But in the eastern Chinese city of Gaoyou—a place synonymous with double-yolked duck eggs—farmers found a way to engineer a vast supply of this local specialty.

Gaoyou, a city with a population of nearly one million, has a long and close relationship with ducks. The duck industry dates back to the 6th century, and locals still gift ducks on occasions ranging from marriages to a child's first day at school. Double-yolked eggs—believed to be more nutritious than regular eggs, as well as a sign of good luck—are held in especially high regard. For generations, locals bred Gaoyou's local duck variety to produce double-yolked eggs, which occur when a fowl ovulates twice in the process of formulating an egg. The resulting duck lays anywhere between 2 to 10 percent double-yolkers.

To check an egg for double yolks, farmers shine a bright light on the shell, which reveals either one gray yolk shadow or two. This process, known as candling, is done on a commercial scale in Gaoyou, where workers pick eggs off a backlit conveyor belt. Once removed from the pack, the special eggs are brined in vats of salt water before gracing lucky tables across the region.

A backlit conveyor belt helps workers identify the duck eggs with two yolks.

NOCTURNAL CRAB CONDIMENT

GHOST CRAB SAUCE • CHINA

On early autumn nights when the tide is low, the beaches off the southern coastal city of Beihai come alive with tiny skittering ghost crabs, darting beneath the moonlight. The miniature crabs, just two centimeters long, have spectral white legs and transparent, ghoulish blue bodies. Also known as sand crabs for their ability to camouflage themselves on the beach, the tiny crustaceans are a species that has remained nearly unchanged for millennia.

During ghost crab swells, Beihai locals put on rubber boots and come out to chase them. Carrying long sticks attached to nets, they scoop the critters however they can, bending to gather them in their hands or swooping them up in their nets. Ghost crabs are incredibly fast, able to sprint about five feet (1.5 m) in a second, so the nocturnal hunt is frenetic, with humans dashing after masses of micro crabs as they try to burrow into the sand.

Ghost crabs, which are sensitive to pollutants, are often a sign of a healthy beach. The people of Beihai like them for their nutrient-rich taste, which they absorb from seawater and algae. Ghost crab sauce is an essential condiment in the southern Chinese city, made from pounding the cleaned and gutted crabs, adding salt and liquor, then letting it ferment for about a month. The pungent, fishy sauce, with its shell-and-meat-studded texture, is used as something of an all-purpose seasoning. The most popular preparation is steamed with cowpeas (a green bean), but the complex, raw, and richly flavored liquid is happily poured over pretty much anything.

How to try it

Ghost crab sauce is highly regional and almost always homemade. The crabs themselves are found on coasts from North America to South Africa.

← 2 cm →

THE WORLD'S OLDEST SANDWICH

ROU JIA MO • CHINA

Rou jia mo, one of China's most popular street foods, has been around since the Qin dynasty (221–207 BCE). Translated as "meat in bread," rou jia mo is widely considered the world's first sandwich, the progenitor of the burger, and one of the tastiest, most interesting foods in the country.

The Han Chinese were the original sandwich makers. Although rice is the starch Westerners most associate with Chinese food, the northern provinces have a distinct cuisine that revolves around mo, or bread. Few details exist about the first rou jia mo, but historical records show the ancient Chinese were combining bread and meat 2,000 years before the Earl of Sandwich. During the Tang dynasty (618–907), the Silk Road originated in the city of Xi'an, now the capital of Shaanxi Province. Traders and merchants from the Middle East and India arrived in the ancient Chinese capital, bringing knowledge and spices, which went into flavoring the world's first sandwich.

How to try it

Anywhere in China, rou jia mo is hard to miss, but around Shaanxi Province, shops sell every imaginable variation. In Xi'an, try Cheng's for "juicy" filling, Ziwu Road Zhang for "chewy" filling, Dongguan Li's for "dry" filling, or Qinyu for just lots of filling.

A Xi'an street vendor prepares lamb rou jia mo.

Traditional, street-style rou jia mo is made with 20 spices, including ginger, star anise, cardamom, galangal, bay leaves, Sichuan peppercorn, cinnamon, and cumin. Swirled into a stock of sweetened soy sauce and Shaoxing wine, the broth is used to slowly braise chunks of pork belly. The stock is the most important part of the dish, used over and over again. Called Thousand Year Old Sauce, the liquid takes on the rich oil of the meat, reducing and growing more profound in flavor with each batch. (This is a technique used in other Chinese dishes such as Chairman Mao's favorite red-braised pork belly, which makes an excellent rou jia mo filling.) The bun, or mo, is a simple wheat flour dough that's formed into hand-size discs, then baked in a traditional clay oven or fried in a pan. Split open and stuffed with meat, cilantro, and vendor-specific toppings, a rou jia mo on the street in China will cost about 5–10 yuan ($0.75–$1.50 USD).

Thanks in part to the Silk Road, modern-day Xi'an is now home to about 70,000 Muslims and a lively Chinese Muslim food scene, awash in hand-pulled noodles and mutton stews. Adapting the regional sandwich recipe to suit their tastes and religious dietary restrictions, they introduced lamb and beef rou jia mo, which are now as ubiquitous in Xi'an as the Han pork belly classic.

Chairman Mao's Red–Braised Pork Belly (Hong Shao Rou)
4-6 servings

2 pounds pork belly, cut into ¾-inch pieces

6 slices ginger (divided)

2 tablespoons oil

3 tablespoons granulated sugar or 40 grams rock sugar, plus ½ teaspoon to finish

3 scallions, diced, with the white and green parts separated

½ cup Shaoxing wine

3 tablespoons light soy sauce

1½ tablespoons dark soy sauce

1 piece of cinnamon

2 star anise

4 bay leaves

1–2 dried chili peppers (optional)

4 cups water

1. Put the pork belly and 3 slices of ginger in a pot, cover with cold water, and bring to a boil with the lid on. Once the pot boils, turn down the heat and simmer for 1 more minute. Drain, rinse the pork belly clean, and set aside.

2. With the wok set over low heat, add the oil and sugar. Slowly melt the sugar, then add the pork belly, the remaining 3 slices of ginger, and the white parts of

the scallions. Turn up the heat to medium and stir, coating the pork in the melted sugar.

3. Add the Shaoxing wine, light soy sauce, dark soy sauce, cinnamon, star anise, bay leaves, dried chili pepper, and water. Stir. Simmer over medium low heat for 1 hour.

4. Add the remaining ½ teaspoon of sugar and green parts of the scallions.

It's said that Chairman Mao (above) ate this dish every day.

The Mandatory Canteens
OF COMMUNIST CHINA

n 1958, Chinese communist cadres descended upon the homes of farmers with an official government mission: to confiscate food supplies and cooking equipment, and to destroy private kitchens. Effective immediately, cooking and eating meals at home became illegal.

The measure stemmed from Chairman Mao Zedong's Great Leap Forward, a series of communist government initiatives intended to revolutionize the Chinese countryside. In order to build a new socialist consciousness in China, Mao pushed agricultural collectivization. He abolished private property, divided all work among households, and grouped farmers into cooperatives of about 23,000 members. The system was called the People's Commune, and it centered around a free canteen system designed to feed commune members.

The People's Commune contained 2.65 million canteens, constructed from confiscated tables, utensils, and kitchen equipment. A ringing bell signified the start of mealtimes, when farmers would line up single file to be served cafeteria-style before sitting down in a central dining

Chinese citizens eat as much as they can at a People's Commune canteen in 1958.

area. The meals were free, but there was no other choice.

At first, the canteens were treated like a miracle. A popular slogan invited diners to "open your stomach, eat as much as you wish, and work hard for socialism." Farmers reveled in the new system and gorged themselves on pork and vegetables, sometimes eating when they weren't hungry. Government propaganda led citizens to believe that more grain was being produced than actually was, and that food was plentiful. Leftovers were thrown away and massive amounts of food were squandered.

Problems arose almost immediately, and signs of famine appeared as early as the winter of 1958. Historically, Chinese farmers maintained food stockpiles to prepare for shortages or slow harvest years. Without them, they were hostage to the dwindling food supply of the canteens.

By spring of 1959, the famine had metastasized beyond control. The carefree days of feasting quickly morphed into hunger. Survivors remember the canteen meals grimly: buns made from corn and bark, served with water. It was not uncommon for laborers, still toiling in the fields to hit massive

quotas, to receive as little as 150–200 grams of food for a meal. Rice was unavailable and was substituted with watery wheat porridge, sweet potatoes and their leaves, and hemp "noodles," made by cutting roots into strands. Farmers also ate the bark from parasol and loquat trees.

Massive exploitation further exacerbated the problem. Corrupt leaders ate as much as they wanted from the canteens. Meanwhile, farmers had little incentive to work because everyone received the same food. By the end of 1960, the rising death toll and drastic food shortages forced the government to acknowledge that the canteen system had failed. After a series of debates with high-ranking officials, Mao finally relented. By 1962, all communal canteens were eliminated. The famine killed an estimated 30 million people, making it one of the worst in human history.

Despite the canteen system's devastating consequences, restaurants that hearken back to Mao's China have opened in cities such as Beijing and Chongqing. Staff don the traditional communist suits and use gimmicks to project nostalgia about a "simpler" time and a China that no longer exists. In an ironic twist, these ultra-capitalist modern restaurants, with their abundance of food, may have been closer to what Mao originally imagined for his communal canteens.

A PERILOUS CUP OF ELEVATED TEA

HUASHAN TEAHOUSE • CHINA

Nestled atop the highest peak of China's holy Mount Hua is a temple that offers a cup of tea—a drink central to Daoist philosophy—more than 7,000 feet (2133 m) in the air. The trek, which has been called one of the most dangerous hiking paths in the world, has attracted pilgrims for centuries. Mount Hua is one of China's five sacred mountains and has been a religious site since the 2nd century BCE, when a Daoist temple was built at its base.

To reach the temple, hikers must first reach the northern peak by climbing a series of steps carved into the mountain known as the Heavenly Stairs, which takes about 4–5 hours. (This is the only leg of the ascent you can take via gondola.) Once at the northern peak, the real work begins. Getting to the southern peak requires another 2–3 hours of climbing, but instead of traditional trails, hikers must sidle along the sheer mountainside, balancing across a thin ledge made of what looks like scrap wood suspended hundreds of feet in the air. (This is called the "plank walk.") At certain points, the planks fall away, leaving nothing but a horizontal chain to hold and some pegs to stand on. Regulations now require hikers to use safety harnesses and carabiners, but the paths are so narrow that climbers often unhook their carabiners to pass each other. Finally, a set of worn stairs leads to the temple, and their sharp grade offers no respite.

Inside the temple, while the monks go about their daily rituals, visitors can sit down for a well-earned cup of tea. In Daoist philosophy, drinking tea facilitates meditation and creates a connection to nature. The tea served at the temple teahouse is made with natural water—collected from rain, melting snow, and mountain springs—or bottled water ferried to the top. Those who have completed the climb say the elevation, view, and temple setting make for one of the most satisfying cups of tea you'll ever experience.

How to try it
The addition of gondolas has greatly increased the traffic to Mount Hua, and there is often a wait to make the climb from the northern peak.

THE WORLD'S LARGEST FLOATING RESTAURANT

JUMBO KINGDOM • HONG KONG

Glistening in Hong Kong's Aberdeen Harbor is Jumbo Kingdom, a floating behemoth of a restaurant that functions more like a city. The kingdom contains a collection of restaurants serving different styles of Cantonese fare, with grand staircases and skinny walkways crisscrossing between the various establishments. Built by Dr. Stanley Ho, known as Macau's "King of Gambling," the complex was completed in 1976 after four years of work and was modeled on an ancient Chinese imperial palace.

The exterior is decked out in neon lights and upturned eaves with yellow flourishes, a color once reserved for imperial buildings. Inside, there is no shortage of dragons, pagodas, and Ming dynasty–era details: In one banquet hall, there is a gold and red "dragon throne" that took sculptors two years to carve. Beyond the dining areas, which can seat more than 2,000 people, there's a seafood tank barge that guests can visit (the daily catch arrives each morning by fishing boat), a 130-foot (40 m) kitchen boat, a cooking school, a Chinese tea garden, and a theme park.

How to try it

Jumbo Kingdom provides free boat shuttles to and from the Aberdeen waterfront. (Don't be fooled by a sampan taxi offering a cheap ride.) Dim sum, served during lunch, is regarded by many as the most lively and affordable meal on offer.

THE COGNAC OF CONDIMENTS

XO SAUCE • HONG KONG

The term XO, when applied to cognac, means "extra old." But in Hong Kong, it simply means luxury. The island's elite have long nursed an obsession with the super-aged French liquor, so when a chef created "XO sauce" in the 1980s, Hong Kongers knew it had to be fancy.

The cognac-inspired condiment is a sweet and spicy, unctuous medley of minced seafood that requires lots of patience and a hefty amount of cash to create. It begins with a wok of hot oil, which must be carefully monitored throughout the lengthy, multi-step frying process. Each ingredient in the sauce goes in separately, is fried until golden, then removed and reserved until the very end. Garlic and shallots get the oil bath first, then the mélange of dried seafood, all of which must be rehydrated and chopped prior to frying. Diver scallops and shrimp are mandatory (cod roe and baby anchovies are happy additions). Jinhua ham, China's version of prosciutto, is the last item to take a dip in the pool. If along the way something gets burned, the sauce is in trouble. Not only are the items pricey (dried diver scallops can go for $300 a kilo), but the fragrant oil is a key ingredient, swirled with the fried bits, sugar, and chili peppers at the end to create the sumptuous alchemy of XO sauce.

Like cognac, a little XO sauce goes a long way. A spoonful atop a steamed fish or a bowl of greens draws out sweet, salty, and savory elements in dishes that would otherwise lack a dynamic range.

How to try it

Bottled XO sauce is available in Chinese grocery stores, but the best versions are homemade.

Farthest Flung
CHINESE RESTAURANTS

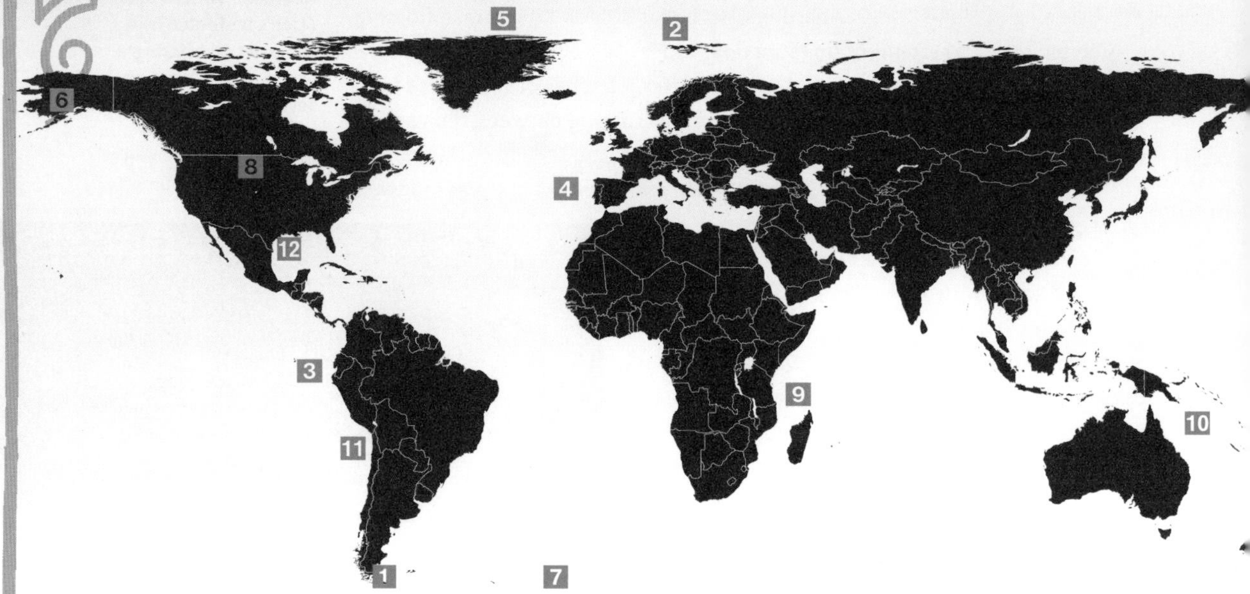

There are more Chinese food joints in the United States than McDonald's, KFC, Wendy's, and Burger King combined. No food has more completely mapped every small town, hamlet, and neighborhood than Chinese cuisine, and it's not just in the United States. Thanks to an expansive diaspora, Chinese restaurants have spread out across the world, and you can find Chinese food from Ecuador to Ethiopia. Here are a few of the farther-flung locations:

1 In Ushuaia, Argentina, at the southern tip of the world, you can get a Chinese buffet at **BAMBOO**. Because it is often the launching point for visiting Antarctica, it isn't uncommon to find large groups of Chinese tourists eating there on their way to the frozen continent.

2 On the island of Tromsøya, above the Arctic Circle, on the fjord-filled northern edge of Norway, you can find **TANG'S**, a traditional Chinese restaurant.

3 Easter Island, with a population of 5,700, has **KAI SUSHI RAPANUI**, a mixed Japanese and Chinese spot.

4 In Lisbon, Portugal, people's apartments form a network of Chinês clandestinos, nonofficial Chinese restaurants.

5 Going to Greenland? Stop at the **HONG KONG CAFE** in Ilulissat, population 4,541, and get some fried spare ribs with your fried rice.

6 **SAM AND LEE'S RESTAURANT** in Utqiaġvik, Alaska, the northernmost city in the United States, may well be the northernmost Chinese restaurant in the world. The restaurant is run by Ms. Kim, who also makes a mean stack of pancakes, reindeer-and-cheese omelets, and the restaurant's own creation, the "Kung Pao" pizza.

7 In Antarctica, although there technically isn't a Chinese "restaurant," the CHINESE GREAT WALL STATION does have a team of Chinese chefs, and researchers from other stations go out of their way for a taste of the roasted mutton and peppery chicken spiced with fresh herbs grown in a soilless base.

8 Montana might not be your first thought when it comes to great Chinese food, but the PEKIN NOODLE PARLOR in Butte is a classic. Immediately identifiable by its iconic glowing neon "Chop Suey" sign, Pekin Noodle Parlor is the nation's oldest continually operating Chinese restaurant. It started serving chow mein back in 1911. On the restaurant's one hundredth birthday, the owner cooked dinner for the whole town.

9 In the city of Mamoudzou, on the island of Mayotte, floating in the channel between Madagascar and the east coast of Mozambique, you can find dozens of Chinese restaurants, including the high-end French-Chinese fusion L'ORIENT EXPRESS. Madagascar was a French colony and also has one of Africa's largest Chinese populations.

10 Visiting Nauru—a tiny island country of 11,347, the second smallest country population in the world behind Vatican City—and worried about getting good Chinese? Don't be—you can choose from one of the more than 138 Chinese restaurants, mostly operated by the 8 percent of the island that are Han Chinese.

11 In the city of Cerro de Pasco, a Peruvian mining town at an elevation of 14,232 ft (about 4,338 m), one of the highest cities in the world, you can still get an egg roll at CHIFA YING FU.

12 In Oklahoma City, beneath the streets is a system of tunnels built in the 1970s known as "the Underground." What's down there? Why, CHINA CHEF, of course, open for more than two decades, despite being notoriously hard to find in the maze of tunnels.

A TRADITIONAL AMIS EATERY

BANAI'S SHOP • TAIWAN

How to try it

Taiwan has three outposts, two in Taipei (Ximen and Shilin) and one in Taichung.

Tucked on a side street off the main drag of Dulan, a small village along Taiwan's eastern coast, is Banai's Shop, a cozy "quick-fry" restaurant specializing in traditional Amis dishes. While the Amis people are Indigenous to this part of Taiwan, a visitor to this popular backpacker town might not immediately guess it from the cute hostels and international eateries that dot its main thoroughfare. Banai's Shop, opened eight years ago by Ms. Ye Shuyuan (Banai is her Amis name), stands out for its tasty, traditional flavors, community-sourced ingredients, and welcoming atmosphere. In addition to Ms. Ye's warm presence, the restaurant's long wooden tables are also often filled with locals who are happy to give tourists recommendations on what to order and aren't shy to share a helping from their plates or a pour of liquor.

Some of the restaurant's more unique offerings include mountain boar stir-fried with bell peppers, cold mountain boar skin marinated in vinegar and topped with fresh cilantro, flying fish fried rice and honey-glazed flying fish (available only during April and May), brook shrimp stir-fried with scallions and chilies, and "Lover's Tears," a green fungus found in the mountains after rainfall, stir-fried with eggs and Thai basil. Traditional millet wine is also available, homemade by local women and sold in tall, unmarked glass bottles. The unfiltered liquor is clean and sweet, making it a great accompaniment to the hearty, bold fare.

TRADITIONAL PYROTECHNIC FISHING

JINSHAN FIRE FISHING FESTIVAL • TAIWAN

How to try it

Tours are about four hours long and offered only in Mandarin. They include an introduction to the history of Jinshan fire fishing, a dinner of noodle soup, and a dazzling view of the fishermen at work.

It's pitch-black on Taiwan's northern waters, when suddenly a boom and blaze of fire explode into the night sky, releasing the sour stench of sulfur. All at once, thousands of tiny sardines leap from the Pacific Ocean, hurling themselves toward the scorching flames. As the fire rages on the boat, several aging fishermen work feverishly to catch the fish before they plunge back into the sea.

Traditional sulfuric fire fishing is a century-plus-old practice found only in Jinshan, a sleepy port city near the northern tip of Taiwan. Fishermen use a bamboo torch and the flammable gas produced by sulfuric rocks (abundant in Taiwan) to ignite a fire fierce enough to drive hordes of sardines to the water's surface. Always timed with a moonless night, when the fish are hungry for light, the fishermen ignite their fire and cast their nets. They work through the night—each playing an essential role such as steering the boat or controlling the flames—for up to 12 hours. The practice is backbreaking, treacherous, and in danger of disappearing.

In its glory days, fire fishing was used by thousands. The technique was first developed by the Pingpu aboriginal tribe and honed during Japanese colonial rule in Taiwan. As of 2019, there are a mere four fire-fishing boats remaining and a dwindling number of fire fishermen, many of them well into their 60s and 70s. The

island's youth have not shown interest in carrying on the fickle, punishing work, which led the government to set up the Jinshan Fire Fishing Festival, where outsiders can witness the nocturnal spectacle.

Like fireworks on the sea, sulfuric flames ignited by Jinshan fishermen attract sardines to the surface.

From May to July, sightseeing tours bring boats of onlookers alongside the fire-fishing boats. The idea is to raise awareness and appreciation for the practice and hopefully save it from extinction. Many fishermen perform the work with a sense of resigned pride, knowing their tradition will inevitably be surrendered to history. For them, fire fishing is both art form and vocation. They feel the cultural significance in what they do, and the strong connection to their island and their ancestors. Yet at its core, fire fishing was a way to make a living, and that way of life is slowly vanishing in a modern world.

PIG'S BLOOD CAKE

ZHU XIE GAO • TAIWAN

How to try it
Find pig's blood cakes at the Rahoe Night Market, one of the oldest markets in Taipei.

In the frenetic, glowing chaos of a Taiwanese night market, all is not what it seems. Propped up on a stick is what looks like a frozen treat, rolled in peanuts and sprinkled with green flecks that, at first glance, you might not recognize as cilantro. Inside is another surprise. The handheld blocks are made of pig's blood and sticky rice, which combine to make a semi-gelatinous, cohesive texture that maintains the integrity of each grain. (The chewiness is reminiscent of Korean rice cakes or Japanese mochi.) Vendors bathe the cake in a pork-soy broth that adds a sweet, umami flavor, then roll it in peanut flour and cilantro. The final product is savory, meaty, herbal, and complexly delicious.

Pantry Staple

BLOOD

Rich in protein and iron, blood is a versatile, shape-shifting ingredient that can thicken or emulsify, congeal into solids, or melt into soup. But when blood goes bad, things get dangerous, which makes for a thin line between healthy and hepatitis.

Gematogen Blood Candy

This soft, chewy stick of molasses-sweet candy wasn't made for pleasure, but for treating low levels of iron and vitamins in Soviet-era Russia, thanks to the primary ingredient: cow's blood. Sold at pharmacies and drugstores, gematogen was dispensed more like medicine than candy. Adults were prescribed daily doses of 50 grams, children under the age of 13 needed an adult's consent, and pregnant women and breastfeeding mothers required a consultation before eating it. These days fresh cow's blood is often swapped out for powdered blood product, but it remains the leading candy bar for anemia, malnutrition, and fatigue.

Blood Tofu

When left out in a clean environment, fresh blood congeals into a jelly-like solid. All it takes is about ten minutes, then the soft block of blood can be cut into pieces and gently boiled to firm up the texture ever so slightly. The result is a silky, ephemeral cube that bursts and melts in the mouth, similar to soft tofu, but with the rich, acerbic flavor of blood. Likely a Chinese invention, blood tofu is eaten across Asian cultures. Duck blood tofu is a staple in hot pot; pig blood tofu tops Thailand's pork blood soup. In the Philippines, chicken blood tofu is cut into rectangular slabs, skewered, and grilled to make a popular street food called Betamax, named after its resemblance to the old-school video cassettes.

Yak Blood

Twice a year, thousands of Nepalese gather in the high Himalayas to drink fresh yak's blood, straight from the animal. At the Yak Blood Drinking Festival, which occurs in the districts of Mustang and Myagdi, local yak owners sell blood by the glass, dispensed from a slit in the animal's neck. The yak is bled alive, without the intention of killing it, and a single animal can provide blood for about 20–50 customers. (In 2019, a glass cost a hundred rupees, or about $1.)

The Nepalese who attend the festival are usually seeking cures for medical ailments. The yaks are known to graze on rare herbs that only grow at staggering altitude, like the wildly expensive caterpillar fungus, and drinking the yak's blood is meant to pass on these medicinal properties. People from around the country arrive with gastric problems, allergies, high blood pressure, asthma, and kidney dysfunction to drink a glass from the source—and many return year after year, citing relief from symptoms.

Blood Clams

When you open a blood clam, you know it immediately. The bite-size cockles are filled with hemoglobin, the dark red protein found in human blood. (Most clams have clear blood.) In places like Asia and Central America, blood clams are a delicacy, generally eaten raw or briefly cooked. But clam blood, like human blood, can carry disease. Hemoglobin allows the mollusks to live in places without much oxygen, but they also must filter a lot of water, making them more susceptible to bacteria and viruses. (In China, a 1988 outbreak of hepatitis A killed 31 people and was linked to contaminated blood clams.) But the ghoulish clams still have a big following and are said to have a cleaner flavor and crisper texture than clear-blooded clams.

Blood Pancakes

Throughout Scandinavia, blood is a common ingredient in breakfast pancakes. The blood—which can be cow, pig, or, in the case of the Sami people of northern Norway, reindeer—whips up nicely into a foam, is packed with protein, and binds the batter almost like an egg. Blood pancakes are nearly black in color, dense, and more nutritious than bloodless pancakes. They're so popular in Europe's northern reaches that the Finnish company Atria makes frozen pig-blood pancakes, available at grocery stores.

Maasai Blood Drinking

Traditionally, the Maasai of southern Kenya and northern Tanzania consume a diet of primarily cow's milk and blood, which is carefully retrieved from the living cow's jugular artery, then quickly resealed. Blood and milk are regarded as "both ordinary and sacred food," used as a regular source of calories and in ritual and ceremony. Cattle blood is considered beneficial for people with weakened immune systems, as well as for hangovers, or simply for breakfast. In a study conducted in 1935, a Canadian dentist found the tribesmen were unusually healthy—entirely free of disease, including cardiovascular problems, and with almost no cavities. (Subsequent studies showed they had half the cholesterol of the average American.) More recently, pasture land has dwindled and many Maasai have been forced to eat more grain and drink less milk and blood, which has shown negative consequences for their health.

A Maasai man dressed in a traditional red shuka holds a gourd full of fresh blood.

CATERPILLAR FUNGUS

YARTSA GUNBU • TIBET

How to try it

Caterpillar fungus is available in many Chinese herbalist stores. It is also sold online, although it's hard to know if you're getting real parasitic fungus.

The Talon Club inside The Cosmopolitan of Las Vegas serves a bowl of "Cordyceps Soup" for $688. It's the most expensive soup in the world, made with chicken, red dates, longan berries, and a quarter ounce of caterpillar fungus. By weight, this tasteless parasitic fungus is one of the priciest substances on earth—more than truffles, more than gold—sourced on the grassy plains of the Tibetan Plateau.

Every May and June, Tibetans spread across the high, grassy plains of the Tibetan Plateau and search for slender brown protrusions that jut from the soil. At first glance, they look like sticks, but they're actually the fruiting bodies of *Ophiocordyceps sinensis*, a fungus that attacks living caterpillars, then consumes them from the inside out. While the ghost moth caterpillar feeds underground, the fungus Tibetans call yartsa gunbu infects it. Once it has consumed most of the body, the fungus takes control of the caterpillar and sends it toward the surface, where the fungus erupts from its head, sending up its "stick." Aboveground, the fruiting body will release spores that go on to infect other caterpillars.

Yartsa gunbu has been a part of Tibetan food and medicine since at least the 1400s, used to treat everything from heart arrhythmias to impotence to cancers. Though little research exists, the fungus is believed to have extensive medicinal properties. Wealthy Chinese buyers have long prized the fungus, but in recent years, the craze has become mainstream.

In the 1990s, stories began circulating about how the fungus helped Chinese athletes break world records. Since then, the value of the parasitic fungus, once traded by locals for food, has increased more than ten times. (A single pound can sell for $50,000.)

The fungal gold rush on the Tibetan Plateau has made a huge impact on the rural region. Some of the change has been positive: Villages have installed solar panels and many households have more money for basics. But the race to find this limited resource has resulted in violent competition, including numerous murders. Many Tibetans have abandoned traditional herding in favor of the fungus hunt, leaving them vulnerable in low-crop years, which are growing more frequent due to overharvesting and global warming.

A Tibetan family digs for valuable caterpillars in the hills of Serxu.

BAMBOO WATERSLIDE NOODLES

NAGASHI SOMEN • JAPAN

n Japanese, nagashi means "flowing." When paired with somen, a cold, white wheat noodle popular during the summer, you get an action-packed meal that requires catching noodles with chopsticks as they float down a bamboo waterslide.

Popularized in the southern town of Takachiho in 1959, the House of Chiho restaurant dreamed up nagashi somen as a way to capitalize on the pure, local spring water. In a tradition that continues today, staff fill long chutes of halved bamboo trunks with cold running water. Once they yell, "Ikuyo!" or "It's coming!" they deposit cooked noodles into the chute for diners downstream to snatch from the current. At most establishments, a basket at the end of the waterworks collects uncaught noodles, and the staff retrieves them for customers. But at the well-known Hirobun restaurant in Kyoto, what you catch is what you get, until red-dyed somen floats through and signals the end of the meal.

Noodle waterslides are not just for restaurants. Home cooks can buy bamboo half pipes to set up nagashi somen in the house. Alternatively, there are special machines that spin noodles around circular basins or send them down miniature waterslides that look like toys. In 2016, the citizens of Gose, in Nara Prefecture, set the Guinness World Record for "longest distance to flow noodles down a line of bamboo gutters." Their nagashi somen chute was 10,871 feet (3,317 m) long.

A woman slurps noodles she successfully snatched out of a bamboo waterslide in Takamatsu, Japan.

How to try it

House of Chiho, located beside a picturesque gorge in Takachiho, still sends noodles flowing through local spring water. It's a 3-hour, 30-minute bus ride from Fukuoka City.

RAILWAY STATION DELICACIES

EKIBENYA MATSURI • JAPAN

t's always a festival (in Japanese, a matsuri) of feasts between tracks 6 and 7 at Tokyo Station. Here, at Ekibenya Matsuri, travelers bustle around choosing from nearly 200 different kinds of ekiben, portable meals meant to be eaten on the Shinkansen bullet train and other local trains that set off from the cosmopolitan city's central train station.

At each train stop in Japan Railways' vast network, vendors sell ekiben containing the specialties of that particular region. In Hyogo Prefecture, this might mean the hipparidako meshi ekiben: a rice, octopus, eel, and vegetables dish served in a miniature takotsubo, modeled on the traditional earthen pot designed to catch octopus in the area. At Shizuoka Station, travelers might line up for the tai meshi, a locally popular dish of sea bream and rice. But circling the displays at Ekibenya

How to try it

The average price of a box at Ekibenya Matsuri is about $10. Ask for a warmed bottle of miso soup when you pay, or grab a bottled matcha, or even single-serve bottles of wine, which they also sell.

Matsuri, you can find most of these region-specific novelties stacked against one another in a single frenetic train station shop.

You can indulge your inner child with an ekiben shaped like a train. Or take advantage of seasonal ekiben, made only with location-specific seasonal produce. Then there's the high-tech self-heating ekiben, packaged in a box that heats up when a string is pulled. Or you might keep it traditional with the Daruma bento, packaged in a box that looks like Daruma, a doll meant to represent Bodhidharma, the founder of Zen Buddhism. The box has a slit at the mouth and can be used as a coin bank, making it a lucky keepsake.

THE ANCIENT ART OF LIFELIKE LOLLIPOPS

AMEZAIKU • JAPAN

How to try it

The Amezaiku Ameshin confectionery is located in the Tokyo Skytree Town mall in Asakusa. For 3,000 yen (about $28), you can also take a two-hour workshop, where a candy artist will teach you to make a rabbit. Instruction is offered only in Japanese.

Within three minutes, the window to make amezaiku is over. Molten sugar is pulled from the pot at nearly 200°F (93°C), just soft enough to manipulate the formless glob into a stunningly lifelike creature. Using just their hands and a pair of tiny scissors, amezaiku masters mold and snip the candy, forming the delicate gills of a goldfish or the three-pronged feet of a frog. The procedure is creative, and it's also precise. Artists can create the same animal over and over again, nearly identical each time. After the candy has cooled, the figurines are painted with food coloring, bringing them further to life with a transparent glaze.

According to candy artist Shinri Tezuka, making the candy is all about thinking ahead, anticipating the next snip and tuck before the candy cools. Tezuka is one of Japan's most prominent and last remaining amezaiku artists. He is also entirely self-taught because there is no longer a school teaching the craft. His Tokyo shop, a neat stall in a high-rise mall, is stocked with classical offerings such as animals and flowers, but in accordance with tradition, Tezuka also makes special orders.

Amezaiku is an ancient practice, brought to Japan from China during the Heian period (794–1185). The ornate sugar sculptures were first used as offerings to the spirits, but during the Edo period (1603–1868), artists took to the streets, snipping and molding their confections as entertainment, often to the specifications of their customer. Tezuka takes pride in the old-school craftsmanship, in knowing the sugar well enough to produce whatever a customer can imagine. As one of the last artisans practicing the art, his shop is one of the few places in Japan preserving the ancient disappearing tradition.

Candy artist Shinri Tezuka's creations—like this pair of koi—are almost too beautiful to eat.

THE ORIGINAL SUSHI

FUNAZUSHI • JAPAN

Sushi has come a long way since the 8th century, when making sushi meant salting a fish and letting it ferment for years. Called narezushi, the earliest sushi was primarily a preservation method: A gutted fish was fermented with salt and uncooked rice, which slowly transformed into a soft and pungent food.

In Shiga Prefecture, traditional narezushi is still the specialty. For centuries, locals have carried on the dying art of making a type of narezushi known as funazushi, made exclusively with the local carp found in nearby Lake Biwa. The fish is gutted, salted, and packed into wooden barrels. After a year, the carp is mixed with rice and packed away again for another two to three years. The result is a cured, prosciutto-like fish with a ripe smell and cheesy flavor.

In Takashima City, a family-run shop has been making funazushi since 1619, and is currently being operated by the 18th generation of the family. Called Kitashina, the shop is one of the few left in Japan preserving the country's ancient sushi.

In 8th-century Japan, an order of sushi looked more like this.

How to try it
Kitashina is located at 1287 Katsuno, Takashima, Shiga. Like most aged products, funazushi can be very expensive.

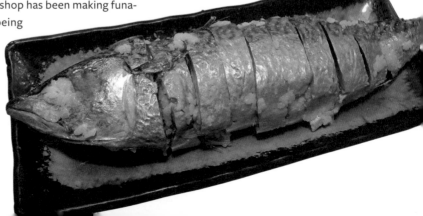

Themed Dining

Tokyo is home to some 160,000 restaurants, the most Michelin-starred restaurants in the world, and these four fantastical haunts where the cuisine is really not the point.

KAWAII MONSTER CAFE feels like a party thrown by the monsters in your closet. Located in Harajuku, Tokyo's fantasy playground, visitors enter through the mouth of a googly-eyed monster and are greeted by a merry-go-round of life-size desserts. The compact space contains a psychedelic "Mushroom Disco" as well as a "Milk Stand," where bunny and unicorn heads drink from baby bottle chandeliers. Monster girls roam, serving food and dancing. (In Japanese, kawaii means "cute.")

ROKUNEN YONKUMI offers a dose of nostalgia by re-creating the Japanese elementary school experience. Upon entry, diners become "students" by putting on a school bag and hat. Seated at wooden desks inside the classroom, "teachers" serve classic elementary school fare like sugary fried bread (agepan) on traditional aluminum dishware. At the end of your meal, you have the option of taking a test.

NINJA AKASAKA is modeled after feudal Japan, where diners step four centuries into the past as silent, black-clad mercenaries guide them across a drawbridge, through winding corridors, past secret doorways, and into the hidden dining room. Patrons order from scrolls, then the ninja-trained waitstaff disappears. But not for long. They regularly reappear, out of thin air, to perform sword tricks and martial arts.

DETECTIVE BAR PROGRESS straddles the line between fantasy and reality. With its yellow "Keep Out" tape across the door and outline of a splayed body on the floor, this bar feels like detective cosplay. But the bartenders here are real detectives. By day, they track down missing people or sleuth around crime scenes, and at night, they'll pour you a drink and tell you about their jobs.

JAPANESE NAVAL CURRY

KAREE • JAPAN

How to try it
Submarine curry is served at the café inside the Japan Maritime Self-Defense Force Museum in Kure. It's a 40-minute drive south of Hiroshima. You can't miss the building—there's a giant black-and-red submarine out front.

The Meiji era, which began in 1868, was a time of increasing foreign influence and domestic militarization. Japan needed to feed its troops, and their current system wasn't working. At the time, eating polished white rice was a sign of refinement and wealth. To attract recruits, the Imperial Navy and Army offered unlimited white rice and many soldiers ate little else, which led to a vitamin deficiency called beriberi. Caused by a lack of thiamine, an essential nutrient absent in white rice, beriberi killed Japanese royals and commoners alike. The deficiency soon became a drastic problem, laying low thousands of soldiers during the 1904–1905 Russo-Japanese War.

To save their sailors, Japanese officials examined the food provided in other navies, particularly Britain's. Many British ships served "curry": a mix of tinned curry powder, butter, meat (typically beef), root vegetables, and a sauce thickened with flour. Because both meat and flour contain thiamine, curry was a silver bullet against beriberi. Served over a heaping portion of rice, it could also feed an entire mess hall.

Japanese naval uniforms, ca. 1908.

Soon, Anglo-Indian curry became a standard meal in the Japanese navy. (Navy officials were more inclined to accept dietary innovation than the army, which suffered beriberi long into the 20th century.) In 1908, the official *Navy Cooking Reference Book* was issued with a recipe for curry that has been enshrined as the traditional gold standard.

The naval curry tradition continues in the Japan Maritime Self-Defense Force, where sailors are served curry every Friday. Each ship takes pride in having a unique curry recipe, many of which have made it ashore. In Kure, Hiroshima, dozens of restaurants serve curry recipes eaten aboard active ships, from the JS *Samidare* to the JS *Umikiri*.

Delicious Diaspora

"YOSHOKU" JAPANESE WESTERN FOOD

In the 19th century, when Emperor Meiji opened his island nation to the Western world, his citizens were shocked to discover how large Europeans and Americans were. Japanese sent to study the West returned with tales of tall, brawny white men who ate not only meat (illegal in Japan until 1872), but a bevy of foods they'd never seen before. The new, modernizing Japan decided to embrace Western-style eating as a means of growing physically strong and internationally competitive.

Yoshoku cuisine, or "Western food," developed from this early contact with the West. Pasta, hamburgers, sandwiches, and deep-fried cutlets are at the foundation of this fare, but tailored to Japanese tastes, these dishes are often unrecognizable to Westerners. Yoshoku defies conventional categorization. It's a nostalgic food, served in family-run restaurants, but it can also be trendy date-night food or high-end restaurant fare. Within Japan, these Western-hybrid dishes are universally known and loved, creating a traditional comfort cuisine inspired by the diets of large foreigners.

Hambagu takes the hamburger and makes it a fork-and-knife (or chopsticks) affair. The beef patty, which is mixed with breadcrumbs and egg, is cooked in a pan and coated in demi-glace, then served with rice and vegetables.

Omurice combines the words *omelet* and *rice*, telling you exactly what to expect. The original combination was simply a mound of rice draped in a sheet of egg, but in recent years the rice is often mixed with ketchup or stir-fried with meat and vegetables, and then the omelet is drizzled with ketchup. Omurice is a classic accompaniment to naval curry (kare). Another variation is omusoba, where soba noodles are covered in an omelet blanket.

Portrait of Emperor Meiji and the Japanese imperial family during the Meiji period, ca. 1900.

Napolitan, named after the Italian city, was one of Japan's earliest pasta dishes and is now a classic. The country is dotted with coffee shops that specialize in the dish, which is made by cooking spaghetti until soft, then pan-frying the noodles with lunch meat, onion, bell pepper, and a ketchup-based sauce. Napolitan is often served with hambagu.

Napolitan

Sando is a Japanese sandwich, an unlikely star on the country's culinary scene. Sando bread is soft, white, and crustless, which hearkens back to the factory-made loaves that substituted for rice during the lean years after World War II. Today, sandos can still be bought for cheap in convenience stores across the country (a classic Japanese sando set is a trio of egg salad, ham and cheese, and tuna fish). Or you could go high-end: Grilled Wagyu beef sandos and fried Wagyu katsu sandos, running about $200 each.

Tacoraisu, or taco rice, hails from the southern island of Okinawa. Relatively new to the Yoshoku canon, the dish was developed by a 20th-century Okinawan cook who began selling tacos to the hundreds of American GIs stationed there. One day, he swapped out the tortilla for rice and piled on the seasoned ground beef, shredded cheese, lettuce, and chopped tomatoes.

Taco rice was a massive hit with both Okinawans and Americans, before spreading to the rest of the country. At the Taco Bell in Tokyo, taco rice is on the menu and comes with French fries.

Tacoraisu

Katsu sando

Hambagu

PAMPERED PERSIMMONS

HOSHIGAKI • JAPAN

To transform persimmons into hoshigaki, the ancient Japanese preserved delicacy, each fruit is painstakingly peeled, then hung by the stem to dry as they dangle in the air. Nearly every day, the fruits are massaged. The gentle handling breaks down the hard internal pulp, which helps create a rich, jammy interior. Regular massages also smooth out wrinkles and air bubbles, where fruit-ruining mold can form, while forcing sugars to the surface. After about a month of coddling, the dried fruits are tender, richly concentrated, and wrapped in a white-frost coating of its own excreted sugars.

How to try it

Hoshigaki are available at supermarkets and department stores around Japan from late autumn to winter.

Luxury Fruit of Japan

The tradition of Japanese gift giving, especially in business, can be something of a competitive sport. Companies vie to procure thoughtful, impressive gifts for their partners and clients, often spending vast sums of money to source something delightfully obscure. Japan has two traditional gift-giving seasons, Ochugen in summer and Oseibo in winter. Given such demand for specialty products, a world of luxury fruit has flourished. Bred and cultivated to be superior in taste and striking in appearance, these wildly priced, edible gems are now power players in the high-end gift-giving game.

DENSUKE WATERMELON

Prized for its black exterior and sweet and crunchy pink flesh, this pricey melon is limitedly grown in Hokkaido.

Average Price: 2,000 yen (about $20)

Sold at Auction in 2008: 650,000 yen ($5,927)

TAIYO NO TAMAGO ("EGG OF THE SUN") MANGO

Allowed to fall naturally from the tree when ripe into a net, they must be 350+ grams and have a high sugar content of 15+ percent.

Average Price: 5,000 yen ($45)

Sold at Auction in 2019: 500,000 yen for two ($4,659)

BIJIN–HIME ("BEAUTIFUL PRINCESS") STRAWBERRIES

The size of a tennis ball, these "scoop-shaped" berries took 15 years to perfect, and about 500 are grown each year.

Average Price: 500,000 yen for one ($4,395)

RUBY ROMAN GRAPES

The size of a ping pong ball, each grape must weigh 30+ grams.

Average Price: 100,000 yen per bunch ($880)

Sold at Auction in 2017: 1.1 million yen for a bunch of approximately 30 grapes ($9,745)

YUBARI KING MELONS

Exclusively from Yubari, only one melon is grown per plant, allowing the single fruit to receive all the plant's nutrients. The melons also wear hats to protect from the sun.

Average Price: 10,000 yen ($91)

Sold at Auction in 2018: 3.2 million yen for two ($29,251)

A seller auctions off Egg of the Sun mangoes in the wholesale market in Miyazaki.

SUMO WRESTLER STEW

CHANKO NABE • JAPAN

Sumo wrestling has no separate weight classes, which means the heavier competitor has the advantage. In recent years, largely due to an influx of Hawaiian and Mongolian wrestlers, the average weight of champions has soared from just under 300 pounds (136 kg) in the 1930s to well over 400 (181 kg) today. To keep up, Japanese wresters eat chanko-nabe—a stew they consume, with ritualistic regularity, at nearly every meal for the duration of their career.

Chanko-nabe is a big communal pot of bubbling broth, to which ingredients are continually added and removed in a process similar to shabu shabu, or hot pot. Each training house typically has a signature broth recipe, which may be chicken, soy, or salt-based. Into the broth goes fish or meat, tofu and vegetables, and chunks of calorie-dense mochi (a starchy cake made from pounded glutinous rice). The sumo stew is cheap, hearty fare and, in ordinary quantities, not intrinsically fattening. But sumo wrestlers skip breakfast to work up an appetite, then eat as many as ten bowls for lunch, washed down with copious amounts of beer. After lunch, the wrestlers nap.

Despite the gluttonous mealtimes, structure and rigor dominate the sumo heya, or "clubhouse." Each wrestler has chores to perform, a surprising number of which revolve around chanko. Junior wrestlers are tasked with setting up the eating area, cycling to buy groceries, or chopping vegetables. (The highest-ranked wrestlers are usually tasked only with making public appearances or entertaining patrons.) While their superiors snooze, junior wrestlers rise early to train and prepare the meal. At lunchtime, the heavyweights sit around the pot first, reaching for soupy morsels they eat with rice. When their rice bowl is empty, they raise their hand and the junior wrestlers, who are expected to watch and anticipate their needs, refill their bowls. Only when a senior wrestler has finished can someone lower in rank sit down and take his place. As a result, junior wrestlers are often left with the dregs of the stew, which they must bulk up with things like instant noodles.

While chanko chores are considered entry-level, being in charge of the kitchen—chankocho—is a position of respect because it gives the wrestler a valuable skillset for his future. Not every wrestler can be a champion, and chanko can be the route into a new profession. Many retired wrestlers work at sumo-themed restaurants called chankoya, where high-end seafood chanko is the main attraction. The most famous wrestlers might even open their own eponymous chankoya, where their stardust is as much of a draw as their stew.

How to try it

The Ryogoku district in Tokyo is where you'll find the sumo stadiums and clubhouses, as well as chankoya. Hananomai Ryogoku Kokugikanmae, located right outside Ryogoku's train station, is shaped and decorated like a sumo dojo.

Sumo wrestlers serve chanko-nabe before a tournament at Osaka's Musashigawa Sumo Stadium in 2007.

GIANT RICE STRAW SCULPTURES

WARA ART • JAPAN

The rural, coastal Niigata Prefecture is the second largest producer of rice in Japan, known for its scenic expanse of rice paddies. Each fall, the rice is harvested and the grain extracted, which leaves a huge amount of leftover rice straw, called wara.

How to try it

The sculptures go on display in late August at the Wara Art Festival in Niigata's Uwasekigata Park. The sculptures remain up until the end of October.

Students constructed a giant gorilla for the 2017 festival's supersize challenge.

Wara doesn't go to waste. The heaps of straw get repurposed as fertilizer, roofing, livestock feed, and most memorably as enormous wara sculptures that transform the rice fields into outdoor art installations. Since 2008, students from Tokyo's Musashino Art University have arrived in Niigata each fall to erect giant fantastical animals from the rice by-product. Made by braiding the straw, then attaching pieces to a wooden frame, the shaggy, golden building material makes strikingly realistic lion manes, gorilla fur, and tarantula fuzz. In 2017, to celebrate ten years of wara animals, the students were challenged to build sculptures twice the size of years past, and so they constructed 20-foot (6 m) dinosaurs and hippos, large enough for visitors to pose in their mouths.

THE REAL MONGOLIAN BARBECUE

BOODOG • MONGOLIA

How to try it

Winter is the traditional season for boodog in Mongolia.

Mongolian warriors carried what little they owned on horseback, which meant they couldn't be weighed down by heavy cookware. To fit food preparation into their nomadic lifestyle, they used an animal's carcass as crockery. The unlucky marmot or goat that got stuffed with its own meat and cooked over an open

Two men drop hot stones into a goat carcass for boodog-style barbecue.

flame came to be known as boodog—the real Mongolian barbecue.

To prepare boodog (pronounced "baw-dug"), a butcher slices the animal, neck to groin, and carefully removes the meat and bones while keeping the rest of the skin intact. After seasoning the meat (including the liver and kidneys), the butcher stuffs it back inside with hot stones and vegetables and reseals the neck.

While ancient Mongolians roasted boodog over a fire, modern cooks use a blowtorch. The flame burns off most of the animal's fur, and what remains is scraped away with a knife. After a couple hours under the blowtorch, when the seal around the neck starts to drip with fat, the animal is ready to eat. But before digging in, diners must first pass around the hot stones; it is believed that holding the warm, smooth rocks reduces stress and fatigue.

With boodog, the animal torso doubles as a serving bowl.

A succulent stuffed goat is enough to feed an army of hungry Mongolians—and it did. According to the president of the Mongolian Chefs Association, Genghis Khan threw boodog banquets when his warriors were victorious.

SHOE SOLE CAKE

UL BOOV • MONGOLIA

When Mongolians celebrate the Lunar New Year with a days-long holiday called Tsagaan Sar, the centerpiece is usually a fabulous ul boov. Ul boov means "shoe sole cake"—a humble name for a towering dessert that's steeped in tradition.

Ul boov is built from layers of fried cakes, each embossed by a wooden stamp that leaves a design like the tread of a shoe. These stamps are passed down through generations and every stamp is unique, which means ul boov designs can identify families like a fingerprint. The height of an ul boov corresponds with age and social status: Young couples make three-layered cakes, elders make seven layers, and most everyone else makes five. (The layers always occur in odd numbers because they symbolize happiness.) The stacking of the cakes is a ritual in itself, performed with the precision and care of lighting a menorah.

To decorate an ul boov, wrapped candies, sugar cubes, and dried milk curds called aarul are placed on top. Fully adorned, the cake is meant to symbolize the sacred Buddhist site, Mount Sumeru.

How to try it
Ul boov is typically a homemade holiday treat. You can find recipes online, but you'll have to borrow a stamp.

NORTH KOREAN DIPLOMACY NOODLES

PYONGYANG NAENGMYEON • NORTH KOREA

How to try it

Pyung Hwa Ok, or "House of Peace," is a restaurant specializing in Pyongyang naengmyeon, located in South Korea's Incheon International Airport.

n many ways, naengmyeon is a simple dish. Typically made from buckwheat flour, the slim, exceptionally chewy noodles are served in an iced beef broth, topped with meat slices, boiled egg, slivers of cucumbers or radish, and seasoned with spicy mustard and vinegar. Created during the Joseon Dynasty, which spanned 1392 to 1910, naengmyeon has been around for centuries. But in April 2018, when the leaders of North Korea and South Korea met for an unprecedented diplomatic summit, the cold noodles were thrust onto the world stage.

For the first time in 11 years, both Korean leaders, North Korea's Kim Jong-un and South Korean president Moon Jae-in, agreed to meet in the DMZ (the demilitarized zone between their two countries). Surprising everyone, Kim Jong-un showed up with a batch of naengmyeon, a noodle maker, and jokes about noodles from a "faraway" land, before conceding that it wasn't that far.

After a 2018 summit, the cold noodles loved on both the north and south sides of the Korean border became a symbol for thawing relations between the countries.

With this simple gesture, the popularity of the humble dish exploded in South Korea. On the day of the summit, the noodles were more talked about than the summit itself, and restaurants that served naengmyeon had lines out the door. Many of the diners expressed that they were eating them in honor of the peace talks. Naengmyeon, after all, was a reminder of their shared heritage.

In North Korea, where the noodles originated, naengmyeon holds special patriotic pride. It's the signature dish at Okryu-gwan, the country's most important restaurant and perhaps the most significant source of North Korea's culinary heritage. During the Korean War, when people fled from the north to the south, they popularized the cold beef broth noodles from their side of the border. (When served with broth made from beef and radish water kimchi, the noodles are considered the North Korean style, "Pyongyang naengmyeon.")

The noodles have long been a refreshing meal in the humid Korean summer, but since the 2018 summit, they have also become an edible symbol of peace, with one restaurant serving the dish as "reunification naengmyeon."

AN ENTIRE UK BREWERY TRANSPORTED TO NORTH KOREA

TAEDONGGANG BREWING COMPANY • NORTH KOREA

The team first arrived in the rural English town of Trowbridge in the summer of 2000. There were two brewers, two engineers, and eight government officials. They were all from North Korea, and they had come to take the brewery.

Their leader, Kim Jong-il (nicknamed "Kim Jong-ale" by the residents of Trowbridge) had recently decided that North Korea needed a proper state-run brewery. But instead of building a brewery from scratch, the North Korean leader decided to go shopping for one.

For £1.5 million, the North Korean bought the 175-year-old Ushers of Trowbridge Brewery. A team of Russians came in to entirely dismantle the brick-walled factory, then the North Koreans shipped all four million pounds of it back to Pyongyang. The crew left nothing, taking every vat, keg, pipe, nut, bolt, tile, and toilet seat in the brewery. They wanted to take the brewmaster himself but had to settle for just his knowledge. Korean translators spent weeks with him poring over beer-making schematics.

A mere 18 months later, in 2002, the Russian team had reassembled the factory on a cabbage field in East Pyongyang. Since named the Taedonggang Brewing Company, the brewery produces seven styles of beer, named pragmatically from light pilsner "Beer Number One" ("Taedonggang 1") to dark, chocolatey dunkel "Beer Number Seven." Taedonggang is considered some of the best beer available on the Korean Peninsula, and even within Asia.

Despite the improved state-run brewing game, most North Koreans still prefer cheaper, harder stuff such as the local liquor, soju. Rural North Koreans must use food rations to buy beer, which makes it a luxury item few can afford. In the country's capital, men receive beer vouchers (usually 1–2 liters a month) that can be redeemed in a Pyongyang bar. But for the most part, beer is still an urban, middle-class affair, more akin to a nice glass of wine than a party beverage.

Although North Korea and the Taedonggang Brewing Company would like the world to focus on their surprisingly good beer, the brewery still remains the property of a mysterious and harsh dictatorship. In 2016, Pyongyang held its first-ever beer festival, which attracted 45,000 visitors. In 2017, however, the festival was canceled by the government without explanation.

How to try it

Taedonggang is very difficult to get outside of North Korea. To try it, you'll have to visit, which makes it an elusive task for many.

A mural of the late North Korean leader Kim Jong-il holding a beer hangs near the entrance of the brewery.

KOREAN NUN CUISINE

JINGWANSA TEMPLE FOOD • SOUTH KOREA

How to try it

Jingwansa is located in Bukhansan National Park, about an hour north of Seoul's urban center. Buses run from Gupabal subway station. Anyone can reserve a stay at the temple, take a cooking class, or tour the property.

Jingwansa, a 12th-century Buddhist temple, sits atop a mountain in Seoul's Bukhansan National Park. Women with shaved heads and gray robes run the entire operation. These Buddhist devotees are renowned for their cuisine, which epitomizes the ancient art of Korean temple fare. It's vegan and free of MSG, garlic, onion, and leeks. Temple food is meant to facilitate meditation, and Buddhist teaching advises eschewing these ingredients because they are believed to incite lust, among other things. Although the kitchens of many monasteries follow similar principles, high-profile visitors from around the world flock to Jingwansa in search of culinary enlightenment.

Korean temple cuisine is far from bland. At Jingwansa, they ferment, spice, dry, marinate, and pickle ingredients to create a wide array of pungent, spicy, and tangy dishes. They also ferment up to 30 different soybean pastes at a time, some of which have been aging beneath the sun for 50 years. Visitors have reported eating more than 25 dishes in one meal, sampling fermented radishes, chestnut stew, crispy greens, marinated tofu, mushroom fritters, and sweet sticky rice squares sprinkled with fruit and nuts—a treat traditionally eaten on the nuns' head-shaving day.

The female order has maintained its status as the preeminent location for temple cuisine for centuries. In Korean Buddhism, monastic mealtime is a practice referred to as baru gongyang, or "offering." Diners eat in silence from a wooden bowl using wooden chopsticks. Historically, Jingwansa hosted suryukje, an annual ritual in which the dead are led to heaven through chanting and food ceremonies. The establishment has become increasingly popular as a culinary pilgrimage site, but the nuns continue to cook with old-school standards and still use vegetables grown on temple grounds.

A quiet sunrise over Seoul's Bukhansan mountains echoes the silent mealtimes at the Jingwansa temple.

Buddhist TEMPLE CUISINE

Respect for animal life and devotion to vegetables is the backbone of Buddhist temple cuisine. Local, seasonal produce, simple hand tools, and zero waste are tenets of religious gastronomy, which seeks to prepare the body for spiritual work. These vegetarian restaurants, all housed within active temples, specialize in nourishment for meditation.

Daitoku-ji Temple • Kyoto, Japan

Izusen Restaurant cooks shojin ryori, or "devotion cuisine," which developed alongside Japanese Zen Buddhism. Elegant, visually striking, and painstakingly prepared, the process of making devotional food is considered a meditative experience in itself. At Izusen, Buddhist cuisine is at its most refined. Surrounded by a tranquil garden on the temple grounds, diners enjoy dainty, impressive courses of wild plants, tofu, seaweed, and vegetables, served in the round lacquered bowls used by monks to collect alms.

Po Lin Monastery • Hong Kong

Located at the bottom of the Big Buddha statue on Lantau Island, the café at Po Lin Monastery is a plant-based paradise in meat-centric Hong Kong. The menu has three options: a general meal, a deluxe meal, or a snack, all comprised of whatever the kitchen has prepared that day. To prevent waste, the quantity of dishes served depends on how many people are eating together. The bean curd, which is made daily, is the monastery's specialty.

Wat Suan Dok Temple • Chiang Mai, Thailand

Just behind the 700-year-old golden-domed Wat Suan Dok is Pun Pun, an organic café serving Thai food made with produce from the restaurant's garden. Beneath the shade of Pun Pun's giant Bodhi tree, watch orange-clad monks pace the temple grounds as you eat coconut milk curry, banana flower salad, and fermented mushroom sausage.

Jiming Temple • Nanjing, China

Perched high on a hill, atop a long staircase fluttering with prayer flags, Jiming Temple is home to a small, cloistered vegetarian restaurant. The simple café surprises with views of Nanjing's ancient walls and Xuanwu Lake, and is especially good at mock meats. While you won't find seitan or tofu "meats" in other Buddhist cuisines (like Japan, where meat eating was taboo until the 19th century), the Chinese have long had a taste for meat and have been making plant-based substitutes for centuries.

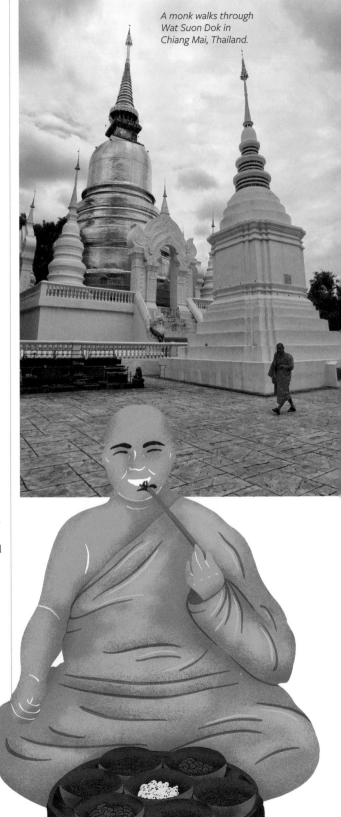

A monk walks through Wat Suon Dok in Chiang Mai, Thailand.

URINE-FERMENTED SKATE FISH

HONGEO • SOUTH KOREA

How to try it

Indongju Maul, a restaurant in Mokpo's east, is a popular place to try fermented skate. It's served with sliced pork, soy-marinated crab, and kimchi.

Back in the 14th century, South Korean fishermen realized the skate they caught could travel long distances without spoiling. While other fish would rot by the time it reached inland, the flat-bodied, bottom-dwelling skate was somehow spared. The side effect to this miraculous preservation, however, was hard to miss. The fish smelled overpoweringly of ammonia, as if it had urinated through its skin—because it had.

Instead of urinating like other animals, skate expels waste by secreting uric acid through its skin, which in turn ferments the flesh. Koreans began eating the caustic-smelling fish as aged sashimi, alongside boiled pork belly and kimchi in a combination known as samhap ("harmonious trinity").

Today, hongeo is polarizing even within Korea. In hongeo's birthplace of Jeolla Province, the dish is considered a luxury item with almost mythical status for its ability to preserve itself. Especially in the port city of Mokpo, where skate fishing is a lucrative business, hongeo is an expensive dish reserved for special occasions, wealthy people, and men in search of libido enhancement. Outside these southwest regions, however, many Koreans find the fish deeply unappealing. The texture, which is chewy with lots of cartilage and mushy bone, is almost as challenging as the smell, which is often compared to an outhouse. Even those who love it recommend breathing in through your mouth and out through your nose when trying to get a piece of hongeo down.

IMPOSSIBLE SLIME FISH

HAGFISH • SOUTH KOREA

Hagfish, with their bald, loose-fitting skin (think naked mole rat), are scavengers who search the ocean floor for dead or dying creatures, burrow inside, and eat their way out. Commonly referred to as both "slime eels" and "snot snakes," hagfish are actually neither snakes nor eels, but rather jawless fish. The misnomers come from their eel-like appearance and their notable ability to excrete up to 20 liters (about 5 gallons) of milky mucus when under stress.

The mucus is a unique defense mechanism that has allowed hagfish to roam the oceans for 300 million years. When a predator attacks, the hagfish's slime coats its gills, suffocating the predator. The slime deters human predators too, but in Korea it's a part of the gastronomic appeal. Hagfish slime, which is fibrous and full of protein, can be used as a substitute for egg whites. To "harvest" the slime, hagfish are sometimes kept in cages, which are rattled to agitate the fish.

In Korean fish markets, it's common to see hagfish skinned alive and grilled with onion and garlic. In a punishing spectacle, hagfish writhe in circles, discharging snot until the hot barbecue kills them. They can also be broiled in sesame oil, salted, and served with a shot of liquor. Like many phallic-looking animals, the hagfish is valued as an aphrodisiac.

But edibility isn't the slime's only virtue. The fibrous thread is an incredibly strong and versatile material, a hundred times thinner than human hair yet ten times stronger than nylon. Researchers are working on ways to use hagfish slime in everything from airbags to bandages to bungee cords. Engineers in the US Navy even hope to create an artificial version of the slime for missile defense systems.

How to try it
Hagfish are available in fish markets around Korea, but Jalgachi Market in Busan is a good place to start.

Hagfish slime is stronger and more useful than it appears.

ARMY BASE STEW

BUDAE JJIGAE • SOUTH KOREA

One of South Korea's most beloved fusion dishes, budae jjigae, began with desperate wartime dumpster diving. Translated as "army base stew," budae jjigae was once made with American throwaways saved by resourceful South Koreans, who transformed the scraps into a one-pot meal that's become a complicated vestige of US imperialism.

During the Korean War, while citizens struggled with food scarcity, a US army base an hour north of Seoul was stocked with ample quantities of American food. Most notably, the Americans had plenty of meat, which most Korean stores no longer carried. Koreans began lining up outside the mess halls, trying to purchase the soldiers' leftovers. Whatever wasn't eaten or bought was thrown away, so many

How to try it
Bada Sikdang near the American army base in Itaewon is a well-known hole-in-the-wall. Their budae jjigae comes draped in a bright-yellow slice of American cheese.

people resorted to scavenging through the dumpsters, picking through cigarette butts and inedible waste to piece together a meal.

What the Koreans found was processed Americana—canned beans, cheese products, Spam, hot dogs, and ham—which they tossed into a pot with kimchi, vegetables, chili paste, and instant noodles. The result was budae jjigae, a surprisingly cohesive stew that was spicy, filling, and sustaining.

After the war, the meat shortage continued. Among the South Koreans who survived, many had developed a taste for budae jjigae, which became even harder to source after the government passed import laws preventing Koreans from buying American products. In response, a black market for army-base stew ingredients flourished. Retail stores for American soldiers stationed in Korea (known as "post exchanges") became sites for illegal trading, facilitated by Korean women involved with American soldiers. American processed meat was the only meat many people had access to, so demand remained high. (Spam was illegal until the 1980s, when a Korean company began producing it.)

The American product ban was eventually lifted, and budae jjigae evolved into a popular comfort food. It's now common on South Korean menus, particularly in college neighborhoods, although even posh neighborhoods such as Gangnam have restaurants specializing in the wartime stew.

Budae Jjigae   *4 servings*

Seasoning Paste

½ packet Korean ramyeon noodle seasoning

3 tablespoons Korean chili flakes

1 tablespoon gochujang

1 tablespoon minced garlic

2 tablespoons soy sauce

½ teaspoon black pepper

Stew

1 can (12 ounces) Spam, sliced

1 can (8 ounces) pork and beans

7 ounces hot dogs or Vienna sausage, sliced

1 package firm tofu, sliced

1 cup sour kimchi, sliced

½ onion, sliced

8 ounces mushrooms, sliced

1 packet Korean ramen noodles

32 ounces low-sodium chicken stock

1 or 2 slices American cheese

white rice (optional)

1. In a small mixing bowl, combine all ingredients for the seasoning paste. Set aside.

2. In a large shallow pot, arrange all the stew ingredients as you please, up to the ramen noodles, which should be set on top.

3. Add the seasoning paste to the pot and pour the broth over.

4. Bring to a boil over medium high heat. When it starts to boil, spread the seasoning paste around the pan, untangle the ramen in the broth, and cook until the noodles are tender yet firm.

5. Drape the cheese over the top. Serve immediately. (Combine with rice for a more filling stew.)

Desperate resourcefulness was the origin of this scrappy, surprisingly delicious wartime stew.

A diver flashes a smile while emptying her net of shellfish.

JEJU ISLAND'S FREE-DIVING SEA WOMEN

HAENYEO • SOUTH KOREA

Jeju Island, the largest island in South Korea, is home to a centuries-old tradition of divers who can plunge 30 feet on a single breath to collect shellfish on the ocean floor. They wear wet suits and goggles but do not use oxygen masks. Called haenyeo, all of these free divers are women, and many of them are in their 80s.

In historically patriarchal South Korea, these deep-diving fisherwomen have become the heads of their households. Their dives yield sea life like sea urchins, abalone, conches, seaweed, and sea snails, which the divers clean and sell to support their families. It's difficult work; the women dive for six to seven hours a day in ice cold water and earn only modest wages. But the practice is also deeply rooted in community and tradition. Many haenyeo carry on in the profession for the intimacy it fosters with fellow divers, as well as with nature.

The haenyeo's numbers are dwindling in modern South Korea, with fewer than 4,000 skilled divers still practicing. (In the 1960s, there were over 20,000.) But in recent years there's been a concerted effort to preserve the women's legacy, and Jeju Island now boasts a haenyeo museum and haenyeo schools.

How to try it
The sea women's home base is next to the volcanic crater of Seongsan Ilchulbong (also called Sunrise Peak). Depending on weather conditions, Beophwan Jomnyeo Village Haenyeo School provides haenyeo experience activities from June to mid-October, offered in Korean/Jeju dialect. The Jeju Haenyeo Museum is open year-round.

KIMCHI-MAKING SEASON

GIMJANG • SOUTH KOREA

How to try it

Gimjang is not a specific day, but a season that occurs between October and November. (The Kimchi Festival takes place during this time.) Seoul's Museum Kimchikan is a great place to dive into kimchi's 1,500-year-old history.

More than a million tons of kimchi is eaten across South Korea each year. Of that, a mere 7 percent is commercially produced. When it comes to kimchi, South Koreans don't mess around. The good stuff is made at home, in staggering quantities, during the annual pickling season known as gimjang.

Every fall around late October, South Koreans begin watching the price of cabbage. National news programs dedicate segments to price spikes and dips, letting their viewers know how much this year's kimchi making will cost. During gimjang, families gather to make pogi kimchi, the most recognizable variety, made by coating heads of napa cabbage with a complex, pungent red pepper paste and aging it, sometimes underground in earthenware pots, sometimes in high-tech kimchi fridges. Farmers' markets pop up around the country, and everyone pitches in, donning rubber gloves to rub the bright red paste into dozens of heads of cabbage. (A typical family might prepare anywhere between 50 and 150 cabbages.)

Volunteers at the 2014 Kimchi Festival slather napa cabbage in bright red paste.

In 2013, gimjang was recognized by UNESCO and added to their list of Intangible Cultural Heritage. The annual pickling affair draws the nation close. Women across South Korea watch the weather, settling on the right day to set up their production, often banding together with other families to make tremendous batches they can divvy up. Another tradition is for new wives to learn their mother-in-law's recipe because many husbands prefer the kimchi of their childhood.

Access to kimchi, which is eaten with nearly every meal, is considered something of a South Korean civil right. The spoils of gimjang are distributed to those who need it, which can be anyone from bachelors to women who are bad at making kimchi but will not suffer the indignity of buying it at the store. At the Seoul Kimchi Festival, which has taken place during every gimjang since 2014, thousands of apron-clad volunteers line up along a sea of tables to make more than a hundred tons of kimchi. The community bounty is presented to those who cannot afford to make it themselves, ensuring that when winter strikes, there will be enough crunchy, sour, slightly fizzy cabbage to sustain many South Koreans through the long cold season.

SOUTHEAST ASIA

STICKY DIPPING PASTE

AMBUYAT • BRUNEI

Eating ambuyat requires a sticky, multistep dance: Using a pair of bamboo tongs called chandas (think cheater chopsticks), diners dip into the starchy goo so that it adheres to the utensil and can make its way from bowl to dipping sauce to mouth, where it's slurped down, no chewing required.

How to try it
Aminah Arif Restaurant in Brunei's capital, Begawan, is the place to twirl and dip to your heart's content.

Made by slowly mixing the interior pulp of the rumbia tree with water, the gelatinous starch has little flavor of its own, which makes it an ideal vehicle for dipping sauce, or cacah. Most typical is binjai cacah, a sour and spicy combination of lime, onions, garlic, and binjai, a local fruit with a sweet-and-sour flavor. Ambuyat is a communal meal, served in a large bowl with several chandas, at least one sauce, and dishes of fresh, raw vegetables for a crunchy interlude between each sweet-and-sour swallow.

CUSTARD-FILLED PUMPKIN

SANG KAYA LAPOV • CAMBODIA

On the outside, it's a pumpkin. On the inside, it's creamy, quivering custard. Known in Cambodia as sang kaya lapov, this is the most elegant dessert you'll ever find hidden inside a squash. The pumpkin, which is hollowed out like a Halloween jack-o'-lantern, makes a perfect, edible vessel for coconut milk custard, which is poured into the cavity. Topped with the pumpkin lid and steamed until

How to try it
Sang kaya lapov is sold in Cambodian markets and sweet shops, generally by the slice. It can also be found in Thailand by the name sangkhaya fak thong.

the custard is set and the pumpkin flesh is soft (between 40 minutes and 3 hours, depending on your pumpkin), this dessert in disguise is a customary centerpiece on Cambodian New Year tables. The recipe likely hearkens back centuries, when Portuguese conquistadores arrived in Cambodia and passed on their affinity for eggy sweets.

The perfect sang kaya lapov will cut into neat, silky slices that hold together like a custard pie. While the preparation may seem straightforward, this is a difficult recipe to master. Custards curdle, pumpkins fall limp, and you won't know until you cut it open.

WORM COURTSHIP FESTIVAL

BAU NYALE• INDONESIA

How to try it

Seger Beach, in the south of Lombok, is the center of the celebration. It can be hard to predict exactly when the worms will emerge, but it always follows February's full moon.

According to legend, there once was on the island Lombok a princess so beautiful that suitors flocked from across the land, igniting a fierce competition to win her hand in marriage. The princess, distraught by seeing her people fight, threw herself into the sea. The villagers waded into the water to search for her, but all they found were thousands of green and purple sea worms. The princess herself was never found, but the discovery of worms brought the village peace because they came together to partake in the bounty.

Inspired by this legend, every year thousands of Sasak people, an ethnic group that lives on Lombok, make the journey to the southern and eastern beaches of their island to catch nyale, or sea worms, and participate in the courting festival known as Bau Nyale (literally translated as "Catch Sea Worm"). Leading up to the event, men engage in ritualistic combat using shields and rattan (a vine-like palm) sticks, athletes race horses on long stretches of beach, and vibrantly dressed women parade through the streets in glittering Sasak regalia. Nearing nightfall, groups of men and women head toward the sea where a game of poetic flirtation called pantun takes place. Using couplets to express their interest in each other, young people call back and forth in a traditional style, their words cheeky and heavy with innuendo.

After a full moon, these sea worms arrive at the water's surface to mate.

As for the nyale, they're also engaged in a courtship ritual. Sometime after February's full moon, the worms are triggered by the lunar cycle. They emerge from their coral homes to release their tails, filled with eggs or sperm, to the water's surface where the mating can occur. (Their bodies stay alive and well.) Equipped with nets and buckets, locals wade into the tides to collect the mass exodus of sea creatures. Eating nyale is said to bring beauty, prosperity, and fertility. The worms can be prepared in a variety of ways, like roasted in banana leaves, fermented with shrimp paste, or cooked in a soup called kalek moren with fresh-grated coconut.

Courtship Foods

Much like humans take dates to dinner, many animals practice a ritual called "courtship feeding," in which the suitor brings an offering of food to a desired mate, who eats it before, during, or after intercourse. Male nursery web spiders, for example, catch an insect (generally a fly) in their web, wrap it in silk, and present it to their chosen female. While she's busy consuming what he's brought, the male begins copulation.

But things don't always go smoothly. Female nursery web spiders are sexual cannibals, which means the male is always at risk of being eaten. Studies have found that the bigger the gift, the lower the risk of being cannibalized. Yet some males are still prone to ungentlemanly behavior: They choose to eat the insect, present the female with a gift-wrapped, nutritionless exoskeleton, and try to get the job done before she figures it out and murders him. (Females are also known to take the meal and run away.)

In the human world, using food as a way to win a mate is generally less cutthroat. Still, there's plenty of innuendo in the type of food, how it's presented, and what's inside.

ARMPIT APPLE: In the 19th century, rural Austrian women attended dances where they would prance with the eligible bachelors, all while keeping a slice of apple tucked into their armpit. When the music stopped, the women would remove the pheromone-soaked fruit and offer it to the man of their choice. To return the compliment, the man had to eat the apple, signaling that he enjoyed the woman's personal fragrance.

SISTERS' MEAL FESTIVAL: Amid the bullfighting, dragon dancing, and horse racing that takes place at the annual celebration in China's Guizhou Province, there is a courting ritual that centers on glutinous rice. Unmarried women from the Miao minority group climb the mountains to pick wildflowers that they use to dye the rice bright colors. They then roll the rice into balls, hiding different symbols inside, and give out their "sister rice" to the Miao men who come to sing to them. Each symbol bears a message for their potential suitors: two chopsticks means love, one chopstick refusal, and then there's cotton, parsley, pine needles, and bamboo hooks, which fall somewhere in between.

CREAMED CELERY: No Amish wedding is complete without creamed celery, the traditional stove-top dish of chopped celery in a white, slightly sweetened sauce. Amish weddings are big affairs with hundreds of guests, so those preparing to marry need a lot of celery (even more if they're making Amish casserole, which they probably are). As Amish weddings are often kept secret until the last minute, the most surefire way to uncover impending nuptials is to check the garden: If it's full of celery, someone's getting married.

BRIK: The North African savory pastry, called brik, is made by wrapping a phyllo-like dough around a filling of tuna, capers, chilies, and a raw egg. The filled pastry is fried just long enough for the egg white to set but the yolk to remain runny. When men in Algeria and Tunisia are ready to wed, they must prove their aptitude for marriage by eating a brik. If they can finish the pastry without spilling a drop of oozing yolk, they are considered husband material.

CZERNINA: If you were a suitor in 19th-century Poland, receiving a bowl of duck blood was a sign that your marriage proposal had been denied. Serving czernina, a thick, black, fruit-and-vinegar-laced blood soup, was a way for peasant families to deliver bad news. The shaming sometimes happened publicly, delivered to the table with other diners who, while enjoying their bloodless soups, understood that the man had been officially rejected.

The Hidden History of the Nutmeg Island Traded for Manhattan

In 1677, the Dutch traded Manhattan to the British for their claim on a tiny island named Run. Less than one square mile, Run is one of Indonesia's Banda Islands—once believed to be the world's only source of nutmeg. At the time, Europeans were crazy for nutmeg. They believed the mysterious brown spice cured everything from the common cold to bubonic plague, and nutmeg was worth more than its weight in gold.

The Bandanese began cultivating the spice early in the second millennium, and the Banda Islands quickly became the key port for the nutmeg trade, frequented by Chinese, Malay, and Javanese. By the 15th century, Arabo-Persian merchants arrived, who sold the spice to Europeans and incited their lust. Eager to cut out the middlemen, Europeans began sailing to the Banda Islands, hoping to take control of the trade.

In the 1510s, the Portuguese were the first to invade but were handily defeated by the Bandanese. Next came the Dutch in 1599, then the British in 1603. The Dutch led a violent, genocidal crusade against the Bandanese, while also warring with the British for claim on the string of islands. In 1677, the British lost the Second Anglo-Dutch War, which ended in the Treaty of Breda. This treaty granted the British the island of Manhattan— then a swampy parcel of land known as New Amsterdam—while giving the Dutch victors what they wanted most: the tiny island of Run, which completed their monopoly of the Banda Islands.

Today, Run is part of Indonesia, which declared independence in 1945. The remote, tranquil island still cultivates what many believe to be the world's finest nutmeg—sweet, warm, and aromatic—while the Dutch go down in history as brokering one of the worst land deals of all time.

CHILI WOOD

MAI SAKAHN • LAOS

How to try it

Mai sakahn is available at morning markets across Laos and easily found in Luang Prabang and Vientiane. Keep in mind that the bark must be used immediately, or else tightly wrapped and kept in the freezer.

Among the lush, wild foliage of northern Laos, the plant known as mai sakahn doesn't stand out—but looking good isn't the main attraction. Also known as chili wood, the bark of the plant contains supercharged, peppery powers. A single sliver of the stuff laces soups and stews with a hot, tingly flavor, similar to Sichuan peppercorns but with even more of a kick.

Mai sakahn is a species of black pepper plant that grows across Southeast Asia. The taste is between pepper and chili, with a hint of herbal bitterness. In Laotian markets, the plant is sold as a woody stem or stump, and cooks splinter the bark themselves just before adding it to the pot. It's the most important ingredient in Laos's famous mor lam, a buffalo stew made with lemongrass, eggplant, and other riverside ingredients.

ONION SOUP MANGO

BAMBANGAN • MALAYSIA

Most fruit enthusiasts have tried only the sweet and tropical common mango, also known as *Mangifera indica*. The bambangan, however, is *Mangifera pajang*. The rare—and endangered—mango variety is found only on the island of Borneo, particularly in the state of Sabah. With their rough brown skin and hefty size (a single fruit can reach more than 5 pounds, or 2.3 kg), bambangans don't look much like the average mango. With their funky, durian-like smell and savory onion-soup flavor, they don't taste like them either.

While some do enjoy the sulfuric fruit on its own, it's most commonly used in dishes such as salads and chutneys. To make bambangan pickles, the fruit is sliced and mixed with chilies, salt, and shavings of the fruit's large white seed. After a week in an airtight container, the pickles are used as an accompaniment to fish dishes.

How to try it

Bambangans make appearances at markets throughout the island of Borneo, but are easiest to find in the East Malaysian state of Sabah. Due to their smell, they are often found alongside durians on the periphery of local markets rather than inside.

MATCHMAKING ORANGE FESTIVAL

CHAP GOH MEI • MALAYSIA

On Chap Goh Mei, the 15th night of Lunar New Year, groups of Malaysian revelers congregate at the edges of lakes and straits, their hands cupping vibrant oranges covered by words written in permanent marker.

At the onset of the New Year, celebrants often give oranges (which represent wealth in the coming year) to their friends and families. But on the last day of celebration, single women in Malaysia co-opt the symbolic orange to help them find love. Starting in the late 19th century, eligible women on Penang Island wrote on the rinds and tossed oranges into the water. Male suitors were meant to pluck a floating orb, then find the affiliated lady. Singles initially performed this ritual so that fate

How to try it

Merrymaking and orange tossing ensues along the waterfront strip of Esplanade on Penang Island. For those not able to attend, a virtual Chap Goh Mei river filled with floating oranges can be accessed from an app called Wowwwz.

might bring them a spouse, but today, women add their phone number or social media handle and try to land a date. Although the tradition started in Penang, groups now gather at bodies of water throughout Malaysia for the annual rite.

Though love is in the air, some participants are guided by entrepreneurial spirit rather than romance. Vendors scoop up oranges from the water, then resell them in the street—contact details and all—to interested bachelors.

EDIBLE BIRD'S NEST FARMING

SWIFTLET HOTELS • MYANMAR

How to try it

Farmed swiftlet nests are a good deal more sustainable than wild ones—but before you stock up, remember it's still a tasteless food with no proven medicinal or nutritional value.

Nestled throughout the southern city of Myeik are boarded-up houses and a few windowless concrete structures. From the outside, they look abandoned, but inside they are fully occupied. Loudspeakers inside the buildings blast a high staccato chirping sound, the mating call of the white-nest swiftlet, and hundreds of the small birds pour out of the sky and in through open windows at the top of the building. They are the swiftlet hotels of Myeik.

Swiftlet nests, which are clear, gelatinous, and made almost entirely of bird saliva, have been prized in Chinese medicine and cooking for hundreds of years. They are the main ingredient in the infamous bird's nest soup and are believed to slow aging, provide disease immunity, and increase sexual vigor. The edible bird's nest industry is massive—estimated to be worth at least five billion dollars annually, with two billion of it generated in Hong Kong alone.

Historically, the nests were gathered in caves in Borneo. Using ropes, bamboo poles, and handmade rattan ladders dangling from the cave's ceiling, the local Ida'an people climbed hundreds of feet in the air to scrape the nests from the cave walls. The work was incredibly dangerous. The pitch-black cave was lit only by torchlight, and people fell regularly to their deaths. Demand quickly outpaced natural resources, and the wild swiftlet population was under severe threat.

In the 1980s, a solution arrived in the form of swiftlet hotels. Typically converted from old houses and abandoned factories, then eventually built to order, these hulking windowless buildings now stretch across Thailand, Vietnam, Myanmar, Malaysia, and Indonesia. There is a get-rich-quick quality to the business model that has helped swiftlet farming grow rapidly. The initial costs are low (an old building, a stereo system), and if the farmer succeeds in establishing a population, it can be quite lucrative. Depending on the source, a kilo of birds' nests can go for more than $2,500.

The rise of swiftlet farming is perhaps the largest avian domestication project in modern history. The empty buildings act like massive artificial beehives, and the swiftlet farmers their keepers. Although the overall result has been an increase in swiftlets, there have been mixed results for wild populations. Wild nests are now even more valued, fetching as much as $10,000 a kilo, and the behavior of swiftlets has changed, with generations of birds learning to seek houses rather than caves.

FLOATING GARDENS

INLE LAKE • MYANMAR

Around a quarter of Myanmar's Inle Lake, the country's second largest body of water, is topped with man-made gardens. Farmers atop boats glide between their plots, plucking produce from patches of "land" that rise and fall with the currents. To create these tiny garden islands, farmers gather clumps of water hyacinth and seagrass from around the lake, which they weave and compress into a flat, raft-like structure. On top, they add a thick layer of silt, then the floating parcel is secured with long bamboo poles that are staked into the lake's muddy bottom. With direct access to the water's vast nutrients, the miniature islands are prime, fertile bits of land.

More than 90 percent of the gardens' yields are tomatoes, which are sold at market hundreds of miles away in Yangon and Mandalay and make up roughly half of the tomatoes eaten in Myanmar. Depending on the season, farmers can also harvest beans, cucumbers, flowers, and gourds, but tomatoes, their most lucrative crop, are given top priority.

The practice of farming atop the lake, rather than around it, is thought to have started in the 19th century before intensifying in the 1960s. The unusual agriculture has boosted the region's economy, but there is increasing concern that chemical fertilizers, pesticides, and runoff are destroying the lake's natural ecosystem, and new measures have been taken to preserve the floating aquaculture.

How to try it

Inle Lake is located in Taunggyi, about 150 miles (241 km) southeast of Mandalay. Many companies offer boat tours of the gardens and the surrounding homes on stilts.

The man-made Kela Floating Gardens on Inle Lake yield produce sold throughout Myanmar.

How to try it

For a culinary demonstration at Atching Lillian's, you'll need a party of ten or more. Reservations can be made through Facebook or by calling 09157730788. In the Kapampangan language, the restaurant is called Kusinang Matua ng Atching Lillian, or the "Old Kitchen of Atching Lillian."

HERITAGE FILIPINO RECIPES IN AN ANCESTRAL HOME

ATCHING LILLIAN RESTAURANT • PHILIPPINES

The province of Pampanga is often seen as the culinary heart of the Philippines, and Kapampangans are rightly proud of their cuisine. Local chef and historian Atching Lillian is a champion of what she calls "Heirloom Recipes," which focus on the rich heritage and stories behind her province's foods. From her ancestral home, where her family has lived for more than a century, Lillian runs a restaurant where she teaches visitors this inherited history.

Lillian prepares adobo, for example, without the customary soy sauce—in accordance to traditional recipes she's discovered. Her signature creations, called San Nicholas cookies, are a religious treat from the Spanish colonial era, made with 100-year-old molds, from a 300-year-old recipe. Many of her recipes were found in archives, and Lillian takes pride in preparing these dishes in the most traditional manner possible. (Just like her ancestors, Lillian doesn't weigh or measure ingredients.) With Lilian as guide, visitors are taken on a rare culinary journey that spans centuries of Pampanga's history, and lets them eat like it's 1699.

BOODLE FIGHT

KAMAYAN • PHILIPPINES

How to try it

Whether called kamayan or boodle fight, the traditional feast is now being served from Manila to the United Arab Emirates to Los Angeles. In the Philippines, Villa Escudero Waterfalls Restaurant in San Pablo City lets diners go barefoot while they eat in the middle of a small river with a waterfall.

Kamayan is a Tagalog word that translates to "by hand" and refers to the traditional Filipino style of eating—communally, and without plates or utensils. Though the practice faded under pressure from colonial rule, kamayan-style banquets are enjoying a resurgence, both within the Philippines and abroad, wherever the Filipino population can sustain a massive free-for-all feast.

A typical kamayan meal features a long table covered in smooth, waxy banana leaves, which all function together as an enormous plant-based plate. Down the middle is usually a foundation of rice, upon which traditional Filipino fare is piled: grilled chicken and pork, fried fish, shrimp, lumpia (a Filipino-style egg roll), pancit (stir-fried noodles), longganisa (sweet sausage), and whatever else will fit. Chunks of fresh fruit are fit into crevices, mango-tomato salsa is

piled on top. Standing, diners scoop their hands into the piles, lifting bites to their mouth that they deposit with their thumb.

Kamayan meals are often referred to as a "boodle fight." The term hearkens back to an American military practice, brought to the Philippines during the US occupation of the country. During a boodle fight, officers of different ranks would engage in ritual eating contests while standing shoulder to shoulder around a table. There is controversy around the term because it turns the traditional style of Filipino eating, without utensils, into a colonial game. But many Filipinos have claimed the word as their own, evidenced by the many boodle fight restaurants and catering services available throughout the country.

MAY MANGO MADNESS

GUIMARAS MANGO FESTIVAL • PHILIPPINES

The province of Guimaras, a small island nestled between Panay and Negros, is the Filipino mango hub. Orchards blanket the island, bearing an abundance of stunningly sweet manga, or mangoes. While a large percentage of these bodacious fruits leave the country, each May Guimaras puts on a two-week celebration for the locals, where the majesty of their mangoes is celebrated in almost every imaginable way.

During the Manggahan Festival, the island comes out to paint the streets yellow. In a mango-themed parade, performers wielding mango props dance in mango skirts. Competitive athletes register for sporting events such as the Amazing Guimarace, the Tour de Guimaras, and a Motocross Challenge. For the true fruit lover, there's the "Mango Eat All You Can," where for a hundred Filipino pesos (about $2), participants are set loose in a space filled with mango treats for 30 minutes.

In 1992, Guimaras was formally recognized as its own province. Locals celebrated the first Manggahan Festival in 1993, in honor of their provincial founding. Two decades later, the festival is bigger and longer than ever. All five municipalities of Guimaras use the event as an opportunity to showcase the island's culture, celebrate their community, and give thanks for the island's natural bounty.

How to try it

The Manggahan Festival takes place each May for two weeks. Outside the festival, you can visit the Trappist Monastery on Guimaras, Our Lady of the Philippines, where the order of monks make mango products that you can buy in the gift shop.

A Filipina dancer at the 2017 Manggahan Festival carries dozens of mangoes on her head.

FOOD PIONEER

MARIA YLAGAN OROSA

(1893–1945)

Ketchup, originally a Southeast Asian sauce, has been made over the centuries with everything from fish to walnuts to tomatoes. In the Philippines, pulped bananas are turned into ketchup, sweetened with sugar, soured with vinegar, and reddened with food coloring. One innovative food scientist is credited with creating a readily available domestic version of the condiment: Maria Ylagan Orosa.

As a young woman, Maria Ylagan Orosa was uncommonly courageous. Boarding a ship to the United States in 1916, she exchanged the warm Philippines and her family for chilly Seattle and her classmates at the University of Washington, where she pursued a degree in chemistry. After graduating, she became an assistant state chemist for Washington.

A bust of Orosa in her hometown of Batangas.

But in a few years, she went back home to the Philippines, taking up a role in Manila's Bureau of Science. (At the time, the US occupation of the Philippines was at its midpoint.) There, she experimented with Filipino produce, developed recipes, and sent economists (often dubbed "Orosa girls") to the countryside to showcase food-preservation methods and ingenious cooking techniques for those with little access to electricity or resources. Meanwhile, she developed hundreds of inventive recipes. In place of imported goods, she made soft drinks from local calamansi limes,

cookies from cassava, and a multitude of ingredients to make ketchup, including the banana. American newspapers reported on her experiments as well, especially about her attempts to ship frozen mangoes to the United States in a time when neither mangoes nor frozen food were especially common there.

All these achievements made her the Philippines' "foremost food specialist and food chemist," as a resolution naming a street in her honor proclaimed. But her life was to be cut unfortunately short. In the midst of World War II, she refused to leave Manila. When the Japanese invaded, Orosa secretly fed guerilla fighters and prison camp internees. But during the 1945 Battle of Manila, the city itself became a war zone. As American and Filipino troops fought to liberate the city, a piece of shrapnel struck Orosa, injuring her and sending her to a hospital. During a fierce artillery battle that pelted the hospital on February 13, Maria Orosa died, along with hundreds of others.

Orosa never commercialized her creations, and banana ketchup became popular only after her death. But she is survived by a large family living around the world, and tributes to her accomplishments have slowly trickled in over the decades. Today, her name adorns a street in Manila, and the nation's Rural Improvement Club considers her their founder. And, of course, there's the ketchup.

How to try it

Jumbo Seafood in Singapore's East Coast Seafood Centre offers yusheng, among other Lunar New Year specialties. Their version is quite large and designed to share with a group.

LUCKY SALAD TOSS

YUSHENG • SINGAPORE

To welcome the Lunar New Year, Singaporeans toss a raw fish and shredded vegetable salad called yusheng, which happens to be a very auspicious homophone. In Mandarin, yu is the word for fish, but it also sounds like the word for abundance. Yu sheng, which literally translates to "raw fish," also sounds like the Mandarin phrase for an "increase in abundance." Playing up the double meanings, many ingredients in the dish also have significance rooted in popular Chinese sayings: lime for luck, peanut crumbs to symbolize gold and silver, green radishes for eternal youth, and shredded white radish for prosperity in the workplace.

The ingredients are added one by one, and with each addition, the salad-maker says a well-wishing phrase. Once all the ingredients have been placed in the dish, all diners stand up and toss the ingredients into the air with their chopsticks while saying "lo hei," a Cantonese phrase that conveys well wishes for the new year. The higher you toss, according to tradition, the higher your fortune will be. Finished with a sweet plum and Chinese five-spice dressing, tossing yusheng might be auspicious for the future, but eating it gives instant returns in the present.

GILDED TOWER OF GIN

ATLAS BAR • SINGAPORE

With its majestic art deco exterior, Singapore's Parkview Square office building has earned the nicknames "Gotham" and "Batman building" among locals. Step inside its lobby and you'll find a warm, ornate space filled with red carpets, leather booths, and a giant golden tower that contains 1,300 bottles of gin from around the world.

This 26-foot (8 m) tall tower is part of Atlas Bar, which opened in 2017. Visitors and workers (the building houses various organizations, including the embassies for Mongolia, Austria, and the United Arab Emirates) can sip gins from regions as far-ranging as Bolivia, Belgium, and Japan, and dating back as far as 1910. Doubling down on its Gilded Age vibe, the bar's cocktail menu revolves heavily around gin and champagne.

How to try it
Atlas Bar is open from 12 p.m. to 2 a.m. daily.

The interior of Atlas Bar allows customers to feel like they are traveling through time and around the world with 1,300 types of gin.

A 45-YEAR-OLD SIMMERING STEW

NEUA TUNE AT WATTANA PANICH • THAILAND

How to try it
Wattana Panich is located at 336 338 Ekkamai Road.

The giant pot of neua tune, a beef stew popular in Bangkok, the Thai capital, has been simmering since owner Nattapong Kaweenuntawong was a child, more than 45 years ago. Growing up, Kaweenuntawong studied the stew's flavor profile and learned its nuances from his father. Today, he balances the flavor himself daily. Employing a centuries-old practice called Hunter's Stew or Perpetual Stew, Kaweenuntawong uses some of the previous day's leftover broth to start the base of the following day's soup. There is no recipe for the dish; he simply tastes until it's right.

A secret blend of spices and herbs, stewed beef, raw beef slices, meatballs, tripe, and other organs swim about the deeply savory, bubbling vat. While new restaurants and high-end condominiums now dwarf the humble one-story bistro in Bangkok's busy Ekkamai neighborhood, the complex, time-enriched flavor of their signature dish keeps Wattana Panich in brisk business.

Kaweenuntawong's mother tends the bubbling vat of stew.

AN ENCHANTING, COLOR-CHANGING EXTRACT

BUTTERFLY PEA FLOWER • THAILAND

How to try it
Butterfly pea flower is ubiquitous across Southeast Asia wherever there are hotels, spas, or markets selling blue dumplings and purple rice. It's also sold online in tea blends, powder form, and as a "cocktail colorant."

The secret to unlocking the transformative powers of butterfly pea flower, or *Clitoria ternatea*, is acid. When dropped into pure water with a neutral pH of 7, the liquid turns a cosmic blue. Add a squirt of lemon, dropping the pH, and the color turns to purple. One more squirt and it changes again, this time into a vibrant magenta. The indigo-colored plant is found across Southeast Asia and has been used for centuries to dye foods and create lava lamp–looking drinks. In Thailand, a blue tea called dok anchan, spiked with lemon and honey, is the traditional welcome drink at hotels and spas.

With a mild herbal taste that's likened to black tea, butterfly pea is gentle in flavor. As with other foods with deep blue hues, the plant is considered extremely healthy thanks to antioxidants called anthocyanins, which combat inflammation and a host of other ailments, including high blood pressure, immune-system issues, and even certain types of cancer. None of this is new to Southeast Asians, especially practitioners of Ayurveda, who have used the blossom medicinally for hundreds of years.

Recently, butterfly pea flower has entered the modern craft-cocktail scene. Using either whole petals or dried flower powder, bartenders have invented drinks that show off the plant's dynamic range of colors. A squirt of citrus might be added before the customer's eyes to make the drink flare lavender, then, as the ice melts and the liquid dilutes, the drink will gradually descend into sapphire.

DICTATOR'S DELIGHT

PAD THAI • THAILAND

Dictators often make unreasonable demands. Plaek Phibunsongkhram, prime minister and military dictator of Thailand, began his reign with a dozen edicts called the 12 Cultural Mandates, meant to build a unified national identity. Beginning in 1939, a year after Phibunsongkhram helped overthrow the Thai monarchy, his countrymen were ordered to start calling the country Thailand instead of Siam, to "eat meals at set times, no more than four daily," to "sleep approximately 6–8 hours," to dress appropriately, to honor the flag, and very specifically, to wear hats. Languages of ethnic minorities were banned, the traditional garments of local tribes were made illegal, and in what might have been his strangest dictate, Phibunsongkhram invented a new national dish called pad thai.

Meant to reduce rice consumption and encourage noodles, which could be made using a fraction of the grain, Phibunsongkhram stated in a speech: "I want everyone to eat noodles. Noodles are healthy, and have a variety of tastes, from sour to salty to sweet. Noodles can be made in Thailand, are convenient to make, and have excellent taste." Before Phibunsongkhram willed it into the world, pad thai was essentially nonexistent.

Rice noodles were most likely brought to the country by the Chinese—ironic for a campaign built on creating a strong Thai identity—but the dish features Thai flavors of tamarind, palm sugar, and chilies. And the name made Phibunsongkhram's intent clear: It was pad THAI.

With the full power of the Thai government and military behind the newfangled noodle dish, the Public Welfare Department began distributing recipes and food carts, from which pad thai was to be sold. (Other foreign food vendors were banned.) Incredibly, his plan worked. Pad thai remains the national dish of Thailand. It's eaten widely across the country and considered the poster child for Thai food abroad. The dictator's noodles were an undisputed success, but not all of Phibunsongkhram's mandates worked so well: Hat-wearing in Thailand is now optional.

How to try it

Pad thai is available in nearly every home-style restaurant in Thailand, as well as at night markets, from street carts, and in food courts across the country.

ALL THEY CAN EAT

MONKEY BUFFET FESTIVAL • THAILAND

How to try it

The Monkey Buffet Festival takes place on the last Sunday of every November, at Phra Prang Sam Yot temple. Be warned: Once the monkeys have had their fill, they're known to get rowdy with the leftovers.

Monkeys jump from table to table and feast on beautiful produce arrangements at the 2010 Monkey Buffet Festival.

On the last Sunday of November, among the ruins of Thailand's 13th-century temple Phra Prang Sam Yot, an exquisite banquet awaits the guests of honor, all of which are monkeys. The province of Lopburi is home to thousands of macaques, and feting them each year is believed to bring good luck to the area and its people.

Known as the Monkey Buffet Festival, the party kicks off with an opening ceremony that features performances by human dancers in monkey costumes. When the real monkeys arrive, hosts remove sheets from the banquet tables, revealing decorative spreads of beautifully ripe watermelons, durians, pineapples, and anything else a monkey could ask for. The macaques jump freely across tables, climbing and feasting on towering pyramids that contain nearly two tons of edible offerings.

Respect for monkeys traces back at least 2,000 years to the epic tale of Rama, the divine Hindu prince, and his struggle to rescue his wife, Sita, from the clutches of a demon lord. According to the tale, the monkey king Hanuman, along with his army, stepped in to help rescue Sita. Since then, monkeys have been revered as a sign of fortune and prosperity, and the annual buffet in Lopburi is a way for Thais to mark their appreciation and to keep the good luck coming.

EGG COFFEE

CÀ PHÊ TRÚ'NG • VIETNAM

In modern-day Hanoi, coffee drinkers rely on a steady stream of condensed milk to smooth out the heavy-duty Robusta brew served in most Vietnamese coffee shops. In fact, ordering a cà phê sữa ("milk coffee") will automatically get you a hot Robusta with sticky-sweet condensed milk. When French colonists introduced coffee to Vietnam in the 1800s, fresh milk was hard to come by. Dairy wasn't part of the local diet, and whatever milk could be found spoiled easily in the tropical heat. Luckily, a New Yorker named Gail Borden invented commercial condensed milk in the 1850s, which the French brought over to Vietnam. The thick, shelf-stable milk became standard in the country's coffee—but in 1946, Nguyen Van Giang didn't have either kind of milk, and so he turned to eggs.

The onset of the French War (also known as the First Indochina War) had caused a milk shortage in Vietnam, and Giang, a bartender working at Hanoi's Sofitel Legend Metropole Hotel, needed something to make a creamy coffee. He whipped in an egg, which foamed almost like milk, and invented cà phê trú'ng, or egg coffee. Today, the rich, fluffy combination is as much a dessert as it is a drink, now made using just the yolks, which are whipped with milk and sugar and heated into an unctuous topping for Robusta coffee. Egg coffee is always served in a small glass, often cradled by a bowl of hot water to keep the treat warm. Otherwise it's cold and strong, like a refreshing glass of liquid tiramisu.

How to try it
Nguyen Van Giang's son, Van Dao, serves the most popular egg coffee in Hanoi at the shop his father opened, called Café Giang. His sister also owns an egg coffee shop called Dinh Café.

Egg coffee can be drunk at any temperature, but it is usually kept warm in a bowl of hot water.

NOODLES DRAWN FROM A SINGLE WELL

CAO LẦU • VIETNAM

Cao lầu, in its traditional form, can never be globalized. While everything in the dish is ostensibly replicable—a bed of greens and herbs, topped with noodles, barbecue pork, crispy rice crackers, pork crackling, and a ladle of pork broth—the traditional rice noodles cannot be made anywhere else but the city of Hội An because they rely on the water from a single well.

All the cao lầu noodles in Hội An, a city of 150,000, are made by a secretive handful of people. The most important cao lầu family has an empire that extends back four generations, when a chef from China taught the current noodle-maker's great-grandfather the recipe. For the first two generations, the water that went into the noodles was drawn from a famous 10th-century well in Ba Le, which has been ascribed mystical and medicinal properties by the locals, thanks to its alum- and calcium-rich composition. In recent years, the family decided to dig their own well to supply their noodle making. (The water, they assure, is just as good.) The second ingredient that makes the noodles hyper-regional is the wood ash they add to the water, made from burning local trees such as the cajuput. Together, the ash-and-water mixture gives the noodles their dense, chewy texture and flaxen color.

How to try it
Cao Lầu Không Gian Xanh is a casual café with an exceptional cao lầu. A bowl is 30,000 dong, or about $1.25.

Every morning, save for one day during the Vietnamese Lunar New Year, called Tet, the family makes cao lầu noodles by hand: boiling and pounding rice, working it into a dough, steaming, kneading, rolling, and cutting. The dough is steamed twice, there's no electric machinery, and few know how to do it outside of a man named Ta Ngoc Em and his family. Fearing that the culinary heritage might be lost if anything were to happen to them, a government official arrived at their home and implored them to share the recipe with others, just in case. The family has since loosened their vow of secrecy and has allowed outsiders to witness their process.

A bowl of cao lầu is always eaten with chopsticks, never with a spoon, because the five spice seasoned broth is meant more as a sauce than a soup. The city's famous noodles, all delivered fresh from the same kitchen, are available at restaurants and stalls all over Hội An—and nowhere else.

Cao lầu noodles are the hyper-regional specialty of Hội An.

Also from a Single Well

BAN SOY SAUCE

The water from the only well in Ban Village is not used for bathing or cooking, but for making a soy sauce many consider the best in Vietnam. Ban soy sauce, a staple of North Vietnamese cooking, is a light, caramel-colored condiment made by fermenting large-grain sticky rice and small-grain soybeans in large ceramic jars. Fermentation takes place during the warmest months, between March and August, when the village yards are packed with hundreds of ceramic jars.

Most people have never tasted traditional fermented soy sauce. Commercial soy sauce is not fermented; rather, it uses hydrochloric acid to break soybean protein into amino acids. While the commercial process takes mere days, fermenting soy sauce takes months, if not years. It allows time to transform the water, grain, soybeans, and mold into a complex and salty, umami-rich liquid.

Compared to other naturally brewed soy sauces, ban soy sauce is milder and sweeter, thanks to the village's pure water and natural resources. The coveted condiment is used as a dipping sauce, a grilling marinade, and a gift for homesick Northerners who now live far from the well.

Africa

NORTH AFRICA · WEST AFRICA
EAST AFRICA · SOUTHERN AFRICA

NORTH AFRICA

WILD PIGEON TOWERS

DOVECOTES • EGYPT

How to try it

You can see clusters of mud-brick pigeon towers in Mit Ghamr, a two-hour drive north of Cairo. Back in Cairo, Kababgy El Azhar Farahat is a classic alleyway restaurant that serves some of the city's best pigeon, including hamam mahshi and pigeon soup.

Dovecotes on the road between Alexandria and Cairo.

Dovecotes rise from Egyptian cities like earthen chimneys, each home to mother pigeons and their young squabs. Pigeons are prized in Egypt for their meat and their excrement, called guano, which makes an excellent fertilizer. The hollow, conical birdhouses have been used in Egypt since ancient times. Dovecotes come in all sizes; some are attached to buildings, others freestanding. Their small alcoves provide a welcoming nest for the flocks of wild pigeons who spend the day flying around looking for food, then return to the dovecote at night to roost.

The dovecotes also provide the country with a steady supply of pigeon meat—a staple of the local diet. Young pigeons, or squabs, are considered the most succulent and are used for the stuffed pigeon dish hamam mahshi. Plucked from their dovecote at around six weeks, often before they learn to fly, the small birds are stuffed with rice or freekeh (a toasted, cracked young green wheat) mixed with onions, chopped giblets, cinnamon, cumin, and nuts. Trussed up tightly, the squab is roasted or grilled until the skin is crispy and the stuffing has soaked up the bird's flavorful juices.

The 2,000-Year-Old Magic of Egyptian Egg Ovens

In 1750, French entomologist René-Antoine Ferchault de Réaumur visited an Egyptian egg incubator and declared, "Egypt ought to be prouder of them than her pyramids." An ingenious—and ancient—system of mud ovens designed to replicate the conditions under a broody hen, these egg ovens could hatch thousands of fertilized eggs in two to three weeks.

From the outside, many incubators looked like smaller, rounder versions of the pyramids. Réaumur wrote a detailed description of what he saw: two symmetrical wings separated by a central corridor, with each wing containing up to five sets of two-tiered chambers. Fertilized eggs were placed in the lower tier and kept warm by a smoldering, dung-fueled fire in the upper tier. Réaumur observed the hatchery workers, who stayed on the premises to monitor the fire and turn the eggs regularly, which kept the embryo membrane from attaching to the shell and creating deformities in the chick. In the final days of incubation, the workers monitored the eggs with additional attention because too much external heat risked causing early hatching. Hens instinctively regulate their eggs' temperature with their bodies. The Egyptian egg hatchers mimicked this process by gently pressing the eggs to their eyelids—one of the most sensitive parts of the human body.

Back in France, Réaumur tried to replicate the Egyptian method, but the cold European climate meant that the hatchers required stronger heat and more fuel than was cost-effective. In 1879, a Canadian farmer named Lyman Byce invented the coal lamp incubator with an electric temperature regulator, which was widely commercialized and used internationally—including in Egypt.

Over the 20th century, most traditional Egyptian egg ovens were replaced with electric incubators, but approximately 200 ovens are still in operation. Although modern advances are slowly creeping in—some hatchery workers now incorporate metal trolleys, automatic egg turners, and thermostats—the 2,000-year-old technology is as effective as ever.

A diagram of the inside of the fire-fueled egg incubator.

Edible Beauty Products

The ancient Egyptians have a reputation for beauty, vanity, and making use of the natural—often edible—world to supply their extensive beautification routines. Cleopatra was rumored to have had hundreds of lactating donkeys to provide milk for her regular anti-wrinkle baths. Egyptians used burnt almonds to fill in their eyebrows and animal-fat creams to moisturize their faces. Cosmetics were so important to Egyptians that many chose to be buried with them.

Body hair, considered a sign of poor hygiene and low class, was deeply undesirable. (An exception was made for eyebrows.) The earliest Egyptians fashioned tweezers from shells and razors from bronze. Around 1900 BCE they came up with a more effective, less painful method for hair removal: caramel wax. Egyptians boiled a mixture of oil and honey until it formed a thick syrup. The cooled caramel was then applied to fuzzy patches of skin, covered with a piece of muslin cloth, and ripped off. The technique (recently rediscovered by the modern hair-removal world and rebranded as "sugaring") soon spread across the Middle East to places like Iran and Turkey. Egyptians may be the most famous ancient beauticians, but they weren't the only ones using edible cosmetics.

MAYA AVOCADO-BANANA HAIR PASTE: During the Maya classical period, which lasted from 250 to 900 CE, head shape was the all-important marker of status and beauty. A high, elongated forehead that sloped

Ancient Egyptian princess Nefertiabet, whose name means "Beautiful One of the East."

SAND-BAKED BREAD

TAGUELLA • LIBYA

How to try it

Due to major unrest in Libya, it's safer to try taguella in neighboring Niger. The desert trade town of Agadez would be a prime place, but violent crime is also common there. Please check travel advisories before making any plans.

For the nomadic Tuareg people of North Africa, the desert is their oven. When they want to bake bread, they spread hot coals over the sand and dig a round, shallow divot in the center. They place their dough—a wet, unleavened mixture of semolina or millet that's been kneaded and shaped into a flat, round disk—into the blazing hollow and cover it quickly with hot sand and stones. A crust will form on the dough before the sand has time to seep into it. After about 20 minutes, the baker will uncover the bread, flip it, and re-cover it to ensure even heat distribution. Called taguella, the chewy, charred bread is a staple of the Tuareg diet. It's typically torn into bite-size pieces, placed in a bowl, and used as a base for stew.

Two Tuareg men baking bread in the Libyan desert.

backward to a point was so desirable that Maya parents would mold the soft skulls of their newborn babies, often strapping two boards to an infant's head to press it into the desired shape. To accentuate a good pointy head, well-to-do women wore high ponytails that they decorated with braids, ribbons, and headpieces, which in turn strained their scalps and damaged their hair. Thankfully, they had avocados packed with vitamins B and E, which facilitate hair growth and repair scalp damage. They also had bananas, with folic acid, to keep their hair shiny and strong. Whipping the two together with a protein-packed egg and moisturizing oil, the Maya made a hair and skull cream that still works today.

ANCIENT GREEK COLD CREAM: Second-century Greek physician Galen is considered the inventor of cold cream, which he made by vigorously blending olive oil, beeswax, and rose water. Called cold cream for its cooling effect on the skin, Galen's invention was a moisturizing marvel for the ancient Greeks. Today, commercial cold cream is made with shelf-stable mineral oils and borax, which keeps the mixture from spoiling and separating, but Galen's original formula can still easily be made in the kitchen. No time for scratch-made

A 19th-century geisha.

cold cream? Modern Greeks are known to use yogurt instead.

CHINESE AND JAPANESE RICE POWDER: Ancient Romans and Greeks used white lead to lighten their skin, which slowly poisoned them, until they made the switch to chalk. The ancient Chinese and Japanese, who also dabbled in lead, eventually settled on rice powder.

Chinese women dusted their faces with the finely ground rice, and geishas mixed the powder with water to paint their faces. (Some geishas would also bathe in rice water.) In modern Asia, rice is still a key cosmetic ingredient. The milky liquid drained from soaked rice, which many believe tones the skin and lessens the effects of sun damage, can be applied to the face with a cotton ball.

VICTORIAN LEMON EYE DROPS: Nineteenth-century England was a time of many treacherous beauty practices. Women bathed in arsenic to keep their skin white, numbed their eyelids with cocaine, and filled out their eyelashes by sewing in hair from their head. They also squeezed lemon juice into their eyes, which dilated their pupils and gave them the desirable big, glassy appearance—and also caused the inevitable corneal abrasions and, with excessive use, blindness.

GRANARY FORTRESS

QASR AL–HAJ • LIBYA

How to try it
Qasr al-Haj is located in a remote area southwest of Tripoli. The granary can be visited, but because it is a functional storage facility, the storage rooms should not be entered without the guidance of the caretaker or permission of the owners.

The Qasr al-Haj is one of the most stunning pieces of Berber architecture in Libya. Even though the name means "Fortress of Haj," the structure is neither a fortress nor a fortified city. It's a 12th-century storage facility—built to warehouse the harvests of the seminomadic people of the region, as well as travelers on the Haj pilgrimage to Mecca—that's still in use today.

From the outside, the circular building is nearly featureless. A single door opens to a vast expanse of courtyard surrounded by 114 cavelike storage rooms. The rooms are arranged on several different levels. The lowest, which lie partially underground, are used to store olive oil, while the upper levels are dedicated mainly to barley and wheat. A staircase leads to the top, where a walkway makes a full circle around the structure. Each room serves as a vault of sorts, much like in a bank, where a family or individual can securely store their foodstuffs. Historically, the granary was also used as a grain "stock exchange," its courtyard a marketplace for buying and trading goods.

Sheikh Abu Jatla, the 12th-century ruler who built the granary, rented the storage rooms in exchange for a small amount of grain, which he is said to have distributed among the poor.

Other Granary Fortresses

For at least 11,000 years, humans have stored grain in bulk. In many societies, a granary was the equivalent of a bank, protecting from local "economic" factors like animals, thieves, and weather extremes. Before formalized currency, grain was one of the earliest forms of money. Ancient Egyptians deposited and withdrew their grain from a centralized collection site, while Babylonians, who used silver as currency, determined its value in relation to barley.

❶ KSAR OULED SOLTANE (TATOUINE, TUNISIA) is a 15th-century Berber granary built on a hill, which protected it from raiders. Divided into two courtyards, the original structure was built entirely of mud (in 1997, the granary was restored using cement) and contains hundreds of storage vaults. Ksar Ouled Soltane rose to international fame when it was used as the slave quarters in the movie *Star Wars: The Phantom Menace.*

❷ AGADIR ID AISSA (AMTOUDI, MOROCCO) is one of Morocco's many spectacular igoudar (the plural form of agadir, which means "granary"), and among the oldest and best preserved. Built some 900 years ago by the Berbers, who are Indigenous to Morocco, Agadir Id Aissa stored not only grain but valuable documents, precious metals, and anything else in need of fortification, including animals, medicines, beehives, and civilians.

Perched high above the small oasis town of Amtoudi, Agadir Id Aissa can be reached only by foot, mule, or donkey. As with all igoudar, the local guardian of the key—which is generally the size of a forearm—grants entrance into the labyrinthine storage facility.

❸ THE HECANG GRANARY (GOBI DESERT, CHINA) is contained within the massive fortress built during the Han dynasty (206 BCE–220 CE) and supported soldiers building the Great Wall. The fortress was designed to disguise itself from enemies in the desert, shielded to the north and south by tall sand dunes. It was also strategically located along a remote part of the Silk Road, and its granary stores helped feed traveling merchants. While the site is now mostly in ruins, it's a rare surviving example of a Han dynasty earthen structure.

PUBLIC OVEN IN A PORTUGUESE FORTRESS

EL JADIDA COMMUNITY OVEN • MOROCCO

How to try it

El Jadida, a recent addition to UNESCO's World Heritage Sites, is a 90-minute drive from Casablanca. The fortress also features a cistern where a scene in Orson Welles's *Othello* was filmed.

Most Moroccans have an oven in their home, yet they leave the baking to the local oven attendant, who makes a living tending to the neighborhood's communal oven.

In El Jadida, a quiet port city on the Atlantic coast, the oven is located in a 16th-century Portuguese fortress. The city, orginally known as Mazagan, was once a colony of Portugal and a stopping point for spice traders on their way to India. Abandoned in 1769, the city stood vacant for half a century. In the mid-19th century, a multicultural mix of Muslims, Jews, and Christians repopulated the town and turned the fortress into a commercial center. They renamed the city El Jadida, or "The New." The wood-burning oven inside the fortress is used for far more than baking bread. Along with their dough, El Jadida's fishermen and homemakers bring in meats, fish, and pizzas to be deftly baked by the oven operator.

El Jadida residents bring their bread dough to the oven attendant, who bakes it in the communal oven.

STUFFED CAMEL SPLEEN

TEHAL • MOROCCO

How to try it

A camel spleen sandwich should cost about 12 dirham, or a little more than $1.

Among the chaos of the Fez medina market, you'll find giant bulging loaves of meat, easily more than a foot in length, hanging out in metal trays. When a customer orders, vendors will slice off a slab and sear it on a griddle. They take requests: Herbs, vegetables, and even an egg can be added to the mix before it is scooped into batbout, a type of Moroccan pita bread.

Holding the meat mass together is a camel's spleen, stuffed taut with ground meat—generally a medley of camel, cow, and lamb—seasoned with spices, olives, and preserved lemon. Called tehal, it has a dark, compacted appearance akin to Scottish haggis. Traditionally, tehal is prebaked in one of Morocco's many communal bread ovens and then sliced and cooked to order in the marketplace. It's a popular lunch for working locals, who line up to grab a quick and portable camel-cinched meal.

A jam-packed camel loaf at the Fez medina.

BATHHOUSE TAJINE

TANJIA • MOROCCO

Tanjia, which is a name for both the cooking vessel and the dish inside it, practically cooks itself. The glazed terra-cotta jug, which resembles the amphorae used to store liquids in ancient Greece and Rome, acts like a single-serving slow cooker. To prepare a tanjia, you will have to make two stops. The first is to the butcher, who will fill your jug with meat, typically beef or lamb. Cuts like collar, neck, and tail work well for this dish because they release fats and gelatins that help braise the meat and create a rich, silky sauce. The butcher also takes care of the seasoning—saffron, cumin, preserved lemon, garlic, a dollop of fermented butter, and a drizzle of olive oil. After sealing the tanjia with a piece of parchment, you'll take it to stop number two: the local hammam, or bathhouse. Give your tanjia to the attendant, who will nestle the jug of meat into the hot ash of the coal-burning oven used to heat the bathwater, and leave it to slowly cook for at least half a day. (Some will drop off their tanjia in the evening and pick it up the next morning.) The long, gentle simmer renders the meat so tender it practically melts and yields a sauce that's bright, fragrant, and unctuous.

Because tanjia requires no cooking skills, it has a reputation for being a bachelor's meal. Traditionally, men who worked at the souk had Friday off and would eat tanjia together after a relaxing morning in the park.

A tanjia filled with lamb and olives, closed at the top with parchment.

How to try it
Marrakech is the city most famous for tanjia. Many butchers will rent you a tanjia to take to the bathhouse, which also charges a small fee for cooking and tending to your meal.

ARGAN OIL ALMOND BUTTER

AMLOU • MOROCCO

How to try it

Amlou is among the many argan-centric products available at APIA, a store in Marrakech's upscale Gueliz district.

Argan oil, the Moroccan cooking staple and internationally prized age-defying cosmetic, is no picnic to produce. The argan tree, which is notoriously thorny, grows exclusively in southwestern Morocco and produces fruit just once a year. The fruit itself is something of a puzzle. Peel the outside flesh to reach the nut. Open the nut, which is extremely hard, to reach the oily kernel (there is often just one, but never more than three). To extract the oil, the kernels must be toasted, ground, and pressed by hand. It can take 20 hours to produce a single liter, which explains the $130 price tag—and the "liquid gold" nickname. Most of the world dispenses argan oil judiciously, or drop by drop as a beauty serum, but southern Moroccans use it to make a sweet nut butter called amlou.

To make amlou the traditional way, toasted almonds and argan oil are ground on a millstone—another laborious process that often requires shifts from the whole family. The pulverized almonds, which release their own fats, thicken the argan oil and create a viscous, nutty liquid that's lightly salted and sweetened with honey. Sticky, silky, and glistening with oil, amlou is used as a dip or spread for whatever needs a little liquid gold.

Amlou

(*about 1 cup*)

¾ cup (104 grams) raw almonds

4–6 tablespoons (32–48 grams) pure argan oil

2 tablespoons (42 grams) honey

Sea salt, to taste

1. Preheat the oven to 350°F (177°C). Spread the almonds on a sheet pan and toast in the oven for about 15 minutes, until they are dark brown and very fragrant. Set them aside to fully cool.

2. Once the nuts have cooled, transfer them to a food processor and pulse until they are very finely ground and oily.

3. Transfer the nut paste to a mixing bowl. Add the argan oil, honey, and salt. Stir well. Store in a tightly sealed container at room temperature. The amlou will keep for up to one month.

The traditional way to make amlou is by hand, using a millstone.

French Doctors Once Feared Tea-Drinking Would Destroy Tunisian Society

TUNISIA

In 1927, at a meeting of the Academy of Medicine in Paris, a French-trained Tunisian doctor, Béchir Dinguizli, announced a "new social scourge" spreading like an "oil stain" across Tunisia. If not stopped by French authorities, the doctor warned, it had the power to corrupt morals and paralyze Tunisian society. Soon after, the French paper Le Matin ran a front-page article about the "new intoxication." The alarming threat? Tea.

Tunisia, a French colony from 1881–1956, was only introduced to tea after the Italo-Turkish War of 1911–1912, which sent an influx of tea-drinking refugees from Tripolitania (modern-day Libya) into Tunisia. When locals began to drink tea, too, French colonists—accustomed to coffee, which they believed was the drink of the Enlightenment—accused them of teaism.

According to Dinguizli, teaism was an addiction comparable to alcoholism, a form of chronic poisoning with nervous tremors, amnesia, palpitations, blurred vision, serious disturbances of the nervous and circulatory systems, a general weakening of the body, and even a marked decrease in birth rates. Later authors delineated additional mental consequences, such as hallucinations, delusions, and even psychoses.

Beyond the medical concern, French colonists believed that tea addicts would do almost anything to satisfy their habit, and those succumbing to the "vice of tea" were potential criminals. They tried banning illegal coffeehouses, which served tea, and increasing custom duties. There were calls for educational posters and films on the dangers of tea, for creating a state monopoly on tea, and for a law making tea a prescription drug available only at pharmacies.

Alas, Tunisians did not respond to the French scare tactics of teaism, and locals continued to drink tea. In 1956, Tunisia gained independence, and today tea is practically the country's national drink.

WEST AFRICA

TASTE TRIPPING FRUIT

MIRACLE BERRY • BURKINA FASO

How to try it

Fresh miracle berries and whole plants can be ordered online. Across West Africa, the fruit is known by a dizzying number of local names.

At first, miracle berries (*Synsepalum dulcificum*) taste like bland cranberries, but eating just one can alter the taste of sour foods for up to an hour, turning them impossibly sweet.

In 1968, scientists isolated the berry's unique protein that turns sour flavors sweet. Named miraculin for its "miraculous" effects, the protein binds to taste buds and lingers on sweet receptors, activating them only in sour environments. The berry must be fresh; heat or refrigeration renders the fruit ineffective.

In recent years, miracle berries have become the stars of "flavor-tripping" parties. Participants (mostly in the United States) kick off the night by scraping the flesh from the fruit with their teeth, letting the juice coat their mouth, and spitting out the seed. Soon a smorgasbord of foods that shouldn't taste sweet do: Lemons become lemonade, and goat cheese morphs into cheesecake.

Though little studied, there are also medical uses for miracle berries. For example, miraculin allows diabetics to enjoy sweetness without ingesting sugar, and it helps chemotherapy patients experience a fuller spectrum of taste.

In Burkina Faso and throughout West Africa, where the berry plant is native, some families and farmers still grow the fruit, but its use has declined. Cheap, plentiful sugar has robbed the miracle berry of its magic.

Another Miraculous Berry

Serendipity

The serendipity berry (*Dioscoreophyllum cumminsii*) is a West African fruit that grows in the rain forests of southern Nigeria and in the tropical regions between Sierra Leone and Eritrea. It contains monellin, a potently sweet protein that's approximately 1,500 to 3,000 times sweeter than sucrose (table sugar), which makes it an exciting natural sugar alternative. Alas, like the miracle berry, the serendipity berry loses its powers when heated above 122°F (50°C), the temperature at which monellin breaks down and the sweetness disappears. For now, extracting the protein is expensive, and commercial viability remains to be seen.

Coating your mouth with the flesh of the miracle berry will temporarily make sour foods taste sweet.

PSYCHEDELIC ROOT

IBOGA • GABON

boga (*Tabernanthe iboga*) sprouts green leaves, bears small fruit, and carries within its roots an important part of Gabon's Bwiti culture: one of the strongest psychedelic compounds in the world.

In powdered form, the dried peelings of the iboga root resemble instant coffee. A small dose works like coffee, too, and Bwiti hunters sometimes use it as a stimulant. In moderate doses, the root is employed to treat a host of physical maladies. In large doses, it becomes a ritualistic substance for initiating a newcomer into the Bwiti religion—a spiritual discipline that incorporates animism, ancestor worship, and Christianity.

When people undergoing initiation enter a Bwiti temple, they're first covered in powdered clay, and then they consume iboga, as dried chips, spoonfuls of powder, or (less commonly) mixed with tea. For the rest of the night—and sometimes for several days—initiates remain under the care of other Bwiti as they experience out-of-body, hallucinatory experiences caused by the plant's active alkaloid, ibogaine. The root-inspired visions help the Bwiti connect with ancestors, which is a central aspect of their religion.

In recent decades, foreigners have developed a reputation for abusing the plant and using it for wild drug trips instead of spiritual journeys. But in 1962, a heroin addict in New York City found a use for the plant that changed his life and many others: After trying ibogaine, he was rid of his desire for heroin, and he spent the rest of his life advocating for the natural medicine. Many addicts now swear by iboga's ability to prevent opiate withdrawal, and while more research is necessary, ibogaine is available at rehab clinics wherever it's legal, from Canada to Mexico to Europe.

How to try it

Iboga is a powerful psychotropic and for practitioners of Bwiti, a powerful spritiural conduit. It is not something to ingest casually.

The hallucinogenic root bark of the iboga plant.

WORLD'S LARGEST LAND SNAIL

GIANT GHANA SNAIL • GHANA

Giant Ghana snails (*Archachatina marginata*) can live for up to a decade, during which time they can grow up to 8 bulky inches (20 cm) long, making them the largest land snails in the world. To maintain their size, these gastropods will eat practically anything, including house paint, stucco, and 500 types of plants. The snails are hermaphrodites, and each lays hundreds of eggs each year, which means that a small group of ravenous giant snails can swiftly turn into a horde of ravenous giant snails. Some countries fear that the snails will destroy their ecosystems (in 2014, 67 snails intended for human consumption were seized at Los Angeles International Airport and promptly incinerated). But in Ghana—where snails are harvested from safe, known locations—the bigger the better because these hefty critters make for delicious meat.

How to try it

Giant snails are easily found in West Africa. They are a popular street food and are generally sold as kebabs or in a spicy pepper sauce.

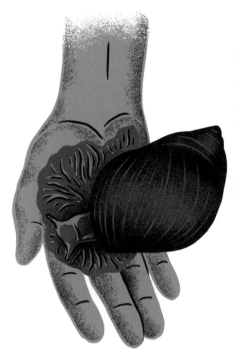

Chili-spiced snails, snail soup, peppered snails, snail kebabs, fried snails, marinated minced snails—all are considered delicacies. In the marketplace, vendors carry metal trays on their heads, hawking snails, while street stalls serve the chewy, briny meat on toothpicks as a quick snack. The snail can be harvested in the wild, but sustainable snailery farms are becoming increasingly common in West Africa.

To shuck the snails, a thin metal stick is inserted into the shell and used to pull out the meat, which is then trimmed and washed in lime juice to remove the slime. The meat is then ready for the pot. The snails are a near-perfect protein—low in fat and rich in iron, potassium, and phosphorus.

PASSENGER JET RESTAURANT

LA TANTE DC 10 • GHANA

Anyone can board the McDonnell Douglas DC-10 jet parked on Airport Road, just outside Accra's international airport—but it won't take you anywhere. Once operated by Ghana Airways and flown to Europe and the United States, the aircraft was impounded in 2005 at London's Heathrow Airport as a result of unpaid company debts. (Ghana Airways is now defunct.) Brought back to Ghana, the jet now serves as a restaurant called La Tante DC 10, known locally as the Green Plane.

Customers board just as they would on an operational vessel, by climbing up a covered stairway. At the top, they are greeted by waitstaff dressed as flight attendants. The first-class seats serve as a waiting area and bar, and the economy section houses the dining room, composed of tables with rows of airplane seats facing each other. (To make room, the plane's capacity was reduced from 380 seats to 118.) While spaghetti and sandwiches are on the menu, the offerings skew largely toward local fare. Under the heading "Proud to Be Ghanaian," the fuselage restaurant offers West African favorites like palm nut soup, jollof rice, guinea fowl, and tilapia. To keep everything as authentic as possible, the restaurant's bathroom is the same tiny one you'd use if the jet was in the air.

How to try it
La Tante DC 10 is located a few minutes away from the terminals at Kotoka International Airport. It's open from noon to 10 p.m.

Before being converted into a restaurant, this plane flew internationally.

SACRED FISHING FRENZY

LAKE ANTOGO • MALI

Fishing is illegal at Lake Antogo except for one day a year, when thousands of men gather at the shore waiting for the gunshot that signals "go." Carrying baskets, the men rush the shallow, muddy lake and capture as many catfish as they can, using just their hands. The scene is dense and chaotic, but it doesn't last long: After about 15 minutes, all the fish in the lake have been scooped up, and the ritual is over for another year.

The Antogo fishing frenzy is a tradition of the Dogon, a Malian ethnic group who inhabit the country's central Mopti region. The Dogon consider the lake sacred because it's a rare oasis in the Sahara, and for a time it provided year-round fishing. Since desertification reduced the lake to its current small size, the annual ritual offers a fair chance for Dogon from all over Mali to come together and capture food from the lake. (Women are prohibited from participating.) The frenzy takes place during the dry season, when the water is low and the fish are easy to capture. After the lake has been emptied, all the fish are presented to an elder from the nearby village of Bamba, who distributes them fairly among the participants.

Once a year, men run into Lake Antogo to catch catfish by hand.

How to try it
The date of the fishing frenzy is determined by the village elders and changes every year, but it generally occurs during May.

GROUNDNUT SNACKS

KULI KULI • NIGERIA

How to try it
You'll most likely find fresh kuli-kuli sold at roadside stands or markets, but you might also find a few packaged brands, such as Kozee, sold in Nigerian grocery stores or online.

In Nigeria, peanuts, colloquially known as groundnuts, form the base for an array of crunchy snacks called kuli-kuli. Every shape of kuli-kuli is made from the same labor-intensive mixture: Peanuts are dry-roasted, stone-ground into a paste, and then mixed with ginger, chicken bouillon, chilies, and other spices. To give the deeply savory snack its iconic crunch, the paste is pressed to remove any excess oil before being formed into its many iterations—skinny sticks, nugget morsels, flat cakes, rings, spirals, noodles—and deep-fried. Kuli-kuli is generally eaten plain or with a sprinkle of sugar. Broken up, it makes a topping for salad or yogurt. Because the peanut-rich fritter is high in protein and fat, it can also be dropped into a blender to pump up a protein shake.

AN ISLAND MADE OF CLAMSHELLS

FADIOUTH • SENEGAL

How to try it
From Joal, the lively fishing village packed with brightly painted pirogues (traditional wooden boats), Fadiouth can be reached by a 1,312-foot (400 m) wooden bridge or by boat. On Sundays, there is a Catholic mass.

Fadiouth, attached by bridge to the mainland fishing village of Joal, is considered a man-made island because it's formed primarily from clamshells. For hundreds of years, the inhabitants of Joal-Fadiouth, as the area is known, dined on clams and threw their shells into the water just off the busy fishing port. The shells' slow accumulation, held together by the roots of baobab and mangrove trees—along with subsequent intentional shell construction—has created an awe-inspiring land mass built from millions of tiny natural pieces that glint white and pearly in the sun.

Apart from being a literal island of shells, Fadiouth has another special claim: In a country that is 90 percent Muslim, the shell island's residents are 90 percent Christian and 10 percent Muslim, and the two live together in harmony. One of the main draws of Fadiouth is the cemetery where people of both faiths are buried side by side, set against a panoramic view of the water. Today, the penchant for natural construction has not been lost: In the afternoons, when the tide is low, women can be seen collecting the shells of mussels, oysters, and clams, which will eventually become building material on the islands.

Fadiouth's cemetery, built from shells.

SENEGALESE EGGROLLS

NEM • SENEGAL

During the French Indochina War (1946–1954), France sent more than 50,000 West African soldiers—recruited from various colonies—to what is now Vietnam, Cambodia, and Laos. Many of these soldiers were Senegalese, and the corps became known as tirailleurs sénégalais ("Senegalese riflemen").

While stationed in Vietnam, some Senegalese soldiers married local women, about a hundred of whom accompanied their husbands back to Senegal after the French were defeated. The tight-knit community of women set up stalls in Dakar's downtown food market, where, among other dishes, they fried nem—small Vietnamese spring rolls filled with glass noodles and ground meat or shrimp.

Today, nem are everywhere in Senegal, sold streetside throughout the city and at countless restaurants. But despite the ubiquity of the spring rolls, Dakar's old-timers say the quality has declined in recent years because most of the community linked directly to Vietnam has passed away. But those who remember the original rolls say that Saveurs d'Asie, a local chain owned by the son of a Vietnamese immigrant, is one of the few remaining outposts still frying up the real deal.

How to try it

Saveurs d'Asie is a small chain with four outposts across Dakar. Le Dragon, one of Senegal's oldest Vietnamese restaurants, has a section on its menu especially for nem.

REGION OF WONDER

Asmara, Eritrea

The local spice blend berbere gives Eritrean spaghetti sauce a fiery kick.

I n 1939, more than half the population of Asmara, the Eritrean capital, was Italian. The African city was the seat of Mussolini's colonialist expansion into Africa, and he encouraged Italians to move to what he called La Piccola Roma, or "Little Rome." Mussolini brought in top Italian architects who erected art deco- and Futurist-style cinemas, cafés, and villas—hundreds of which still stand today. When the Italians left in the 1940s, control shifted to the British and then the Ethiopians, until finally Eritrea gained its independence in 1991. There is little tourism and no free press, which means the capital's wide, bicycle-filled boulevards and modernist buildings, in varying states of beauty and disrepair, are rarely seen by outsiders. (In 2017, Asmara became a UNESCO World Heritage Site, making it the first modernist city to receive the accolade and the preservation assistance that comes with it.) Beyond the architecture, the cuisine of this time-capsule city—which traditionally features boldly spiced, aromatic stews and curries—was also marked by Italian influence. Many Italian staples have

been folded into Eritrean cuisine—some of them remaining faithful to the traditions of the European colonizers, some of them taking on an Eritrean twist.

Spaghetti al sugo e berbere is the Eritrean take on the Italian classic. Tomato sauce is laced with the local spice mixture berbere, which includes chili peppers, ginger, nigella, and fenugreek. The fiery powder, which makes an appearance in many Eritrean dishes, is also

commonly melted into butter for a simple, spicy spaghetti sauce. In Asmara, berbere-spiced spaghetti can be eaten with your fingers using a piece of injera, the local crepe-like bread and universal carb.

Lasagna is a ubiquitous Asmara party food, especially prevalent during the holidays. (The sweet Italian Christmas bread panettone is also traditional.) Recipes hail from an older generation who worked in the homes and business of Italians,

A man buying breakfast pastries for sale at a café in Asmara.

The Fiat Tagliero service station, built by Italian engineer Giuseppe Pettazzi in 1938.

picking up culinary knowledge along the way. Over the years, Eritrean lasagna has morphed into a dish that accommodates local ingredients: less cheese, more berbere-spiced beef (never pork). The cheese is generally mozzarella or cheddar, rarely ricotta, and the final casserole has a spicy, meaty density unique to the Eritrean lasagna-making tradition.

Coffee is served ceremonially in most of Eritrea: Hosts roast the beans by hand, grind them with a mortar and pestle, brew the coffee in a special clay pot, and then serve it in three leisurely rounds. In Asmara, coffee culture skews more Italian, and java is enjoyed quick and small as espresso-based drinks at any of the numerous bars around the city. The machines are old, with the same Eritrean baristas manning

the machines for years. Along with coffee, the clientele enjoys the pastries they inherited from the Italians, like cream-filled, flaky sfogliatella.

A Gaggia espresso machine at Asmara's Bar Impero.

FALSE BANANA

ENSETE • ETHIOPIA

How to try it
Kocho is easily found in the Gurage region in southwestern Ethiopia and in the country's capital, Addis Ababa. If you find kocho outside Ethiopia, it will generally have been pit-fermented in the traditional manner before being exported.

The ensete looks like a banana plant, is harvested like a root vegetable, and tastes like flatbread. It's a cousin of the banana, but this plant's inedible fruit is nothing like that sweet yellow berry (banana is indeed a berry). Betrayed by the ensete's misleading appearance, English speakers named it the "false banana." But the fruit is not what makes the ensete worth planting.

The most prized part of the ensete is the starchy pith inside the plant's pseudo-stem and corm—the bulbous organ that grows underground, at the stem's base. In order to harvest the pith, the entire plant must be pried from the dirt and dismantled by hand. The corm and stem are scraped with a bamboo hand tool to collect the white fleshy pith, which is then combined with yeast, buried in a pit lined with ensete leaves, covered with more leaves and rocks, and left to ferment for at least three months and up to two years (it gets better with age). The subterranean fermentation yields a doughy paste, called kocho, that is made into porridge, drinks, and most commonly a flat, bread-like disk that's also called kocho. Kocho bread can be eaten in its pure, sticky form, or it can be toasted to a crispy, cracker-like texture.

Although almost unknown outside Ethiopia, ensetes are a staple crop for roughly 20 million people in the country's southwestern region. The plant's ubiquity, utility, and nutritional value make it a critical commodity. The plants can be harvested throughout the year, which provides a buffer against famine when seasonal crops fail. Fermented ensete paste is sold and traded at market, and ensete pits are regarded as commercial assets. After the dismantling and pulping process, the tough leftover fiber is turned into ropes, mats, and sacks—making ensete a plant that provides just about everything but bananas.

A Dorze woman preparing traditional bread, called kocho, from the ensete plant.

BEER, WINE, AND SODA MIX

TURBO • ETHIOPIA

Walk into any dive bar in the Ethiopian capital, Addis Ababa, and you're likely to see a group of jubilant souls sitting around a jug of turbo, a perennial favorite among locals who want their booze cheap and potent.

Turbo is simple to prepare: Take a plastic jug and pour in a bottle of local white wine (typically the Awash brand), a large bottle of local Bedele Special beer (look for the spider monkey on the front), and a bottle of Sprite. The large-format cocktail is part of the Ethiopian culinary tradition of spris, the Amharic word for "mix." Spris applies to cocktails (red wine and Coca-Cola is another favorite), but the concept extends far beyond the bar. Order a spris in an Ethiopian café and you'll get a cup that is half tea and half coffee. A spris in a juice shop will be a seasonal mix of three freshly squeezed fruits. But none of these spris will get you dancing as fast as turbo, which is light, sweet, and notoriously drinkable.

How to try it

Jambo House in Addis Ababa is a sweaty and riotous underground bar known for its dance scene and free-flowing jugs of turbo.

ETHIOPIAN BEEF TARTARE

KITFO • ETHIOPIA

If you visit one of Ethiopia's kitfo houses, you will notice that the menu offers just one dish: kitfo, finely ground, lean raw beef mixed with a clarified herb butter called kibbeh and a spicy chili blend called mitmita. The beef is almost always grassfed, which provides maximum herbal, meaty flavor and a smooth, unctuous texture that requires almost no chewing. The glistening beef is typically served with gomen (collard greens), ayib (Ethiopian cheese), and a piece of injera (spongy sourdough flatbread) that is meant to be used as a delivery vessel.

There are risks associated with eating kitfo, including worms, so butchers often take the meat from between the shoulders of an ox because it's traditionally thought to be a worm-free part of the body. In Ethiopia, raw meat is an important, often celebratory food. Another dish, tere siga, translates as "raw meat," and it is exactly that: a slab of uncooked meat, generally beef, cut into pieces and dipped in mitmita.

Ethiopian children are generally allowed to eat raw meat at around the age of five or six, when their systems are deemed strong enough to defend against foodborne illness. But old or young, some never develop a taste for it, which is why kitfo can also be slightly cooked, in a preparation known as lebleb.

How to try it

Yohannes Kitfo, a restaurant in Addis Ababa, is famous for the dish. A serving costs about $6 and serves two or three people.

A plate of kitfo with typical side dishes, collard greens and cheese.

LAST OF THE WILD ARABICA PLANTS

MANYATE COFFEE VILLAGE • ETHIOPIA

How to try it

Bale Mountains National Park is located 250 miles (402 km) southeast of Addis Ababa. Directions are available on the park website.

Protected within Bale Mountains National Park is Harenna Forest, a tangle of dense greenery hidden beneath the shroud of often-present, low-lying clouds. Ethiopia is the birthplace of coffee, and within this forest are some of the world's last wild coffee plants.

Most people have never tasted wild coffee, and they probably never will: According to a 2017 study, the wild plants are at a "high risk of extinction" in the next few decades, largely due to climate change's negative effects on coffee-growing land. For now, arabica flourishes in the high-elevation, mountainous reaches of the Harenna Forest, where massive, mossy trees provide the shade that the wild plants need. About 3,000 farmers living in the area depend on the crop, known as "forest coffee," for income. The plants produce bright-red fruit, called cherries, which harvesters collect and then spread out on frames to dry naturally beneath the sun. The wild coffee they gather has not been well studied, and its wildness has been a subject of beguiling speculation among many coffee professionals, who believe the forest holds more than a hundred untapped varieties of arabica.

At Manyate Coffee Village, situated on Harenna's southern edge, you can sample a cup of wild coffee. Residents of Manyate have established a community group, known as the Sankate Association, to better develop the forest's small-scale industries. Sankate's coffeehouse offers traditional Ethiopian coffee ceremonies, and during harvest season, guests can pluck their own ripened coffee cherries.

Gushuralle Peak in Ethiopia's Harenna Forest.

The Controversy of Caffeine

Caffeine is the most commonly consumed psychoactive drug in the world. Despite scientific evidence that caffeine is habit-forming, performance-enhancing, harmful in large doses, and difficult to quit, it goes unregulated around the world. But caffeine wasn't always universally accepted. Catholics once deemed the drink "satanic" because of its association with Islam and Mecca, and 17th-century sultan Murad IV was known to dress as a commoner and walk the streets of Constantinople decapitating subjects he found drinking coffee. Since then punishment has eased, but caffeine still has its detractors.

MORMONS: The Doctrine and Covenants, one of the scriptures of Mormonism, contains a section called the "Word of Wisdom" in which God delivers a revelation to Joseph Smith about what Mormons are allowed to eat. "Strong drinks" (which Mormons agree means alcoholic beverages) were expressly forbidden, and tobacco was banned unless used medicinally. But what was the meaning of the third prohibited item, "hot drinks"? Coffee and tea, literally hot, were removed from the Mormon diet, but this linguistic ambiguity incited a debate about whether or not caffeine was the offensive "hot" (i.e., stimulating) substance. Some Mormons avoid caffeine altogether and, until 2012, the sale of all caffeinated drinks, including sodas, was banned on the campus of the predominantly Mormon Brigham Young University. In the 1970s, Brigham Young University students hid a secret "black market" Coke machine in the theater department, which had to be moved regularly to avoid detection. Since then, the university has loosened its stance on soda, but the issue is far from resolved. During the 2012 US presidential election, Mormon candidate Mitt Romney caused a media stir when he drank a Diet Coke on camera and confessed to enjoying a scoop of coffee ice cream.

NAZIS: The Third Reich championed decaf coffee so heartily that you might think it was an Aryan health drink. The nonstimulant brew was the invention of Ludwig Roselius, a German national and aspiring Nazi. After his father's death, which he attributed to the overconsumption of coffee, the inventor figured out how to remove caffeine from coffee beans. (Many reports claim his discovery was accidental.) Roselius patented his invention in 1905 and marketed it as a luxury good and healthy coffee alternative.

The Nazis bit, and decaf drinks became state policy, served at Nazi festivals and Hitler Youth camps. Despite their fondness for his coffee, however, the Nazis twice denied Roselius membership in their party. But inventor and invention did just fine, with the drink soon hitting shelves across the world as Sanka, short for "sans caffeine."

OLYMPIC ATHLETES: Before 2004, if an Olympian tested positive for high levels of caffeine, they risked being ejected from competition. This was not an empty threat: In 1972, Mongolian judo silver medalist Bakaava Buidaa was stripped of his title for excessive caffeine. The World Anti-Doping Agency considers caffeine, at high levels, to be a performance enhancer that improves speed and stamina. As innocuous as coffee seems, studies have shown that caffeinated athletes do indeed perform better—showing about a 1 to 2 percent improvement, running slightly faster and jumping slightly higher. Throughout the years, the upper limit for caffeine has vacillated between 12 and 15 micrograms per liter of urine, which is a lot, approximately the equivalent of six to eight cups of coffee consumed within a few hours. A threshold this high, many argue, should separate the casual drinkers from the caffeine dopers, but it's still contentious territory because all bodies process the stimulant at different rates, making the line between cappuccinos and cheating a moving target.

FUTURISTIC CLIFF RESTAURANT

BEN ABEBA • ETHIOPIA

How to try it

Ben Abeba is open from 7 a.m. to 10 p.m. General manager Habtamu Baye also operates a local transportation company that can arrange transfers to the restaurant from local hotels.

Lalibela is a holy city and a UNESCO World Heritage Site, famous for its 12th-century churches cut into the rock of the Earth. A short walk away you'll find another architectural stunner: Ben Abeba, a snail shell of a building that looks like a spaceship that landed on a rock. Perched high on a hill on the north side of town, the restaurant has been compared to everything from a bouquet of flowers to a futuristic amusement park ride.

Ben Abeba was the dream of owner Susan Aitchison, a retired home economics professor who came to Ethiopia from her native Scotland, initially to help a friend set up a school. Faced with leaving Lalibela, she opted to stay and open a restaurant with her Lalibelian business partner, Habtamu Baye. Aitchison worked with local architects to bring her vision to life. They built a central spiral staircase that leads to multiple levels of curved open-air decks, each of them offering unobstructed views of the breathtaking river valley below.

The award-winning restaurant serves a menu of traditional Ethiopian dishes and Western fare, sometimes combining the two. Ben Abeba prides itself on being eco-friendly and community-minded: The restaurant has planted 50,000 trees in the valley around the restaurant, trains young Ethiopians looking to become food service professionals, and sources local ingredients, many of which are grown in the garden on the premises.

ALL-OUT MEAT EXTRAVAGANZA

CARNIVORE RESTAURANT • KENYA

How to try it
Carnivore is near Nairobi's Wilson Airport on Langata Road. The "Beast of a Feast" dinner, which comes with unlimited meat and an array of accompaniments, costs 3,600 Kenyan shillings, or about $36.

Enter Carnivore, twice named one of the world's 50 best restaurants by *Restaurant Magazine*, and you'll be faced with a giant roasting pit, where traditional Maasai swords are laden with hunks of meaty goodness from just about every animal that's not on the endangered species list: beef, lamb, pork, chicken, turkey, camel, crocodile, ostrich, ox, and more.

After guests are seated and introduced to a double-decker revolving tray of sauces, servers swarm them, swords in hand, offering a cut of whatever strikes the customer's fancy. The meat is unlimited, and visitors are encouraged to eat until they can take no more, signaling their surrender by lowering a white flag provided for them in the center of the table. Servers will then bring around dessert and coffee to those who are up to the challenge.

Besides the meat extravaganza, Carnivore also offers a concert venue, gardens, a playground for children, an events area, an African heritage gallery, and believe it or not, a vegetarian menu. The decor is indoor/outdoor, with tropical plants and streams weaving around tables. For your birthday, the staff will even gather around your table with drums and sing the Kenyan song "Jambo Bwana," sometimes called "Hakuna Matata" (no relation to the song from *The Lion King*).

At Carnivore Restaurant, meat is roasted on Maasai swords.

FERMENTED RUNNER'S MILK

MURSIK • KENYA

How to try it
Mursik can be found in small restaurants around the high-elevation city of Eldoret (also known as the "home of heroes") in western Kenya.

Kenyans have a reputation for dominating long-distance footraces. When the heroes and heroines return to their villages after winning trophies and breaking world records, the first part of their congratulatory reception is often a sip of mursik, a traditional fermented milk.

Mursik is an integral part of the culture and heritage of the Kalenjin community, which has produced many of Kenya's renowned runners, and the tangy fermented milk has become synonymous with the country's athletics. With a history tracing back more than 300 years, the drink likely began as a way to preserve milk during times of surplus production. To make mursik, dairy farmers boil milk (typically from cows, but sometimes from goats or sheep) and, once it has cooled, pour it into a calabash gourd, known as a sotet, that has been lined with charcoal from local tannin-rich trees. (In the past, animal blood was also sometimes added to the milk.) The gourd is sealed and then stored in a cool, dry place for at least three days to allow the milk to ferment.

The charcoal in the sotet imparts a unique smoky flavor and a bluish color, which is of high aesthetic value to Kenyan connoisseurs of mursik. The fermented milk should be smooth and sour, but the flavor can vary significantly because it's heavily dependent on which tree bark is used and the quality of the original milk.

Pantry Staple

MILK

Whether produced by humans or barnyard animals, milk has earned a reputation for being nature's perfect food, which makes it an ideal substance for intrepid marketing, weird science, and unconventional applications.

Skim Milk

Before World War II, skim milk was nothing more than a pesky by-product of making butter. The cloudy liquid waste was fed to farm animals or cast into nearby creeks, where it would eventually clog the waterways, sour, and attract swarms of flies. By the 1920s, American dairy towns smelled like the spoiled contents of an unplugged refrigerator, or the preferred term at the time, "dairy air." Instead of investing in expensive industrial sanitation, dairy producers partnered with organic chemists to turn the by-product into something drinkable. The result: skim milk. First released as a powder, skim got a lucky break from a wartime contract that sent tons of powdered milk to the front lines. When the war ended, the former dairy waste got a second makeover. Fresh skim milk was repositioned as "diet milk," the best way to stay slim and healthy—a reputation that remains to this day.

Animal Wet Nurses

Mythological brothers Romulus and Remus are classically portrayed beneath a she-wolf, suckling at her teats. While the image is meant to bestow a kind of folkloric ferocity to the founding of Rome, animals nursing human babies is not hyperbole. When a mother in ancient Europe was short of milk, or a baby was abandoned by its mother, nursing was sometimes outsourced to a lactating animal. In southern Africa, the Khoikhoi people were known to strap their babies to the bellies of goats, where they would drink directly from the animal. In the 18th and 19th centuries, with the rise of syphilis, goats were sometimes more sanitary than people: European foundling hospitals of that era used skilled goats as wet nurses, training them to stretch above the infants in their cribs in order to bring milk straight to their mouths.

Milk, trusted and beloved for centuries, has become inherently good in the minds of many.

Kumiss

Even Genghis Khan was raised on milk. The storied horseman drank the traditional fermented milk of the Central Asian steppes called kumiss, made by agitating the sugar-rich milk of a mare until the liquid is acidified and slightly alcoholic, and tastes like a cross between sparkling wine and sour cream. Without this fermentation, mare's milk contains so much lactose that it is essentially a laxative. During Genghis's day, kumiss was often agitated in a horsehide container strapped to a galloping horse, but today's kumiss makers churn the milk in a vat or barrel, much like butter. In Central Asia, a bowl of kumiss is not only a gesture of hospitality but a cure for whatever ails you. This reputation gave rise to "kumiss cure" resorts—medicinal lodges tucked high in the mountains, where visitors ranging from wellness vacationers to the terminally ill come to drink fresh kumiss by the gallon in the hope of purifying their bodies.

Competitive Milk Weight Gain

To celebrate their new year, the Bodi tribe of Ethiopia selects an unmarried man from each of their 14 clans to compete in the Ka'el Ceremony, or "Ceremony of Fat Men." The contestants seclude themselves for six months, gorging on a mixture of cow's milk and blood, in an attempt to gain as much weight as possible. The cow is sacred to the Bodi, and the mixture of the animal's vital secretions is a cherished food source. On the day of the competition, the men emerge from their huts, substantially heavier, prepared to compete in physical and acrobatic challenges. Naked and smeared with clay and ashes, the men run for hours under the watchful eye of the village elders. The most impressive man is crowned "Fat Man of the Year" and becomes a village hero.

Participants in the Ka'el Ceremony spend six months gaining weight before the big day.

THE OBSCURE LANGUAGE OF THE
Lake Kivu Fishermen

Most nights, just before sunset, a group of fishermen emerge from the green terraced hills of Kibuye, Rwanda, get in their boats, and paddle toward the center of Lake Kivu, an idyllic lake shared by Rwanda and the Democratic Republic of Congo. They set out in teams of three boats, attached by long eucalyptus rods that the fishermen cross like balance beams. Beneath the boats, they stretch a net for catching sambaza—a small fish similar in taste to tilapia but resembling a sardine—and light gas lanterns. The bright, winking light attracts the fish to the boats and creates a nightly spectacle on the horizon.

While working, some men sing in Amashi, the language that practically marks them as fishermen. The little-used language is spoken ubiquitously on Lake Kivu, where most everyone is a fisherman, and is taught Amashi by family members. (Rwanda's national language is Kinyarwanda, which is spoken by 93 percent of the population.) Most believe the language is a product of the shared border between Rwanda and the Democratic Republic of Congo. Amashi is a language from the Abashi people of Eastern Congo, historically located around Bukavu, a bustling Congolese city on the southern tip of Lake Kivu that borders Rwanda. Amashi, however, is no longer the predominant language in Bukavu, though it's alive and well on both sides of the border that divides Lake Kivu. The dialect changes around the lake, but if an outsider wants to learn the fishing trade, they must also learn some basic Amashi.

When the nets are set and the lanterns lit, the sun dips low and the fishermen relax. They have several hours until it is time to pull the nets—the first pull of several they make each night. When it's time to haul the catch, they communicate, of course, in Amashi.

Concerned about Amashi's potential disappearance, some fishermen have recorded amasare, or work songs of the fishermen. They use these songs most when paddling out, singing in unison as they set up. A different member of the crew leads each night, favoring their treasured melodies, some of which incorporate intricate harmonies and whistles. Although the lyrics change, "be mighty" features frequently, as does "may God watch over us." Some songs include exultations of God, and prayers for family and fish. When a fisherman slowly starts to sing, everyone quickly joins in.

DROPLET CHILI OIL

AKABANGA • RWANDA

Bright orange and flaming hot, Akabanga is so spicy that workers are required to wear face masks while making it. The Rwandan hot sauce is generally packaged in small plastic eyedropper bottles to keep dosages under tight control. With a heat rating of more than 150,000 Scoville units, a single drop is a good place to start. (For comparison, jalapeños score about 5,000 on the Scoville heat chart.)

In the past few decades, this fiery sauce has garnered a cult following, but its rise to fame was largely unintentional. In the early 1980s, a young Rwandan vendor named Sina Gerard was selling mandazi (fried savory doughnuts) from his roadside stand. To help his snacks stand out, he decided to make a condiment to serve with them: a chili oil made from local Scotch bonnet peppers, picked and pressed when ripe and yellow. Gerard named his creation Akabanga, roughly translated from the Kinyarwanda language to mean "secret," in reference to the beguiling hit of heat. Earthy, smoky, and painfully addictive, the chili oil soon had customers flocking to his stand. Today, Akabanga is Rwanda's iconic and ubiquitous spicy condiment, and the travel-size eyedropper bottles are commonly kept, at the ready, in purses and pockets.

How to try it

Akabanga is sold in convenience stores in Kigali, Rwanda's capital, or it can be ordered online.

····· FOOD PIONEER ·····

SINA GERARD

b. 1963

Sina Gerard's first enterprise was a roadside stand where he sold bread and doughnuts he baked himself. He then expanded into fresh juice from his family's orchard. And then came Akabanga, the hot sauce that became a runaway hit and bankrolled the rest of his endeavors.

Today, the self-made millionaire is described as a "pig farmer, timber trader, bakery owner, supermarket owner, spice maker, and philanthropist." His myriad businesses are all run within Rwanda because he is devoted to building his country's economy. Self-taught and self-made, Gerard is known to apply eccentric methodology to his enterprises. At his piggery, for example, he plays music on speakers mounted to the wooden beams of the sty (a mix of R&B, rap, and local hits). He says the music keeps the pigs happy and makes them more productive. To prove it, he set up a control group of pigs without music, and indeed, those pigs did not feed, mate, or deliver piglets with the same

ease and pace. Instead of staple crops, Gerard experiments with higher-earning produce like strawberries, apples, and grapes for wine. (He also makes banana wine.)

The hot-sauce millionaire circulates his money, knowledge, and agricultural innovations within the country that made him rich. His central objective is to help his fellow Rwandans, 75 percent of whom are engaged in farming. To that end, he gives out seeds and fertilizer to local farmers, teaches them to grow the crops, and then purchases what they grow. Much of this gets processed into higher-value products at his factories.

Gerard himself still lives in his hometown of Nyirangarama, having built his business headquarters on the same land where he once slung doughnuts from a stand. He constructed the town's first school, which is free, and hopes the students will come to work for him. Akabanga, his celebrity hot sauce, is still made in Nyirangarama—now in industrial quantities.

LAST OF THE INDEPENDENT MILK BARS

KURUHIMBI • RWANDA

How to try it

Kuruhimbi is located at KN 204 St. 14. The bar is cash only. The hours are inconsistent; typically, it's open every day from 6:30 a.m. to 9:00 p.m., but that is dependent on how many customers are in the bar at any given time.

Kuruhimbi is one of Kigali's most popular bars, and it doesn't serve a drop of liquor. Instead, milk is on tap. Located in the city's Kimisagara neighborhood, Kuruhimbi is a milk bar, a Rwandan stalwart, and one of the last of its kind.

Inside, frothy cups of milk are poured from a big metal drum and served hot or cold. Ikivuguto, a thick fermented milk similar to probiotic yogurt, is one of Kuruhimbi's specialties, and locals swear that the bar brews the best in the city. Condiments—honey, sugar, and cocoa powder—are readily available.

The bar seats no more than ten people at a time, but customers pop in and out quickly, just long enough to throw back a half liter of milk or fill up a jerry can for takeout. Kuruhimbi is one of the community watering holes, and many nearby residents spend late mornings and afternoons chatting in the shop. The owners have lived in the neighborhood for decades, and they source Kuruhimbi's milk from farms just outside Kigali's city limits.

Milk bars are unique to Rwanda. When rural citizens left their cows behind as they took up urban life, the milk bar was born as a way to keep Rwandans connected to their dairy heritage.

Independent Kigali milk bars, once ubiquitous, are slowly being replaced by Inyange Milk Zones, a sterile, government-backed chain. Kuruhimbi is one of just a few operational neighborhood milk bars still standing.

WEDDING CAMEL JERKY

MUQMAD • SOMALILAND

How to try it

Muqmad can be bought at the market in Hargeisa, the capital city of Somaliland, but to try your hand at the xeedho, you'll have to marry into a northern Somali family.

Muqmad is the Somali version of jerky, made by slicing meat into thin strips, hanging the strips out to dry in the sun, then chopping the meat into cubes and deep-frying them into salty, chewy morsels that can keep for more than a year. Typically made from camel (but sometimes beef), muqmad began as a preservation method for Somali nomad communities and is now a symbolic part of many northern Somali wedding ceremonies.

To dress up camel jerky for a wedding, muqmad is placed in a xeedho, a wood-and-leather container prepared by the bride's family. The vessel, which represents the bride, is then wrapped in white cloth, bound by intricately knotted rope, and given as a gift to the groom and his family. On the seventh day after the wedding, members of both families gather for the opening of the xeedho, and a relative of the groom is tasked with untying the knots. If the relative fails, the bride's family has the power to claim her back, and the reputation of the groom and his clan will suffer. If successfully opened, the xeedho reveals another, smaller container made of mashed and hardened dates, which in turn contains the muqmad. The jerky is distributed to the guests, along with parts of the date container, and only then can the marriage be truly celebrated.

BAOBAB SEED CANDY

UBUYU · TANZANIA

When you've been snacking on ubuyu, Zanzibar's favorite baobab candy, the evidence is left on your red-stained tongue, lips, and fingernails. To make the candy, the nutrient-rich seeds of the baobab tree, which have a natural citrus kick, are coated in red-dyed sugar syrup that's laced with salt, black pepper, cardamom, and vanilla. As you suck on the candies, the morsels give off alternating bursts of sour, spicy, and sweet. The ride is over when you reach the seed, which should be spit from your bright-red mouth.

How to try it
Babu Issa is a famous ubuyu producer that sells cups of candied seeds throughout the islands of Unguja and Pemba, as well as on mainland Tanzania. A 300-gram (10.5 oz.) serving goes for 1,000 Tanzanian shillings (about 44 cents).

HIGH TIDE ISLAND RESTAURANT

THE ROCK · TANZANIA

Once the site of a fisherman's post, The Rock restaurant sits perched atop its namesake, just off the eastern coast of Unguja Island in the Zanzibar archipelago. At low tide, the raised eatery hovers above the sand on Michamvi Pingwe beach. At high tide, water rushes beneath and the restaurant becomes an island. Depending on the time of day, guests arrive on foot or by boat.

A wooden staircase leads up to The Rock, a small structure with 12 cozy tables beneath a makuti (palm tree leaf) roof. Diners enjoy unobstructed views of the Indian Ocean; during high tide, the back patio is surrounded by turquoise water on three sides. The restaurant serves lunch and dinner, so visitors can time their meal reservations to match the desired tide level.

The menu is largely European-inspired, with local seafood and house-made pasta, but the restaurant also aims to impart the flavors of Zanzibar and the surrounding region in every dish. The fish carpaccio is served with coconut, lime, and chili pepper. Most desserts come topped with "Zanzibar spices" ice cream. The beef, spices, and vegetables are all farmed nearby.

While dining at The Rock is exponentially more expensive than dining elsewhere in Zanzibar, the restaurant sponsors the Kichanga Foundation, an organization that teaches community members to swim and focuses on sustainability programs like waste sorting and recycling.

How to try it
The Rock offers two lunch seatings (at noon or 2 p.m.) and two dinner seatings (at 4 p.m. or 6 p.m.), both by reservation only.

OVERSTUFFED CREPE BOAT

ZANZIBAR PIZZA • TANZANIA

How to try it

Prices range from 4,000 Tanzanian shillings ($2.00) for a basic vegetarian pizza to up to 15,000 shillings ($7.50) for a mixed seafood pizza. The Forodhani Night Market is a good place to find them.

A cook prepares Zanzibar pizza in Stone Town's Forodhani Gardens.

Pizza purists may balk at a dish that veers so far from the original, but on the Tanzanian islands of Unguja and Pemba, "Zanzibar pizza" is a loose interpretation made with pride. More like a mash-up of a crepe and a savory pancake, these tasty fried pockets of dough house a dizzying array of fillings. Avocado with squid and tomatoes. Lobster with cheese. Vegetables with egg and mayo. Snickers with banana and Nutella. Anything is possible with a Zanzibar pizza.

Vendors flatten a ball of dough, layer on a second smaller piece of dough to reinforce it, and then pile on as many meats, sweets, spices, and vegetables as the customer desires. After folding up the sides, they fry the pizza in clarified butter on a hot tava (a large flat or concave frying pan). When the fillings are hot and the crust crispy, the pizza is slid onto a paper plate and smothered with fresh, spicy mango-chili sauce.

You can find at least 30 Zanzibar pizza spots on Unguja and Pemba. It's a popular late-night snack said to have been invented nearly 30 years ago by a cook, Haji Hamisi, who traveled to Mombasa and was inspired by the Kenyan city's famous egg chapati (a stuffed, pan-fried meat omelet). Zanzibar pizza is also similar to Nairobi's mkate wa nyama (meat bread) and the mutabbaq (stuffed grilled pancakes) made in Saudi Arabia, Iraq, Yemen, and India—but Zanzibar's version sets itself apart with its local sauce, meshing of styles, and unrestricted stuffing combinations.

ROLLED EGGS

ROLEX • UGANDA

How to try it

The city of Kampala holds an annual Rolex Festival in August, where thousands of rolex fans gather to enjoy rolled eggs of all sizes and flavors.

Step up to a street stand in Uganda, say "roll eggs" as fast as you can, and you'll get a rolex—the ubiquitous omelet whose name arose from a misunderstanding. A rolex is exactly what the original name implies: a beaten egg cooked flat on a charcoal-heated skillet, rolled up in a freshly griddled chapati, and served blistering hot. The rolex vendor, often beneath a colorful umbrella, will have some omelet additions on hand, like onions, tomatoes, and cabbage. But if you're near a market and have something special, like an avocado, in your basket, obliging vendors will fold your shopping into the eggs and make a deluxe, personalized rolex. In Uganda, omelets are eaten throughout the day and into the night, and rolex is often available until dawn.

Reviving the Almost Lost Art of Bigwala Gourd Trumpets

Bigwala is the music of the Basoga kingdom, one of the traditional monarchies of Uganda. In the local Lusoga language, *Bigwala* is an all-encompassing term, referring to the dance that accompanies the music, the music itself, and the instruments—five differently sized trumpets fashioned from gourds that were nearly lost to history.

For centuries, Bigwala trumpets were considered royal instruments, their joyful sound played at any important event for the Basoga kingdom. But Bigwala was also a music for the people, and performances invited participation: Men thumped on drums, creating a beat for the smooth, deep blast of the trumpets as women danced in a circle around them.

But in 1966, Ugandan prime minister Milton Obote imposed a new constitution that, in an effort to unify the country, abolished the kingdoms and banned Bigwala. The traditional monarchs were demonized, and those playing the king's music were arrested. Bigwala performers went into hiding, and their music largely disappeared. By the time President Yoweri Museveni restored the kingdoms in the 1990s, royal musical traditions were on the brink of extinction.

In 2005, a Ugandan academic named James Isabirye made it his mission to revive the tradition among the younger generation. Isabirye won Bigwala a spot on UNESCO's List of Intangible Cultural Heritage in Need of Urgent Safeguarding. Working with elderly musicians, Isabirye set out to teach young people to play the trumpets, but he quickly ran into a problem: The seeds needed to grow the gourds to make the trumpets were lost.

Isabirye organized community leaders to search the country for the seeds. They looked and looked, farther and farther, traveling hundreds of miles by motorbike, until they found an old woman with a gourd on her fireplace—the exact type of gourd they were looking for. Inside were 36 seeds, which were planted and grew to produce the first new generation of trumpets.

As of 2013, only four master practitioners of Bigwala were still alive. But since 2015, with support from UNESCO, more than a hundred young people from different villages in the Busoga region have been trained in making gourd trumpets and performing Bigwala music. (Gourds are grown to maturity, gently dried above a fireplace for a month, and then glued to form trumpets of various lengths.) The new generation of Bigwala players has performed at coronation anniversaries and other events to mark Kyabazinga (King) Day. Against all odds, young Ugandans are taking up an ancient musical tradition that was once in danger of losing its instruments.

Musician James Lugolole (left) and friend with Bigwala gourd instruments.

THE WORLD'S LARGEST EDIBLE MUSHROOM

TERMITOMYCES TITANICUS • ZAMBIA

In Zambia, where mushroom gathering is a part of life, *Termitomyces titanicus* is especially beloved. *T. titanicus* is the world's largest edible mushroom, with a cap that can reach more than 3 feet (91 cm) in width. The genus name, *Termitomyces*, refers to where the mushroom grows—inside a termite hill. These fungi have a symbiotic relationship with the insects: They grow on termites' fecal matter and in turn break down plant material for the termites to eat. (Termites also chomp away at decayed mushroom tissue.) The colossal mushrooms have a savory, smoky flavor and meaty texture, and they flourish during the rainy season.

How to try it

The Mutinondo Wilderness Lodge in Kalonje offers mushroom-gathering expeditions, but keep in mind that the mushrooms grow only during the winter rainy season.

SOUTHERN AFRICA

INSECT NEST OVEN

TERMITE MOUND OVENS • BOTSWANA

Termites are prolific builders, constructing dirt mounds that can stand as high as 30 feet (9.1 m). The insects don't actually live inside these structures; the sturdy but porous towers serve as "lungs" for the colonies below, letting carbon dioxide out and oxygen in.

A fire-burning termite mound oven.

In parts of Africa, Australia, and South America, these impressive works of insect architecture double as outdoor ovens for baking bread and pizza. (In the past, they were used to cook meats, from emu to snake.) To turn a termite mound into an oven, first confirm that the mound has been fully abandoned. Then cut a hole at the base of the hill, stuff it with newspaper, light a fire, and wait about 10 minutes for the whole thing to heat up. Toss in a steak and cover up the hole, and in an hour you'll have dinner.

How to try it

African Horseback Safaris in Botswana's Okavango Delta lead horseback tours that include a stop for pizza made in a termite hill oven.

Hunt Like a San
A MARATHON BEFORE DINNER

On hot days in the Kalahari Desert, men of the San tribes will head out on runs of 20 miles (32 km) or more. They are the world's last persistence hunters, engaged in what is likely humanity's first form of hunting. Over the course of a day, they will chase an antelope on foot, literally exhausting their prey to death by covering more ground than a marathon.

The San have long lived in the Kalahari, where they hunt, gather, and live a traditionally seminomadic lifestyle largely governed by the scarcity of water. When San men go out on persistence hunts, they follow a millennia-old playbook:

TIMING: The right time to hunt is when the animal is at its weakest. The hunt always begins in the middle of hot days, when the heat will wear down the animal until it collapses in a panting heap. Other good times are after a full moon, when an animal may be tired from being up all night, or late in the dry season, when there is less to eat.

TRACKING: San hunters are expert trackers. When telltale signs such as a hoofprint or bent blade of grass are absent, they crouch down, imagine themselves as the antelope, and predict its actions.

TOOLS: Hunters carry enough supplies for a night in the bush, including a blanket, firesticks, and water vessels. Their small bows look diminutive, but the arrows are tipped with poison made from the larvae of a local beetle and can bring down a giraffe. Hunters also carry spears. Working in small groups and using hand signals, they usually select a lone hunter to make the final run and spear the exhausted animal after hours of pursuit.

Colonization and environmental neglect have changed the San way of life. Boreholes risk depleting the already limited water supply, ranchers have set up fences that disrupt the once-massive migrations of wildebeest and other animals, and the San have been banned from hunting in many areas. Most persistence hunters are middle aged or older, and they lament that young men are not learning the traditional skills.

WILD DESERT WATERMELON

TSAMMA • NAMIBIA

For the hunter-gatherer San tribe of southern Africa, hunting season is made infinitely better by the wild, desert-growing tsamma melon. It's said that between its nutritious seeds and the high water content of its flesh, a person could survive for six weeks, if not longer, on nothing but tsamma. (The 19th-century missionary and explorer David Livingstone wrote of desert-dwelling tribes he encountered in southern Africa who survived on tsamma for several months.)

The perennial fruit was first domesticated hundreds of years ago in Africa. It's typically pollinated by bees and flies and, once sown in the rainy season, can start to germinate within a week. From the outside, the tsamma looks like a watermelon—which it is. But inside, the flesh is the pale, cool green of a honeydew. Some tsammas taste vaguely sweet, but most are flavorless.

The San use all parts of the tsamma: The flesh is dried and cooked into stews, and the protein-packed seeds are roasted and eaten plain or ground into flour. The seeds are also pressed for their oil, which can be used for cooking and for moisturizing skin, and the melon's leaves can be cooked like spinach.

How to try it
The name *tsamma* refers to the species *Citrullus ecirrhosus*, or Namib tsamma, which grows wild in the Kalahari and Namib Deserts.

A BREAD LOAF STUFFED WITH CURRY

BUNNY CHOW • SOUTH AFRICA

Bunny chow, called a bunny for short, is a hollowed-out chunk of soft white bread filled to the brim with curry. The dish emerged from the large Indian community in Durban, South Africa, but the facts get a bit confused from there. Some say the inventors were the Indians known as banias, or merchants, and that "banias' chow" slipped linguistically into "bunny chow." Others believe Indian sugarcane laborers came up with the cheap, edible way to transport their lunch. Some think it was golf caddies who couldn't break for lunch.

Whichever story you believe, the dish dates back to the mid-20th century, a time when South Africa was racially segregated by apartheid. Beginning in 1948, both Indian and black South Africans were banned from entering many establishments, including restaurants, and bunny chow became a cheap meal that could be passed through a window and required no silverware. (Eating utensils were also segregated into sets for whites and nonwhites.) Over time, bunny chow transitioned into a food ordered out of desire rather than necessity, but its history remains rooted in a dark time of South African history.

Bunny chow is typically ordered based on the protein and the quantity of bread. A "quarter mutton," for example, will get you a quarter loaf filled with mutton curry. The hunk of bread that is scooped out so that the interior of the loaf can be filled with curry is served alongside the order and used for dipping. Using utensils is frowned upon, so these bunnies need to be eaten quickly before the bread becomes too soggy to handle.

How to try it
Canecutters in Durban is a popular bunny chow restaurant. You can order its bunnies by the quarter and half loaf, filled with mutton, chicken, prawn, or vegetarian curry.

MILK TART

MELKTERT • SOUTH AFRICA

How to try it

February 27th is National Melktert Day. Melkterts are available at bakeries across the country, and there are dozens of recipes online. The melktert at Checkers, a South African grocery store chain, gets high marks among the supermarket varieties.

When Dutch colonizers arrived on the Cape of Good Hope in the 17th century, many of them became dairy farmers. They used their milk to make a custard pie called melktert, a now quintessential South African dessert found at supermarkets, bakeries, bake sales, church events, and most every celebration. The combination is simple but timeless: silky, vanilla-scented milk custard poured into a shortcrust or puff pastry shell, chilled, and then dusted with cinnamon before serving. Most recipes are quick and straightforward, but even with such a simple preparation, everyone's family recipe is a little different.

Melktert

Makes 2 tarts

Crusts

5 ounces (142 grams) butter, at room temperature

½ cup (100 grams) sugar

2 eggs

2¼ cups (272 grams) flour

2 teaspoons (8 grams) baking powder

A pinch of salt

Filling

4½ cups (1 kilogram) milk

3 tablespoons (42 grams) butter

3 eggs

¾ cup (150 grams) sugar

3 tablespoons (21 grams) cornstarch

3 tablespoons (23 grams) flour

1 tablespoon (13 grams) vanilla extract

Topping

2 tablespoons (25 grams) sugar

1 teaspoon (2 grams) ground cinnamon

1. Preheat the oven to 400°F (204°C).

2. To make the crusts: Cream together the butter and sugar. Add the eggs and mix well. Add the flour, baking powder, and salt, and stir until the mixture forms a dough. Divide the dough in half

and press each piece into a 9-inch (23-centimeter) pie plate. Prick the crusts all over with a fork. Bake for 10 minutes, then remove from the oven and set aside to cool.

3. To make the filling: Combine the milk and butter in a medium saucepan over medium heat, and heat until the butter melts, stirring often. Allow to cool for 10 minutes.

4. Combine the eggs with the sugar, cornstarch, flour, and vanilla in a large bowl and beat well. Whisking the egg mixture continuously, slowly drizzle in half a cup of the hot milk mixture. Add the rest of the hot milk mixture in this way, half a cup at a time, never forgetting to whisk. (Whisking while slowly adding the hot milk tempers the eggs, allowing you to bring them up in temperature without scrambling them.)

5. Pour the custard mixture into the saucepan you used to heat the milk and set it over medium heat. Cook, whisking constantly, until the custard thickens, about 8 minutes.

6. Pour the thickened custard into the prebaked pie shells. Combine the sugar and cinnamon and sprinkle over the tart as a topping.

7. Allow to cool completely, and then refrigerate.

MOPANE WORMS

AMACIMBI ∘ ZIMBABWE

Like many places in the world, bugs are a hot commodity in Zimbabwe. After the seasonal rains, which arrive between November and January, local families race to harvest the outbreak of mopane "worms"—which are not technically worms, but the caterpillar form of the emperor moth (*Gonimbrasia belina*). The worms spend nearly their entire lives on mopanes, trees with butterfly-shaped leaves that are native to parts of southern Africa. The insects lay their eggs on the tree's leaves, which the larvae gorge on from the moment they hatch. After literally eating until they burst (they molt their skin four or five times), the worms grow to about 4 inches (10 cm) and are ripe for the picking.

The flesh of the mopane worm contains up to three times the amount of protein as an equivalent mass of beef, and a skilled collector can gather between 55 and 110 pounds (25 and 50 kg) of worms each day. Once picked, the worms are pinched open at one end and squeezed to expel a vibrant green mass of half-digested leaves and innards. The empty bodies of the worms are dried and then smoked, roasted, pickled, or fried to the cook's taste. These protein-packed morsels last throughout the year and are vital to the country's economy and nutrition. The flavor varies slightly with the terroir, but the earthy, vegetal taste has a savory element some compare to that of a well-done steak. However, compared to beef, which is among the world's most resource-intensive proteins, mopane worms are exceedingly sustainable, requiring about 6 pounds (3 kg) of mopane leaves to bring 2 pounds (1 kg) of worms to edible maturity.

How to try it
Prepared mopane worms can be found throughout Zimbabwe, especially in the capital city of Harare, where vendors sell them from baskets. Mopane worms can also be ordered online.

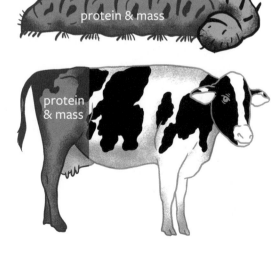

THE MASSIVE FORBIDDEN FRUIT

COCO DE MER • SEYCHELLES

How to try it

Because the coco de mer is endangered, we don't recommend buying products containing it. The Seychelles government allows a small number of (nonedible) seeds to be sold to visitors as souvenirs—they go for hundreds of dollars each. The approved seeds have an anti-counterfeit holographic sticker and an export permit attached. Stores near Anse Lazio beach on the island of Praslin may have them.

The coco de mer, a most unusual palm tree, produces the largest seed of any plant in the world. Weighing up to 60 pounds (27 kg), the seed is also remarkable for its distinctive shape, which resembles a woman's shapely buttocks. In 1881, British general Charles Gordon encountered the sensuous seeds and concluded that the coco de mer was the tree of knowledge, and its seed the original forbidden fruit.

Coco de mer palms are incredibly rare, growing naturally on just two islands in the Seychelles, an archipelago off the coast of East Africa. The International Union for Conservation of Nature (IUCN) classifies the species as endangered. The government strictly monitors these trees, and anyone with a coco de mer palm growing on their land must follow certain rules: The seeds may be given as gifts, traded, or eaten, but money can't be exchanged for the unprocessed seed.

At its best, the coco de mer fruit contains a milky jelly that tastes like a sweet, slightly citrusy coconut with the texture of soft Turkish delight. Alas, this flavor manifests (and passes) before the interior seed reaches maturity, and harvesting the jelly from the young fruit means losing the potential to plant a new coco de mer tree. As a result, few have tasted the fresh natural jelly. Instead, the mature fruit is often hollowed out and sold as a decorative husk, and the mature flesh is dried and shipped abroad to places such as China and Hong Kong, where it's sold as herbal medicine. Over the centuries, the curvaceous seed has taken on something of a mythical status—its husk prized by Roman emperors and European royalty, and its flesh used around the world as an aphrodisiac, a skin whitener, and an ingredient in medicines like cough syrup.

Conservationists fear that treating the fruit as food will create a demand that will further devastate the sparse tree population, so for now it's better to enjoy the seeds with your eyes.

The coco de mer grows exclusively on two islands in the Seychelles.

Oceania

AUSTRALIA · NEW ZEALAND

PACIFIC ISLANDS

AUSTRALIA

DINING ABOARD THE HISTORIC GHAN TRAIN

QUEEN ADELAIDE RESTAURANT • AUSTRALIA

The Ghan train serves local specialties throughout its 1,850-mile (3,000 km) journey across the middle of Australia.

How to try it

Voyages on the Ghan aren't cheap, with overnight trips starting at AU$1,099. Occasionally, while at a station, the Queen Adelaide opens for a pop-up, so travelers without the budget or time for a train journey can experience the restaurant.

The Queen Adelaide is a white-tablecloth restaurant aboard the Ghan, a train that traverses the Australian Outback from north to south. The menu, inspired by the country's native flora and fauna, includes dishes like crocodile sausage, kangaroo steak, grilled barramundi fish, bush tomatoes, and quandong (wild peach) pancakes.

To score a table at the Queen Adelaide, travelers must book a train journey, which can range from a quick overnight jaunt from Darwin to Alice Springs to a two-week transcontinental expedition from Adelaide to Darwin and back. The menu changes daily and often reflects the local offerings at each stage of the train's journey. While in the north, for example, the chefs serve curry made with buffalo, an animal that was introduced to the Northern Territory in the 19th century. In the south, diners feast on lamb from Kangaroo Island, a nature reserve southwest of Adelaide.

Depending on the train's route, travelers can stop for other regional food experiences, like a tour of a Top End cattle farm or an underground lunch with the opal miners of Coober Pedy.

A DELICIOUS, IMPRACTICAL STRAW

TIM TAM SLAM • AUSTRALIA

How to try it
The Tim Tam website has a handy Tim Tam locator to help you find retailers near you.

n 1958, a horse called Tim Tam won the Kentucky Derby. Six years later, the Australian biscuit manufacturer Arnott's named its (now) iconic cookie after the horse. Inspired by the British Penguin cookies, Tim Tams feature two biscuits, a creamy filling, and a chocolate coating. This structure, though seemingly unremarkable, gives Tim Tams the ability to become an edible straw.

After biting off opposite corners of the cookie, snackers can suck liquid—usually coffee or tea—through the center. The liquid dissolves the creamy filling and creates a straw-like passageway. This process happens quickly, so the molten cookie must be "slammed" before it falls apart. (Slamming means shoving the whole cookie—or biscuit, as Arnott's prefers—into your mouth.) The Tim Tam Slam has since spread internationally. According to astrophysicist Neil deGrasse Tyson, the sensation is "a moment in your life experience that you can chalk up and say, 'That was different from anything else I've ever experienced.'"

The Tim Tam cookie doubles as a straw—but only if bitten at both ends.

HOME OF THE LAST PUREBRED LIGURIAN BEES

KANGAROO ISLAND BEE SANCTUARY • AUSTRALIA

How to try it
Kangaroo Island is open to visitors, and there's no shortage of opportunities to taste Ligurian honey. Island Beehive, one of the biggest organic honey producers in Australia, offers beekeeping tours.

n the 1880s, a group of Italian queens moved to Kangaroo Island, about 10 miles (16 km) south of mainland Australia. With its Mediterranean-like climate and largely unspoiled wilderness, the sunny island was the perfect home for these Ligurian royalty, all of which were bees.

Today, Kangaroo Island is home to the last surviving purebred Ligurian bee population. The island's isolation, coupled with an 1885 act of Parliament that designated the land a bee sanctuary, has kept the bees from disease and interbreeding. Today, the Australian government prohibits outside bees, honey, pollen, and used beekeeping tools from entering the island to keep the bee lineage pure and the honey pristine.

The taste of the honey reflects the natural environment, changing with the season and the flowers the bees visit. On Kangaroo Island, the Ligurian bees that feed from eucalyptus flowers tend to produce intensely flavored, amber-hued honey. The sugar gum eucalyptus yields the island's most well-known variety, which is lighter in color, softer in flavor, and more floral than other eucalyptus honeys. In the spring, bees feed on flowers such as canola and capeweed and make more delicate honeys.

HONEY

Honey is one of the few known edible substances with an everlasting shelf life. Thanks to its high acidity, low moisture content, and naturally occurring hydrogen peroxide, honey has antibacterial properties that have been tapped to treat flesh wounds and embalm bodies since ancient times. Making honey, however, is punishing work. The typical honeybee lives for just six weeks, during which time it produces a literal drop of honey ($\frac{1}{12}$ of a teaspoon, or less than a gram). After flying miles to gather nectar, honeybees deposit the liquid, via a relay of bee-to-bee regurgitation, into a honeycomb within the hive. To thicken the fresh nectar, the bees must flap their wings like tiny fans, pulling water from the sugar syrup before it's sealed within the comb and ready to be harvested and enjoyed by humans around the world.

Bilbila Giyorgis

Ethiopia's holy honey church is occupied by bees that, according to local lore, took up residence shortly after the church was completed in the 5th century. Since then, the bees have been cared for by a continuous succession of priests. Their honey is considered holy by the congregation and is used to treat both physical and psychological ailments. Typically administered by the head clergy, the holy honey is either ingested or applied to the skin. Dark amber in color and studded with bits of grit, honeycomb, beeswax, and tiny dead bees, this honey is believed to help with conditions as serious as leprosy. The town of Lalibela, just south of Bilbila Giyorgis, is named after a king whose name means "the bees recognize his sovereignty."

White Kiawe Honey

Brought to the Big Island (also known as Hawaii) in 1823, the kiawe is a desert mesquite tree native to Ecuador and Peru. It grows up to 60 feet (18 m) tall and flowers throughout the year, providing year-round nourishment for the bees that make this smooth, creamy, rare white honey. The honey is 99 percent monofloral—which means the bees that make it feed almost exclusively off the kiawe flower. Some say that the aftertaste carries a hint of menthol, while others taste vanilla and almond.

Tupelo Honey

Tupelo honey hails from the wetlands of the Florida Panhandle, where Ogeechee tupelo gum trees grow. Their flowers are in bloom for just two to three weeks each year, during which time beekeepers scramble to bring their bees to the often-remote nectar collection sites. Some bring their hives in by truck; others transport them by boat or set them up on barges to reach the more secluded stands of trees in the swamps. Pure tupelo honey is fruity and buttery, with notes of pear and rose water, and a sweetness that inspired Van Morrison's song "Tupelo Honey."

Florida's Ogeechee tupelo trees are known for their high-maintenance honey, but they also produce limes.

Honeybee Fences

These fences are cropping up on farms in Africa and India as a humane way to keep elephants away from crops. Elephants are frightened by bees, whose stings can cause serious pain on the soft inside of their trunk. Even the sound of bees makes elephants retreat, so a wall of beehives makes an effective barrier against the otherwise unstoppable giants. The beehive fences are far cheaper than concrete or electric walls, and there is a massive added benefit: bees. The honeybees pollinate the crops and can produce enough honey for the farmers to sell as a cash crop.

Beehive fences in southern Kenya provide sweet protection from crop-eating elephants.

These towering, ancient trees once fed dinosaurs.

GIANT PINE CONE NUT

BUNYA • AUSTRALIA

Bunya pines are the stuff of legend. Roaming dinosaurs likely snacked on these towering evergreens, and the trees have been an Aboriginal food source for centuries. Native to Queensland, where they thrive in the state's wet, tropical soils, these pines can grow to more than 150 feet (46 m) tall, with a trunk that is more than 4 feet (1.2 m) in diameter. Every few years, they produce pine cones the shape of an egg and the size of a football. Each one weighs as much as 22 pounds (10 kg) and is filled with anywhere from 30 to 100 husk-covered edible nuts.

Traditionally, Aboriginal Australians threw massive celebrations every three years when the bunya nuts were ripe. Groups would put aside their differences to gather together and trade, arrange marriages, and, of course, feast on the bunya nut, which can be eaten raw, roasted, boiled, or ground into flour and baked. These festivals—and bunya-eating culture itself—faded away in the early 20th century as European colonizers relocated Aboriginal people to government settlements and started logging bunya pine timber.

Today, Queensland's Bunya Mountains are still home to the country's largest stand of these enormous ancient trees, and the bunya nut is making a slow culinary comeback. You can often find it at food markets featuring Indigenous foods (or "bush tucker," as it's called), and there's talk of reviving the traditional Aboriginal bunya nut festival.

How to try it
Something Wild, an Aboriginal foods purveyor in Adelaide Central Market, carries bunya nuts when they're ripe.

Bunya nuts are dry and crunchy with a taste similar to chestnuts.

FIELD RATION EATING DEVICE

FRED • AUSTRALIA

The "field ration eating device," a multipurpose gadget distributed to members of the Australian military, is either a great invention or utterly useless depending on whom you ask. Those who fall in the latter camp have been known to call it a "fucking ridiculous eating device." In either case, the acronym FRED is the tool's common moniker.

Introduced in the early 1940s, FRED has three functions: can opener, bottle opener, and spoon. On one end, a small blade is engineered to puncture the lid of a can and then saw around the perimeter until the top is liberated. (This function is considered FRED's best feature.) In the center, a hook-shaped opening works as a bottle opener, and the opposite end serves as a spoon. The spoon is where things get controversial: It's so shallow that using it to get food to your mouth is a perilous undertaking. Users agree that FRED opens rations with military precision, but using it to eat what's in the can is where FRED falls apart.

As of 2020, FRED was still standard issue in ration packs for the Australian military.

How to try it
FREDs are sold online, but genuine military-issue models are prized possessions earned through military service, so many owners are reluctant to part with them.

Try eating a bowl of soup with this.

Bush Tucker

The word *aboriginal* comes from the Latin *ab* and *origine*, which together mean "from the beginning." The Aboriginal people, along with the Torres Strait Islanders, were Australia's first people and have lived off the land and its incredible array of Indigenous resources for an estimated 65,000 years. For those who know where to look, the Australian bush can be a wonderland of obscure and edible delights, many of which have natural health benefits.

WITCHETTY GRUBS

These thick, white, thumb-size worms—the larvae of the cossid wood moth—are harvested from inside the woody roots of the witchetty bush. The grubs are about 15 percent protein and 20 percent fat, with a nutty flavor and crunchy skin when skewered and barbecued.

Crushed into a paste, witchettty grubs are used topically as a treatment for burns and wounds.

DEAD FINISH

The name of this spiky acacia tree refers to its most impressive trait, which is its ability to withstand a drought until the "dead finish"—the very end. As the last tree standing in times of scarcity, it's a highly valued bush food. Aboriginal Australians use its seeds to make seedcakes.

The tree's needles have antiseptic properties; when inserted into a wart, they can cause it to shrivel up and dry, making it easy to remove.

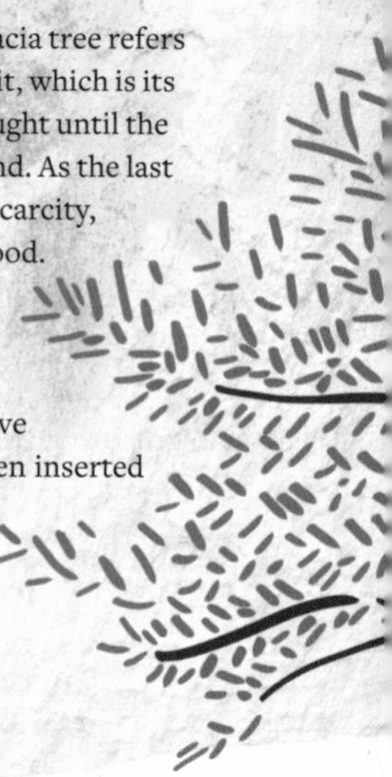

MACADAMIA NUT

While Hawaii produces about 70 percent of the world's macadamia nuts, a 2019 study revealed that all Hawaiian macadamia plants are likely the descendants of a single tree in the nut's native Queensland. This remarkable lack of genetic diversity makes macadamia crops vulnerable to disease and climate change. But Australia's wild macadamia population remains relatively robust, providing a genetic safety net for the crumbly, buttery nuts.

Macadamia nuts are packed with the mineral manganese.

FINGER LIME

Inside this oblong microcitrus are tiny, caviar-like bubbles that pop when chewed, releasing a tart explosion of lime juice. Native to the rain forests of South East Queensland, these elegant fruits have provided folate, potassium, and vitamins C and E to Aboriginal groups for thousands of years. Finger limes reach an average length of 3 inches (7 cm) and grow in shades of green, red, yellow, purple, and pink.

Finger limes are rich with antioxidants, which help fend off disease, and contain three times more vitamin C than a mandarin orange.

WATTLESEED

An edible type of acacia—a bush with hundreds of varieties—the wattleseed produces small, flat pods containing seeds that taste like a mix of chocolate, hazelnut, and coffee. Typically cooked in the pod or ground into powder (and then baked into "bush bread"), the seeds have been an Aboriginal staple food for at least 40,000 years.

Wattleseed is considered a superfood of the bush; it's loaded with protein, potassium, calcium, iron, and zinc. It also has a low glycemic index.

FOOD PIONEER

EDWARD ABBOTT

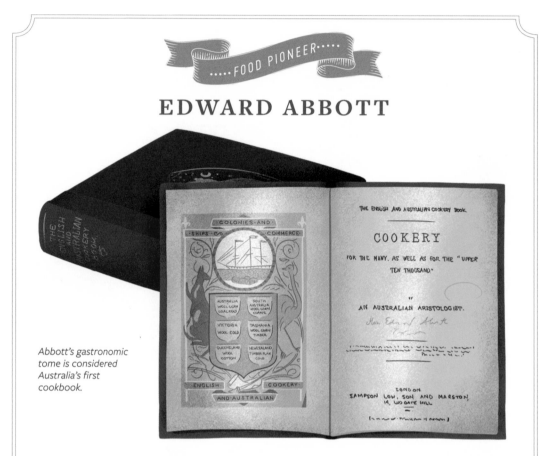

Abbott's gastronomic tome is considered Australia's first cookbook.

When Europeans colonized Australia's shores, many were wary of the island's native foods. Local ingredients were often seen as novelties or last resorts; most colonizers preferred to cook familiar dishes from home. Edward Abbott, an Australian of Canadian parentage, wanted to change that. In 1864, Abbott anonymously published *The English and Australian Cookery Book*, the world's first Australian cookbook. The byline read simply, "by an Australian aristologist," or an expert in cooking and fine dining.

At more than 300 pages, the book was an impressive tome with a big promise: "cookery for the many, as well as for the 'upper ten thousand.'" (The "upper ten thousand" is a 19th-century term for high society, coined by American writer Nathaniel Parker Willis in reference to the 10,000 wealthiest residents of New York City.)

Born in Sydney in 1801, Abbott lived most of his life on the island of Tasmania. He worked as a clerk for his father, a deputy judge advocate, before eventually becoming a newspaper publisher and landowner. An eccentric man, Abbott famously spent 30 years squabbling with colonial authorities over the land rights to a swamp and was notorious for having attacked the premier of Tasmania with an umbrella. It was only in his final years that Abbott turned to writing the cookbook that would become his greatest legacy.

The English and Australian Cookery Book is crammed full of European preparations, but Abbott also lovingly lays out recipes that make good use of often-overlooked native Australian ingredients. There's roast wombat and fricassee of kangaroo tail. There's also Slippery Bob, or breaded kangaroo brains fried in emu fat. There are recipes that call for echidna, turtle, ibis eggs, and "kangaroo ham."

Abbott's long and strange love letter to food includes quotes from Shakespeare, advice on smoking, musings on the British Empire, and multiple pages of advertisements. It is also practical and includes many recipes that might appeal to the modern chef. Fewer than 3,000 copies were printed, and while Abbott planned more books, he died in 1869. His cookbook was largely forgotten until its recent sesquicentennial, when it was reprinted and found a new generation of admirers.

AN INNOVATIVE INDIGENOUS MARKET

SOMETHING WILD • AUSTRALIA

How to try it
Something Wild is stall 55 at the Adelaide Central Market, open Tuesday through Saturday.

Within Adelaide's lively Central Market is Something Wild, one of Australia's premier purveyors of Indigenous Australian foods and beverages. The company supplies its food to restaurants, caters events, and, at their outpost in the Central Market, sells their Indigenous goods straight to the consumer.

In the meat case, there's kangaroo, emu, and camel. As an alternative protein, there are green ants, sold either dried or in a bottle of Green Ant Gin. Beyond sourcing Indigenous ingredients, Something Wild excels at giving these traditional foods a contemporary twist. Wattleseed lager, for example, is made from the seeds of Australian acacia plants, while recipes for Wallaby Stroganoff and Kangaroo Chili con Carne can be found on the company's website.

Part-owner and General Manager Daniel Motlop, himself Aboriginal and Torres Strait Islander, makes a priority of hiring Aboriginal employees. He hopes that in spreading Indigenous cuisine, he can also deliver economic benefits to Australia's Indigenous community.

A WHIMSICAL FRUIT PLAYGROUND

BUNDABERG BOTANIC GARDENS • AUSTRALIA

How to try it
The town of Bundaberg is a 4.5-hour train ride, or 1-hour flight, north of Brisbane, Queensland's capital. Bundaberg is also famous for its rum and (non-alcoholic) ginger beer.

The Bundaberg Botanic Gardens are an incredible, edible playground. Visitors to these grounds, located on Australia's Queensland coast, are welcome to roam and pluck freely from the offerings—including some impressive and unusual fruits.

Among the bounty is the fabled peanut butter tree, or *Bunchosia glandulifera*. During the Australian winter (June–August), these trees yield bright red-orange fruit that tastes and smells like peanut butter, and even has a similar texture.

Other garden residents include the fruit of the rain forest plum tree, the prickly and citrusy soursop fruit, the bulburin nut, and the panama berry—whose taste has been likened to "fairy floss," otherwise known as cotton candy. Those up for a taste adventure should seek out the miracle berry. This West African fruit contains a protein called miraculin that makes sour foods taste sweet: To experience the science, simply eat a berry, then bite a lemon.

WORM-FILLED, COCONUT-FLAVORED TREE TUMOR

BUSH COCONUT • AUSTRALIA

This "coconut" is neither coco nor nut—it's technically a tree tumor.

A grub-like coccid insect, usually *Cystococcus pomiformis*, settles on the branch of a desert bloodwood tree. She—and it's always a she—irritates the tree until it defends itself by sprouting a knobby tumor known as a gall. The gall grows around the grub, who spends the rest of her life within the fortress, drinking tree sap and mating with male grubs via a tiny air hole.

How to try it

Alice Springs Desert Park in the Northern Territory is a great place to see (and taste) a bush coconut.

Together, the gall and the worm form the bush coconut, sometimes called the less appetizing "bloodwood gall." Lumpy and small, this faux coconut is named for the gall's coconut-flavored flesh. Foragers typically eat both gall and worm, which has a sweet, juicy taste. In the northern savanna woodlands, the bush coconut has long been a source of nutrition for Aboriginal Australians.

WATERMELON ATHLETICS

MELON FESTIVAL • AUSTRALIA

How to try it

The Chinchilla Melon Festival takes place every other year in February.

Watermelon skiers get pulled down a slippery track at the 2015 Chinchilla Melon Festival.

Watermelon skiing is the main event at Chinchilla's biennial Melon Festival. Aspiring fruit athletes don a helmet, slip each foot into a hollowed-out watermelon, and hold on tight. The rope they grasp is held on either end by volunteers, who pull the skiers down a long, slippery tarp strewn with smashed melons until they belly flop (common) or make it to the end of the line (rare). Those who are truly ambitious can attempt the Melon Iron Man, which includes four events: watermelon skiing, pip spitting, watermelon bungee (four people struggling within a big elastic band to retrieve melons in competing directions), and a watermelon race (a 984-feet/300-m race while holding a 17-pound/8-kg watermelon).

The Curious Case of August Engelhardt, Leader of a Coconut Cult

In 1902, 26-year-old August Engelhardt set sail from Germany with a suitcase full of books and a peculiar mission: to establish a new Edenic order on the sunbaked shores of Papua New Guinea. Engelhardt's formula for happiness was simple: abandon earthly possessions, move to a tropical island, become a nudist, and eat only coconuts.

From his newly purchased island home, Engelhardt established a cult called Sonnenorden, or the Order of the Sun, a religion that worshipped the sun, which he saw as the ultimate giver of life, and coconuts, which he believed to be the tropical transubstantiation of God's very flesh. The principles of Sonnenorden are meticulously outlined in Engelhardt's collection of writings, *A Carefree Future: The New Gospel*. The obsessive text contains page after page of wild theories that extol the virtues of the coconut and adoring, devotional poems with titles like "The Coconut Spirit" and "How to Become a Coconut Palm."

Engelhardt's coconut obsession was rooted in a thin theory. The coconut, with its spherical shape and furry shell, is the fruit that most resembles the human head, and therefore the most ideal fruit for man's consumption. According to Engelhardt, coconuts are "vegetal human heads, and they alone are the proper human nourishment." But despite his devotion, Engelhardt's cult attracted no more than 15 disciples, all of whom were German. Together, in their quiet life of island devotion, they sunbathed for hours, swam in the cool waters of the Pacific, and ate their holy fruit.

Alas, paradise was not without its perils, and Engelhardt's cult was short-lived. Unaccustomed to the warm climate and stringent coconut diet, several of his followers died, and others contracted malaria. Engelhardt himself grew seriously ill, and despite his recovery, the remaining cult members disbanded and returned to Germany. Engelhardt blamed his followers' illnesses on their deviation from the coconut diet.

In response to the cult's ruinous outcome, the German government issued a stern warning banning anyone else from joining Engelhardt on the island. Engelhardt was left alone, scribbling lengthy treatises on the healing powers of plants and studying the dietary habits of the island's natives. An emaciated nudist, he was treated as something of a sideshow by visiting tourists who would occasionally ask him to pose for photographs.

Little is known about the eventual fate of Engelhardt. It is widely assumed that he died in his mid-40s, nearly 17 years after setting foot on the island. While no trace of a gravesite or memorial remains, his body is believed to have been discovered on the shores of Papua New Guinea in May 1919, his legs riddled with ulcers.

August Engelhardt believed coconuts were the secret to everlasting health and communion with the divine.

THE WORLD'S MOST STUNNING

In the coastal city of Port Pirie, housed within a 19th-century stone church, is a most glorious outpost of Barnacle Bill—a popular South Australian seafood chain. Outside, the church spires loom over Barnacle Bill's logo: a portly sailor balancing a tray of fish on one hand and a ship's wheel on the other. Inside, the pulpit is now a deep-frying counter, and the pews have been replaced by tables and a salad bar. The former Congregational church, which opened in 1879, shut its doors around 1991, and the building lay abandoned for five years. It was about to be razed when the current owners, Kevin and Kym Spirou, bought the building and turned it into a Barnacle Bill franchise—entering it into the pantheon of the most stunning fast-food restaurants in the world.

STARBUCKS NINENZAKA YASAKA CHAYA (KYOTO, JAPAN): Within this two-story, 100-year-old town house is a Starbucks with tatami floor seating, where visitors must remove their shoes before they caffeinate.

LINDA MAR TACO BELL (PACIFICA, CALIFORNIA): This 1960s wooden building is now a beachfront Taco Bell with surfboard parking, an indoor-outdoor fireplace, and pristine ocean views.

Fast-Food Restaurants

MCDONALD'S IMPERIAL (PORTO, PORTUGAL): Imperial, once an iconic 1930s Portuguese coffeehouse, now houses an art deco McDonald's with vaulted ceilings, a soaring stained-glass window, and crystal chandeliers.

MCDONALD'S (BATUMI, GEORGIA): The winner of an architecture award, this futuristic McDonald's is covered in 460 glass panels and surrounded by a reflective pool.

Delicious Diaspora

CHINESE IN AUSTRALIA

The Chinese have a long history of immigration to Australia. While some historians believe that Chinese contact with the continent predated Captain Cook's 18th-century arrival, it was the gold rushes of the 1850s and '60s that brought an estimated 40,000 Chinese to Australia's shores. Largely indentured and contract laborers, the goldfield-bound men were met with European resentment and racism. The Chinese formed enclave-like camps, where they tended small plots of fruits and vegetables to feed themselves and supplement their income. European miners, who had little access to fresh food, bought the produce, and when the gold rush ended, many Chinese immigrants found their next opportunity in market gardening—growing produce on a small scale for sale at local markets.

By the late 19th century, Chinese-owned market gardens had spread across Australia, especially in the growing suburbs. The Chinese cornered much of the produce market and opened restaurants and green grocery stores. In 1901, when Australia became a federation, the government passed the White Australia Policy, which discriminated against all non-European immigrants. But there was a loophole—Chinese cooks were allowed into the country. Australia, while fostering a deep-seated racism against the Chinese, had developed a fondness for their

cooking, and by the turn of the 20th century, approximately one in every three cooks in Australia was from China.

These days, Chinese food remains one of the most popular cuisines in Australia. While traditional Chinese

market gardens are now largely lost to time and industrialization, one historic garden remains in La Perouse, a suburb of Sydney. Here, Chinese farmers have been cultivating the land since the 1870s, and for the last 80 years, it has been passed generationally through three families. They work the crops by hand as they have since the beginning. The heritage-listed site has been under threat, most recently from a cemetery expansion project, but locals have fought hard to protect this historical plot.

Melbourne's Chinatown, established in the 1850s, is considered the oldest Chinatown in the southern hemisphere.

THE WORLD'S OLDEST EMU FARM

FREE RANGE EMU FARM • AUSTRALIA

When Australia began granting licenses to raise emus commercially in 1987, Kip and Charmian Venn received one of the first and used it to open Free Range Emu Farm. Endemic to Australia and valued for millennia by Aboriginal Australians, the enormous flightless birds were an exciting new industry that promised lean meat, healthy oil, and eggs eight times larger than a hen's. Emu farms sprang up across the country, but demand for emu products did not keep pace, and many farms closed.

Today, emus are making a commercial comeback. Chefs covet their dark, glossy eggs for their impressive size, rich flavor, and deep-orange yolks. Raising emus for their meat, which many say tastes like beef, is a far more sustainable enterprise than raising cows. (Emus are rapid breeders, laying multiple clutches of six to ten eggs throughout the breeding season.) But it's emu oil, made from the bird's fat, that's driving the growth. Emu oil has long been used by Aboriginal people to treat skin conditions. Although modern clinical testing is still in early stages, emu oil has gained fandom across the world thanks to its purported ability to moisturize skin, protect against sun damage, and treat burns, scars, and wounds.

At Free Range Emu Farm, now the oldest emu farm in Australia, visitors can see a hundred or so emus at any given time. The birds breed and lay eggs from April to August, hatch from July to October, and run through acres of pasture land all year long.

How to try it

Free Range Emu Farm is located at 681 Clackline Road in Toodyay, Western Australia. It is open to the public every day from 10 a.m. to 4 p.m., and visitors can purchase emu meat, eggs, oil, feathers, and even live chicks.

Emus are the second tallest bird in the world, outranked only by the ostrich.

How Australia Came to Have the Largest Feral Camel Population in the World

In the 19th century, British colonists were stumped by the desert expanse of Australia's vast interior. Was it flat or mountainous? Dry or a giant inland sea? European modes of transportation, like horses, weren't suited to the new terrain and early expeditions were unsuccessful. But a solution arrived from elsewhere in the empire: Camels, which the British encountered in colonial India, were an ideal solution for traversing the dry, rugged island.

In 1858, the Victorian Exploration Committee tasked horse dealer George Landells with recruiting camels and their drivers from India and bringing them to Australia. Over the next few decades, an estimated 20,000 camels were imported to the continent, along with about 3,000 camel handlers, who together enabled the settlement of Australia's interior. The hardy, steady animals could trek for hours under brutal sun with little water, and they became integral to the overland network of goods, labor, and infrastructure. But the Muslim migrants—dubbed "Afghan cameleers" by white Australians, despite not always being from Afghanistan—were the target of rampant discrimination.

On January 1, 1901, Australia became an independent country and enacted a set of new, decidedly racist immigration laws. Collectively called the White Australia policy, these laws halted almost all nonwhite immigration, and by the 1920s, the vast majority of cameleers had fled the country. Left behind, some of the camels were shot under the South Australian Camels Destruction Act of 1925. Others were released into the wild, where their descendants continue to live today.

Australia is now home to the largest feral camel population in the world, with estimates around one million. Left to roam, the animals pose a threat to delicate native ecosystems and water supplies. The Australian government has sponsored aerial camel culls in which feral camels are shot down by helicopter. But many argue for another solution: use the animals as food.

The Australian market for camel meat is growing, but its success hinges on capturing the camels and transporting them to processing facilities, which is expensive. The lean meat, which many people liken to a cross between lamb and beef, is sold to many Middle Eastern and North African countries and their diaspora communities. The animals are typically processed at an abattoir, and the meat is distributed to butchers both domestic and international.

Indian camels and their drivers were brought to Australia for work in the late 19th century, but when the drivers fled the country, the remaining camels ran wild.

WILD RICE CONSERVATION ART

MOMI-2010 • AUSTRALIA

Wander into a certain part of the Australian bush and you'll encounter enormous carvings blasted into the terrain. Lizards and insects crawl along the sides of granite boulders and below, carved into the floodplain, is a gigantic 269-foot-long (82 m) stalk of wild rice.

Found in the Mount Bundey area of the Northern Territory, this is the work of Mitsuaki Tanabe, a Japanese sculptor who dedicated much of his art to the importance of wild rice. (He called his wild rice sculptures "Momi.") Tanabe's works dot the globe, often depicting seeds or other organisms that help raise awareness about biodiversity. While working in Australia in the 1990s and early 2000s, he dreamed up a new project.

With the cooperation of the Australian government, Tanabe began work on these carvings in 2010. For ten years, he traveled to Australia during the dry season to work on the project. Tragically, Tanabe passed away before he could finish the work, but his son, Takamitsu Tanabe, along with some sculptor friends, completed the pieces in 2016.

How to try it

The carvings are located to the north of the Arnhem Highway. The wetlands are flooded for several months of the year, so check the ground condition before planning a visit.

NEW ZEALAND

LAMB MASQUERADING AS GOOSE

COLONIAL GOOSE • NEW ZEALAND

A plump goose with its elegant neck, roasted until golden brown, was a hallmark of the English holiday table. When homesick 19th-century British colonizers in New Zealand found themselves craving goose dinner, they had to get creative. With the island's lack of geese and preponderance of sheep, inspiration struck: Why not make a goose from a sheep?

Colonial goose, now a classic New Zealand dish, is a stuffed and marinated leg of lamb that's trussed up to look like a goose. While most recipes tell you to debone the shoulder, cooks serious about faking poultry leave in a length of shank bone to approximate the goose's neck and head. Stuffed with a mixture of breadcrumbs, herbs, onions, and honey, the lamb is tied up tight and marinated in a red wine mixture, which makes the outside glossy and goose-like. Goose on the outside, lamb on the inside, this wacky roast is sliced like a loaf of bread and is every bit as delicious as it is confusing.

How to try it

Colonial goose is served at restaurants during New Zealand's midwinter festivities, which take place in June and often feature English-inspired spreads.

UNDERGROUND MAORI OVEN

HĀNGI • NEW ZEALAND

How to try it

Whakarewarewa is a living Maori village located in the geothermal area of Rotorua. Open to visitors every day from 8:30 a.m. to 5 p.m., the village heats its hāngi with geothermal power. Residents also harness the heat of the mineral pool to boil vegetables and seafood.

The Maori people landed on the shores of New Zealand around the 13th century, likely hailing from central-eastern Polynesia. With them came a method of underground cooking known as hāngi.

This traditional fire pit technique requires digging a large hole, heating volcanic stones in a large fire, and placing the hot stones in the bottom. Early hāngi masters would set kai (food) that they'd foraged, hunted, or grown on top of the stones and then cover everything in foliage and soil to trap the steam inside. A few hours later, they had tender, smoked meat and vegetables that emanated an earthy, almost ashen aroma. In areas of New Zealand rife with geothermal activity, such as Rotorua, a region now known for Maori culture, hāngi masters employed natural springs to heat their stones.

Historically, the Maori people roasted fish, shellfish, chicken, and turtle alongside banana, sweet potato, and other starches in the hāngi. (When they arrived in New Zealand and encountered its enormous flightless birds, their ovens grew larger.) Today, hāngi masters also include pork, lamb, pumpkin, cabbage, and stuffing.

The centuries-old hāngi method of fire cooking uses volcanic stones.

When the Maori First Settled New Zealand, They Hunted Flightless, 500-Pound Birds

Before the arrival of humans, New Zealand was a land of birds. With no large carnivores on the island, an avian hierarchy flourished, from the burrowing muttonbirds to the gigantic but now extinct Haast's eagle, which perched at the top of the food chain. And then there were the moas: nine species of flightless birds, the smallest the size of turkeys, the largest 10 feet (3 m) tall and more than 500 pounds (227 kg). During its time, the giant moa was the tallest bird to walk the earth, and moa species proliferated across New Zealand, inhabiting different ecosystems suited to their size and diets.

The hierarchy was upended in the 13th century with the arrival of the early Polynesians, now known as Maori. Starting in Asia, most likely Taiwan, they traveled across the Pacific by canoe for thousands of years, populating islands along the way. New Zealand was the final stop, and as the last major uninhabited landmass to be settled by humans, it proved to be fertile hunting grounds.

Without wing bones, moas couldn't fly from their new foes. But they did have large leg bones, which has led to speculation that they were fast runners with a powerful kick. The newly arrived Maori had yet to develop bows, and so researchers have used archaeological and anthropological findings to piece together how these birds were hunted. Some believe that the Maori used snares to snag their prey, while others think they had help from dogs that either hunted moas themselves or drove the birds to locations where they could be cornered and killed.

After a successful hunt, Maori base camps functioned as butchering sites. (Enormous quantities of leftover bones have been found buried with the trash from these campsites.) While smaller moas could be carried away whole, hunters dealt with the 500-pounders by separating and carrying away only their meat-heavy legs. Researchers believe that the meat was cooked underground, likely in a hāngi fire pit, using koromiko wood as kindling.

Before the arrival of the Polynesians, an estimated 160,000 moas roamed New Zealand. Within 150 years, they were gone—annihilated in what a University of Missouri study calls "the most rapid, human-facilitated megafauna extinction documented to date." The moas had few natural predators (other than the giant eagles), and it's possible they weren't very afraid of humans. The birds laid few eggs—only one or two every breeding season—and took a long time to reach maturity. Hunted faster than they could reproduce, the moas were soon extinct.

When British naturalist Richard Owen confirmed the existence of moas in 1839 from a single bone, his revelation sparked something of a moa craze. The birds were as unique as the kiwi, as extinct as the dodo, and more monumental than any other avian species. Twenty years later, a workman unearthed the largest moa egg ever known: the Kaikoura egg, which had been nestled next to a body in a Maori grave. It likely weighed almost 9 pounds (4 kg) when fresh, and it is now on display at the Te Papa museum in Wellington, New Zealand.

The largest eagle known to exist once hunted the moose-sized moa in New Zealand.

A feral pig messes with the nest
of a white-capped albatross on
Auckland Island.

The Livestock Living at the End of the World

In the spring of 1866, the USS *General Grant* struck the western cliffside of Auckland Island, a remote, subantarctic mass of rocky land in the middle of the South Pacific. Trapped inside a rocky cavern, the ship began its fateful plunge into the frigid water, dragging most of its passengers down with it. Things looked bleak for the few who survived, but on the island, the castaways found a surprising resource that helped keep them alive for 18 months: a herd of long-haired, narrow-faced pigs.

The origin story of the strange swine begins in the early 19th century, when whalers and sealers sailed to the Auckland Islands—more than 360 miles (579 km) south of the mainland of New Zealand—to hunt the fur seals, sea lions, and whales drawn to its cold shores. According to lore, the whalers and sealers intentionally mischarted the islands to keep their hunting grounds secret. That cartographical distortion had devastating effects. Within the span of a century, sailors on at least nine ships, believing themselves to be in open seas, ended up smashing into the islands' cliffs.

In 1806, when British mariner Abraham Bristow happened upon the archipelago, he worried about the well-being of future castaways. A year later, he returned with a shipful of pigs and released them on the island. More pigs were plopped ashore in 1843, and again in the 1890s. By the end of the 19th century, the feral pig population was thriving. And while they did indeed feed a few castaways, the pigs also scarfed down plant roots, albatross eggs, and penguins, and generally began to wreak havoc on the island's flora and fauna. According to New Zealand's Department of Conservation (DOC), they're largely responsible for the disappearance of more than 30 native bird species.

Following the pigs, goats were released in multiple locations, then a colony of rabbits and a small herd of cattle. For nearly two centuries, the stranded animals lived in isolation with few natural predators, running completely unchecked until the DOC decided to intervene. In 1991, a sharp-shooting crew was deployed to kill cattle, and by 1992, goats had been eradicated from the main Auckland Island. To get rid of rabbits, they dropped poison pellets in the grazing areas.

But eradication efforts then paused in deference to another type of conservation: livestock biodiversity. In the face of climate change, maintaining a diversity of breeds able to adapt to different weather, temperatures, soil compositions, and overall environments is critical. As agriculture increasingly prioritizes size, yield, and productivity, the number of minority breeds grows smaller and smaller. The Auckland Island animals, which developed in relative isolation, showed incredible adaptive behaviors. The Auckland Island goat is among the largest in New Zealand, while the pigs are small and markedly athletic. When the rabbits ate most of the grass on the island, cattle were driven to higher ground and steep cliff faces in pursuit of vegetation. (Some claim they even ate seaweed.)

The most valuable trait of some of these animals, however, isn't one they've acquired but one they lack. Thanks to 200 years of seclusion, the Auckland Island pigs had never been exposed to the viruses and bacteria common in modern pigs—pathogens that could potentially be transmitted to humans and have been a major obstacle to xenotransplantation, or the grafting of cells from animals for use in human therapies. On the mainland of New Zealand, biotechnology firm Living Cell Technologies (LCT) retrieved a small herd of the feral pigs and began breeding them in a secure, high-tech quarantine facility. These pigs are worth hundreds of thousands of dollars.

As of 2019, most of the Auckland Islands are free of the nonnative pests, but the main island continues to bear feral pig and cat populations. In 2018, conservation minister Eugenie Sage pledged NZ$2 million to complete plans for restoring the vast, rugged island to its predator-free status. If all goes according to plan, within the next decade the pigs will disappear—from the Auckland Islands, but not from the world—and the albatross will be left to safely nest, the penguins to roam, and the plants to grow.

NEW ZEALAND'S FINEST BIVALVE

BLUFF OYSTER • NEW ZEALAND

How to try it

Beginning in March, Bluff oysters are everywhere around New Zealand, until they run out. Bluff's festival is held in May, but be sure to check for the exact dates—and to make sure that the year's harvest went well.

You'd be hard-pressed to find the famed wild Bluff oysters outside their native New Zealand. The big, sweet, minerally mollusks are available only between March and August, when they're harvested from the ice-cold Foveaux Strait between the town of Bluff and Stewart Island—a perilous stretch of rough, unpredictable waters that has taken many lives over the years. The annual harvest, which is about ten million oysters, falls short of the tremendous demand. (Helicopter couriers are not uncommon.) To guarantee a taste of the hyper-local, hard-won oyster, many people travel to the tiny town of Bluff for its annual oyster festival.

Bluff is the southernmost port town on mainland New Zealand, and its citizens are the hearty descendants of whalers, traders, and missionaries. They speak with uncommon Southland accents that feature a strong Scottish burr, and only about 2,000 of them live in the town. On oyster festival day in May, well-heeled Aucklanders arrive by morning flight, gorge themselves on the seasonal bounty, and depart in the evening. Adhering to the town's heritage, the festival kicks off with the oysters being "piped in" (brought in on a platter, serenaded by bagpipes). Next, a man in a tam-o'-shanter and tartan trews performs the traditional "Ode to the Oyster," exclaiming, "We put you on a pedestal, O Oyster from the Sea." What follows is a quirky mix of oyster eating (regular and competitive), a maritime-themed fashion show, and liters and liters of beer and wine.

Plates of New Zealand's prized shellfish at the Bluff Oyster and Food Festival.

AN ODE TO 16TH-CENTURY LIQUOR PROOFING

GUNPOWDER RUM • NEW ZEALAND

In the 18th century, when sailors in the British Royal Navy wanted to test the potency of their daily allotment of rum, they employed a 16th-century technique: Mix a pinch of gunpowder into a small amount of liquor and strike a match. If the wet gunpowder still caught flame, it was "proof" that the spirit had sufficient levels

of alcohol. If it didn't, the sailor knew that it was watered-down swill. (The liquor term *proof* comes from this practice.) "Navy strength" is generally defined as 57 percent alcohol by volume (ABV), which is the dividing line between booze that will and will not burn gunpowder.

In New Zealand, this fiery practice inspired the Smoke & Oakum Manufactory's Gunpowder Rum, made from a secret recipe that incorporates the three main elements of traditional gunpowder: saltpeter (potassium nitrate), sulfur, and charcoal. Blended with nicotine-free tobacco and chili peppers, the dark rum has notes of smoke and chocolate, and flavors of spice and molasses. (It should be noted that potassium nitrate, which is occasionally used as a preservative, is dangerous when consumed in large quantities.)

Smoke & Oakum's Gunpowder Rum is an homage to the dark, full-bodied rums consumed by most sailors—be they navy men, pirates, or smugglers—centuries ago. These rums were produced without standardization and bottled in whatever was available, which is why Smoke & Oakum's Gunpower Rum comes in a motley crew of bottle shapes, all wrapped in brown paper. At 51.6 percent ABV, however, this rum is just shy of navy strength.

How to try it

Smoke & Oakum's Gunpowder Rum is released in limited batches. Check the store locator on the company's website to find a retail location, then contact that store to be sure the rum is in stock.

PACIFIC ISLANDS

FIJI ASPARAGUS

DURUKA • FIJI

In the swampy marshes of Fiji, a nation comprised of hundreds of islands, you'll find the tall, grassy stems of *Saccharum edule*, a cane shoot closely related to sugarcane. Peel back the slim green sheaths and you'll find duruka. Nicknamed Fiji asparagus for its resemblance to the slender vegetable, duruka is actually the flower of the cane shoot. It has a sweet flavor, reminiscent of corn.

Duruka is a favorite ingredient in curries. About 40 percent of Fiji's population is of Indian ancestry, descendants of the indentured Indian laborers who worked the sugar plantations in the late 19th century. The fleshy seasonal flower holds up well in soups and stews but is also excellent roasted over charcoal or simmered in coconut milk.

How to try it

Duruka season is in April and May. Vendors at the Suva Municipal Market, in Fiji's capital, sell it in huge wrapped bundles.

YAM HOUSES

BWEMA • PAPUA NEW GUINEA

Off the coast of Papua New Guinea is Kiriwina, the largest of the Trobriand Islands, where yams represent wealth, prestige, and power. The tubers lie at the heart of Trobriand cultural life, and are so important that they're given houses of their own. Known as bwema, these stylized wooden structures are arranged in concentric circles, with the innermost houses typically decorated with intricate carvings etched into logs painted red, white, and black.

Nearly every Trobriand household has a yam house, as well as a garden, called a kaymata, used exclusively for growing yams. Yams are not easy to cultivate. They require frequent thinning and can be grown only once a year. Trobriand Islanders sometimes call on the help of yam-growing spells performed by a towosi, or a professional gardening magician. The local culture revolves around a traditional system of giving and receiving, so the yams are always grown for someone else in the community. When they're ready, they are transported, sometimes in a parade accompanied by a dance, to the recipient's yam house.

There is little life the tuber does not touch: yams pay land rents, celebrate weddings, bless births, and structure the calendar year, which revolves around the yam harvest. When someone dies, family members save up yams for months, in yam houses, and give them out during mortuary feasts.

The tall, skinny storage houses are built of logs and raised high above the ground. Their walls have plenty of open space to optimize air circulation, allowing the yams inside to stay fresh for months. In a show of power, village chiefs have the biggest, most decorated yam houses.

Climate change has made Trobriand yam-collecting on the island of Kiriwina more difficult, and more meaningful, than ever.

VOLCANIC EGG INCUBATOR

EGG FIELDS OF SAVO • SOLOMON ISLANDS

From Honiara, the capital of the Solomon Islands, Savo Island is reached by a 90-minute boat ride across Iron Bottom Sound—so named for the dozens of ships and planes that sank in it during World War II. The 11-square-mile (28-sq-km) island is home to an active, steaming volcano that attracts megapodes—chicken-size black birds that make use of the volcanic heat to incubate their eggs.

In the sand fields surrounding the nearby village of Panueli, megapodes arrive at dawn to lay and bury their eggs. The volcanic earth keeps the eggs warm, which frees the mother birds of their brooding duties. But when the mothers leave, men from the village arrive, digging more than three feet down to unearth the birds' nests. They dig by hand, taking care not to damage the eggs, and wrap them in banana leaves for safekeeping. Afterward, women fill in the holes and level the sand.

Megapode eggs are relatively large—about the size of duck eggs—and each one is worth about $2 in the local economy. They were once abundant around Panueli, but overharvesting has led to an unsustainable system. As of 2017, only one egg-laying sand field remains in the area, and the yield is sparse. Visitors can still come at dawn to witness the incredible egg-laying scene, but they should abstain from purchasing or eating the eggs.

How to try it

The most common way to get to Savo Island is by boat from Visale, a town at Guadalcanal's northern tip. From there, the trip takes about 30 minutes, so day-trippers eager to see megapodes lay their eggs should depart before dawn. Those who would rather arrive the night before can stay at the Sunset Lodge, which is the main accommodation on the vehicle-less island.

Megapode eggs are buried deep in the sand so they can be warmed by the volcanic heat of Savo Island.

GIANT *Egg-Shaped* WONDERS

WINLOCK EGG (WINLOCK, WASHINGTON, USA)

Named the "World's Largest Egg" in 1989 by Ripley's Believe It or Not!, this colossal structure has been built four times. In the 1920s, to celebrate the area's booming egg industry, the egg was constructed out of canvas stretched over a wooden frame. That egg was replaced by a plastic version in the 1940s and a fiberglass model in the 1960s. The current edition, made of cement, was built in 1991. It is 12 feet (3.7 m) long and weighs 1,200 pounds (544 kg).

THE EGGS OF MERRY BAY (VIKURLAND, ICELAND)

In 2009, Icelandic artist Sigurður Guðmundsson created 34 enormous granite eggs in honor of the 34 species of native bird that nest in eastern Iceland. Perched atop a slab of concrete, each stone specimen accurately depicts the shape, patterns, and colors of the bird egg that it represents.

RIVERSIDE ROUNDABOUT (LOS ANGELES, CALIFORNIA, USA)

In the Cypress Park neighborhood of LA is a traffic roundabout filled with granite egg sculptures, each containing a human face. The 2017 installation is not only a visually engaging art piece but was also designed as a stormwater retention landscape. Each face is sculpted from the image of an actual member of the local community, randomly selected from hundreds of applicants.

SOLAR EGG (KIRUNA, SWEDEN)

In one of the northernmost towns in Sweden, a 15-foot (4.5-m) golden egg stands in the middle of a field of snow, reflecting the white expanse from 69 panes of glass. Inside, the egg is a sauna where local residents can bask in the heat, relax, and talk. Heated by wood, it seats eight people and is free of charge. The egg sauna was a gift from the Swedish government as repayment for massive sinkholes they left in the area while extracting iron ore. Beginning in 2017, the Solar Egg embarked on an extended tour with stops in Copenhagen, Paris, and Minneapolis.

DALÍ THEATRE–MUSEUM (FIGUERES, SPAIN)

From the outside, this museum looks like a dream-logic breakfast castle, complete with giant eggs on the parapets and loaves of bread decorating the walls. Designed by Salvador Dalí himself, the egg fortress is home to the world's largest collection of the Spanish artist's work.

SHRUB-BASED TINGLE TEA

KAVA TEA • VANUATU

How to try it

Port-Vila, Vanuatu's capital, is filled with kava bars. El Manaro is a rustic option, with open-air thatch-roofed seating areas and a communal atmosphere. A recommended dose for newcomers is three to four coconut shells. (Locals might have twice this.)

Kava is typically served in a coconut shell.

t's just after dusk on the island of Espiritu Santo in the Melanesian archipelago of Vanuatu. Before grabbing dinner in the stalls of the Luganville marketplace, local men, expats, and visiting divers walk into a thatched hut on the hillside above. Inside, there's a wooden counter next to a large, sink-like basin and behind the counter, a length of stretched pantyhose with a giant lump in the bottom dripping gray fluid into a bowl below.

One by one people line up, chug some of the gray liquid from half a coconut shell, rinse their mouths with water, and spit a few times into the basin. Then they all take seats on benches, lean back, and start to tingle. This is the nightly Vanuatu ritual for kava, a mildly psychoactive drink made from the root of the *Piper methysticum* shrub. It creates a warm anesthetic feeling, starting at the lips and radiating outward, enlivened by little spikes of euphoria. Kava contains 15 or more active compounds, known as kavalactones, and Vanuatu is known for having the most potent varieties.

Kava has a long history across the Pacific—from Hawaii to Tonga to Micronesia—though some consider Vanuatu its spiritual home. Its usage ranges from casual relaxation to medicinal and ceremonial purposes. Modern purveyors prepare fresh kava root by grinding it against a rough coral cone, though traditionally it was prepared by women who chewed pieces before spitting them into a woven sieve.

Canada

WESTERN CANADA · EASTERN CANADA

WESTERN CANADA

A TOWERING FIBERGLASS DUMPLING

THE WORLD'S LARGEST PYROGY • ALBERTA

How to try it

Take Highway 28 to Glendon, about two hours northeast of Edmonton. It's located in Pyrogy Park, which is on Pyrogy Drive.

n the small village of Glendon, a 27-foot (8.2-m) dumpling weighing 6,000 pounds (2,721 kg) stands in the middle of a community park, a mammoth fork stabbed through the filling. The Giant Pyrogy, as it's known, is one of the "Giants of the Prairies," a collection of massive sculptures scattered across western Canada (among them "Giant Potato" in Vauxhall and "World's Largest Mushroom" in Vilna). Unveiled in 1991, the sculpture is Glendon's tribute to the eastern European

THE EXPANSIVE WORLD OF

Scottish Clootie Dumpling

Vietnamese Bánh Bao

Uzbek Chuchvara

Bolivian Salteña

Chinese Shumai

Indian Modak

dumpling—one of the most popular imported foods in Canada. According to Johnnie Doonanco, who dreamed up the sculpture when working as the town's mayor, the original design needed a little help. "People went by and they responded that it looked like a cow pie or something," Doonanco said, so he added a fork to let them know it was a pyrogy.

Next to the Giant Pyrogy sculpture is a café (one of two restaurants in Glendon) serving smaller, edible versions of the fiberglass dumpling.

Dumplings

Russian Pelmeni

American Baked Apple Dumpling

Italian Raviolo Gigante

Georgian Khinkali

Turkish Manti

West African Kenkey

DRINKABLE SPAGHETTI ALLE VONGOLE

CAESAR • ALBERTA

How to try it

The Calgary Inn is now the Westin, but they still serve a Caesar (with cherrywood-smoked tomato puree).

Alle vongolle (spaghetti with clams) is a traditional Italian preparation that Walter Chell, manager of the Calgary Inn, ate in Venice and never forgot. In 1969, when asked to create a signature drink for the inn's new Italian restaurant, Chell made a clam spaghetti–inspired cocktail. He began with a base of mashed "clam nectar," then added tomato juice, vodka, lime, spices, Worcestershire sauce, and hot sauce. He named his invention the Caesar, and although Chell was not the first person to put clams in a cocktail (recipes exist from as early as 1900), it was his blend that really took off.

Around the same time, a drink called Clamato (a portmanteau of clam and tomato) hit the market, invented by Californians who, like Chell, found their muse in a seafood meal: Manhattan clam chowder. When word reached Canada that the United States had a shortcut for mixing Caesars, the country clamored for Clamato. By the mid-1990s, cases of Clamato poured into western Canada, 70 percent of which was being poured into Caesars. Since then, the beverage has become a vital part of Canadian bar culture. Three hundred and fifty million Caesars are imbibed each year, making it the country's favorite mixed drink. (And in 2009, it became the official cocktail of Canada.)

Comparisons to the American Bloody Mary are inevitable, but Canadians insist their beloved Caesar is far tastier and more complex, as Americans remain stubbornly squeamish about drinking clams. What researchers call "the clam barrier" is real. Clamato sales are still meager among Americans, but Canadians are happy to absorb all the extra bottles.

A REVIVAL OF FLUORESCENT SOCKEYES

OSOYOOS LAKE SALMON • BRITISH COLUMBIA

For thousands of years, the Sylix, or Okanagan, people of the Pacific Northwest have eaten the sockeye salmon of Osoyoos Lake. The fish are known for their bright red skin, which appears as they prepare to spawn, and their distinct taste, which is light yet rich with buttery flavors, thanks to a diet rich in plankton and crustaceans.

How to try it

Okanagan Select Tasting Room (105-3535 Old Okanagan Highway) is a store affiliated with the Okanagan Nation Alliance. They sell salmon from Indigenous fishing groups and take orders online.

Alas, due to overfishing and climate change, the local sockeye population took a major downturn. In 2003, the Okanagan Nation Alliance launched a repopulation initiative dubbed Kt cp'elk' stim' (Sylix for "cause to come back"). Through the program, they re-outfitted dams to allow the sockeyes' passage, cleaned up the water, and incorporated Indigenous cultural practices such as feeding the local eagles and owls. By 2010, their efforts had paid off: For the first time in more than 75 years, the sockeye population was deemed sustainable and measured in the hundreds of thousands.

Osoyoos Lake sockeye season is fleeting—from July through part of September—but for those who can't get it fresh, the fish are also candied with sugar, salt, and syrup.

Delicious Diaspora

RICHMOND NIGHT MARKET

Starting in the 19th century, Chinese immigrants, mainly from Guangdong Province, began arriving in western Canada to mine for gold and work on the Canadian Pacific Railway. Despite the racist legislation and sentiment of the time, many chose to stay, establishing a Chinese Canadian community that developed and flourished over the next century. Today, the population of Richmond is more than 50 percent ethnic Chinese, and the city is home to the largest Asian night market in North America.

From May to October, when the sun goes down, some 300 vendors at the Richmond Night Market sell snacks, clothing, and trinkets in a setting modeled after the bustling night markets of Asia. Steam billows from food stands selling fish balls, crab claws, pork hocks, dumplings, bubble tea, and countless other snacks from around the world such as Mexican churros, Japanese takoyaki, and Filipino sisig. Each night the market plays host to 5,000–8,000 visitors, all eating their way through some of Asia's finest midnight munchies.

How to try it
Richmond Night Market sets up at 8351 River Road and is open for business Friday, Saturday, and Sunday nights, from May to October.

THE BATTLE FOR BISON ENERGY BARS

PEMMICAN WARS • MANITOBA

How to try it

Canadian Prairie Bison makes pemmican (original, and varieties with sunflower seeds and berries) at the University of Saskatchewan. You can buy it at Canadian supermarkets such as Safeway.

For more than 200 years, spanning the 17th to 19th centuries, European powers battled for prime fur-trading territory in northwestern Canada. But in order to push operations into the subarctic regions, Europeans faced a significant nutritional challenge. A single man needed 4,000 to 6,000 calories every day, and the weevil-infested flour and spoiled meat coming from Europe wasn't nearly enough to sustain an expedition. They turned to pemmican—the energy bar of the Indigenous North Americans.

Pemmican is made from dried, finely ground animal meat that's mixed with the animal's rendered fat. It's nutritionally dense, lightweight, shelf-stable, and contains about 3,500 calories per pound. Although any meat (or even fish) can get the pemmican treatment, bison fueled the fur trade. The Métis, an aboriginal group descended from First Nations people, and Europeans from the colonial era produced much of the pemmican. After a big bison hunt, they made the dried meat and fat mixture, and then stuffed it into buffalo skin bags, a concoction they called a taureau. One taureau contained 300,000 calories and could keep, unrefrigerated, for as long as a decade. Pemmican was sold to trading posts around the region and became pivotal in the expansion of Europe's commercial beaver hunting empire—so much so that it started a war.

In the early 1800s, a new colony connected to the British fur traders (the Hudson's Bay Company) attempted to pass a law stating that all provisions, including pemmican, could not be taken out of the region. This cut off the supply to their rivals, North West Company, and incited two years of pemmican-related fighting, ending with the burning of two forts and dozens of deaths. But the Pemmican Wars weren't the most devastating consequence of the compacted meat-and-fat business: Pemmican became so essential to commercial beaver hunting that it nearly wiped out the Canadian bison herds north of the Missouri River.

Beyond Indigenous North Americans and European fur trappers, pemmican found its way into the packs of explorers in the Antarctic, and Robert Peary carried it to the North Pole. He later proclaimed his appreciation for the food, saying that "Too much cannot be said of the importance of pemmican to a polar expedition."

Buffalo meat being dried over an open fire, later to be ground and used in pemmican.

New Iceland

Traditional Culture Frozen in Canada

In the late 19th century, Sigtryggur Jónasson led a group of Icelandic immigrants to the remote shores of Manitoba's Lake Winnipeg. The expedition hoped to find a suitable place in Canada to begin a new settlement, abundant with farmland and natural resources, and not so different from the Nordic landscape of Iceland. Over the next few decades, following an Icelandic volcano eruption that devastated the local economy, some 20 percent of Iceland's population emigrated to North America. In Manitoba, newcomers faced brutal winters and many perished in the early years. But those who survived—largely thanks to help from First Nations people—were determined to build the community now known as New Iceland.

In New Iceland, it's often easier to find traditional Icelandic foods than it is on the Nordic island. Rúllupylsa, a dish of pounded lamb flank rolled into a log, is rare in Iceland but relatively abundant in the Canadian region, sold at general stores and supermarket chains. The potent Icelandic liqueur brennivin flows freely at bars, and the shelves of local stores are stocked with dried fish, homemade slátur (a kind of Icelandic haggis), and crepe-like ponnukokur.

There is an intriguing disconnect between New Iceland and Iceland. After World War II, Iceland entered into a relationship with NATO and the United States that modernized the country very quickly, while New Iceland maintained a largely traditional way of life. This is especially evident in the region's food culture. Vínarterta, for example, is a multilayered prune jam and cardamom cake that was at the height of fashion in 1875, when the first wave of immigrants arrived to Lake Winnipeg. In Iceland, making vínarterta is a fading practice, but in New Iceland, bakeries, gift shops, and most every amma (grandma) bakes the old-style treat.

Iceland and New Iceland share a friendly fascination with each other. The Icelandic prime minister makes a point of flying over for the annual Icelandic festival each year. The Canadian settlement attracts busloads of curious Icelandic tourists and visitors from the country's diaspora, all looking to experience their traditional culture, set in a place that feels preserved in amber—stuck in a time closer to the 19th-century volcanic explosion than to modern Iceland.

A 15-foot Viking statue in Gimli, Manitoba, pays tribute to the area's large Icelandic population.

Vínarterta, an Icelandic cake popular in the 19th century, is still handmade at shops like the Hnausa General Store in New Iceland.

PERMAFROST COLD STORAGE

TUKTOYAKTUK ICE HOUSE • NORTHWEST TERRITORIES

How to try it
The Ice House is no longer open to the public, but the village is conducting a feasibility study in hopes of reopening with additional safety precautions.

The village of Tuktoyaktuk sits in the extreme north, a place so cold it's not uncommon to see locals taking a snowmobile to the store. Families rely on hunting, fishing, and trapping to sustain themselves, and must work with the weather to survive. In the summer, they fish. In the fall, they hunt caribou. All year round, they use an underground labyrinth of rooms dug from permafrost as their freezer.

Looking at the small, outhouse-like structure, it seems unlikely this building could lead to much. But go inside and look down: Cut from the floor is a square opening like a trapdoor, the walls fuzzy with ice, descending into frozen darkness. To store your meat, you must carry it into that hole and lower yourself, step by step, carefully down a wooden ladder. At the bottom, the space opens dramatically, revealing a catacomb-like passageway caked in frost and crystals. This is the Tuktoyaktuk Ice House, the village's communal cold storage.

Dug in 1963, the Ice House is carved 30 feet (9 m) deep into the permafrost. Three hallways lead to 19 separate rooms where locals stash their excess meat after a hunt. The rooms hold at a fairly steady 5°F (–15°C), making them perfect freezers.

Before electricity, most northern villages had ice houses of their own. In recent years, many have shut down in favor of modern refrigeration, but Tuktoyaktuk chose to preserve theirs, adding the small entrance structure to protect it. Each year, as ice falls from the ceiling to the floor, the passage gets smaller, and locals must duck a little lower to get to their reserves.

HOCKEY ARENA COMMUNITY GARDEN

INUVIK GREENHOUSE • NORTHWEST TERRITORIES

How to try it
Members pay $25 a year and must volunteer for ten hours. Visitor tours are $5.

The climate of Inuvik, located 120 miles (193 km) above the Arctic Circle, is extreme in every way. Temperatures swing between –40 and 80°F (–40 and 27°C) throughout the year. During the summer, the days are literally endless, with more than 50 days of 24-hour sunlight. Harnessing this brief yet powerful season, Inuvik residents rescued an old hockey arena from demolition in 1998 and turned it into Canada's northernmost commercial greenhouse.

The semicircular, glass-windowed structure is divided into two distinct sections: A 4,000-square-foot (370-sq-m) commercial greenhouse uses half the space and funds the second half, a community garden. About 180 individual plots are tended by residents of the town. They grow spinach, lettuce, tomatoes, strawberries, squash, and many other plants that wouldn't otherwise survive in the Arctic. A portion of the raised beds is allocated for groups such as town elders, children, and local charities. The growing season is short, just May to September, but the seasonal abundance brings valuable nutrition and food security to the far-flung community.

THE FRANKLIN EXPEDITION'S EERIE LEFTOVERS

BEECHEY CAN CAIRN INDENTATION • NUNAVUT

On the rocky shore of Beechey Island, high above the Arctic Circle in Nunavut, there is a circular depression covered in patchy moss, roughly 12 feet (3.7 m) in diameter. This is all that remains of what was once a 7-foot-tall (2 m) pyramid of tin food cans, and among what little remains of the arctic expedition that stacked them there.

How to try it

You can now fly across the Northwest Passage to Beechey Island.

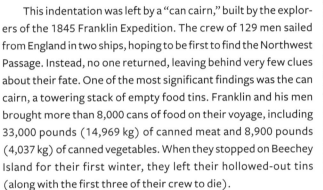

This indentation was left by a "can cairn," built by the explorers of the 1845 Franklin Expedition. The crew of 129 men sailed from England in two ships, hoping to be first to find the Northwest Passage. Instead, no one returned, leaving behind very few clues about their fate. One of the most significant findings was the can cairn, a towering stack of empty food tins. Franklin and his men brought more than 8,000 cans of food on their voyage, including 33,000 pounds (14,969 kg) of canned meat and 8,900 pounds (4,037 kg) of canned vegetables. When they stopped on Beechey Island for their first winter, they left their hollowed-out tins (along with the first three of their crew to die).

A woodcut illustration of the McClintock Arctic Expedition of 1857, one of several search and rescue missions to find Franklin and his explorers.

When Franklin's crew still hadn't returned to England three years later, numerous search parties were sent to find them. In 1851, teams landed on Beechey Island and discovered the cans and the three graves. At the time, preserving food in metal tins was new technology, and the tins Franklin and his crew ate from were thin and soldered closed with lead. For years, these tins were implicated in the crew's downfall, many believing the men suffered from lead poisoning. Since then, science has largely debunked lead as the main cause of death, and most research now points to a combination of malnutrition, hypothermia, tuberculosis, and starvation.

The cans have since disintegrated into the earth below them. In their wake is a verdant patch of moss, thriving on the minerals the cans left behind. The circular depression is all that's left of the Franklin Expedition can cairn, but not far away you can see another cairn with sturdier food tins, left behind by the search parties who came to rescue them.

INUIT BLUBBER CUBES

MUKTUK • NUNAVUT

According to Inuit legend, the whales, seals, and walruses that swim the northern waters were once the fingers of Sedna, goddess of the sea. By some accounts, Sedna's father panicked in the face of an oncoming storm and threw his daughter overboard, severing her fingers as she tried to hold on to the edge of the kayak. It's generally believed that Sedna is a vengeful goddess (in part because of the severed fingers) and that respect for the ocean's animals—once pieces of the goddess herself—is key to appeasing her. This respect often means using the entire animal as either food or tools.

How to try it

Muktuk, usually shared among Inuit people, has recently become available at country food markets in Nunavut, where hunters sell traditional Inuit foods.

Muktuk is one such dish that makes use of the whole animal. A traditional Inuit food, muktuk consists of the skin and blubber of a whale, usually a bowhead, beluga, or narwhal. It's typically served raw in tiny cubes, but it can also be deep-fried, pickled, or stewed.

Depending on the type of whale, muktuk may look like a black cap of skin with soft, pinkish-white blubber or striated layers of gray, white, and pink—similar to pork belly. The skin is frustratingly elastic, but it's often scored to make chewing somewhat easier. The blubber, however, melts gently as you chew, giving off an essence of the ocean without being overly fishy or briny.

Inuit tribes have been snacking on narwhal blubber for centuries.

WILD BERRIES FOR BARTERING AND PIE

SASKATOONS • SASKATCHEWAN

How to try it
Nine miles (15 km) north of downtown Saskatoon is the Wanuskewin Heritage Park—an active archaeological site and museum dedicated to preserving and celebrating the culture of the Northern Plains First Nations people. They also serve a mean saskatoon berry pie.

In River Landing, Saskatoon, there's a statue of the city's founder, John Lake, crouched beside Chief Whitecap of the Dakota First Nation tribe. With his arm outstretched, Chief Whitecap gestures to the land before him—an expanse that was once so full of saskatoon berries, they named the city after them.

Saskatoons (*Amelanchier alnifolia*) are small purple berries with a sweet almond flavor. They grow wild in North America and played a key role in the diets of Indigenous peoples and early colonizers, who pounded them into cakes and used them as a sweetener. According to an account from 1900, the berries were once so valuable that ten saskatoon cakes could be traded for one large buckskin.

Like other berries, saskatoons are great in jam, wine, and beer, but the most iconic application is pie. A filling of saskatoons tossed with a little lemon juice, sugar, and flour is a common preparation. But as humans encroach on saskatoon habitats, the berries are becoming harder to find, which means a pie packed with saskatoons is a precious, labor-intensive commodity.

Since the 1990s, attempts to domesticate the saskatoon have been underway in both Canada and the United States. This dual cultivation has caused a bit of a cultural conflict because American farmers felt that saskatoon, as a word, would not work in the US market and rebranded it the Juneberry. In Canada, the *saskatoon* remains the saskatoon.

Country Food Markets: The Untraditional Way to Save Traditional Food

Walking into a country food market in Nunavut, Canada, you'll find a display of caribou heads and hearts, chunks of narwhal fat with the skin still attached, Arctic char (smoked, frozen, or made into dried chips called pitsi), igunaq (fermented seal meat), ground umingmak (musk ox), and frozen flatfish called turbot—among the most asymmetric vertebrates to ever live, with both eyes mashed on one side of its head. Known as "country food," this high-fat, vitamin-rich fare has sustained the Nunavummiut people for thousands of years. But until recently, it couldn't be bought at a store.

Country food is the Nunavummiut way of life: hunted, fished, or foraged, then shared within the community. In an inhospitable climate like the Canadian north, this lifestyle has always been precarious, and insufficient hunts have led to conditions like "rabbit starvation," a deadly protein poisoning that occurs when the body is deprived of fats. Today, the region is changing. Previously semi-nomadic communities have settled into permanent towns, and Nunavummiut children are spending less time learning migration patterns and reading sea ice. On top of everything, global warming is changing and shortening hunting seasons, which means country food is growing rare, and 70 percent of children in Nunavut live in food-insecure households.

In less remote regions, losing the ability to hunt might be remedied by the grocery store. But in Nunavut, where all commercial goods must be flown in, a single bunch of celery can cost a staggering nine dollars. Commercial food prices are two to three times more in Nunavut than in the rest of Canada, and local families simply can't afford it.

In an attempt to encourage hunting and create an economic incentive for country food, nonprofits such as Project Nunavut and Feeding Nunavut stage pop-up markets where hunters and fishers can come and sell their meat to the public. The creators of Project Nunavut were unsure if the concept would work, but at their first country market in 2010, they sold out in less than ten minutes. A few years later, permanent shops have opened in the area, selling whatever meat has been hunted that day at reasonable prices.

Traditional food markets are not unique to Nunavut. Nearby Greenland has had them for more than 150 years, but in Nunavut, the concept has been controversial because country food is meant to be shared, creating bonds and mutual reliance across the community. Selling seal or whale or char is still, to some extent, seen as a betrayal of traditional values.

Other attempts to revive country food include government-subsidized hunts, programs for teaching traditional hunting methods, and community freezers open to all. But as locals work to bolster time-honored pathways to food and nutrition, the country food market gives the Nunavummiut community a way to keep their traditional foods alive and accessible in a rapidly modernizing Canada.

Huntsmen in Nunavut transport a shot musk ox on a sledge.

A STORIED APPENDAGE SERVED IN A GLASS

SOURTOE COCKTAIL • YUKON

How to try it

The Sourtoe Cocktail is served in the Sourdough Saloon at the Downtown Hotel in Dawson City. The cost is the cocktail you order, plus $5 CAD for the toe.

The Sourtoe, the city of Dawson's signature cocktail, is served every night at the Sourdough Saloon. It can consist of any liquor your heart desires and has just one nonnegotiable ingredient: a human toe that's dropped into the glass and must touch your lips as you tip the drink back. The same toe, pickled by time and alcohol into a sterile human appendage, goes into each cocktail. The enduring practice is the life's work of a self-proclaimed bastard, asshole, and professional wolf-poisoner named Captain Dick Stevenson, a man who once toured the country for 80 days with his sourtoe.

Captain Dick first encountered a stand-alone human toe when cleaning out a cabin once owned by Prohibition rum runners, the Linken brothers—one who froze his toe while bootlegging and one who cut the frozen toe off. Captain Dick was a fan of boozing himself, and one night he decided to drop the toe into a beer glass of champagne and try to get people to drink it. The Sourtoe Cocktail Club was born, admittance given to anyone willing to touch their lips to the toe.

Over the years, toes have been lost to hijinks. The first was accidentally ingested by a miner attempting to set a record by drinking 13 beer glasses filled with champagne and the toe. On the thirteenth glass, he fell over backward, hit his head on the deck, and swallowed the toe. As Captain Dick searched for a new toe, he substituted a pickled bear's testicle and used the "pecker bone" as a swizzle stick. (He named this the "Better Bitter Bear Ball Highball," which was used intermittently as a stand-in between lost toes.)

For admission into the Sourtoe Cocktail Club, intrepid drinkers must let this severed human toe touch their lips.

The second toe came from a foot with an inoperable corn, but it vanished shortly after. Captain Dick ran newspaper ads offering $300 for a new toe, while imploring Canadian police to search for the old one. After administering a polygraph test to ensure the lost toe wasn't a publicity stunt, police received a tip that the toe was being served in Memphis, Tennessee. They tracked it to Texas, recovered it, and eventually returned it to Canada. A third toe, donated by another frostbite victim, was briefly in service until swallowed by a baseball player. Then, in an unexpected windfall, a miner lost a leg and gave all five toes to Captain Dick. With the new wealth of toes, he started the SourFoot Club, for those willing to put all five nubs in their cocktail.

In 2009, Captain Dick wrote an "au'toe'biography" detailing his experience sourtoeing around the country. He never made much money off his antics (which included "the first nude beauty contest north of the 60th parallel" and a failed business trying to sell pet rocks), but his legacy lives on in the blackened, mummified toe that regularly touches the lips of those looking to join his senseless, yet exclusive, club. In 2019, Captain Dick died at the age of 89.

Klondike Supply List
A TON OF GOODS

When gold was discovered in the region of Klondike in the summer of 1896, prospectors from around the country scrambled to the Yukon to make their fortune. To get there, they sailed hundreds, sometimes thousands of miles in overloaded boats, typically in conjunction with brutal stretches of mountainous terrain they traversed by foot.

With a stampede of people rushing toward a barren landscape, Canadian law required anyone entering Yukon territory to bring a year's supply of food. Added to their camping gear, the average prospector (man or woman) was responsible for hauling about 2,000 pounds (907 kg). The majority of explorers couldn't afford pack animals or the services of locals, so they carried the goods in 50–80 pound (23–36 kg) loads, trekking back and forth between their personal stockpile and the next frontier. Often, they walked a thousand miles to move their supplies 30 miles (48 km) away.

The packing list for a year of groceries, opposite, was published by the T. Eaton Company, once Canada's largest department store chain, in an 1898 catalog.

Prospectors at Chilkoot Pass in 1898, bound for the Klondike gold fields.

500 lbs flour	$12.00
200 lbs bacon	$19.00
75 lbs sugar	$3.00
10 lbs coffee	$3.00
10 lbs tea	$2.50
10 lbs baking powder	$1.00
12 lbs soap	$.40
3 doz yeast cakes	$1.44
1 lb mustard	$.40
25 lbs candles	$2.50
100 lbs beans	$1.67
10 lbs barley	$.25
10 lbs split peas	$.25
25 lbs rice	$1.05
15 lbs evaporated apples	$1.43
12 lbs evaporated vegetables	$2.16
1 doz beef extract	$3.00
1 doz condensed milk	$1.50
5 tins assorted soup	$3.00
20 lbs salt	$.20
1 lbs pepper	$.15
50 lbs rolled oats	$1.04
20 lbs corn meal	$.29
21 lbs baking soda	$.63
1/2 gal lime juice	$2.49
5 boxes matches	$.50
10 lbs prunes	$.63
20 lbs evaporated apricots	$2.20

RESTAURANT

EASTERN CANADA

AN OBSCURE PIECE OF COD

COD TONGUES • NEWFOUNDLAND AND LABRADOR

How to try it

Nanny's Root Cellar Kitchen in Elliston serves fried cod tongues topped with scrunchions—bits of crispy fried pork eaten across Newfoundland.

Although "cod tongues" may not sound all that appetizing, this misnomer is more charming than what they actually are: small, meaty muscles extracted from the back of a cod's neck. The two-pronged morsels are a Labrador delicacy. They have a flavor similar to scallops, a slightly rubbery texture, and when floured and fried, they make a pricey dish served throughout the coastal province.

Back when the Labrador Sea was packed with cod, most fishermen didn't bother scooping out the neck muscle from their fish. It was often enterprising children who would parse through the piles of discarded cod heads and remove the fleshy bits to sell for pocket money. But by the early 1990s, rampant overfishing led to the near-extinction of local cod, and the Canadian government placed a moratorium on commercial fishing off Labrador's shores. The new law left thousands jobless and even more cod-less.

Though several small fisheries have been established in recent years, cod is no longer the free-flowing food it once was. Now every part matters and must be treated with respect, even the small, gelatinous muscle from the back of the throat.

When Labrador was overflowing with cod, children would sift through piles of fish, cutting out the "tongues" to sell for pocket money.

A VERSATILE BAG OF PUDDING

BLUEBERRY DUFF • NEWFOUNDLAND AND LABRADOR

How to try it

There are many recipes for blueberry duff online; assemble the ingredients, grab a pillowcase, and get started.

The word *pudding* has described an array of dishes across history, from sausage and haggis to steamed cake and custard. The term has evolved to signify primarily desserts, but blueberry duff plays by nobody's rules: The Newfoundland pudding is interchangeably lunch and dessert.

A blueberry duff is the classic accompaniment to a traditional midday Sunday meal called "Jiggs dinner," made by boiling salt beef and root vegetables in a big pot. As the meat and vegetables simmer, the duff comes together much like a cake batter, with flour, eggs, sugar, and blueberries. The mixture is poured into a cotton bag (a pillowcase will do in a pinch), the bag is tied, and the whole thing is dropped into the Jiggs dinner pot to cook. The result is a pale, spongy cake that's sweet from the batter and savory from the beef-laced liquid.

Once cooked, the duff can be taken in two directions. As a side dish for the Jiggs dinner, the cake is simply sliced and plated with the stewed meat and vegetables. To serve the duff as dessert, top it with rum sauce and serve it with tea.

PICKLES WORTH PANICKING OVER

MUSTARD PICKLES • NEWFOUNDLAND AND LABRADOR

Sitting down for Sunday dinner in Newfoundland, you'll likely be asked, multiple times, to pass the mustard pickles: big chunks of cucumber, onion, and cauliflower, brined and mixed together in a thick yellow sauce. They're sweet, they're spicy, and you'd better not say anything bad about them, because in this province, mustard pickles are under perpetual protection from slander.

How to try it
Bick's Sweet Mustard Pickles are available online and in Canadian grocery stores.

The pickles' popularity is the result of Newfoundland's often cold and always rocky climate. Without the benefit of grocery stores, the island province's early residents relied on preserved foods—salted meats, puddings, and root vegetables—to get through the long winters. On a plate like that, a dollop of mustard pickles was a ray of zesty, welcome sunshine. (The traditional Newfoundland Sunday meal, the Jiggs dinner, is still served with mustard pickles.)

The brined vegetables are so entrenched in the local cuisine that a recent hiccup in their production caused immediate grief and panic. In 2016, Smucker Foods of Canada announced the company would end production of two of their mass-produced mustard pickle brands—the acidic Zest and the more robust Habitant. The news precipitated a wave of mourning across Newfoundland. ("Kiss your pickle goodbye" read a headline in one local paper.) Fans cleared out supermarket shelves, the Heritage Foundation of Newfoundland and Labrador began stockpiling family recipes, and at least one devotee wrote a musical elegy for the beloved condiment. In the end, pickle enthusiasts had nothing to fear. Smucker's simply increased production of the company's third mustard pickle variety, Bick's Sweet Mustard Pickles, which some experts say "tastes the same."

Pantry Staple

PICKLES

Not only do pickles taste amazing and last years without refrigeration, they are nutritional wonders. Celebrated Roman senator Cato the Elder recommended pickled cabbage first thing in the morning to remedy joint disease. Second-century Greek physician Galen believed eating brined olives and fermented fish sauce before a meal cleaned and reinforced the digestive system. These early pickle advocates weren't wrong. Fermented pickles are packed with vitamins and are an incredible source of probiotics, which have helped keep people alive and healthy throughout history.

Ancient luminaries like Greek physician Galen of Pergamon touted the benefits of pickled foods.

Sauerkraut

Popularized in Europe around the 18th century, sauerkraut was one of the Dutch navy's methods for preventing scurvy. When salted, pressed, and allowed to ferment, the pickled cabbage retained its high vitamin C content. British captain James Cook adopted the sauerkraut supplement on his ship, but at first his crew refused to eat it. To increase the cachet of the sour cabbage, Cook served it to just the high-ranking officers. Afterward, his crewmen agreed to eat it, too, and all of them were spared from scurvy.

Umeboshi

The prized Japanese dried and pickled plum umeboshi has been used to nourish the nation's fighters for centuries. Rich in acids and minerals, umeboshi is used to combat fatigue, stomachaches, dehydration, and hangovers. The mysterious assassins we now call ninjas ate "thirst balls" made from umeboshi pulp. Samurai took the salted fruit on long crusades and, since the 16th century, an umeboshi comes standard issue in the military rations of Japanese soldiers.

Naem

Thailand's sour sausage is made by fermenting seasoned pork, pork skin, and sticky rice for up to a week, until it develops its signature tang. The sticky rice, which becomes a breeding ground for lactic acid bacteria and yeast, acts as the souring agent, while the salt keeps the pork from going too sour. The result is spicy, sour, garlicky, and often eaten raw.

Pickle Juice

At least in America, pickle juice is no throwaway liquid. Americans use the briny, après-pickle fluid to relieve cramping and muscle ache after a strenuous workout. Packed with sodium and potassium, pickle juice helps replenish electrolytes much like commercial sports drinks. In 2000, when the Philadelphia Eagles beat the Dallas Cowboys in punishing 109°F (42.8°C) heat, the victors called upon pickle juice to keep them in optimum form.

Kimchi

These spicy fermented vegetables at the heart of the Korean diet may be what saved the country from severe acute respiratory syndrome (SARS). In 2003, SARS broke out in China and spread rapidly, killing 774 people across seven countries. Yet South Korea, whose citizens regularly travel to China, did not experience a single fatality. Many South Koreans, including doctors and scientists, believe the scores of healthy bacteria in a kimchi-rich diet are responsible for killing the SARS microbes and keeping the Korean public from infection.

In 2016, the average South Korean ate about 80 pounds of kimchi.

A RUM AND COD INITIATION

SCREECH-IN • NEWFOUNDLAND AND LABRADOR

How to try it

Christian's Pub on George Street in St. John's is known for its educational and moving screech-ins led by Keith Vokey, the son of the ceremony's "inventor."

An English captain once wrote that the cod around Newfoundland were "so thick by the shore that we hardly have been able to row a boat through them." Starting in the 16th century, European sailors came by the thousands to fish for cod, salting the abundance and then selling it to Europe and its colonies. The British West Indies became an important buyer: Plantation owners needed protein to feed their enslaved workers, and salt cod provided a cheap, nonperishable solution. In return, Jamaica sent barrels of their local specialty: rum.

"Screech" is the name for rum in Newfoundland. While no one knows exactly why, legend goes it was named for the screeching sound emitted by an American GI after taking a shot of the 80-proof rum. Screech has become so ingrained in Newfoundland life that locals created an elaborate, tongue-in-cheek ritual known as a "Screech-In" that welcomes newcomers to their province.

To become an honorary Newfoundlander (or "Newfie") and be inducted to the Royal Order of the Screechers, you must first introduce yourself and allow the locals to mock you. Next you kiss a cod (salted, frozen, or fresh), eat some bologna (known as Newfie steak and nearly as popular as Screech), and when asked, "Is ye a Screecher?" answer proudly, "Deed I is, me old cock, and long may your big jib draw!" Although this response may sound uncouth, it is simply Newfie slang for "Yes, indeed, my friend, may your big sail always catch the wind." The inductee then takes a shot of Screech, and the deal is done.

Kissing a cod is the only way to become an honorary Newfie.

INDIGENOUS COMFORT FOOD

SEAL FLIPPER PIE • NEWFOUNDLAND AND LABRADOR

How to try it

Flipper pie is often available during the Lenten season (which coincides with seal-hunting season). Bidgood's Market in Goulds bakes meat pies all year, including flipper.

The meat of a seal flipper is rich, dark, and delicate. The flavor is simultaneously gamey and fishy, akin to duck, and when slowly braised in a gravy studded with vegetables, seal flippers make a filling to rival any potpie.

The Indigenous and maritime cultures of Canada have long relied on seals for their livelihood. Seal pelts provided waterproof material for coats and boots, seal oil was used for lamps, and seal meat contained valuable iron and vitamins that fended off scurvy. The flippers, however, had no obvious commercial value, and so they became pie.

Flipper eating has its detractors. Animal rights groups criticize the traditional seal hunt that takes place every spring, calling the ritual inhumane. Those who support the practice cite the strict regulations of the hunt and the growing seal

population. Seals are not endangered in Canada, and in many parts, the number is actually on the rise. Although seals are unlikely to be adopted as pie filling outside of Newfoundland, many argue that within the region, seal meat is one of the most sustainable meat sources available.

PREHISTORIC COCKTAIL COOLER

ICEBERG ICE • NEWFOUNDLAND AND LABRADOR

Newfoundland sits in Iceberg Alley, the famed stretch of the Atlantic Ocean known for ushering icy monoliths, calved from Greenland glaciers, southbound to the open sea. Starting in the early spring, when the icebergs begin rolling through, many locals get out their tools to begin harvesting the frozen, seasonal slabs.

While larger companies often use cranes, boats, and nets to do the job, smaller ice harvesters get creative when wrangling up "bergie bits." (One technique is shooting the ice with a rifle.) After the chunks are brought ashore, they're broken into smaller bits using a hammer or a mallet and a thin pin, which shapes the pieces into tiny icebergs.

Iceberg ice is used just like freezer ice. It's often coupled with alcoholic beverages, perhaps to kill off any sneaky prehistoric pathogens that might be inside. Aside from the fact that chilling a drink with a 12,000-year-old specimen is undeniably cool, people love iceberg ice for its taste—or rather, lack thereof. Many claim that pre–Industrial Revolution water and air, free of modern pollutants, give the ice its highly coveted tastelessness.

How to try it
If you're not into harvesting your own bergie bits, general stores (like B.J.'s General Store in Fogo) often sell it by the bag.

For these fishermen in Bonavista Bay, the big catch of the day is an iceberg chunk.

ACADIAN GATHERING PIE

RAPPIE PIE • NOVA SCOTIA

How to try it

Some Acadian restaurants, such as La Cuisine Robicheau in Saulnierville, Nova Scotia, serve rappie pies. To make it at home, there's an abundance of traditional recipes online, with fillings from poultry to seafood.

Rappie pie is no everyday food. The recipe calls for 20 pounds (9 kg) of potatoes, which must be peeled, grated ("râpé" in French), and wrung out in small batches to remove their liquid. Once dry, the potatoes are rehydrated with hot stock, which generally comes from a pot where a chicken's been boiling for hours. Once the liquid transplant is complete, the chicken-infused potatoes are poured into a casserole dish, topped with shredded chicken, more grated potatoes, hunks of salt pork, and dollops of butter, then crisped in an oven. Processing 20 pounds of potatoes requires time and teamwork, both in the making and the eating, which is precisely the point of a rappie pie. This casserole is an exercise in fellowship—a way to gather the dwindling Acadian community.

The Acadians are descendants of the early French colonists who settled in what is now Nova Scotia, New Brunswick, and Prince Edward Island starting in the 17th century. As the decades passed, Acadians formed a close-knit community largely independent from European influence. But in 1713, France ceded control of Acadia

to the British, who feared the Acadians would remain loyal to France. In 1754, the two European powers went to war, and when France lost, the Brits forced out the Acadians in a violent series of events called the Great Expulsion.

More than 10,000 Acadians, many of whom died along the way, were forced from their homes. They took refuge in Louisiana, the Caribbean, and the English colonies along the Atlantic seaboard. Some went back to France. When the Acadians were permitted to return to Canada in 1764, they were given new land that was rocky and difficult to farm. The resettled community began to grow potatoes, which bore the tradition of making a dish with 20 pounds of potatoes and a lot of kinship.

Rappie pie has become a symbol of the Acadian plight. It's a dish that represents adversity, resilience, and ingenuity, while displaying French technique in a deceivingly humble presentation. And while rappie pie is delicious, the real importance lies in its ability to connect generations of displaced people.

SOAP-FLAVORED GUM

THRILLS GUM • ONTARIO

How to try it

Thrills is still sold in candy stores and online.

If you're tired of coworkers, friends, and family always asking you for a piece of gum, try handing them a purple nugget of Thrills. Canadians say the retro, rosewater-flavored chewing gum tastes like soap, and the company agrees. The box bears the reassuring slogan: "It still tastes like soap!" Fans cite not having to share as a major plus of chewing it.

For much of the 20th century, the O-Pee-Chee Gum Company, which also sold trading cards, provided Canadians with Thrills. In the 1950s and '60s, perfumed flavors like teaberry and violet were common at the candy store, and rosewater-flavored Thrills fit in perfectly. Although floral gum is less desirable these days, if you're lucky enough to like it you'll likely get the whole pack to yourself.

····· FOOD PIONEER ·····

SAM PANOPOULOS

(1934–2017)

Sam Panopoulos, inventor of the notorious Hawaiian pizza, left Greece on a boat bound for Canada in 1954. Along the way, the boat stopped in Naples, where Panopoulos encountered pizza for the first time. When he arrived in the small Ontario town of Chatham, he opened the Satellite Restaurant and began serving the kind of food people ate in midcentury Canada: pancakes in the morning, burgers and fries for lunch, and liver and onions for dinner. But Panopoulos was eager to delight his customers with new dishes. First, he hired an Asian cook and put American Chinese food on his menu. Then, he checked out Detroit and Windsor's up-and-coming pizza scene and began his own experiments.

Pizza was still totally foreign to most Canadians. (A 1962 recipe from the *Toronto Star* includes a recipe for "Spanish pizza," made with yellow rice and Vienna sausages piled on a dough made from biscuit mix.) At the time, pizza boxes didn't exist, so Panopoulos cut circles out of cardboard boxes from a furniture seller next door, placed the pizza on top, and wrapped the whole thing in aluminum foil.

He mixed and matched toppings to see what worked. And although some of his discoveries, such as olives and anchovies, were simultaneously discovered by other pizza pioneers, the use of pineapple was something entirely his own.

In the 1960s, Hawaii loomed large in the fantasy of North Americans, fueled by the tales of returning soldiers who had seen the South Pacific paradise. Tiki culture became hugely popular, and canned pineapple, which was advertised extensively in Ontario's newspapers, became a staple of Canadian households. According to Panopoulos, sweet and sour was a rare flavor, available only in Chinese dishes. With the Satellite already serving Chinese food, he thought his customers might appreciate a sweet and savory pizza. In 1962 he opened a can of pineapple, drained it, and threw the pieces of fruit on a pie. He named his creation the "Hawaiian pizza," and amazingly, the ham and pineapple combination caught on.

Panopoulos passed away in 2017, but he never stopped loving his signature pie. When asked, at the age of 81, if he still ordered it, Panopoulos said, "Yeah, I do. I still like it."

Hawaiian pizza is neither Hawaiian nor Italian.

A PLASTIC BAG OF MILK

BAGGED MILK • ONTARIO

How to try it

In Ontario, milk bags are available in every grocery store and are commonly called "milk bladders."

There are pluses and minuses to buying milk in a plastic bag, which happens to be Ontario's prevailing milk packaging. The dairy section in the province's grocery stores is a display of plump, rectangular sacks of milk, often bundled three to a pack. At home, Ontarians deposit a milk sack into a special plastic pitcher, snip a corner, and pour from the homemade "spout." The upside is that bagged milk can be easily stored in tight spaces where a carton would not fit, and the minimal packaging reduces waste and transportation costs. The downside is that the bag cannot be resealed and so must be drunk relatively quickly, and the flimsy, makeshift spout is prone to accidents. Canada is far from the only nation with this system (other milk-bagging regions include eastern Europe, South America, India, and China), but the Canadian practice emerged almost by accident, when transitioning from British weights and measures.

Debuted in the late 1960s, milk bags weren't truly embraced until the 1970s, when Canada switched to the metric system. Redesigning machinery to manufacture glass bottles and cardboard cartons in liters, rather than gallons, was costly and time-consuming—but resizing plastic bags was simple. Milk companies started offering free plastic pitchers to entice Canadians to switch to bags, and many did. Today, Canadians drink about half their milk from a bag, and in the province of Ontario, it jumps to around 80 percent.

A POTATO TRUCKER'S THEME SONG

"BUD THE SPUD" • PRINCE EDWARD ISLAND

How to try it

The Canadian Potato Museum is located on Prince Edward Island. Their café serves everything PEI potato, from french fries to potato fudge.

Folk and country artist Stompin' Tom Connors made a long, distinguished career with his Canadian-centric music, crooning about union strikes, gold mining in the Yukon, and hockey. From the 1960s on, Connors wrote more than 300 tunes, among them the 1969 breakout hit "Bud the Spud," featuring a truck driver named Bud who hauls "the best dog-gone potatoes that's ever been growed" from Prince Edward Island. He travels the country, meeting people and delivering his spuds. The Ontario police chase him down the highway, but Bud is just a fun-loving potato hero doing important work: bringing the PEI potato to tables across the country. The song became so popular it inspired a children's book and cemented the PEI potato's place in Canadian life.

Canada's smallest province, Prince Edward Island, is known for its serene, pastoral landscape of rolling hills, woodland, and windswept coastline. The lush island grows more than a hundred potato varieties, which make up 25 percent of the Canadian crop. Local farmers say their weather (warm summers, cool winters, plenty of rain) coupled with their signature soil (deep red and iron-rich) makes the potatoes uniquely delicious. It's also an island of small family plots, with relatives passing their hard-won knowledge generationally. (Only about 300 farmers manage the entire crop.) In the words of the great Stompin' Tom Connors:

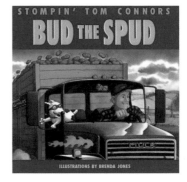

> Now I know a lot of people from east to west
> And they like the spuds from the island best
> Cause they stand up to the hardest test –
> Right on the table;
> So when you see that big truck rollin' by
> Wave your hand or kinda wink your eye
> Cause that's Bud the Spud, from old PEI.
> With another big load of potatoes!

A BETTER WAY TO SEASON LIVER

MONTREAL STEAK SPICE • QUEBEC

If you've ever enjoyed the peppery-sweet taste of a ribeye seasoned with Montreal steak spice, you can thank a Canadian grill cook known as the Shadow.

Like many cured-meat seasonings, the popular blend has its roots in eastern European cooking. Montreal steak spice features pepper, garlic, coriander, and dill—all common in recipes from Romania. It makes sense, then, that most accounts trace the origin of the spice blend to Schwartz's, a deli founded by a Romanian immigrant that's now the oldest, and arguably the most famous, deli in all of Canada.

According to *Schwartz's Hebrew Delicatessen: The Story* by Bill Browstein, every deli employee was allowed to eat their fill of only one item: cooked liver. It was perhaps this limited diet that made a cook named Morris Sherman so thin that he earned the nickname the Shadow. (His coworkers joked that if he turned sideways, only his shadow would be visible.) One day, according to Canadian deli legend, Sherman used a new blend of spices to make the liver more appealing, and customers liked it so much, they started requesting it on other items, especially steak. Montreal steak spice quickly became a seasoning classic, and Schwartz's, known for its smoked meat sandwiches, rose to Jewish deli fame. (In 2012, Céline Dion became a part owner.)

How to try it
For those who want to try Montreal steak spice at the source, the lines at Schwartz's can be long. Otherwise, it can easily be found in the grocery store and online.

Schwartz's was established in 1928 by Reuben Schwartz, a Jewish immigrant from Romania.

MAPLE SYRUP HOGWARTS

SUCRERIE DE LA MONTAGNE • QUEBEC

How to try it

In Rigaud, about an hour west of Montreal, the Sucrerie de la Montagne is open all year. After a heavy night of syrup, you can sleep in one of the sugar shack cabins.

Maple syrup runs through the veins of the Quebecois. They produce more than 90 percent of Canada's golden liquid supply, which makes up more than 70 percent of the world's maple syrup. To extract 150 million pounds of syrup from trees, much of the process has become high-tech: Computer-controlled vacuum tubes connect trees to reverse osmosis machines, before the syrup is cooked down in huge evaporators to a precise 66 percent sugar content. Much of the natural beauty has been lost to automation, but tucked in the woods about an hour west of Montreal is Sucrerie de la Montagne, an authentic sugar shack making syrup as it was done by early French arrivals, using tree taps, buckets, and a wood-fired evaporator.

Think of Sucrerie de la Montagne—with its log cabins and rural, whimsical setting—as a Maple Syrup Hogwarts. After a tour of the syrup production, you are welcomed into an immense banquet hall built of stone and massive wooden beams. A sugar shack feast arrives at the long communal tables. It's an all-you-can-eat spread of crusty bread, pea soup, maple-smoked ham, wood-fire baked beans, omelet soufflé, sausage, meatball stew, crispy-fried pork rinds, mashed potatoes, tourtière (a Canadian meat pie), homemade fruit ketchup, and pickles. On the table, you'll find jugs of maple syrup that are constantly refilled, to pour over anything your heart desires. For dessert, there is maple taffy, made by pouring syrup over fresh snow.

The Sucrerie de la Montagne even has its own Dumbledore, founder Pierre Faucher, who with his enormous white beard, wide-brimmed field hat, flowing flannel layers, and antique wool sash (known as a ceinture fléchée), and accompanied by his three-quarters wolf, one-quarter husky Louploup, seems like the human embodiment of maple syrup.

Pierre Faucher's sugar refinery collects sap for maple syrup the old-fashioned way, with buckets attached to maple trees.

The Great Canadian Maple Syrup Heist

It was a nearly perfect crime. Replacement barrels were painted the exact same shade of white. Replica stickers were printed. A specialized forklift was rented. Under the cover of night, dozens, then hundreds, then thousands of 600-pound (272-kg) barrels were extracted, drained, refilled, and brought back, neatly replaced into the towering six-barrel stacks. For months, this process happened over and over, undetected. Then someone realized maple syrup doesn't sweat.

The Canadian Maple Syrup Reserve, spread across multiple rural Quebec towns, is a string of huge warehouses that hold the country's excess supply of syrup. The reserve is controlled by the Federation of Quebec Maple Syrup Producers, an organization that oversees every aspect of the Quebec syrup business, including supply and price. (Some compare the federation to OPEC, the organization of oil-producing countries, others to the Mafia.) In July 2012, a federation representative was climbing stacks of 600-pound barrels inside the syrup reserve when one nearly slipped from under his feet. The barrel, he realized, was empty. He began inspecting other barrels and found rust, along with rings of condensation. (Maple syrup never sweats.) Suspicious, he opened the barrels. They were full of water.

Two hundred fifty investigators arrived to check every barrel in the reserve. They found nearly 10,000 barrels filled with water, which meant 18 million Canadian dollars' worth of syrup was missing. The Great Canadian Maple Syrup Heist, as the theft is commonly known, was the largest robbery in Quebec history.

Established to protect the industry from price swings and bankruptcy, the federation dictates how much syrup each producer can make, whom they can sell it to, and for how much. All syrup produced in excess is put into the Maple Syrup Reserve, also controlled by the federation. If a syrup producer refuses, or sells directly to the buyer, they are fined or have their syrup seized. This restricted system prompted a maple syrup black market, where smugglers known as "barrel rollers" are tasked with moving syrup into places such as the United States and Europe, beyond the reach of the Federation.

In 2017, after an extensive investigation, three major guilty sentences were finally obtained. Avik Caron, whose wife owned the property on which the reserve warehouse was rented, was fined $1.2 million CAD and sentenced to five years in prison. The barrel roller was Richard Vallières, a hotshot in the world of syrup smuggling, who took the barrels to a small sugar shack and siphoned the syrup. He was fined $9.4 million CAD and sentenced to eight years in prison. Étienne St-Pierre, who received the syrup in New Brunswick and sold it abroad, was sentenced to two years home imprisonment and fined more than a million dollars.

Shockingly, about two thirds of the "hot" syrup was recovered. The other third remains missing, likely poured over pancakes or otherwise enjoyed by unsuspecting diners across New England. After the arrests, tensions between the federation and the rebels only intensified. In a country where marijuana is legal, and even hard drugs are decriminalized, an increasing number of producers want to know why selling maple syrup is a crime.

THE FROZEN APPLE LIBATION

ICE CIDER · QUEBEC

When apples freeze, their juice becomes concentrated, and when that sugary, golden liquid is painstakingly pressed from the fruit then slowly fermented, it becomes ice cider, Quebec's gift to the world of libations. The amber liquor is made using one of two techniques. The first, which is riskier and more labor-intensive, leaves the apples in the orchard until about January, waiting for them to reach a temperature of −10°C (14°F). The apples grow gradually shriveled and hard as they dry out, then the frozen apples are pressed (a process that can take

How to try it
Ice cider is generally served as an aperitif or paired with a dessert course. Bottles of Montreal's finest can be ordered online.

hours) and the extracted juice is fermented. The second method juices fresh apples, then puts the juice outside in the cold, allowing the water to crystalize and separate from the sugary liquid. Then, with the water removed, the concentrated juice is fermented.

Both methods require huge amounts of apples: Nearly 10 pounds (4.5 kg) goes into every 375 ml bottle of ice cider, or about five times what's needed for regular hard apple cider. The taste is a rich distillation of apples coupled with the warmth of alcohol, sweet without being saccharine, sharp with a velvety texture.

The Beaver Club's Extravagant Dinners

In 1785, the Fur Barons of Montreal, a group of early European settlers in the beaver pelt industry, established a notoriously opulent dining club. The objective of the Beaver Club, according to their official rules, was "to bring together, at stated periods during the winter season, a set of men highly respectable in society, who had passed their best days in a savage country and had encountered the difficulties and dangers incident to a pursuit of the fur trade of Canada."

All dinners commenced at 4 p.m. with the passing of a calumet, an American Indian ceremonial pipe, followed by five toasts: to Mary Mother of All Saints, to the king, to the fur trade, to the voyagers and their families, and to absent members. From there, there was typically a Highland piper to play out the servants carrying a flaming boar's head on a velvet dais. Then the feasting and imbibing would begin in earnest with a table overflowing with country food and enough wine to drown each man. (Some meals ended in a final course of "a cheque for a sum of money" served on a plate.)

The Beaver Club was known to get rowdy as they danced on tables and broke china and crystal engraved with the club's insignia. In the wee hours,

Founder Joseph Frobisher (bottom left) allowed only the most "respectable" fur traders to join his decadent Beaver Club.

they often sat single file on the floor and pretended to row an imaginary canoe in a tradition called "The Grand Voyage." They sang voyageur songs and used fire pokers and walking sticks as paddles—while dressed in ruffled gold lace, gold-clasped garters, and silver-buckled shoes.

One night in 1808, 31 members and guests went out for dinner and racked up the following bill:

32 dinners

29 bottles of Madeira

19 bottles of Port

14 bottles of Porter

12 quarts ale

7 suppers

Brandy and gin

Cigars, pipes, tobacco

Three wine glasses broken

Total................ £28.15

The exclusive club was both picky and formal about who they let in. When auditioning a new member, they invited him to dinner, got him drunk, and when he left, they voted (also drunk). If the prospective member earned a unanimous yes, he was let in. Over four decades, they inducted about a hundred members, but never exceeded 55 men at a time.

The United States

WEST COAST, ALASKA, AND HAWAII
FOUR CORNERS AND THE SOUTHWEST
GREAT PLAINS • THE MIDWEST • THE SOUTHEAST
THE MID-ATLANTIC • NEW ENGLAND

WEST COAST, ALASKA, AND HAWAII

THE NOAH'S ARK FOR CITRUS

CITRUS VARIETY COLLECTION • CALIFORNIA

How to try it

The Citrus Variety Collection hosts occasional public education events featuring tastings of hybrid fruits and their "parents."

The citrus collection at the University of California, Riverside, is the largest in America, containing more than a thousand different citrus varieties across 22 acres. And like the animals on Noah's Ark, they keep two of each species.

The thousands of specimens on display exhibit the staggering diversity of citrus, remarkable given that most modern citrus stems from just three ancient varieties: the Malaysian pomelo, the North Indian citron, and the Chinese mandarin. The sweet supermarket orange, for example, was produced through multiple crosses between a pomelo and a mandarin. The grapefruit was made by crossing a pomelo and a sweet orange.

When breeders want to create a new type of citrus or experiment with multiple varieties, they come to UC Riverside to play with the genetic material. Yellow-and-green-striped lemons, football-size pomelos, heart-shaped grapefruits with deep red veins, and fruits so small they look like peas—they all thrive in the orchard. When cut, some varieties ooze a mucosal slime. Others have tiny juice bubbles with a caviar-like pop. Whatever happens, it's all by design.

THAI FOOD IN A TEMPLE PARKING LOT

WAT THAI MARKET • CALIFORNIA

How to try it

Wat Thai market, located at 8225 Coldwater Canyon Avenue, is open on Saturdays and Sundays from 8 a.m. to 5 p.m. To purchase food, you must exchange cash for tokens, which are accepted by the vendors.

Since the 1980s, Wat Thai market in Los Angeles has sold some of the best Thai food outside of Thailand. Located in the parking lot of a Buddhist tem-ple, these outdoor food stalls were conceived by a handful of Thai grandmothers who wanted to share their family recipes. Today, this weekend-only market has trans-formed into a bustling Thai street scene with a devout following of Californians. Make your way through the thick, sweet-and-smoky air to find classics like pad thai and papaya salad, as well as the lesser-known but equally delicious crispy mussel pancake, sour Isaan sausage, meaty larb, and sweet coconut fritters.

·····FOOD PIONEER·····

BROWNIE MARY

(1921–1999)

The *New York Times* compared Mary Jane Rathbun to American domestic goddesses Betty Crocker, Mrs. Field, and Sara Lee—with one big difference. Rathbun's signature baking ingredient was cannabis.

Born in 1921, Mary Jane—her real name—Rathbun spent 50 years working as a waitress. In the early 1970s she started selling pot brownies on the side. Her homemade flyers, decorated with squiggles and stars, advertised her "magically delicious" brownies. The marketing tactic brought police to her door, which she opened only to reveal dozens of brownies in her kitchen. Rathbun's first words to the cops were: "Oh, shit." At 57, she already had a sweet, elderly appearance, and reporters thrilled at the idea of a grass-slinging granny (Rathbun liked to smoke marijuana as well as bake it). Her arrest made national headlines.

Charged with possession and sale of illegal drugs, Rathbun was sentenced to hundreds of hours of community service and became a fixture on the volunteering scene. In the 1980s, when San Francisco was hit hard by AIDS, Rathbun spent her time at San Francisco General Hospital, caring

Brownie Mary wearing her signature marijuana leaf button as she shows off her healing baked goods.

for AIDS and cancer patients. She called them her "kids," and to help alleviate their pain and nausea and stimulate their appetites, she baked them her signature pot brownies. In 1982, Rathbun was arrested again for bringing brownies to a cancer patient, but that didn't stop her—it's said that she baked some 1,500 brownies a month for patients. In 1986, the hospital named her "Volunteer of the Year."

Her third arrest, in 1992, also made the news, but this time headlines portrayed her as an AIDS activist who worked intimately with patients. Rathbun was ultimately acquitted of the charges, and August 25, 1992, was officially declared Brownie Mary Day.

Rathbun never gave up her signature brownie recipe. "When and if they legalize it, I'll sell my brownie recipe to Betty Crocker or Duncan Hines," she told a reporter, "and take the profits and buy an old Victorian for my kids with AIDS."

When Brownie Mary, the "angel of mercy," died of a heart attack in 1999, hundreds of people showed up to a vigil in her honor, hailing her as a social justice hero and a totally tubular baker.

INDIGENOUS CUISINE IN A BOOKSTORE

CAFE OHLONE · CALIFORNIA

Cafe Ohlone, a restaurant resurrecting local Indigenous American cuisine, was founded by two members of the Ohlone tribe whose ancestors hunted and gathered in the area centuries ago. Vincent Medina and Louis Trevino met at a 2014 conference on native languages and bonded while listening to records of tribal-elder interviews from the 1930s. Struck by the detailed information on disappearing culinary techniques, Medina and Trevino set out to re-create the recipes themselves. In 2018, they served their first meal on a patio behind Berkeley's University Press Books, where Cafe Ohlone still operates today.

How to try it

University Press Books closed in 2020 and Cafe Ohlone is looking for a new home in the Bay Area. In the meantime, they offer takeaway dinner boxes that contain prepared meals as well as ingredients you can use to make some of their dishes at home. You can reserve your box at makamham.com.

Founders Louis Trevino (left) and Vincent Medina (right) plating traditional Ohlone food at their café in Berkeley.

The Cafe Ohlone experience offers a glimpse into a little known Indigenous culture. Each meal begins with a solemn prayer in the Chochenyo language and a brief history of the native peoples of the East Bay Area, who preserved their culture despite persecution from successive Spanish, Mexican, and American governments. At each meal, Medina and Trevino introduce the dishes, which are based on wild ingredients gathered locally by native people. The menu changes seasonally, but it might include a cress, sorrel, and amaranth salad, venison meatballs with local mushrooms, an acorn flour brownie, and plenty of tea made from local herbs. Many meals close with songs or a fast-moving round of an ancient gambling game.

Cafe Ohlone's menu and hours are dependent on how much wild food they can sustainably source, so the restaurant updates their hours and offerings about three to four weeks in advance.

ENCRYPTED INEBRIATION

THE ZOMBIE • CALIFORNIA

How to try it

For an old-school experience, go to the tiny, cash-only Tiki-Ti in Los Angeles, which opened in the '60s. For the 21st-century spin, visit Jeff Berry's Latitude 29 in New Orleans, open since 2014.

The Zombie has a reputation for subduing its victims. The rum-based cocktail, invented at Hollywood restaurant Don the Beachcomber in 1934, packed such a punch that customers were cut off after two. And, for decades, proprietor Donn Beach—Zombie inventor and "father" of tiki—was the only person who knew what was in them.

Beach kept his liquors, elixirs, and proprietary mixes unlabeled behind the Beachcomber's bar. Each mystery bottle was given a number. The bartenders knew which bottles to pour and in what amount, but not what was in them. In other establishments, bartenders cobbled together fruit juices, syrups, and rum in a loose approximation of the original.

In 2007, tiki cocktail connoisseur and author Jeff "Beachbum" Berry solved the mystery. After finding a black book of coded recipes from Beach's restaurant, he worked with former Beachcomber staff to reverse engineer the cocktails. He published the decrypted Zombie recipe, nearly two decades after Donn Beach died, in the book *Sippin' Safari: In Search of the Great "Lost" Tropical Drink Recipes . . . and the People Behind Them.*

The Talented Groceries of
HOLLYWOOD POST-PRODUCTION

In the 1920s, when Universal Studios was transitioning from silent movies to sound, crewman Jack Foley showed them the way. His technique, now called "Foley art," was to lay an audio track over the film in post-production, adding sound effects like footsteps and slamming doors. Foley used unconventional methods to create convincing sounds, and today Foley artists reach for anything and everything to simulate the crunches, splashes, and thuds in the movies, which means food has been tapped to play some serious Hollywood roles.

When freezing a wig and ripping Velcro didn't work, Foley artists turned to frozen lettuce to engineer the sound of Rose's ice-covered hair breaking as she clung to the headboard, waiting to be rescued after the shipwreck in *Titanic.*

The Foley artists working on **Fight Club** tried out many ways to mimic the sound of a physical brawl. One of the winners was punching a raw chicken stuffed with walnuts. The movie nabbed an Oscar for Best Sound Editing.

Terminator 2: Judgment Day opens with a postapocalyptic shot of Los Angeles in 2029, after a nuclear fire has killed three billion people. Shells of cars and human remains litter the ravaged landscape. From above the frame, a robotic foot crashes down, smashing a skull with a shattering succession of fractures and cracks. It sounds eerily like human bone. How did they do it? Pistachios.

Steven Spielberg wanted **E.T.** to sound "liquidy and friendly" when he moved, which inspired a Foley artist to wander a grocery store scouting for slippery, cheerful sounds. She found that packaged liver fit the bill, which, when mixed with the sound of jelly swishing in a wet towel and popcorn shifting gently in a bag, became the sound of the alien's movements.

When John Goodman lifts Jeff Bridges from his wheelchair in **The Big Lebowski**, Lebowski's back cracks audibly and he screams in pain—but it's just celery. Stalks of the green stuff are twisted and snapped to simulate breaking bones.

In **Jurassic Park,** a velociraptor hatches from its shell to the sound of an ice-cream cone being crumbled. The subsequent sound, of the baby dino emerging from its egg, was made by two gloved hands covered in liquid soap squishing the flesh of a melon.

OREGON'S
Mysterious Mycology

Oregonians hunt for mushrooms on vacation, take mushroom-cultivating classes at mushroom schools, attend fungus festivals, and occasionally ascend to the vocation of professional mushroom hunter. For the amateur aficionado or mycology maven, Oregon forests supply a buffet of unusual fungus ready to be identified, picked, and sautéed with brown butter.

BEAR'S HEAD TOOTH (*HERICIUM AMERICANUM*) is a mushroom that resembles a white, dripping mass of wax. The easily identified mushroom sprouts from trees and often takes up residence in recent cuts or wounds to the wood. When cooked, the soft spines are tender and sweet and taste vaguely of seafood.

CAULIFLOWER MUSHROOMS (*SPARASSIS CRISPA*) have curly, leafy lobes that grow into big spongy bushes. Once you've found a cauliflower mushroom, remember the place because they tend to grow in the same spot. After a meticulous cleaning, they're great simmered in flavorful liquid or broth, which brings out their lasagna noodle-like texture.

A HONEY MUSHROOM (*ARMILLARIA OSTOYAE*) that has been slowly growing in Oregon's Blue Mountains for more than a thousand years is the largest living organism in the world. It occupies more than 3 square miles, extending a meter into the ground and weighing, some estimate, up to 35,000 tons (the equivalent of 200 gray whales). Honey mushrooms are edible, though they have a bitterness that makes them less appealing than daintier spores.

LOBSTER MUSHROOMS (*HYPOMYCES LACTIFLUORUM*) are not technically mushrooms but rather a parasitic fungus that grows on mushrooms. They appear after a heavy rain, often under hemlock trees. Prized for their cooked-lobster color and lobster-like flavor and aroma, they pair well with seafood dishes.

BLACK TRUMPETS (*CRATERELLUS CORNUCOPIOIDES*) are hollow, funnel-shaped mushrooms with a dusty black-gray exterior. Finding them can be tricky because they blend into the forest floor, but their rich, buttery, and woodsy flavor makes them them a darling of the wild mushroom world. When dried, they emit notes of black truffle.

SAFFRON MILK CAPS (*LACTARIUS DELICIOSUS*) are convex orange-capped mushrooms with delicate gills. When they're sliced open, the flesh excretes a milky, sunset-colored latex liquid. When bruised, they turn green. Milk caps are loved around the world for their firm, almost crunchy texture, and have been eaten in Europe for millennia. Russians like to preserve them in salt, while the Spanish panfry them in garlic and olive oil. Find them in pine forests or near other conifers.

APRICOT JELLY (*GUEPINIA HELVELLOIDES*) is a bright, salmon-colored, ear-shaped mushroom with a smooth, gelatinous texture. Find it on the ground, generally near a conifer tree. The thin, petal-like flesh is tasty when raw in salads, as well as pickled or candied.

A GIANT PHALLIC CLAM

GEODUCK • WASHINGTON

Geoducks are harvested along coasts in the Pacific Northwest and have shells that can grow up to 8 inches (20 cm) long.

The geoduck (pronounced "gooey-duck") is the world's largest burrowing clam, found only in the coastal waters around Washington, British Columbia, and Alaska. The appearance of the hulking, wrinkled mollusk draws plenty of suggestive comparisons, but that doesn't deter its adoring international fan base.

By weight, geoducks are worth more than foie gras. Many characterize the clams as the ideal seafood: The meat is sweet and briny (without being fishy) and has a clean, snappy bite that's much crisper than other clams. Much of Washington's live geoduck is exported to restaurants in Asia. In China, geoducks are a prized hot pot ingredient, while in Japan they're eaten as sashimi. What stays in Washington is bought up quickly by locals, who make it into anything from chowder to carpaccio.

The area's Indigenous American Salish tribes gave the clam its name, which derives from gweduc, meaning "dig deep" in the Lushootseed language. As the geoduck grows, it uses its tiny foot to burrow into the seafloor, leaving only its neck above ground. With few natural predators, geoducks are one of the longest-living animals in the world. (The oldest phallic clam recorded was 168 years old.) Recently, scientists have been using the shells to study climate change. Much like trees, geoducks grow a ring each year and the width of that ring chronicles the temperature of the year.

How to try it
You can order a fresh 2-pound (1-kg) geoduck from the Washington company Taylor Shellfish Farms for $70.

AN OPEN-ACCESS EDIBLE PARK

BEACON FOOD FOREST • WASHINGTON

How to try it
Beacon Food Forest is located at 15 Avenue South and South Dakota Street. The Sound Transit Link Light Rail and the King County Metro routes #50, #60, and #36 are within walking distance of the forest.

The Seattle neighborhood of Beacon Hill is home to seven acres of public land teeming with trees, perennials, and annuals—a forest that provides the community with unlimited free access to fresh produce.

The Beacon Food Forest, among the largest public edible permaculture gardens in America, grows more than 350 species of plants and vegetables. Food forests are meant to mimic the natural, plant-based food production cycle of woodland ecosystems. All plants are positioned in a way that helps create harmony in growth. The canopy from large fruit trees, for example, shades smaller berry bushes, while root vegetables provide mulch. The plants are "layered," which means that vertical space is maximized. Ground vegetables grow beneath shrubs, which grow beneath dwarf trees, which grow beneath large trees. This diversity and density of plants ensures rich soil and copious amounts of food.

Anyone is allowed to forage in the Beacon Food Forest. Historically, residents of Beacon Hill have struggled with access to affordable local produce, and the open-door policy of the food forest is meant to remedy this nutritional deficit. There is no prerequisite for harvesting and eating, and no responsibilities in the form of gardening or volunteering. In this way, Beacon is distinguished from community gardens, where yields are often accessible only to those who manage the crops. Those who do work in the forest are given small plots of land for personal gardens, which cannot be bought, only worked for.

Food forests exist across the world, from Canada to Morocco to Vietnam, and have fed communities for thousands of years. Depending on the geography and climate, they all look a little different, but each design follows the basic rules of density, diversity, and layering in their pursuit of sustainable food security.

Beacon Food Forest breaking ground in 2012.

ESKIMO ICE CREAM

AKUTAQ • ALASKA

After a successful hunt, groups of Native Alaskan women gather to vigorously stir bowls of fat (generally from moose or caribou) and oil (usually from a seal) into akutaq, also known as Eskimo ice cream. From the Inupiaq word for "mixed together," akutaq is made by beating the fat and oil—and sometimes a bit of water or fresh snow—into a texture similar to whipped frosting.

Akutaq is made in two varieties. Savory meat-based akutaqs contain dried fish or ground caribou, which gives it a salty, often gamey taste. Berry-based versions, classically made with salmonberries or blueberries, are sweet yet briny, from the oil base. What goes into akutaq is dictated by the flora and fauna of the nearby terrain. In the North, there might be hints of caribou, bear, and musk-ox fat, while coastal akutaqs might use saltwater fish, and Southwestern akutaqs might include candlefish—an oily smelt that, when mixed with oil and fresh snow, creates an ephemeral frozen treat that lasts just minutes before collapsing.

How to try it
Check with the Yupiit Piciryarait Cultural Center in Bethel, Alaska, which is known to serve akutaq at events. The Alaska Native Medical Center offers the ice cream to patients as a part of the room-service menu. It can be ordered with or without fish.

RESCUING HIGHWAY MOOSE MEAT

ROADKILL SALVAGE PROGRAM • ALASKA

How to try it

Salvaging roadkill for human consumption is currently legal in 28 US states, although many require permits. Confer with local state laws before doing any highway harvesting.

In a state with nearly 200,000 roaming moose and high-speed roadways running through their habitat, vehicular moose collision is inevitable, especially during the coldest months when roads are icy and sunlight scarce. About 800 moose die in these impacts every year, along with the occasional bear, mountain goat, or caribou. Conservatively speaking, that leaves a million pounds of animal meat scattered across the state, which locals do not want to go to waste.

Alaska's solution was the Roadkill Salvage Program, launched in the 1970s and still thriving today. Every time a state trooper finds a big animal dead on the road, they report it to dispatchers who contact citizens and charities who have expressed interest in collecting moose cadavers and turning them into food (the lean red meat can be used like beef in stews, sausage, and burgers). Whoever can come fastest, usually with a flatbed truck and a winch, gets to salvage the animal and reap the spoils.

Kenai Peninsula has one of the highest rates of moose-vehicle collisions in Alaska; signs like this are updated regularly.

For institutions like food banks, where protein is difficult to come by, the roadkill program is a blessing. Alaskans also happen to love moose meat. Hunting moose for personal consumption is a popular Alaskan pastime, so eating an animal freshly slaughtered on the road is hardly a radical prospect. Many locals are also versed in recognizing a dead moose that's been corrupted by heat, time, or damage to internal organs—which keeps things safe and sanitary.

Although many states could benefit from a roadkill salvage program, Alaska's system likely isn't replicable elsewhere. In more populous areas, deer strikes happen in the tens of thousands, spread across road systems far more extensive than Alaska's. The biggest hurdle is that eating roadkill is a difficult sell in the lower 48 states, and perhaps for good reason: Deer and other big game outside Alaska have higher disease rates, and the weather is not as reliably frigid to prevent spoilage.

UNDERWATER PRODUCE

SEA PEACHES • ALASKA

How to try it

Sea peaches are found in the northern Pacific Ocean, from the Arctic Sea to the Puget Sound, 130–330 feet (40–100 m) below the surface. They're farmed commercially in Japan.

Suspended in the Bering Sea, Saint Lawrence Island experiences powerful fall storms that churn the deep surrounding waters, gathering the sea's contents and heaving it onto the shoreline. For the Yupik people, Indigenous Alaskans who have lived on the island for centuries, autumn is a delicious time of year because the beach becomes blanketed with salty edibles. The Yupik call them sea foods or sea vegetables, but many of them are technically animals:

spineless invertebrates called tunicates that look like colorful organs and live on the sea floor.

The most popular "vegetable" is perhaps the sea peach, which looks like a human heart with two open valves and tastes like salty ocean with a rubbery chew. Sea peaches live stationary lives, attached to rocks, so it takes a good storm to dislodge the creatures and send them flying. When there isn't enough shoreline treasure to go around (the beach tends to be crowded after a squall), serious fans tie a long rope to a rake and either comb the water from the shoreline or get in a boat and drop the rake into the sea.

Other Underwater Produce

SEA PINEAPPLES

These oblong, sunset-colored creatures are covered with pointy knobs that squirt water when squeezed. Sea pineapples attach to rocks and grow rubbery shells to protect a soft, oozy meat that resembles an oyster but tastes briny and bitter with a slightly metallic aftertaste. Sea pineapples are popular in Korea and Japan, where they're eaten raw with vinegar-based sauces. The sea pineapple's agriculture was developed in the 1980s and has since become big business: About 21 tons are collected every year.

These so-called fruits and vegetables have a devoted following on dry land.

SEA GRAPES

Nicknamed "green caviar," these tiny verdant pearls pop in the mouth, releasing a burst of saline and seaweed. In Asia, where they're primarily eaten, the algae clusters are mixed into salads and used as a topping for sushi, rice bowls, and noodles. The residents of Okinawa, Japan, are especially fond of what they call umi-budō. They eat the green orbs in abundance and live longer than most people on Earth, which correlates with the food's other nickname: longevity seaweed.

SEA CUCUMBERS

A $60 million market, most sea cucumbers are harvested by hand, dried, and sold as a delicacy to Asian countries. There are more than a thousand species of the bottom-dwelling brainless hermaphrodites, but only a few are commercially valuable. Sea cucumbers are used in traditional Chinese medicine to treat everything from impotence to kidney issues. The mild-flavored, fishy-smelling critter has a slippery texture that takes some getting used to, but many have and are willing to pay up to $1,000 per kilo to eat them.

SPICED HAM STREET PARTY

SPAM JAM • HAWAII

How to try it

Waikiki Spam Jam takes place every April. Admission is free, and proceeds benefit the Hawaii Food Bank.

Every April, Spam fans from across the globe make their way to the island of Oahu to pay homage to the beloved mystery meat. The Waikiki Spam Jam, a massive food festival and the largest Spam celebration in the world, has been delivering Spam fantasies since 2002, and it's only getting hammier.

Invented in the Midwest, Spam was brought to Hawaii during World War II by American soldiers, where it found its most enthusiastic fan base. Hawaiians eat seven million cans every year, and a typical grocery store may carry a dozen varieties including Turkey Spam, Chorizo Spam, and Hickory Smoke Spam.

With a population this devoted, the Spam Jam is a big deal. Spread along Waikiki's posh Kalakaua Avenue, flanked by high-end shopping and luxury hotels, the festival is a big event on the local social calendar. Larger-than-life Spam cans walk the street, waving happily at festivalgoers who stand in line for Spam musubi (a kind of Spam sushi), Spam pizza, buttery Spam pastries, Spam fries, macadamia nuts covered in powdered Spam, coconut Spam custard, and chocolate-covered Spam. Live music and hula dancers take the stage with Spam-loving celebrities. This is a festival with no tipping point: The more Spam T-shirts, Spam tattoos, and Spam animal mascots, the better.

The Hawaiian love for Spam is true, unironic, and deeply felt. Despite its reputation elsewhere, there is no social stigma against Spam in Hawaii, and the over-the-top festival, which attracts 35,000 people each year, feels like a natural expression of the islands' reverence for the delicious, versatile, inimitable canned meat.

A PERFECT PINEAPPLE

SUGARLOAF PINEAPPLE • HAWAII

How to try it

On Kauai, you can find sugarloafs at Banana Joe's Fruit Stand. Or the farm Kauai Sugarloaf Pineapple will mail a pineapple, picked that day, anywhere in the continental United States. One perfect pineapple costs about $30.

If a tangy, juicy, yellow pineapple has any flaws, it's the unpalatable core and the prickly feeling left in your mouth after eating too much. In both cases, bromelain is the culprit. The enzyme is known to irritate the mouth, and aside from the stem, the highest concentration is found in the pineapple's core.

But the issues that plague the traditional pineapple are nonexistent in the sugarloaf, a variety that grows on the islands of Hawaii. The white, creamy flesh is unfathomably sweet with almost no acid, the core is edible, and no matter how much you eat, the aftertaste is clean. The variety also grows in South America and West Africa, but Hawaii is the sugarloaf's main stage. The rich, volcanic soil and long history of pineapple cultivation make the islands, and the islanders, especially adept at coddling the finicky fruit. A new plant requires 18 to 24 months to bear its first fruit, and because pineapples produce no seeds, they can only be grown through hard-won propagation material.

Delicious Diaspora
HAWAII'S PLATE LUNCH

Hawaiian cuisine is easily misunderstood. Outsiders tend to think of pineapple-glazed meats and flaming cocktails. Traditionally, Hawaiian food means pounded taro and coconut pudding, smoked octopus, and earthen ovens. But contemporary Hawaiian food, known colloquially as local food, is something quite different.

Since the 1850s, when migrant workers began arriving from around the world to work the sugarcane and pineapple plantations, the cuisine of Hawaii has evolved into a distinctive mishmash of foreign influence—and the plate lunch is the ultimate expression of how locals really eat.

The Hawaiian plantations of the 19th century were a hotbed of cultural exchange. Chinese, Japanese, Koreans, Filipinos, Puerto Ricans, and Portuguese lived in migrant communities where shops and grocery stores catered to the multitude of ethnicities. The Japanese bento, the traditional portable meal, is believed to be the foundation for the Hawaiian plate lunch. Because the workers were predominantly Asian, rice was the cheap and comforting starch of choice that accompanied a main dish from their home countries. With time, the patchwork community began to exchange recipes and a distinct cuisine emerged. Korean kimchi was served alongside Japanese chicken katsu, Chinese chow mein beside Filipino pork adobo and native Hawaiian kalua pork. The options continued to evolve: After World War II and leading up to Hawaii's statehood, Spam became a standard addition, followed by continental American classics like chili and hamburger steak.

The plantation work eventually came to an end, but plate lunches stuck around, becoming the default lunch of day laborers and construction workers before establishing itself as arguably the island's favorite meal. Thanks to lunch wagons and restaurants, a universal format took shape. Plate lunch, to this day, always includes a protein, two scoops of white rice, and one scoop of macaroni salad. (Ice-cream scoops are standard operating equipment.)

Plate lunch, with its many cuisines sharing a limited space, provides an easy metaphor for contemporary Hawaiian culture. Hawaii is an island—a collision of cultures in a finite area—working to form a unified community while remaining distinct and honoring the cultures' separate identities. Unlike fusion food, plate lunch keeps recipes and traditions intact. The idea is to make room on the plate for everyone.

Though the foods span many cultures, they all find a home on the plate.

FOUR CORNERS AND THE SOUTHWEST

GIANT ORGAN PIZZERIA

ORGAN STOP PIZZA · ARIZONA

How to try it

Find Organ Stop Pizza at 1149 E. Southern Ave. in Mesa.

Each night in Mesa, Arizona, the largest theater pipe organ ever created rises on a rotating hydraulic elevator above a 700-seat dining room filled with patrons enjoying pizza, pasta, and sandwiches. Played by a virtuoso theater organist, the 276-key instrument is linked to a mind-boggling series of xylophones, glockenspiels, gongs, and cymbals.

The landmark attraction was the brainchild of the late William P. Brown, a real-estate developer, pizza enthusiast, and accomplished theater organist. The original Organ Stop Pizza opened in Phoenix in 1972 and was so popular, Brown opened a second, larger outpost in Mesa. Today, the eccentric Mesa pizzeria is owned by longtime employee Mike Everitt, who has expanded the organ so much that the show had to be moved to its current largest location in 1995.

While diners sup below, four industrial blowers pump pressurized air through the 6,000 pipes of the 1927 Wurlitzer organ, which is insured for $5 million. The performance hall restaurant serves 300,000 visitors each year, while the organ plays classics like "The Flight of the Bumblebee," "The Hills Are Alive" from *The Sound of Music*, "Under the Sea" from *The Little Mermaid*, and the theme from *Star Wars*.

A COMPETITIVE DISPOSAL OF TERRIBLE CAKE

THE GREAT FRUITCAKE TOSS · COLORADO

How to try it

The event is held in late January. Entrance costs one nonperishable food item for a local charity. Those who ate their holiday fruitcake can throw a "rental" for a dollar.

There is an American Christmas tradition of gifting a fruitcake, which endures despite the other American tradition of disliking fruitcake. All too often, the sweet, dense, and artificially flavored loaf gets tossed in the trash—which gave the residents of Manitou Springs a brilliant idea.

In 1996, a group of fruitcake haters gathered in a public park to dispose of their unloved Christmas cakes. Instead of the trash, they launched them across the park, which sparked a local competition that's been going strong for two decades. The annual January celebration has grown to include a slew of events. In addition to the classic hand toss, there has been a fruitcake slingshot (with robotic, mechanical, and three-man divisions) and a pneumatic weapon launch. In 2007, a team of Boeing engineers shot a cake 1,420 feet (433 m) using a mock artillery piece. (By comparison, the hand toss winner that year clocked 124 feet / 38 m.) Children have their own division complete with targets, as well as speed and balance games. Those less athletically inclined can enter the fruitcake costume competition or the "Too Good to Toss" bake-off.

ELVIS PRESLEY'S CROSS-COUNTRY INDULGENCE

FOOL'S GOLD SANDWICH ∘ COLORADO

Elvis Presley once ate a sandwich made with a whole jar of blueberry jam, a whole jar of peanut butter, and an entire pound of bacon. The novelty item, served at the now-defunct Colorado Mine Company in Denver, was known as the Fool's Gold. It cost $49.95 and was served in an entire hollowed-out loaf of bread.

The King never forgot the sandwich. On February 1, 1976, he went back for a second round. Rather than re-create the Fool's Gold at Graceland (his home in Memphis, Tennessee), he took his private jet to Denver and back in one night. The owners of the Colorado Mine Company recall bringing 30 gargantuan loaves directly to the plane. Elvis and his comrades ate and drank from the comfort of the Combs hangar at Stapleton International Airport (also defunct), then flew back home.

How to try it
Nick's Café in Golden, Colorado, is run by a chef who cooked for Elvis as a teenager, then went on to open this Elvis-themed diner where you can order the Fool's Gold.

Nick Andurlakis served the King a Fool's Gold sandwich in 1976, and now he whips them up in his diner in Golden.

AN OLD WEST EATERY ON THE PONY EXPRESS

MIDDLEGATE STATION • NEVADA

How to try it

Middlegate Station is located at 42500 Austin Highway. They open daily at 7 a.m. and serve until 9 or 10 p.m.

Alongside a stretch of the historic Lincoln Highway, US Route 50, dubbed the Loneliest Road in America, is an isolated Wild West–style saloon announced by a wooden sign that (accurately) describes its location as "in the middle of nowhere."

This rustic restaurant in the heart of the Nevada desert, decorated with bull skulls, a neon "BAR" sign, and an antique wagon, is Middlegate Station, a historic eatery created in the 19th century as a stop on the Pony Express. Founded in 1857 by James Simpson, the restaurant that stands today was once an active station and rest stop along the historic trail. When the Pony Express ceased operations in October 1861, Middlegate Station stayed open, serving as a stage and freight stop for gold and silver mines. Since then, the outpost has survived as the only gas station for nearly 50 miles (80 km) in either direction and a rare roadside eatery along the Lincoln Highway. Their Middlegate Monster Burger is legendary, so big that anyone who finishes it wins a T-shirt.

Another attraction of Middlegate Station is the ceiling covered in cash, where you can leave a donation of your own. According to the owner, the cash ceiling started because there was no bank nearby. Regulars would attach dollar bills to the ceiling, write their names on them, and leave the cash to spend on another visit.

Middlegate, an unincorporated Nevada community, has a population of 17.

THE WORLD'S ONLY HOT PEPPER SCHOOL

CHILE PEPPER INSTITUTE ∘ NEW MEXICO

New Mexicans are known to put chile sauce on anything. Made from one of the state's official vegetables (despite technically being a fruit), chile sauce is suitable for sandwiches, pizza, stew, pasta, and even wine. New Mexico chiles are roasted and pureed into green sauce or dried and reconstituted into red sauce and ladled on everything from burgers to enchiladas. New Mexico was the first state to adopt an official state question: red or green? When asking for both types of chile sauce, the answer is "Christmas."

This abundance and fervor for chile sauce is largely thanks to the Chile Pepper Institute at New Mexico State University. Mexican-born horticulturalist Fabian Garcia, a member of the first graduating class in 1894, was appointed director of the Agricultural Experimentation Station in 1913. He dedicated much of his work to breeding chiles, and successfully cultivated the first pepper with a standard pod and heat level, which he called "New Mexico 9." This pepper became the catalyst for the state's booming chile industry, which now grows on about 8,000 acres. The Science Center, where the Chile Pepper Institute is located and peppers from around the world are researched and bred, is named after the pioneering pepper maven.

The Chile Pepper Institute is a nonprofit program whose objective is to educate the public about chiles—from growing and picking to tasting, cooking, and extinguishing a burning mouth. The world's largest pepper, the foot-long Numex Big Jim, was developed at NMSU in the 1970s; in 2001, NMSU tested the hard-to-find Bhut Jolokia pepper from northeastern India and declared it the world's hottest pepper. Outside, in the Teaching Garden, the program grows more than 150 varieties of peppers. It not only showcases beautiful, flourishing peppers from classic green to vibrant violet, it's a teaching ground for how to fight against disease and treat prevailing problems. The institute also sells obscure chile pepper seeds, offers chile sauce tastings, and hawks Bhut Jolokia brownie mix and frozen bags of roasted peppers.

How to try it

The institute is located in room 265 of Gerald Thomas Hall. The Teaching Garden can be found at 113 West University Avenue, Las Cruces. To visit, call to make a reservation. You can also shop their online store, which ships chiles across the United States.

Paul Bosland, longtime director of the Chile Pepper Institute, oversaw experiments like creating a "spiceless" jalapeño.

TRADITIONAL FOOD OF TAOS PUEBLO

TIWA KITCHEN • NEW MEXICO

How to try it

Tiwa Kitchen serves lunch from 11 a.m. to 4 p.m. and is closed on Tuesdays.

Phien-tye is a dish of blue corn fry bread stuffed with buffalo and covered in chili.

The Indigenous American Taos people have continuously inhabited the legendary Taos Pueblo, a collection of multistoried adobe buildings, for more than 1,000 years. Located just off the highway en route to this UNESCO World Heritage Site, Tiwa Kitchen is as close as it gets to being invited for lunch at a local family's table.

Owners Ben and Debbie Sandoval began constructing the Pueblo adobe building by hand in 1992. Out back, they constructed an adobe oven, called a horno, for baking traditional breads, cookies, and pies. A rare outpost for home-style Pueblo and New Mexican comfort food, Tiwa Kitchen serves dishes that have been passed

from generation to generation—taught to Ben by his grandmothers.

Ben, who grew up in Taos Pueblo, incorporates local ingredients into the menu. The Pueblo's bison herd supplies meat for their burgers, served on buns baked out back in the horno. Homegrown blue corn adds a crisp coating to local trout and appears in hard-to-find specialties such as Phien-tye (pictured to the left) and steaming mugs of grits-like, periwinkle atole. Even popular New Mexican dishes, such as the restaurant's heirloom red chile stew, are crafted using crops harvested from Pueblo land.

24-HOUR FULL-SIZE PIES

PECAN PIE VENDING MACHINE • TEXAS

How to try it

Berdoll Pecan Candy & Gift Company is located at 2626 TX-71, where the vending machine is always open.

To find an all-night pecan pie machine, look for the squirrel as tall as a house.

If you're driving through Texas down Highway 71, keep an eye out for a sign pointing the way to a giant squirrel statue holding a pecan. Once you've seen the 14-foot (4.3 m) squirrel (her name is Ms. Pearl), make your way to the less flashy but equally glorious landmark beside her: a vending machine stocked with full-size homemade pecan pies.

Both Ms. Pearl and the pie vending machine belong to the nearby Berdoll Pecan Farm. Their pecan pies are in such high demand that the business put in a 24-hour vending machine to satisfy pie lovers around the clock. The pecan pie machine—the only one of its kind in the United States—is located out front of the Berdoll Pecan Candy & Gift Company shop. It's restocked every day with freshly baked pies and other pecan treats, with even more frequency during the holiday season. Those visiting during business hours can do their shopping inside the store.

COW'S HEAD BARBECUE

BARBACOA DE CABEZA • TEXAS

In northern Mexico, the word *barbacoa*, or barbecue, still typically refers to goat's meat. Central Mexicans associate the word with lamb, while the people of the Yucatàn prefer barbecue pork. And in Texas, where the Mexican culinary influence runs deep, barbacoa often means barbacoa de cabeza, or cow's head barbecue.

Borrowing from the traditional Mexican technique, cows' heads are wrapped in water-soaked burlap and maguey leaves, then buried in pozos, or wells, heated by wood embers. The pit is covered with more maguey leaves, and the swaddled head is left to cook for hours until the meat is tender and glistening with fat.

Almost every piece of meat on a cow's head is edible. The lengua (tongue) is fatty and luscious. The cachete, or cheeks, are tender and beefy. The brain is creamy. The eyes are gelatinous. The gristle and cartilage counter the soft, silky bits, and the head as a whole—when chopped up and nestled in a warm tortilla, as is the fate of all proper barbacoa—is brightened and balanced by a topping of salsas, cilantro, and onions.

How to try it
Vera's Backyard Bar-B-Que in Brownsville makes barbacoa de cabeza using the old-fashioned pit technique. They go through about 65 heads every weekend.

THE POTATO DOUGHNUT

SPUDNUTS • UTAH

During the 1930s, brothers Al and Bob Penton were living in California, working unfulfilling jobs, and dreaming up ways to reinvent the doughnut. Bob, who had served in the navy as a baker, had a German doughnut recipe that called for potatoes. The brothers began experimenting with spuds—adding potato water to the doughnut dough, mixing in mashed potatoes—before landing on a mix with dehydrated potatoes. The brothers returned home to Utah and set up shop.

Spudnuts, as the brothers named them, were large, fluffy doughnuts fried in shortening and glazed. The potatoes in the mix absorbed moisture, which kept them tender, while their starchy consistency held air and made them light. Instead of giving up their secret formula, the Pentons decided to franchise by selling their dry doughnut mix, and by the end of the 1940s, there were more than 200 Spudnut shops across the country.

Spudnut was the first doughnut chain in America and, for many years, it was also the largest. (At its peak, there were more than 300 stores across the United States, Canada, and Japan.) But their decline came almost as quickly as their success.

How to try it
Spudnut shops now use various dough recipes because the mix became unavailable when Bake-N-Serv went under. In Utah, try Johnny O's Spudnuts, which has outposts in Layton and Logan.

In 1968, the Penton brothers sold their company to Vancouver-based Pace Industries, and in 1973, Pace sold the company to North Dakota–based Bake-N-Serv. When the Bake-N-Serv owner was convicted of fraud and conspiracy in 1979, the company closed and all the Spudnut franchises were orphaned.

Spudnuts, made with dehydrated potato, were all the rage in mid-century America.

A CASSEROLE FOR MORMONS IN MOURNING

FUNERAL POTATOES • UTAH

How to try it

No one has to die for you to eat funeral potatoes. The Hoof & Vine steakhouse in Salt Lake City serves them at dinner Monday through Saturday.

A death in the Mormon community is eased with a warm, comforting casserole of potatoes (shredded or cubed), canned cream soup (chicken or mushroom), butter, sour cream, and grated cheddar cheese. On top, there is always a crunchy sprinkling of corn flakes.

While no one's exactly sure where funeral potatoes originated, most sources attribute their spread to the Relief Society, a women's organization within the Church of Jesus Christ of Latter-day Saints. Society members attend to the needs of the bereaved, including meals, and the ingredients of funeral potatoes were almost always stocked in a Mormon pantry. Mormons are urged to maintain a three-month food supply at all times. The stockpile is intended to hedge against hard times, which could be a layoff, a natural disaster, or a funeral.

Funeral potatoes—with their creamy starchiness—provide a soothing hit of comfort. But this dish isn't just for Mormons, and the recipe has spread throughout Utah. In 2002, when Salt Lake City hosted the Winter Olympics, the official pins featured little casseroles of funeral potatoes.

Anti-Masturbatory Food

Presbyterian minister Sylvester Graham was one of the leading voices of the anti-alcohol temperance movement of the early 19th century—but his real passion was vegetarianism, which he hoped would cure Americans of "self-abuse" (more formally known as masturbation). His Graham Diet eschewed all foods that provided pleasure or could be associated with indulgence. He called these foods "excitants" because he believed they fired the blood, and they included all spices (even salt and pepper), condiments (like vinegar and mustard), candy, eggs, and most dairy. To combat these thrilling foods, he invented the graham cracker— a coarse unbleached flour, bran, and wheat germ biscuit meant to dull the senses and keep people from touching themselves. Graham died in 1851, at the age of 57, before his graham cracker was commercially processed with sugar and used as a vessel for chocolate and marshmallows.

One of Graham's most fervent followers was John Harvey Kellogg, anti-masturbation health activist and actual medical doctor. Kellogg, who spent most of his life as a Seventh-day Adventist, also believed a bland vegetarian diet would curb sexual urges and keep people pure. He ran a sanitarium in Battle Creek, Michigan, where he experimented with recipes for bland breakfast food. Around 1877 he baked a wheat, oat, and corn dough that he crumbled and sold as "granula." But Kellogg's biggest break was in cereal flakes, a process he and his brother discovered when they ran a sheet of stale dough through the rolling machine. Cereal became a health trend, a cold plain food in direct opposition to the era's standard morning meal of meat, potatoes, cake, and pie. Kellogg believed eating his cereal would keep the public from carnal impulses, and it might have worked had not his brother, Will Kellogg, insisted on adding sugar to the flakes and advertising them as fun, tasty food. (It was Will, not John, behind the Kellogg Company that brought sugary cereals mainstream.)

GREAT PLAINS

IDAHO STURGEON ROE

WHITE STURGEON CAVIAR • IDAHO

How to try it

White sturgeon is now being farmed in other states such as California and Maine. For the Idaho variety, get in touch with the Fish Breeders of Idaho, who take orders by phone and email.

Idaho caviar is something of an industry secret. Most of the world still associates the luxury product with Beluga sturgeon, which was severely overfished in the 20th century and is now critically endangered. In 1988, Idaho fishermen found their rivers made a prime habitat for white sturgeon, a species native to North America, and set out to farm the fish sustainably. Like Beluga, white sturgeon is enormous and commonly grows to 7 feet (2 m) and more than 1,000 pounds (454 kg). The impressive size means impressive eggs: large, shiny globules that pop clean, sweet, and briny in the mouth.

Idaho now boasts a number of caviar farms, each with their own technique. At Leo Ray's in Hagerman, the sturgeon live in a pool that is perpetually refreshed with cold mountain streams and warm geothermal water, impeding the growth of unwanted algae that muddies the flavor. The egg harvest is timed just before the fish would lay them herself (harvest too early and the flavor is undeveloped; too late and the eggs lose their taut, poppable quality). In the days leading up to the harvest, the fish is biopsied using a plastic tube, so a small sample of eggs can be examined. Patience and accuracy is of the essence because the sturgeon must be killed to harvest its eggs. When the time comes, the sacs are removed by hand from the belly and the eggs gently separated from the membrane, rinsed, salted, and canned. The rest of the fish is also sold.

Researchers tag a great white sturgeon in the Snake River in Hells Canyon.

Delicious Diaspora

BASQUES IN IDAHO

The Basques, who occupy a small autonomous region on the border of France and Spain, are thought to be the oldest civilization of Europe. (Their language, Euskera, is the oldest European language.) The Romans report contact with them as early as 200 BCE, but the Basques did not keep written records, so their origins are cloaked in almost impenetrable obscurity. It's also difficult to track their diaspora because most censuses don't differentiate between Basque and Spanish. But in Idaho, where Basques began to settle in the late 1800s, their presence is well known, and the state is now the unlikely home to the most concentrated Basque population outside of Basque country—with around 15,000 in Boise alone.

Drawn to Idaho as sheepherders and silver miners, early Basque immigrants cultivated a community, bringing over wives and workers to help develop the sheep industry. The first Basque boardinghouses opened in 1900, offering rooms to shepherds. As the life of a shepherd was solitary, these houses became lively, social places for Basques to gather and speak their language, eat their foods, and drink the wines of their home country. The Basque American style of large-format, family-style meals originated in these boardinghouses.

Along downtown Boise's Basque Block, the glory of the cuisine is on full display. Bar Gernika specializes in chicken croquetas and classic sandwiches like solomo (marinated pork loin with pimento peppers), beef tongue, and chorizo. Along with cooking classes, the Basque Market offers pintxos (Basque for tapas) and a tasting flight of the region's best wines. Leku Ona is where you'll find the family-style platters that hearken back to the boardinghouse days, featuring lamb stew, meatballs, and fried cod. Perhaps the most Basque of all is the kalimotxo, which is easily found in every bar along the street and delivers a perfect combination of Basque and American influence: half red wine, half Coca-Cola.

The Oinkari Basque Dancers perform at the Trailing of the Sheep Festival in Hailey, Idaho.

THE FIRST
American Fireworks

Long before Americans celebrated Independence Day by lighting up the night sky, the earliest European colonizers gathered to watch nocturnal displays of pyrotechnics. "Such a fire is a splendid sight when one sails on the rivers at night while the forest is ablaze on both banks," wrote Adriaen van der Donck, a prominent early resident of New York. These weren't modern fireworks—they were annual burns set by local Indigenous American tribes to transform the surrounding landscape on an epic scale.

Across the continent, different tribes set fires for different reasons. Fires warded off rattlesnakes and mosquitoes, cleared land for homes, and denied enemy tribes cover they could use in an attack. Fire also played a key role in North America's food system.

BISON HABITATS

Early American colonizers were astonished by the abundance of buffalo roaming the stretch of land that came to be called the Great Plains. The Plains Indians used fire to increase the buffalo's habitat, essentially creating a man-made game park.

HUNTING

Annual burns cleared out undergrowth, making American forests as pleasant and easy to walk through as planned parks. This increased the number of deer, bison, and other prey. But fire was used in the hunt itself, too. Whether pursuing moose, alligators, rabbits, or grasshoppers, tribes could cut off their prey's escape with fire.

BERRIES AND NUTS

Burning created the conditions to gather huckleberries, strawberries, blackberries, and raspberries. It also increased the availability of nuts, especially acorns. Fires cleared way for oak trees that produced nuts that could be gathered each fall to make porridge and bread.

FARMING

North America is one of the most wooded places on Earth, which made fire an essential tool for clearing land to plant crops such as squash, beans, or maize, the dominant grain of the Americas. Fires on existing fields also killed pests and weeds, while providing ash that acted as fertilizer for the next crop.

European artist Karl Bodmer's painting Bison Hunting on the Prairie *depicts Indigenous American hunters in the 19th century.*

NATURE'S SPICE RACK

AMERICAN SPICEBUSH • KANSAS

Bite into a berry from the American spicebush and experience a spice rack exploding in your mouth: The small, round fruit contains notes of mace, pink peppercorn, sassafras, and the seasoning known as allspice. But the berry is not the only flavorful part of the North American plant—the bark and leaves, once used by Indigenous Americans to flavor meat and brew medicinal teas, have a peppery taste with a warm kick of cinnamon.

How to try it
In Kansas, the spicebush is native to the southeast, growing in moist soil along riverbanks and in wetlands. Outside of Kansas, it can be found in similar conditions from the East Coast to Texas. The plant blooms in early spring.

With its collision of familiar flavors, the versatile spicebush has also served as a handy seasoning substitute. During the Revolutionary War, when reserves of the Caribbean-derived allspice ran low, home cooks simply plucked the fruit growing in their backyards, ground it into a powder, and swapped it into their recipes.

THE HISTORICAL VACATION BERRY

HUCKLEBERRIES • MONTANA

Huckleberries, the blueberry's wild doppelgänger, have never been commercially farmed. The tart, sometimes bitter fruit with crunchy seeds thrives on steep slopes among heavy brush. The huckleberry plant requires a finicky balance of sunlight, warmth, and moisture in order to bear fruit during its fleeting two-month season.

How to try it
Around midsummer, you can start picking huckleberries in the Flathead Valley in northwest Montana. Picking in the Flathead National Forest is free and does not require a permit, unless you plan to pick more than 10 gallons a person.

Montana huckleberry yields are some of the highest in the country. Indigenous tribes drew the connection between productive harvests and intermittent burning. After a fire, the huckleberries would go fallow, but eventually the ashy, nutrient-rich soil would bring an explosive crop. For centuries, Indigenous Americans burned areas and then reaped the fruit, relying on the berries as a staple of their diet. Using the backbones of salmon, they made combs to cull the fruit from the bush and stockpiled the berries in massive quantities, drying them and mashing them into cakes.

In 1910, an enormous wildfire blazed through northern Montana. Two decades later, the area reaped massive huckleberry returns. Indigenous Americans set up camp on one side of the land, erecting hundreds of tepees, while other locals grouped together and pitched tents across the way. When the season opened, the buzzy atmosphere was compared to the California Gold Rush.

These days, huckleberry picking is still a competitive sport. Most seasons there aren't enough berries to go around, and so the huckleberry's value resets every year.

While huckleberries are mostly used in the same way as blueberries (in pancakes, muffins, pies, jams), fans of the huck say they pack more flavor, texture, and character than the standard blue supermarket variety. For the devoted, the inaccessibility is part of the huckleberry's charm.

Agriculture That Changes the Weather

Corn Belt Climate Change

The American "Corn Belt"—the Midwest's unfathomable expanse of cornfields—is the world's most productive agricultural region. In recent years, corn yields have been explosive: From 1950 to 2010, production increased from 3 billion to about 10 billion bushels each year.

Nebraska farmers have since sensed shifts in the weather. Summers have been wetter and 100°F (37°C) days fewer than before—observations that contradict many predictions of global warming.

The new weather patterns have to do with what farmers call "corn sweat." As plants open their pores to let in carbon dioxide, they also release water. This process, called transpiration, cools the plant and the air surrounding it, while also increasing the amount of water in the air, which will eventually return as rainfall. More corn means more transpiration, which accounts for the cooler, wetter weather.

By studying observed data and modeling the region's climate, MIT researchers found that the intensified corn production has increased the region's summer rainfall by 5 to 15 percent, and decreased the temperature by as much as 33°F (1°C). While temperatures around the world have risen, the study confirmed that eastern Nebraska has gotten cooler thanks to the heavy agriculture, which has counteracted the effects of greenhouse gas emissions. (In China, similar effects have been observed in rice-growing regions.)

The region's explosive agricultural growth is unsustainable. Only so much corn can grow on the limited amount of land, and greenhouse gas emissions have no real limit. Eventually, the mitigatory effects produced by agriculture will be overtaken. For some farmers, knowing this helps them prepare for the future, which likely includes the return of droughts. Until then, many are working on reducing fuel consumption and increasing efficiency during the window of favorable weather.

Nebraska, Iowa, Minnesota, and Illinois are the heart of the Corn Belt.

THE INTERNATIONAL ART OF
Corn on the Cob

Corn, known as maize in most of the world, was domesticated 10,000 years ago by the Indigenous people of modern Mexico. It was revered as a gift from the gods, a motherly substance, and even life itself. Corn was uniquely Mesoamerican until the 15th century, when the plant caught the attention of European voyagers. Columbus brought corn back to Spain, where it slowly spread north. Around the same time, Portuguese traders carried the plant east to Africa and Asia. In each place, corn kept moving. By the end of the 16th century, the Ottoman army was eating maize, China was drawing pictures of it, and it was growing in Germany, India, and Thailand.

Corn flourished almost everywhere it went. While some, namely Europeans, first mistrusted the new plant as food, corn found an essential place in diets across the globe. The versatile, resilient vegetable-cum-starch was adopted and transformed by countless culinary traditions, which is apparent in the myriad ways an ear of corn is eaten around the world.

TAIWANESE

Basted with garlic soy paste and sweet chili sauce, blackened on the grill, then slathered with lard.

PERUVIAN

Giant kernel white corn (choclo) boiled and served with a slab of fresh cheese and an herbaceous sauce called huacatay.

KENYAN

Grilled and doused in lime, rolled in ground salt and chilies, and served in its own husk as a carrying case.

KOREAN

Glutinous waxy corn steamed or boiled in salted, sugared water until the texture is sticky and chewy.

AMERICAN SOUTH

Whole ear pushed onto a stick, dipped in cornmeal batter, and fried until crispy.

PERSIAN

Blistered on a grill, then dunked in hot salt water to season.

Corn on the cob is a popular street food worldwide, from the Shilin Night Market in Taipei, Taiwan (left), to the chocolo vendors in Cusco, Peru (right).

NEBRASKA'S BEEFY HAND WARMER

RUNZA • NEBRASKA

How to try it

Runzas are readily available in Nebraskan bakeries. Runza the restaurant chain uses scratch-made dough and local beef sourced primarily from Nebraska. Their flavors include Swiss and mushroom, BBQ bacon, and BLT (bacon, lettuce, and tomato).

Runza history begins with Catherine the Great, a German princess who married into the Russian royal family in 1745. During her three-decade reign as empress of Russia, she invited Germans to move to her adopted country, enticing them with the promise of autonomy. No men would serve in the army, no family would pay taxes for 30 years, and all immigrants would have full governmental control of their villages and schools. Many Germans accepted her offer and came to farm the Volga River Valley. They began making something called bierok, a yeast dough filled with meat, which became the portable meal of choice for field workers. The Volga River Germans stayed for about a century, until Alexander II came to power and repealed his great-grandmother Catherine's law. Throughout the 1870s, Russian Germans were stripped of their special privileges. Rather than bend to the new regime, the Germans sent scouts out into the world to find a new place, similar to the Volga River Valley, to live. When the scouts returned, they recommended Nebraska.

The German word *runza* means "bun shape" and became the Nebraskan term for bieroks. Members of the Russian German Nebraskan community opened small shops dedicated to the handheld spiced meat pocket, which grew so popular that it spawned a chain. The first Runza store opened in 1949. Today, there are about 85. Locals eat runzas regularly, but they are especially abundant at football games, where they're used as edible hand warmers.

A COWBOY DATE NIGHT

PITCHFORK FONDUE • NORTH DAKOTA

How to try it

Medora, a city in the Badlands of North Dakota, does outdoor Pitchfork Fondue dinners during the summer months.

If you're familiar with Swiss fondue, the cowboy style can be made with a few simple adjustments. Instead of a quart-size ceramic pot suspended above a tiny flame, use a 30-quart metal cauldron on an outdoor gas burner. The cowboy version requires no cheese sauce, just a lot of oil poured into the cauldron. Heat up the oil and it's time to dip. And in country fondue, there's only beef. Steaks get skewered onto a pitchfork, then plunged into the hot oil. A rare steak with a dark crunchy exterior will be ready in three minutes. Medium takes about five.

When Eating Crow Was an Oklahoma Food Trend

In the 1930s, there were too many crows in Tulsa, Oklahoma. Hordes of the birds were raiding fields and covering the town in their droppings. To combat the aggressive flocks, former county health superintendent Dr. T. W. Stallings decided to promote crows as a food. The doctor began holding banquets where he peddled the main ingredient as quail. By the time locals developed a taste for "quail," they didn't mind Stallings's big reveal. Even as crow, they carried on eating it. One of the most outspoken fans was the governor of Oklahoma, who founded the Statehouse Crow Meat Lovers Association.

Stallings's winning recipe involved rubbing lard on the plucked crows to combat their dryness, cooking them in a sealed cast-iron pan with celery, then finishing them off with lots of gravy.

Stallings's passion for eating crow caused a craze. In 1935, the *Pittsburgh Post-Gazette* reported that a "wave of enthusiasm for crow" had swept Oklahoma. In the trailing days of the Great Depression, eating crow provided both a welcome source of protein and a way for farmers to rid their fields of serious predators. For many, the dark meat was pleasantly gamey and relatively tasty. Cultivating this sentiment was no easy battle because scavenging crows are liable to eat meat and garbage—but people pressed on. Crows were plentiful and easy to hunt, and for years, the "black partridge" stayed on the Oklahoma dinner menu. Luckily for the crows, the trend eventually fizzled, likely because times got less desperate.

A QUAPAW TRIBE FARM-TO-TABLE RESTAURANT

RED OAK STEAKHOUSE · OKLAHOMA

The Quapaw Indigenous American tribe has a reputation for agricultural excellence. Settling in the junction of the Arkansas and Mississippi rivers (in modern-day Arkansas), they developed a special relationship with the area's fertile soil, perfecting agricultural techniques over centuries to yield prodigious amounts of flavorful produce. As guardians of the region's breadbasket, the Quapaw strengthened their ties with neighboring tribes and later earned military support from the French. Their crucial role in the early American food economy helped them survive to modern day with their traditions intact—traditions you can still taste in the tribe's very own casino in Oklahoma.

While the US government forced the Quapaw from their ancestral homeland after the Louisiana Purchase, the menu at Downstream River Casino's Red

How to try it
Red Oak Steakhouse is nestled within the tribe's casino, Downstream River Casino, in Quapaw, Oklahoma.

The restaurant's produce is grown in on-site greenhouses.

Oak Steakhouse is a tribute to their agricultural legacy. Meat from the tribe's 1,000-strong herd of cattle and bison is prepared in their own on-site processing plant. Greens, herbs, and spices are sourced from the tribe's five greenhouses, just a short walk from the kitchen. Honey is produced by the tribe's own bee colony, and it makes its way into cocktails and salad dressings. The tribe roasts its own coffee and brews its own beer, too—all available in the adjacent steakhouse. True to nature, the dishes on Red Oak's menu rotate to suit each ingredient's peak season.

FREE PHEASANT FOR SOLDIERS

PHEASANT SALAD SANDWICH • SOUTH DAKOTA

South Dakota's Game, Fish, and Parks website claims the state is known for two things: pheasants and Mount Rushmore—in that order. Their headliner, Pheasants, were introduced to the United States from their native China in 1908. By the 1940s, the bird's population had boomed in South Dakota. So much so that the city of Aberdeen made use of the teeming bird population and began giving away pheasant salad sandwiches by the thousand. They dubbed themselves the World's Standout for a Handout.

Throughout World War II, soldiers traveling toward training or deployment on the Chicago, Milwaukee, and St. Paul Railroad all passed through Aberdeen, where the local canteen became known for its free pheasant salad sandwiches. Volunteers, most of them housewives, operated the facility every day from 8 a.m. to midnight, even on holidays. Their signature filling contained carrots, onions, celery, sweet pickle relish, hard-boiled eggs, and mayonnaise, but it was the pheasant that made the sandwich a standout. Industrialized farming had yet to mass-produce chicken, and so America was still smitten with poultry, which was expensive and considered the lavish alternative to red meat.

The Aberdeen canteen closed in 1946, but the pheasant salad sandwich remains a South Dakota specialty. In the city of Brookings, the aptly named Pheasant Restaurant still serves the dish, and because the sandwich is no longer a handout, it's been upgraded with apple, dried cranberries, and roasted pecans.

How to try it

Pheasant Restaurant, established just three years after the Aberdeen canteen closed its doors, features live music and pheasant salad sandwiches.

AN IMMERSIVE BISON EXPERIENCE

TERRY'S BISON RANCH • WYOMING

Have you ever dreamed of boarding an old-fashioned dining train and enjoying a leisurely Sunday lunch while chugging through open pastures of bison? At Terry's Bison Ranch in Cheyenne, this dream could be yours. Established in 1993 as a bison farm, their property has a history that extends much further: In 1910, when the land was owned by F. E. Warren, Wyoming's first territorial governor, bison enthusiast Theodore Roosevelt came to dine. The menu from Bison meal, which included game broth and trout, is on display at the ranch's steakhouse.

Today, Terry's Bison Ranch is a working farm with interactive bison experiences and award-winning bison ribs. Custom-built trains take visitors through bison country, meandering past ostriches and camels before the main event: petting and feeding bison. You can also see the sights on horseback or on an ATV, then head inside for a bison burger.

Feeding the bison, then feeding on bison, may seem like an incongruous experience, but the practice of raising bison like cattle was a key factor in keeping the species from extinction. At the end of the 19th century, the American bison was nearly wiped out and conservation efforts, which focused on finding protected habitats, moved slowly. But around the 1970s, American ranchers made a concerted push to raise the animals like cattle, and today the number of bison raised for food is about 20 times the number being traditionally conserved.

American bison (scientific name: *Bison bison*) have lived in North America for hundreds of thousands of years and are the national mammal of the United States. Growing up to 6 feet (1.8 m) tall and 2,000 pounds (907 kg), they are majestic to behold, especially in their native land, and at Terry's Bison Ranch, you can do it all from the comfort of a slow-moving train.

How to try it

Terry's Bison Ranch is located at 51 I-25 Frontage Road. The regular train tour takes about 90 minutes and runs multiple times a day. The lunch train departs at 12 p.m. on Sundays and requires a reservation.

THE MIDWEST

ONE OF THE WORLD'S WORST LIQUORS

JEPPSON'S MALÖRT • ILLINOIS

How to try it

Ninety percent of Jeppson's Malört is consumed in Chicago. The traditional way is to take a shot, but wormwood cocktails are cropping up around the city.

n the early 1930s, Swedish immigrant, cigar shop owner, and heavy smoker Carl Jeppson peddled a homemade alcohol called Jeppson's Malört—an astringent, foul-flavored spirit, and one of the only things Jeppson's tobacco-dulled mouth could actually taste.

In Swedish, *malört* means "wormwood"—a bitter herb used to treat worms. It is the alcohol's only flavoring, and it is appalling. During Prohibition, law enforcement allowed Jeppson to continue selling it because they couldn't conceive that something so terrible-tasting could be anything but medicinal.

CULINARY GIFTS FROM THE
Chicago World's Fair

n 1893, the city of Chicago hosted the World's Columbian Exposition—an ambitious, staggering showcase of culture and innovation—to commemorate the 400th anniversary of Christopher Columbus's arrival in the New World. Over six months, more than 27 million people came to stroll the promenades of the newly erected fairground city while inventors, entrepreneurs, scientists, and artists showed off their newfangled goods and ideas—a few of which went on to become seminal products of 20th-century America.

Lore has it that the beer, Pabst Select, was renamed PABST BLUE RIBBON after the company won a first-place award at the Chicago fair. By the time of the fair, the Milwaukee-born company had already won numerous awards for its beer and had been tying blue silk ribbons—at great expense—around every bottle. Whether they really took the top prize in Chicago is uncertain, but Pabst launched the prizewinning name, and after the fair, it became one of America's most popular beers. (Until the silk shortage of World War I, Pabst churned through more than a million feet of ribbon every year.)

SHREDDED WHEAT also made its public debut at the Chicago fair. The inventor, Ohio lawyer Henry Perky, was a man plagued by diarrhea. He conceived of the nourishing, wholesome food after seeing a man eat boiled wheat with cream. He pitched the idea to a machinist friend and

together they invented a machine that could churn out "little whole wheat mattresses." The pair came to the Columbian Exposition to sell the shredded wheat machine, but the public was far more interested in the wheat snack itself. After the fair, Perky moved east and started the Shredded Wheat Company, which he sold to Nabisco in 1928.

Austrian-Hungarian immigrants Emil Reichel and Sam Ladany brought their then-novel

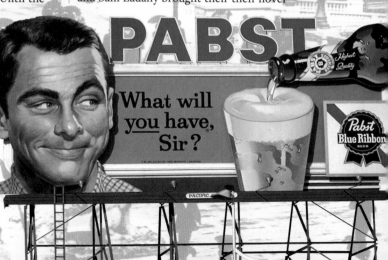

The taste, which has become sport to describe, is almost universally hated. Bug spray, gasoline, and burnt vinyl are often used as comparisons. For many years, the back of the bottle read: "Most first-time drinkers of Jeppson Malört reject our liquor . . . Our liquor is rugged and unrelenting (even brutal) to the palate." And yet it's one of Chicago's most distinguished libations, served ubiquitously at bars across the city.

The most common reaction is "Malört face," wrinkled, stunned, and disgusted. But as Jeppson's marketing goes: "For the braggart who stays the first few rounds . . . odds are he'll be Jeppson's forever." The citizens of Chicago (and only Chicago) have developed a fondness for the hard stuff. The astringent libation is used as both a rite of passage for out-of-towners and a way for locals to prove their ability to take a shot like a champion.

Josephine Cochrane with a later version of her dishwasher.

of a machine that would do the job gently and efficiently and set out to build it with a mechanic. Her invention was the first successful hand-powered DISHWASHER, which she presented at the Chicago fair. Her dishwashing contraption (called Lavadora, then Lavaplatos) won an award for design and durability. The Lavaplatos were primarily sold to restaurants and hotels until the 1950s, when housewives began to bite. Eventually, Cochrane's machines became known under a different name: KitchenAid.

Milton HERSHEY was also in attendance—but at the time, he was a caramel maker. At the fair, he encountered a German chocolate-making machine so impressive he eventually sold his thriving caramel business, Lancaster Caramel Company,

(to American audiences) all-beef hot dogs to the Chicago fair and, to their surprise, sold millions of sausages from their street cart. With their profits, they opened the first VIENNA BEEF shop a year later, then began distributing their hot dogs to vendors all over the city. In the 1930s, some Vienna Beef stands started advertising a hot dog with "salad on top," which led to the famous Chicago-style hot dog: mustard, onion, sweet pickle relish, a dill pickle spear, tomato, sport peppers, and celery salt.

for the incredible price of one million dollars (the equivalent of about $30 million today) and poured all his resources into chocolate.

William Wrigley Jr. came to Chicago as a salesman for the Wrigley family business, which at the time was known for soap and baking powder. To drum up sales, he started throwing in a free stick of gum with each purchase and soon found his customers were more excited by chewing gum than household supplies. In 1893, he brought his own line of gum to the Columbian Exposition, where he gave the public their first taste of JUICY FRUIT.

Josephine Cochrane, a wealthy Illinois socialite who liked to entertain, was fed up with her servants breaking her very nice china when they washed it by hand. In 1887, she conceived

THE BURMESE COMMUNITY CENTER

CHIN'S GROCERY • INDIANA

How to try it
Chin Brothers is located at 2318 E Stop 11 Road, on the south side of Indianapolis, and is open nearly every day.

In Myanmar (or Burma, as it was known before 1989), most socializing happens in tea shops, but there were none to be found in Indiana when Than Hre arrived in 2002. He was part of the first wave of Chin people—a Burmese Christian ethnic group—to arrive in Indianapolis. Many Chin followed in his steps, fleeing religious persecution in Myanmar. Today, there are so many Chin in Indianapolis it's earned the nickname "Chindianapolis."

In 2007, after working for five years and saving his money, Hre decided the burgeoning Chin community needed a space of their own. Despite having no business experience, he bought a grocery store and set out to fill it with food from his home country. But in 2007, Myanmar was undergoing sanctions and nothing could be imported. With great trouble and expense, Hre sourced Burmese products packaged in Thailand, Vietnam, or Cambodia and managed to stock his store with things like lahpet (fermented tea leaves), rakhine noodles, ngapi (dried shrimp powder), and htoe mont (glutinous rice cake). Chin people came to shop, and within a year and a half, Hre added a restaurant.

With Chin chefs in the back and Hre's wife out front, Chin Brothers Restaurant caters to a largely Burmese clientele. In the morning, they serve the traditional breakfast pe pyot, a sprouted yellow bean boiled with turmeric and fried onion, eaten with ei kya kway (Chinese fried dough sticks), or with breads like naan or paratha. Later in the day, there's the Chin specialty sabuti (ground white corn that's stewed with beef or pork bones, offal, and split peas), vok ril (Chin pork blood sausage), and mohinga (fish soup with noodles). At one table, there might be a family from Hre's tiny village in Chin State, and beside them, a Midwestern couple eating Chin food for the first time. At breakfast, it often looks like a Burmese community center.

The name Hre gave his business, Chin Brothers, was decided on a whim at the registration office. He hadn't thought about a name, but coming from a country with painful divisions along religious and ethnic lines, he wanted to make a statement about inclusivity. "We are all brothers and sisters," Hre explains. "We are all Chin."

Than and Biak Hre spread Chin culture with their grocery store and restaurant.

AN HEIRLOOM SEED SANCTUARY

SEED SAVERS EXCHANGE • IOWA

How to try it
Seed Savers Exchange sells hundreds of seeds on their website, seedsavers.org. When possible, Heritage Farm welcomes visitors, but call ahead to make sure.

The Seed Savers Exchange—one of the largest non-governmental seed banks in the United States—is dedicated to preserving and exchanging seeds in order to protect and perpetuate plants that might otherwise be lost. Headquartered on Heritage Farm, an 890-acre organic farm, the exchange houses more than 20,000 plant varieties. Each year they work to regenerate rare plant species, keeping a detailed directory and historical record of every seed they've conserved. Plants grown from the seeds are kept in a refrigerated central collection,

while seeds themselves are frozen in an underground vault. The apple orchid is perhaps the best representation of the exchange's mission: More than a thousand heirloom apple varieties grow side by side in what is essentially a living collection of apple heritage.

Seed Savers Exchange regenerates rare plant species.

AMERICA'S LAST NIGHT LUNCH WAGON

THE OWL • MICHIGAN

In the late 1800s, most restaurants closed at 8 p.m., which left all manner of hungry people wandering the street. Sensing an opportunity, a Rhode Island man named Walter Scott began peddling sandwiches and coffee from a basket, then a push-cart, and finally, once business began to boom, from a horse-drawn wagon. His idea caught on and soon the "night lunch wagon" swept the country.

The wagons averaged about 8 by 14 feet (2.4 by 4.3 m) in size, allowing just enough space for a small counter with cooking equipment and a handful of patrons. Many lunch wagons were lavishly designed with murals and elegant carvings, and attracted a diverse clientele. (The fancy interiors did not match the menus, which typically consisted of humble sandwiches, pies, and coffee.) Many wagons could not withstand the wear and tear of moving around town, so the wagons began to stay put, evolving into what we now know as diners.

The last known surviving wagon is the Owl Night Lunch Wagon. Henry Ford, who was once an Owl Night customer, purchased the wagon in 1927 when Detroit banned lunch wagons (restaurants lobbied against the roving entrepreneurs) and installed it at Greenfield Village, an out-door historical village that is part of the Henry Ford museum. Ford put the Owl to its former use, and for years it was the only place to buy food in Greenfield Village's sprawling grounds.

In the 1980s, the Owl underwent a full renovation. Gigantic red-and-blue letters now decorate the sides, and etched-glass windows depict owls perched atop crescent moons, an ode to the nighttime eateries of the past.

How to try it

The Henry Ford Museum is located in the Detroit suburb of Deerfield, Michigan. Greenfield Village is open seven days a week, from 9:30 a.m. to 5 p.m.

Before roadside diners, night lunch wagons like the Owl fed late-night appetites.

Instant Salads of the Midwest

In the American heartland, the term *salad* adheres to regional vernacular and often has nothing to do with vegetables. These iconic preparations hail from the retro era of processed foods, when recipes were passed from friend to neighbor on handwritten cards. While the glory days may be over, these salads still make appearances at summer potlucks, church basements, and holiday gatherings around the Midwest.

COOKIE SALAD was invented in Minnesota, where the cookie of choice is the Keebler Fudge Stripe—a thin, tire-shaped shortbread with a chocolate drizzle. The crushed cookies get bathed in buttermilk, vanilla instant pudding, and whipped cream topping, followed by a can of mandarin oranges and, if you're feeling fancy, a sliced banana.

WATERGATE SALAD has nothing to do with the Nixon scandal, except perhaps that the pistachio pudding is meant to "cover up" the other ingredients. The recipe, published by General Foods in 1975, mixes bright green pistachio instant pudding with whipped cream topping, which makes an excellent disguise for the canned pineapple, pecans, and miniature marshmallows.

JELL-O SALAD rose to prominence as an easy, affordable way for housewives to prepare something new and stylish—marketed as a refined preparation derived from the aspics of the Victorian era. Using a packet of instant Jell-O, these molded salads could contain almost anything, sweet or savory, from shrimp and olives in lime Jell-O to cottage cheese in orange Jell-O.

GLORIFIED RICE can still be found in deli counters across the upper Midwest. Cooked white rice becomes glorified when anointed with whipped cream and canned crushed pineapple, stirred, then topped with the popular regional garnish of marshmallows and maraschino cherries.

THE CASSEROLES OF MINNESOTA LAWMAKERS

CONGRESSIONAL HOTDISH COMPETITION • MINNESOTA

How to try it

The hotdish competition, held in Washington, D.C., isn't open to the public, probably because people would become overwhelmed with excitement. After the winner is declared each year, authenticated recipes are posted on an official government website.

In 2010, then Minnesota senator Al Franken challenged the ten members of his state's congressional delegation to a hotdish cook-off. Six members answered his call, gathering with homemade, Minnesota-style casseroles in a bid to prove their talents beyond the realm of politics. Trash talk ensued. Casserole rivalry was established.

The hotdish—a Depression-era, easy, and thrifty way to feed a crowd—has become one of Minnesota's most emblematic foods. The one-baking-dish meal combines a starch, a meat, a canned or frozen vegetable, and a can of creamy soup. Canned tuna, frozen peas, egg noodles, and mushroom soup, for example, is a classic tuna hotdish. Another standard, Tater Tot hotdish, is made with ground beef, canned corn, frozen tater tots, and cheddar cheese soup.

On competition day, congressional members turn all their legislative energy toward casserole. In 2013, Representative Michelle Bachmann told Al Franken: "I will smoke you."

The event has quickly become a Capitol Hill favorite. Along with the classic components, the entries must include an ingredient from their home state, so the hotdishes remain decidedly Minnesotan, from Senator Amy Klobuchar's I Can't Believe It's Not Spam Pepperoni Pizza hotdish (Spam hails from Minnesota) to Representative Tim Walz's Hermann the German hotdish, with local bratwurst and Schell's beer.

The grand prize is a personalized Pyrex dish, which comes with a year's worth of showboating privileges. Walz, who has won three times, entered the 2018 competition trailed by three staffers holding up the baking dish trophies from his previous victories.

WINNERS OF THE CONGRESSIONAL HOTDISH COMPETITION

2012: A tie between Senator Al Franken's Mom's Mahnomen Madness hotdish and Rep. Chip Cravaack's Minnesota Wild Strata hotdish

2013: Representative Tim Walz's Hermann the German hotdish

2014: Representative Tim Walz's Turkey Trot Tater Tot hotdish

2015: Representative Betty McCollum's

Turkey, Sweet Potato, and Wild Rice hotdish

2016: Representative Tim Walz's Turkey Taco Tot hotdish

2017: Representative Collin Peterson's Right to Bear Arms hotdish

2018: Representative Tom Emmer's Hotdish of Champions

2019: Representative Betty McCollum's Among Friends hotdish

Senators Amy Klobuchar and Tina Smith and Representative Angie Craig sample entries from the 2019 Hotdish Competition.

A BUTTER SCULPTURE FOR A DAIRY PRINCESS

PRINCESS KAY OF THE MILKY WAY • MINNESOTA

How to try it

The Minnesota State Fair takes place in the Falcon Heights suburb of St. Paul from late August to early September. Engrossing butter sculpture action happens every day.

Each spring, nearly a hundred aspiring Dairy Princesses from around Minnesota vie to be crowned Princess Kay of the Milky Way. The women (all unwed and under the age of 24) must be hometown dairy ambassadors, either working in the industry or the direct kin of dairy-producing people. Twelve finalists are interviewed and give speeches before the crowning, and the winner becomes the state's traveling dairy diplomat for the next year. But this is a competition with no losers because all finalists receive the honor of having their likenesses carved from 90-pound (41-kg) blocks of Grade A butter.

For more than 40 years, Linda Christensen has been the resident butter sculptress. During her residency, she's carved more than 500 sculptures from 32,000 pounds (14,515 kg) of butter. For the 12 days of the Minnesota State Fair, Christensen sits in a glass-walled booth and carves the women, one by one, producing a "butter head" each day. Princess Kay goes first. Dressed in warm layers, she sits for 6 to 8 hours in the 40°F (4.4°C) showroom, posing for her sculpture as spectators watch from outside the glass. Christensen uses knives and other sculpture tools to slowly coax the princess's features from the block of fat.

Each finalist gets to keep her butter head. Some choose to preserve and care for them as art, while others like to eat them, donating their heads to big community meals like pancake breakfasts and corn feeds.

2008 Princess Kay of the Milky Way Kristy Mussman poses for her official butter sculpture at the state fair.

..... FOOD PIONEER .....

CAROLINE SHAWK BROOKS

(1840–1913)

I n November 1877, about 2,000 spectators gathered in an auditorium in Des Moines, Iowa, to watch a unique demonstration. Onstage a woman in her mid-30s perched on a stool. She held several wooden paddles and a straw brush. Before her was an easel and a metal milk pan filled completely with butter. Next to her was a full brass band.

The show began, and the musicians struck up "La Marseillaise," the national anthem of France. The woman scraped and brushed with her paddle, creating the wide cheekbones and distinct forelock of Napoleon. When the band switched to a more American song, the artist quickly reshaped the face with the furrowed brows and strong nose of George Washington. A sudden low note from the tuba rattled the easel and Washington's shoulder began to slide off. The artist calmly caught it, stuck it back on, and the room erupted in applause.

Brooks carves butter at a Boston exhibition in 1877.

Caroline Shawk Brooks, aka the Butter Woman, was the world's premiere butter sculptor. From the mid-19th through the early 20th century, her unusual talent brought her widespread renown.

Brooks had always shown a knack for unorthodox materials—as a kid in Ohio, she sculpted a bust of Dante out of mud from a nearby creek. When she married and moved to a farm in Arkansas, she took up butter sculpting out of economic necessity. Women farmers were often responsible for making and selling butter while their husbands worked the fields. In 1867, when her farm's cotton crop failed, Brooks distinguished her butter by carving it into intricate animals, shells, and faces. A grand departure from the premade molds used by

the other farm wives, neighbors were eager to buy Brooks's elegant butter shapes.

In 1873, Brooks found the character that would become her lasting muse: Iolanthe, the blind princess at the center of a popular play titled *King Rene's Daughter*. The play moved Brooks, and for the first time, she took up her butter tools solely out of inspiration. *Dreaming Iolanthe* was put on display in a local Cincinnati art hall where 2,000 visitors paid 25 cents each to see it. The piece also attracted the attention of the *New York Times*, who called it "a face that may yet make [Brooks] famous."

Lucy Webb Hayes, the future first lady and a big fan of Brooks, commissioned her to carve a *Dreaming Iolanthe* for the Women's Pavilion at the 1876 Centennial Exposition in Philadelphia. The sculpture drew such large crowds that Brooks was asked to demonstrate her techniques for an audience. Under the gaze of reporters and judges, Brooks carved her 12-pound (5.4-kg) block of butter into a relief bust, shuffling the piece back and forth to the refrigerator to restore the desired texture.

Over the years, as Brooks gained fame and popularity, critics urged her to switch to what they viewed as "real" material. And while she did eventually try new mediums, even spending seven years with marble-cutting artisans in Italy, she never gave up butter. "I had previously modeled in everything workable, in clay, sea sand, mashed potatoes, putty and so on," she told the *Akron Daily Democrat* in 1893. "[But] I began my best work in butter, and with butter I shall end."

THE BREAKOUT DESIGNER APPLE

HONEYCRISP • MINNESOTA

How to try it

During the fall, the Applehouse store at the University of Minnesota sells honeycrisps as well as rare and experimental apples grown at the university.

When you bite into a honeycrisp apple, the flesh bursts with sweet, tart juice—all by design. The scientists at the University of Minnesota apple breeding program engineered larger cells that act as liquid capsules, delivering maximum mouth-watering apple flavor. They also endowed the honeycrisp with a thin skin, a vibrant blushing color, and a long shelf life. The result was what many consider to be the world's first celebrity apple.

The honeycrisp apple took 30 years to get ready for market. When it came on to the 1990s apple scene, Americans went crazy for the designer fruit. They learned

to call it by name and grew accustomed to paying three to four times more than they would for a standard supermarket apple. The taste for honeycrisp spread quickly, and soon it was the most glamorous apple in the country, with orchards, farm stands, and markets setting up big seasonal displays of the fruity jewels.

The success of the honeycrisp ushered in a new era of apple branding. While bananas and blueberries remained bananas and blueberries, apples grew identities. Pink Ladies were bright, tart, and effervescent. Jazz apples were firm, snappy, and juicy. Apples have long been America's most popular fruit (each person eats about 16 pounds/7 kg a year), but the honeycrisp set a new bar for what a humble apple could do in the marketplace.

A GOLF-CART BAR IN A BAT-FILLED CAVE

BAT BAR • MISSOURI

How to try it

Carts are available for rent from 8:00 a.m. until 45 minutes before sunset. Drivers are permitted alcohol, but not before signing a liability waiver.

Top of the Rock, a mountaintop bluff in the Ozarks, is the entry point into the area's finest watering hole—a bat-filled bar that's accessible only by golf cart. After renting a two- or four-person vehicle, visitors make their way through a 2.5-mile (4-km) woodland path over streams and bridges, with the option of stopping at a butterfly garden and a scenic outlook. Shortly into the trip, the trail dips into the Lost Canyon Cave, which contains this one-of-a-kind bar.

While everyone on the journey must stay in the golf cart, the ride is filled with surprises: The lantern-lit cave contains a natural waterfall, a live bat colony, and skeletons of both a saber-tooth tiger and a short-faced bear. When it's time for a drink, park beside the wooden bar and order up a Bat's Bite (strawberry and peach lemonade) or a John L's Lemonade (vodka, grapefruit, lemonade, and grenadine), then go for a loop around the waterfall pool.

Missouri's premier mountaintop cave bar is accessible only by golf cart.

Depressing Dishes of the Great Depression

Penny restaurants offered a dignified alternative to breadlines during the Great Depression.

When the stock market crashed in 1929 and the economy nosedived, sourcing regular meals became a grim and perpetual challenge. To aid the hungry masses, "penny restaurants," where humble foods like pea soup and bread could be had for a cent, began popping up across the country. These restaurants were charitable projects, intended to restore dignity to people growing accustomed to waiting in endless breadlines. In New York, weightlifter and fitness pioneer Bernarr MacFadden opened a four-story penny restaurant with health-conscious offerings like prunes and whole wheat bread. In California, Clifton's Cafeteria made it a mission to feed penniless diners in accordance with their slogan "Dine free unless delighted." In its first three months, Clifton's (which is still open in Los Angeles today) served 10,000 people for free. The service was formidable and a welcome supplement to the scrappy, unconventional home-cooked meals born out of scarcity.

MOCK APPLE PIE was an apple pie made without apples. Instead of fruit, butter crackers were boiled in a sugar syrup, mixed with cinnamon and lemon juice, and baked in a crust. The sweet, spiced crackers made a surprisingly moist and satisfying apple replacement, although they provided no vitamins or minerals.

PEANUT BUTTER AND MAYONNAISE SANDWICHES were once as popular as PB&Js, valued for the high-calorie combination of protein and fat that provided incredible nutritional density for little money. By the 1960s, Hellmann's Mayonnaise was advertising ways to jazz up the classic PB&M. A "double crunch" added bacon and pickles, while a "Crazy Combo" meant salami, sliced eggs, and onions.

POUDING CHÔMEUR, or "unemployed person pudding," was created by women factory workers in the French-speaking province of Quebec. They took stale bread, soaked it in brown sugar sauce, and baked it until golden and caramelized. Despite its belittling name, the dish provided a bowl of comfort; and pouding chômeur remains a popular dessert, although it's now more often made with a batter than with stale bread.

NORTH AMERICA'S MANGO

PAWPAW FRUIT • OHIO

Native to the central and eastern half of the United States, pawpaws are a little bigger than an avocado and comparably heavy. A ripe pawpaw has an almost liquid texture with a pungent, sweet smell and a taste reminiscent of tropical fruits like mangoes and bananas. (They're sometimes referred to as the poor man's banana or hillbilly mangoes.) Advocates praise pawpaws' creamy, tropical taste, while detractors find their puckery flavor more suitable for those with blunted palates.

Pawpaws are the largest edible fruit native to North America—millennia ago, they fed mastodons. Fruits and vegetables such as corn, strawberries, and carrots were small and bitter before humans tediously grafted and bred them for size and flavor. But wild pawpaws were large and one of the most nutritious fruits, providing a good source of potassium, several amino acids, vitamin C, iron, and copper. Pawpaws were a staple of many Indigenous American diets, and Lewis and Clark were content to live off them during a leg of their 1804–1806 journey across America. George Washington was also an enthusiast.

But the pawpaw is persnickety in its own way. The trees are harvestable only from late August to mid-October, and if kept at room temperature, the fruit ripens to the point of fermentation within three days. Pawpaws bruise easily, and the only effective way to ship them is frozen. Once the shortcomings of apples and strawberries were bred away, the pawpaw fell out of favor.

That doesn't mean there aren't still fans. Every year, the Ohio city of Albany hosts a Pawpaw Festival, where the pawpaw flows freely and growers enter their fruit for awards.

How to try it
The Pawpaw Festival happens in September near Albany's Lake Snowden. Otherwise, finding pawpaws requires persistent seasonal hunting at farmers' markets.

THE WORLD'S MOST BITTER ISLAND

WASHINGTON ISLAND • WISCONSIN

How to try it

Nelsen's Hall Bitters Pub is located at 1201 Main Road on Washington Island. It's open seven days a week.

The standard way to enjoy bitters is in moderation—a dash or two in a Manhattan or a Sazerac for a sharp, earthy tang. But on Washington Island, a remote islet in Wisconsin's share of Lake Michigan, locals prefer to drink it straight, as they have for a hundred years. Their brand of choice is Angostura—the yellow-capped bottle found in nearly every bar in the world—and they drink so much of it that tiny Washington Island (population 700) has acquired the title of world's largest consumer of bitters. According to an Angostura representative, they do upward of 10,000 shots every year.

The tradition began with Tom Nelsen, a Danish immigrant who arrived on the island in the late 1800s. After traversing the northernmost reaches of Wisconsin and surviving the choppy, treacherous stretch of water known as the Death's Door Strait (for the many shipwrecks that occur there), Nelsen decided to settle down and open a dance hall and bar, where he sold drinks until Prohibition made it illegal in 1920. At first, Nelsen despaired. Then, he got a pharmaceutical license.

Bitters, despite containing alcohol, could be classified and sold as "stomach tonic for medicinal purposes." With a pharmaceutical license, Nelsen could legally sell bitters without a doctor's prescription, and so he began pouring shots of the 90 proof "medical tincture" for his "patients." The tonic was extremely popular, unearthing hundreds of previously undiagnosed stomach ailments. Patients kept coming, Nelsen kept pouring, and Nelsen's Hall Bitters Pub stayed open all through Prohibition—making it the oldest continuously operating tavern in Wisconsin.

When Prohibition was repealed in 1933 and the pub resumed normal operations, locals didn't give up bitters. Angostura shots become a local drinking tradition and remained one of the best-selling items on the menu. (Nelsen himself is said to have consumed up to a pint of bitters, or about 16 shots, every day until he passed at the ripe age of 90.)

In the mid-20th century, Nelsen's pub was passed on to his nephew, Gunnar, and Gunnar's wife, Bessie, who founded the

Bitters Club. To join, you must take a shot. First-timers to the island often make Nelsen's a priority because the shot comes with an official Bitters Club card that states you are "now considered a full-fledged islander and entitled to mingle, dance, etc. with all the other islanders." The card is notarized by the bartender, who sticks a thumb in the dregs of the empty shot glass, then stamps a thumbprint on the card and writes the new club member's name in a ledger.

THE SOUTHEAST

THE SUMMER SEAFOOD WINDFALL

MOBILE BAY JUBILEE • ALABAMA

Each summer, on a sultry, full moon night, residents around the coastal region of Mobile Bay are roused from sleep by news of a wondrous natural phenomenon. Along a 15-mile (24 km) stretch of Alabama coast, a bounty of seafood rises from the Mobile Bay floor. Catfish, shrimp, and flounder wash onto the sand, still alive, writhing at the water's edge while eels and crabs scuttle around them. This exodus of sea life provides residents with as much seafood as they can gig, net, or scoop, and the atmosphere is so celebratory they call it a jubilee.

Jubilees have a legendary quality to them, but science backs the annual windfall. Estuaries contain layers of water with different densities and salinities. Jubilees occur when the bottom layer of water, which is salty and low in oxygen, gets pushed by easterly winds into the shallow shoreline area of Mobile Bay. In response to the movement and increased summer salinity of this inhabitable water, sea creatures flee in front of it, toward the shoreline, where they eventually wash up.

The oldest records of jubilee dates back to the 1860s, and after so many years, residents say they can feel them coming. They tailgate after midnight at the dock when signs suggest one might manifest. If they're lucky enough to be right, locals alert their neighbors, and hundreds of people, along with flocks of sweeping pelicans and gulls, arrive in their pajamas to sweep the shoreline of its seafood. Jubilees are the only time of year fishing quotas go unpoliced. Employers and schools are also known to be more lenient the day after a jubilee, when the town is busy steaming fish, cracking crab, peeling shrimp, and generally enjoying the free onslaught of good eating.

How to try it

Time magazine, CNN, *National Geographic*, and other outlets have come to Mobile Bay over the years, trying but failing to document the event. But those willing to wait out a summer will likely be rewarded—years without a jubilee are extremely rare.

Locals make the most of each seafood jubilee, like this harvester during a recent bounty in Point Clear in 2012.

A CELEBRATION OF GOOBERS

NATIONAL PEANUT FESTIVAL • ALABAMA

When the National Peanut Festival debuted in 1938, the guest speaker was celebrity peanut heavyweight George Washington Carver, famous for his sensational 1918 agricultural bulletin, *How to Grow the Peanut and 105 Ways of Preparing It for Human Consumption*. Carver played a significant role in reviving Alabama's agricultural economy. Cotton, the state's historic cash crop, had depleted the region's soil and was being ravaged by boll weevils. At Carver's advice, Alabama farmers switched to peanuts and now the booming industry produces 400 million pounds (181 million kg) of peanuts annually.

The National Peanut Festival—a ten-day peanut party for 200,000 people— is about as American as it gets. There's a cheerleading competition, a gun show,

How to try it

The National Peanut Festival takes place every fall, typically in November, as a way to honor the farmers and welcome the harvest season. General admission is $7. A cup of boiled peanuts is $3.

A mural in Alabama's Dothan Historic District commemorates the local peanut industry and festival.

a demolition derby, a professional chainsaw sculptor, army helicopter rides, a "greased pig scramble" where students must catch a pig in an arena and coerce it across a finish line, a parade of peanut-themed people atop peanut-themed floats, and an abundance of foods celebrating the mighty peanut. The most serious competition is perhaps the Miss National Peanut beauty pageant, whose contestants must hail from peanut-producing states like Alabama, Florida, or Georgia. The women compete on the large civic center stage where they're judged, according to the official rules, on "Appearance, Poise, Communication Skills, Personal Interview, and of course, Knowledge of Peanuts."

PERFECT PORK FROM A FAMILY HOME

JONES BAR-B-Q DINER • ARKANSAS

The Jones family has been perfecting barbecue for more than 100 years.

Jones Bar-B-Q, a two-table eatery in the town of Marianna, is one of only two restaurants in Arkansas to ever receive a prestigious James Beard Award. The owners, James and Betty Jones, hadn't even heard of the award before winning the "America's Classics" category in 2012.

The small diner takes up the ground floor of the couple's home. The sign out front reads "since 1964," but the family operation dates back to at least 1910. James Jones's recipes are the same ones that his grandfather used when he sold barbecued meat out of his home and that his father used when he opened up an earlier iteration of the restaurant, known as the Hole in the Wall (so-called because his father served everything through a window).

Today, James runs the pit and restaurant, while a man named Sylvester chops wood and operates the attached smokehouse, which is a shed. Oak and hickory logs burn in a cinderblock barbecue pit, where pork shoulders—the only meat Jones sells—smoke for 12 hours at a time. The menu includes pork by the pound and sandwiches: pork dressed in a slightly sweet vinegar sauce and served between slices of white bread. Beyond slaw, sides are nonexistent. But with smoked pork this perfect, they're also unnecessary.

How to try it

Jones Bar-B-Q is located at 219 W. Louisiana Street. The restaurant opens at 7 a.m. and closes when it sells out. This could happen at 10 a.m., so plan to eat pork for breakfast.

..... FOOD PIONEER .....

GEORGIA GILMORE

(1920—1990)

Before Rosa Parks was arrested on a segregated bus in December 1955, sparking a citywide bus boycott by African Americans, Montgomery native Georgia Theresa Gilmore had begun a protest of her own. Two months earlier, a white driver had kicked her off a bus for using the front door, then drove away with her fare. "I decided right then and there I wasn't going to ride the buses anymore," Gilmore said.

When the city's bus boycott began in earnest, the organizers (known as the Montgomery Improvement Association, or MIA) needed money. Hundreds of cars, trucks, and wagons were required to transport protestors across the city. To support the cause, Gilmore assembled a group of women who pooled together $14 to buy chicken, bread, and lettuce, then sold sandwiches at a rally. When the sandwiches were a hit, they expanded into pound cakes, sweet potato pies, fried fish, and greens, which they sold door-to-door.

Georgia Gilmore's living room restaurant became a clubhouse for civil rights leaders.

The MIA threw biweekly rallies, and Gilmore's fund-raising updates were one of the highlights. Twice a week for more than a year, she sauntered down the aisle singing "Shine on Me" or "I Dreamt of a City Called Heaven," then emptied the club's earnings into the collection plate, announcing the amount to jubilant applause and stomping feet. Her food raised $125 to $200 each week, or the equivalent of $1,100 to $1,800 today. She is believed to have raised more money for the boycott than any other person in Montgomery.

Gilmore eventually testified against the white driver who kicked her off the bus—an act that cost Gilmore her job at the National Lunch, a segregated restaurant. But a fan of her cooking stepped in to help: Dr. Martin Luther King Jr. lived

a couple blocks away and encouraged Gilmore to open a restaurant. With his financial support, she transformed her dining room into a makeshift restaurant, which served as a clubhouse for civil rights leaders.

Every morning, Gilmore woke around 3 or 4 a.m. to prepare a rotating menu of ham hocks, stuffed pork chops, potato salad, collard greens, candied yams, bread pudding, and black-eyed peas. By noon, her house was crowded with customers. About a dozen people could squeeze around her dining room table, but everyone else had to eat standing up in her living room or kitchen. "Georgia House" became the unofficial office and social club of Dr. King, who held clandestine meetings around her table.

Between her no-nonsense attitude and notorious sense of humor, Gilmore became as much of an attraction as her food. She often greeted her guests by calling from the kitchen, using nicknames like "heifer" (for Dr. King) and "whore" (for the Reverend Dixon). In response, Dr. King affectionately called the large woman "Tiny."

Gilmore remained active in the civil rights movement for the rest of her life, using her food to fuel social change. She died on March 7, 1990—the 25th anniversary of the Selma to Montgomery march. Against doctor's orders, she had risen early to prepare chicken and potato salad for the people marching in commemoration. Instead, her family served the food to people who came to mourn her. Years later, Gilmore's sister Betty remembered: "Lots of people brought food to the house, too, but everybody ate Georgia's chicken and potato salad first. Nobody could fix it better."

HORSE-DRAWN KITCHEN GALLOP

CHUCKWAGON RACES • ARKANSAS

How to try it

Admission to the Chuckwagon Race grounds is $20–35/day, but once you're in there's free camping, roping clinics, rodeos, karaoke, cowboy mounted shooting, barrel racing, horseshoeing, and "cowboy church service." The party lasts eight days, with three days of chuckwagon racing.

Scattered across America is a collection of preserved chuckwagons—the portable "field kitchens" used in the 19th century to feed traveling workers or pioneering settlers. Strapped to horses, the wooden wagons transported pantry items and cooking equipment, and while they're still used on occasion for their original purpose, the chuckwagon at its core is a four-wheeled vehicle. And where there are vehicles, eventually there will be a race.

On Labor Day weekend in Clinton, Arkansas, chuckwagons from near and far gather to compete in America's premiere wagon race. What began as an impromptu competition between friends in 1986 has blossomed into a weeklong outdoor blowout for some 30,000 people and hundreds of racers. In Arkansas, chuckwagon racing involves teams of three: a driver, a cook, and an outrider. The cook and the outrider begin on the ground, while the driver is in the wagon. With a signal from a judge, the cook loads the stove into the wagon and hops in. With a gunshot, the outrider loads the tent into the wagon, then mounts his horse (the racers are almost exclusively men). The driver and the cook take off in the kitchen, galloping around a grassy field while the outrider tries to overtake them on his horse. The outrider must pass his teammates before they cross the finish line, and the chuckwagon must retain its stove and tent in order to receive a qualifying time.

Chuckwagon racing was born in Canada in 1923, where the sport remains a huge draw at the Calgary Stampede—a ten-day rodeo that draws a million people. The high-speed competitions have drawn criticism from animal welfare groups, as the intense courses and unwieldy kitchen equipment have ended in the injury and death of horses. Those arguing for the sport's survival claim that losses are a part of ranching, farming, and keeping horses.

Fourche Mountain Rough Riders racing in the 1994 National Championships.

A MASSIVE TROPICAL FRUIT EMPORIUM

ROBERT IS HERE • FLORIDA

In 1959, Robert Moehling's father, a Florida farmer, tasked his son with selling his surplus cucumbers on the side of the road. Robert was six years old, and the cars speeding past took no notice. To draw attention to the makeshift operation, his father spray-painted a message on a hurricane shutter and placed it beside the cucumbers: "Robert Is Here."

More than 60 years later, that statement remains true, but what was once a ramshackle stand is now the Disney World of tropical fruit. Just off US 1, this kitschy, massive shop features produce, jams, souvenirs, animals (including goats, emu, iguanas, and birds), a picnic area, and live music on the weekends. The barn-like emporium has become a local landmark for those visiting the Everglades or traveling the long stretch of highway to Key West and the Florida Turnpike. Robert, now well into his 60s, still works there alongside his immediate family and grows much of the fruit himself.

The stand specializes in unique fruit varieties, like egg fruit, dragonfruit, *Monstera deliciosa*, and sugar apples. Whimsical descriptions accompany each product, such as soursop, which is described as tasting like "pineapple cotton candy." But the most beloved offering might be the milkshakes, made from Robert's fresh fruit, milk, yogurt, and soft-serve ice cream. During peak season, they sell about 1,400 shakes each day.

How to try it
Robert Is Here is located at 19200 SW 344th Street in Homestead.

Robert Moehling is still here, arranging the produce at his eponymous fruit stand.

Florida Grows the Most Diverse Fruit in the United States

The South Florida city of Homestead is hot, humid, and just two degrees north of the Tropic of Cancer, making it the perfect climate for growing tropical fruit. The land is farmed by an international community of people—from Latin America to Africa, the Caribbean to Asia—that has turned Homestead into a global fruit lovers paradise. Within the patchwork of farms, you'll find dozens of varieties of mangoes and avocados, as well as lychees, longans, jackfruits, green papayas, sapotes, tamarinds, starfruits, and guavas.

THE WORLD'S LARGEST COLLECTION OF METAL-SIDED NOSTALGIA

LUNCH BOX MUSEUM • GEORGIA

The original children's metal lunch pail was plain and utilitarian, modeled after the cheerless vessels of the workingman. In 1935, all that changed when Mickey Mouse debuted on the side of a lunch box, and other brands followed suit. Licensed characters began to appear on lunch box sides, exploding with the 1950s television boom. Suddenly there were hundreds of choices, from Snoopy to

A vintage Flintstones lunch box and thermos, ca. 1962.

How to try it
The Lunch Box Museum is open Monday–Saturday, 10 a.m. to 6 p.m. Woodall takes pride in the hands-on aspect of his museum: All the lunch boxes are meant to be picked up, unfastened, and played with.

Annie Oakley to the Beatles. But by 1985, metal lunch boxes were largely replaced by cheaper plastic or vinyl versions, leaving a legacy of some 450 old metal boxes with distinctive character designs.

Collector Allen Woodall, who operates the Lunch Box Museum in Columbus, Georgia, has all 450. Now the world's largest collection of lunch boxes, the museum contains more than 3,000, many of which are accompanied by their matching thermoses. Archie & Friends, Arthur & Friends, the Avengers, Pac-Man, Cabbage Patch Kids, the Smurfs, the Beatles, King Kong, and Knight Rider—Woodall has them all. Some of the rarest pails are valued at more than $10,000. He's perpetually culling his main collection, which he organizes alphabetically.

With so many lunch boxes, many of them are duplicates or replicas. Woodall keeps a "barter room," where he'll sell certain pails to the public, or trade lunch boxes with other aficionados.

THE CHEESE SANDWICH SCANDAL OF THE MASTERS TOURNAMENT

PIMENTOGATE • GEORGIA

How to try it
WifeSaver restaurants still sell their secret-recipe pimento cheese. The Junior League of Augusta, Georgia, published the included recipe in their cookbook, *Par 3 Tea-Time at the Masters*, which many hail as the closest to the original.

Pimento cheese—the heady blend of cheese, mayonnaise, and pimento peppers—is a thick, spreadable delicacy that's known as the paté of the American South. And though the main draw to the Masters Tournament is arguably golf, the pimento cheese sandwich is a quintessential part of the experience. The tradition began in the mid-1950s, when South Carolina caterer Nick Rangos began selling his sandwiches to hungry attendees, gradually cultivating a fan base that came to associate the golf tournament with his signature sandwich. His pimento cheese reign lasted nearly half a century, until 1998, when the tournament gave the sandwich contract to local restaurant WifeSaver. Rangos, jilted from his position, refused to give up his beloved recipe (in fact, he took it to his grave), and so WifeSaver set out to reconstruct it. Recipe testers ordered dozens of cases of cheeses for experimentation and delivered attempts to the tournament's concession committee—all were rejected. Eventually, a woman who worked for the Masters stepped forward. She had been saving a batch of the original recipe in her freezer, and with this sample (and some tips from Rangos's suppliers), WifeSaver was able to reverse engineer a pimento cheese that satisfied the golf fans.

But in 2013, the tournament brought the sandwich-making in house. WifeSaver, like Rangos, refused to surrender its formula, and this time, without a frozen sample, the tournament was out of luck. The pimento cheese sandwich, while still $1.50 and sold in the iconic green plastic sack, is decidedly different: more heavily spiced, some say looser with mayo. Fans were shaken by the abrupt end to an era. An ESPN article covering this final change quoted one disgruntled fan, who said "I am fine with adding the female members, and I am tolerating the belly putters, but changing the pimento cheese recipe is taking change too damn far."

Masters-Style Pimento Cheese Sandwich

Makes 8 sandwiches

3 cups shredded white cheddar cheese

2 cups shredded yellow sharp
   cheddar cheese

4 ounces crumbled blue cheese

1 cup shredded parmesan cheese

1 (4-ounce) jar sliced pimentos,
   drained

1 cup light mayonnaise

2 tablespoons dijon mustard

1 loaf white bread

Combine cheeses, pimentos, mayonnaise, and mustard in a food processor and process until smooth. Cover and chill. Spread on bread slices.

A DEGREE IN DISTILLATION

MOONSHINE UNIVERSITY ○ KENTUCKY

Back in the day, when bootleggers wanted to sell their moonshine, they might put jars of the illegal homemade hooch in a hollowed-out tree stump in the woods. Within a day or two, they'd come back to find the shine gone and their money waiting in the stump. The unregulated liquor, distilled across the homes and backwoods of the American South, was a centuries-old game of production and evasion. Moonshine developed a dangerous reputation, which was only aided by the practice of using dicey machinery like car radiators as condensers and harmful additives like lye. Rebellion runs deep in whiskey-making history: In 1791, when distillers in Pennsylvania (the birthplace of American whiskey) were slapped with a liquor tax, they revolted against the tax collectors, tarring and feathering them and attacking the home of a prominent inspector in what's now known as the Whiskey Rebellion.

But in 2010, moonshine—now a term that refers to clear, unaged whiskey—was legalized in the United States, and in Louisville, Kentucky, there's a school to teach you how to make it.

How to try it
The six-day Distiller Course, held at the Distilled Spirits Epicenter in Louisville, is offered four times a year and costs $6,250.

Moonshine University is intended for people looking to get into the distilling business. Students study the science and business side of the industry, then get immersed in the production: milling grain, cooking mash, measuring, tasting, and smelling. After an intensive six-day course, graduates come away with a body of knowledge meant to prepare them for starting a distillery of their own. As the state that produces 95 percent of the world's bourbon and exports more than a billion dollars of whiskey every year, many consider Kentucky the whiskey capital of the world. Now that moonshine is legal, Moonshine University is a crash course in what promises to be a much bigger business than wads of cash in hollowed-out tree stumps.

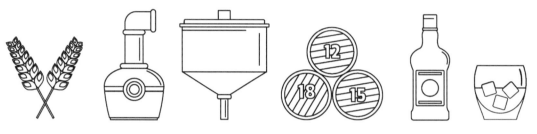

THE ARM WORKOUT COCKTAIL

RAMOS GIN FIZZ • LOUISIANA

How to try it
New Orleans's Sazarac Bar serves a supremely fluffy Ramos Gin Fizz.

In 1888, Henry C. Ramos purchased the Imperial Cabinet saloon in New Orleans and a year later introduced the world to the New Orleans Gin Fizz. His namesake version, the Ramos Gin Fizz, graced the menu of his next saloon: the Stag. Located near the popular St. Charles Hotel, it became a New Orleans destination and the Ramos Gin Fizz an emblem of the city.

The Ramos Gin Fizz takes the standard combination of gin, sugar, lemon juice, and club soda and adds egg whites, orange flower water, lime juice, cream, and powdered sugar (in place of cane sugar). In drink lore, the subsequent step was 12 minutes of cocktail shaking, although experts agree 5 minutes was probably more accurate. Nonetheless, his namesake drink wasn't perfect until it reached a near-whipped state.

With a process so laborious and time-consuming, Ramos hired several full-time "shaker boys" to help prepare his gin fizzes. Especially around Mardi Gras, dozens of shaker boys would shake continuously, for hours on end, trying to keep up with the demand.

Despite the craze, Ramos did not tolerate drunken tomfoolery. He enforced a policy against drunkards and a strict 8 p.m. closing time. The saloon was a calm space and a stage for fine cocktails—not a place for late-night debauchery and disorder. Ramos followed the rules, and with the ratification of the 18th Amendment, he shut down the bar for good in 1919. He died before Prohibition ended.

A 1928 issue of the *New Orleans Item-Tribune* published advice from the late Ramos, who insisted that the key to the cocktail was care, patience, and quality ingredients. Readers were instructed to "shake and shake and shake until there is not a bubble left, but the drink is smooth and snowy white and of the consistency of good rich milk. The secret in success lies in the good care you take and in your patience, and be certain to use good material."

A FRENCH TRADITION IN LOUISIANA

GIANT OMELETTE CELEBRATION • LOUISIANA

The land that makes up Abbeville, Louisiana, was purchased for $900 by a French priest named Father Antoine Désiré Mégret in 1843. With the help of the Acadians—descendants of the French Canadian colonists who settled in Louisiana in the 18th century—Mégret set out to design a rural, French-style village, gathered around a main place he called Magdalen Square. For nearly two centuries, Mégret's square has served as a gathering place for the community and, in the last few decades, as the location of a new French tradition called the Giant Omelette Celebration.

Every November, the Confrérie d' Abbeville ("Brotherhood of Abbeville") gathers to crack and scramble 5,000 eggs, which get poured into a 12-foot (3.7 m) pan over a blazing wood fire and fed to anyone who shows up to celebrate. This French tradition dates back to Napoleon Bonaparte, who was said to have eaten such a delicious omelet while traveling through the south of France, he ordered one the next day large enough to feed his army. In the town of Bessières, where Napoleon fell for the omelet, the Confrérie Mondiale des Chevaliers de l'Omelette Géante ("World Brotherhood of Knights of the Giant Omelette") puts on a 15,000-egg spectacle every Easter. They also appoint new "omelette knights" for foreign chapters around the world.

In 1984, three Abbeville natives attended the Bessières celebration and decided to bring the tradition to Louisiana. While the Abbeville chefs still uphold the primary practices of making the omelet in the town square and sharing it among the townspeople, the Abbeville omelet is distinctly Cajun (as the Louisiana Acadian descendants are known). The Southern version is made with 50 pounds (23 kg) of onions, 75 pounds (34 kg) of bell peppers, and 15 pounds (7 kg) of Louisiana crawfish tails. And while the base is still scrambled eggs, those eggs are spiked with a healthy dose of Tabasco, Louisiana's signature hot sauce.

How to try it

The Giant Omelette Celebration takes place every November in Abbeville's Magdalen Square. With each new celebration, they add one egg to the original 5,000. In 2018, they cracked 5,034.

Abbeville chefs were inspired by the Knights of the Giant Omelette of Bessières, France, shown here.

How to try it
Notable venues still in business include the Apollo in New York City, the Howard Theater in Washington, D.C., and Southern Whispers in Greenville, Mississippi, which is also a stop on the Mississippi Blues Trail.

ENTERTAINMENT SAFE HOUSES IN JIM CROW AMERICA

THE CHITLIN CIRCUIT • MISSISSIPPI

Pig intestines, or chitlins, were a staple for enslaved African Americans. Chitlins required intense cleaning, and slaveowners preferred the choicest cuts that required little work, like the upper portions of the leg and the back (hence the affluence-denoting phrase "high on the hog").

West Africans were particularly accustomed to eating every part of the animal, so intestines were nothing new. Chitlins were deep fried, simmered in soup, and paired with cornbread and collard greens—all recipes that belong to the culinary tradition of soul food, a confluence of Indigenous American, African, European, and Southern cooking developed by African Americans during the time of slavery.

Under Jim Crow, from about 1930 to 1950, chitlins gained a new significance. For black performers traveling through the country, the hog intestines became a kind of insider code, as they knew that establishments serving chitlins would welcome them. This collection of restaurants, music venues, and nightclubs became known as the Chitlin Circuit. Stretching from Texas to Massachusetts, it functioned as a touring route for black performers. Big-name acts occasionally made the rounds, but the establishments were mostly mom-and-pop places, often in small towns, that offered an informal stage for aspiring performers.

With so much talent traveling along the same route and appearing in the same rooms, the Chitlin Circuit was fertile ground for promoters and managers, who began to champion their favorite acts. Some performers, like Louis Jordan and Roy Brown, had so much success that they climbed the Billboard charts. Today, America's love for blues, swing, and rock and roll is largely thanks to the black performers who came up through the soul food circuit.

Performers like Floyd Smith (top) and Dick Wilson (bottom) graced the stage of the Howard Theater in the 1940s.

Arnett Cobb and Walter Buchanan, Apollo Theatre, New York, NY, ca. Aug. 1947

Music and the warm welcome of soul food drew crowds from Texas to Massachusetts.

KOOL-AID BRINED PICKLES

KOOLICKLES • MISSISSIPPI

The quirky combination of dill pickles and Kool-Aid, America's iconic beverage powder, hails from the Mississippi Delta, where the psychedelic spears are sold at community and convenience stores for a dollar. Known locally as koolickles, the sweet and vinegary pickles are generally loved and widely eaten. Cherry is the classic flavor, but koolickles are limited only by the assortment of Kool-Aid on hand: The line includes pink lemonade, watermelon, peach mango, and strawberry kiwi.

To make a batch of koolickles, drain the brine from a jar of pickles into a bowl. Into the brine, mix a package of unsweetened Kool-Aid powder and some sugar, then pour it back into the jar. Soaking whole pickles creates a corona of color around the circumference of the pickle. Slicing pickles lengthwise before curing allows the Kool-Aid to dye the interior a bright jewel tone. Either way, devotees recommend leaving pickles in their Kool-Aid bath for at least a week.

How to try it

The Mississippi-based convenience store chain Double Quick sells them as "Pickoolas."

ALL-YOU-CAN-EAT DEPRESSION BURGERS

SLUGBURGER EATING CHAMPIONSHIP • MISSISSIPPI

How to try it

The Slugburger Festival is held every July in downtown Corinth. First prize is $1,500. Participants must be 18 or older and abide by the rules of the MLE.

During the lean days of the Great Depression, "meat extending" was a necessary practice. Burger joints in Mississippi began cutting their ground meat patties with potato flour, deep-frying them, and sliding them into buns laced with mustard and onion. It was a surprisingly satisfying burger that was crispy on the outside and soft on the inside. The slugburger, which sold for a nickel, was so popular that even after the Depression, Mississippians kept extending their meat out of sheer pleasure.

Since 1987, the town of Corinth has been throwing the Slugburger Festival, a three-day event to honor the divine union of beef, starch (now soybean meal), and a hot vat of fat. There's a Slug Idol singing competition and a cornhole throwing contest, but the glitziest draw is the World Slugburger Eating Championship.

Since the contest debuted in 2012, celebrity eaters ranked by the Major League Eating (MLE) association have arrived in Corinth to compete for the international title of Slugburger Champ. Matt "the Megatoad" Stonie from San Jose took

home gold for the first three years, setting the world record in 2014 when he ate 43 slugburgers in ten minutes. In 2015, when Stonie took a year off, first place went to the eminent Joey "Jaws" Chestnut, the reigning king of the Nathan's Hot Dog Eating Contest (in 2018, he set the world record with 74 hot dogs in ten minutes). Chestnut, who ate his first slugburger during competition in 2013, said he enjoyed the burger but had more trouble swallowing than anticipated. While signing autographs, he apologized to fans, saying, "Next year I'll come back and know what I'm getting into and eat more." (He did; in 2014 he ate 42, a dozen more than the previous year.)

The Great Eater of Kent

Before competitive eating was rife with bigwigs and fanfare, there was Nicholas Wood, the Great Eater of Kent.

Wood's career, which spanned the early 17th century, was mostly chronicled by the English poet John Taylor, who was so taken by Wood he later became his manager. Taylor's awe is embodied in his pamphlet, *The Great Eater, of Kent, or Part of the Admirable Teeth and Stomach Exploits of Nicholas Wood, of Harrisom in the County of Kent His Excessive Manner of Eating Without Manners, In Strange and True Manner Described*.

The story goes that Taylor first encountered Wood at an inn in Kent, where he watched him devour 60 eggs, a good portion of lamb, and a handful of pies, before declaring himself still hungry. Wood, who was a farmer by trade, had a local reputation as a superhuman feaster and was known to perform at town festivals and take dares and wagers from nobles. While he had emerged victorious from many feats (he once ate seven dozen rabbits in a single sitting), Wood was far from invincible. During a challenge with a man named Sir William Sedley, Wood ate so much he fell over, passed out, and was put in the stocks—a punishment for his failure. In another instance, a man named

John Dale fed him 12 loaves of bread that he'd soaked in ale, and Wood got so drunk, he passed out and was humiliated once again.

Despite these losses, Wood was a kind of celebrity in Kent. The poet Taylor made Wood an offer, reasoning that they could both make money if they took his talents to London. Taylor would provide payment, lodging, and massive amounts of food, and Wood, in return, would perform daily feats of overeating at the city's Bear Gardens, which at the time hosted animal fights. (Suggested meals included a wheelbarrow full of tripe, and as many puddings as would stretch across the Thames.)

But Wood declined. He was reaching the end of his youth and with it, the end of his intensive eating career. He'd recently eaten an entire mutton shoulder—bones and all—and the experience had left him with only one tooth. He wasn't confident he could perform, so he turned down the enterprising poet.

Though Taylor never got his shot at big city fame, his admiration for Wood never wavered. In his writings, he compares Wood's monumental feats of gluttony to the achievements of Charlemagne and Alexander the Great, declaring he "doth well deserve the title of Great."

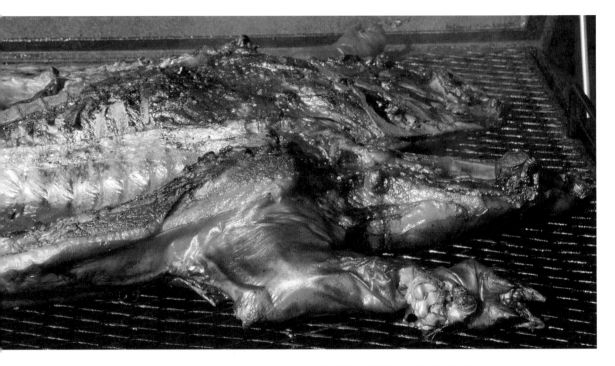

WHOLE HOG HOEDOWN

PIG PICKIN' • NORTH CAROLINA

How to try it

The annual Jamestown pig pickin' event is open to the public. Past themes include Swine & Shakespeare, Cork & Pork, and Hammin' & Jammin'.

In North Carolina, the word *barbecue* is a noun and it always means pork. *Pig pickin'* is also a noun, and in this state it means a party featuring a succulent, slow-cooked whole hog with meat so soft, guests can pick it right off the pig.

Before the Civil War, Southerners ate 5 pounds of pork for every pound of beef. Pigs were left to live in the forest until one was needed for food, when it would be hunted, butchered, and cooked on an open fire. Often, at the helm of these cookouts was an enslaved African, who expertly tended to meat and fire in a technique their masters would claim as their own. In West and Central Africa, smoking and roasting animals was a common practice, and the knowledge enslaved Africans brought to the American South is what made North Carolina pig pickin' what it is today.

By the 19th century, pig pickin's were adopted by politicians as a way to gather big crowds to listen to their speeches. Politicians vied for popularity by bringing the most food to a pig pickin', which led to the phrase "going whole hog." In North Carolina especially, pigs and politics became fully entrenched, and attending a rally became synonymous with feasting on pork.

These days, pig pickin's still draw crowds. They also draw a lot of opinions. Cooking a whole hog requires teamwork, about eight hours, and agreement over several major issues. Some pit masters prefer the even cooking heat of propane, while others like the smoky flavor of charcoal or the aroma of wood. In the Piedmont region of North Carolina, hogs are basted with a tomato sauce. To the east, locals use a thin vinegar and pepper sauce. And though state can't always agree on what to put on or around the pig, the pig itself remains an almost holy facet of North Carolina's culinary heritage, shaped by centuries of European, African, and political influence.

A TIMES SQUARE ALTERNATIVE

NEW YEAR'S EVE PICKLE DROP • NORTH CAROLINA

At the corner of Cucumber and Vine street, hundreds of revelers gather to ring in the New Year outside the Mt. Olive Pickle Company. At the stroke of 7 p.m., they cheer as a 3-foot-long (1-m) fluorescent pickle drops from a 45-foot (14-m) flagpole into a redwood pickle tank. The tank sprays a delicate fountain of liquid as the pickle hits and the crowd goes wild, blowing on noisemakers and applauding the spectacle.

Since 1999, the Mt. Olive Pickle Company has been dropping the massive celebratory pickle. The event attracts families, older adults, and anyone else wanting to line dance to live music under the glow of a magnificent pickle while also getting to bed at a reasonable time. Seven p.m. Eastern Standard Time happens to be midnight Greenwich Mean Time, which makes the countdown official and justifies the early bedtime.

How to try it

The pickle party starts at 5:30 p.m. at 1 Cucumber Boulevard in Mount Olive. Part of the event is a canned food drive, where all participants are entered to win an inflatable pool pickle.

AFRICAN SESAME COOKIES

BENNE WAFERS • SOUTH CAROLINA

Benne (pronounced "benny") means "sesame seed" in Bantu, a family of languages spoken in sub-Saharan Africa. In the 1700s, when slave traders brought Africans to work the fields of South Carolina, they loaded the ships' cargo holds with African crops intended to feed the captives during the long transatlantic passage. Among these crops was sesame—a buttery, protein-rich seed that the Africans later planted in South Carolina and pressed into cooking oil.

While plantation owners explored sesame's potential as an alternative to imported olive oil, sesame-based substitutes gained little traction until the

How to try it

Olde Colony Bakery in Mount Pleasant uses a 100-year-old recipe, which they claim is the original recipe for benne wafers.

19th century. Instead, South Carolinians developed a fondness for benne wafers, a light and crispy cookie made by toasting sesame seeds, mixing them with brown sugar, butter, and small amounts of flour, and baking them into small nutty discs. Over the last two centuries, benne wafers have become a Low Country staple, tied to the regional cuisine of South Carolina and sold at bakeries and gift shops around the state. Yet many never realize the sweet and salty snack is a vestige of slavery, a tradition owed to those who planted, tended, and popularized the sesame seed.

Benne Wafers from the historic Charleston City Market, established in the 1790s.

CORNMEAL MUSH ENTRAPMENT COMPETITION

ROLLING IN THE GRITS • SOUTH CAROLINA

How to try it

There are two age divisions for Rolling in the Grits: 12 to 16, and 17 or older. Prospective rollers can register at the festival. It's advisable to book your accommodations early because the town's population increases to 45,000 people during festival days.

The small hamlet of St. George has a population of 2,000 and one big claim to fame: They eat more grits per capita than any other place on Earth. To celebrate their town's passion for the Southern dish, St. George hosts the annual World Grits Festival and invites honored members of the community to roll around in an inflatable pool with 3,000 pounds (1,361 kg) of grits.

The object of the competition, called Rolling in the Grits, is to trap as many grits on your body as possible. Participants have taken to wearing grits-catching clothes: sweatshirts with big hoods worn backward, sleeves rolled and duct-taped into pockets, and baggy sweatpants that cinch at the ankle. Contestants are weighed before and after diving into the grits, and the largest weight gain wins. In the pool, they have ten seconds to do their best work, swimming, rolling, and scooping. (The rules state: "Once ten seconds is up, roller must stand up slowly with their arms upward and no grabbing the pants.") In 2015, the world record was set when Tiffany McGirr gained 66 pounds (30 kg) of grits.

Preparing the grits for competition is a challenge in itself. Twenty-seven cases of grits are cooked until just thick enough to hold a paddle upright. Each year, depending on the weather, the recipe is adjusted. (Hot weather, for example, dries out the grits, and they require extra time for cooling.) Since the inaugural contest in 1986, the competition has always used plain grits. But the cook, a man named Philip Ranck, who's been preparing the grits since 2001, recently expressed interest in trying a shrimp base.

With only ten seconds per attempt, contestants try to maximize their grits hoarding ability with baggy clothes.

A REPLICA OF THE FIRST MODERN GROCERY STORE

PIGGLY WIGGLY AT PINK PALACE MUSEUM • TENNESSEE

Before 1916, shopping for groceries was a time-consuming, social endeavor: A clerk served customers one by one, pulling their items from the shelves. Nothing was marked with prices and tallying the bill was done by hand. Clarence Saunders, a flour and grain salesman, conceived of a self-service grocery store where customers would shop autonomously. In 1916, he opened the first Piggly Wiggly. Saunders advertised in newspapers and on billboards, telling the public that grocery shopping was about to change forever. On opening day 487 customers bought groceries—an impossible feat in a clerk-serviced store. Within a year, eight more stores opened in Memphis and by 1923, there were 1,200 stores across the country and countless copycats. Although Saunders's prophecy was right that his self-service concept would change grocery shopping in the United States forever, it's unlikely that he foresaw his own financial ruin. In 1923, with Piggly Wiggly public on the stock exchange, Saunders made some risky trades and lost the company along with millions of dollars.

At the time Saunders lost his grocery-store fortune, he was building a palatial mansion outside Memphis, faced with pink marble. Plans included a ballroom, shooting gallery, and indoor pool, but the unfinished house was taken by his creditors and later donated to the city of Memphis. Now the Pink Palace Museum, visitors to the house can see a replica of Saunders's early Piggly Wiggly stores and step back into a time when grabbing groceries off the shelf (and knowing their price) was a novelty.

How to try it

The Pink Palace Museum is located at 3050 Central Avenue, Memphis, TN. Piggly Wigglys still operate in the southern and midwestern United States.

BEER STEIN HOME-MUSEUM

STEINS UNLIMITED • VIRGINIA

How to try it

From the road, the museum is entirely nondescript, but GPS will get you there. Although technically open every day from 8 a.m. to 5 p.m., Adams is a one-man show, so it's best to call ahead.

ocated just outside Pamplin, a tiny 200-person village along an isolated stretch of Virginia's US 460, the Steins Unlimited home-museum is advertised by two hand-painted signs—one hanging from the mailbox, the other rising from the edge of the yard.

Visitors step into a large two-room outdoor shed and are greeted by an array of floor-to-ceiling shelves brimming with some of the most ornate and historically significant drinking vessels ever made. The collection of 10,000-plus rare beer steins is George Adams's lifelong obsession, which took more than 50 years to compile.

Adams uses his formidable collection to tell the story of beer drinking from 1350 to modern day. He's the museum's only host, and quick to offer a "bottomless pint" of America's oldest beer, Yuengling, from an on-site kegerator. (Beer and admission are free, though donations are welcomed.) For about an hour, Adams guides guests down a rabbit hole of German and American beer history. A tour typically covers the institutionalization of the stein via 15th-century sanitation laws (following the Black Death), the ensuing "golden era" of European beer drinking, the rise of beautifully crafted steins as status symbols, American prohibition, the drinking habits of the Third Reich, and much more.

Adams's finest treasures are displayed within his home, a four-bedroom brick rancher. The keystone of the collection is a room containing about 500 vessels that include hand-carved wooden steins, silver steins, and even gold-lidded steins, many of which are hundreds of years old.

THE MID-ATLANTIC

AN INSIDER'S JAM

BEACH PLUM JELLY • DELAWARE

To get your hands on some beach plum jelly, chances are you'll have to forage for beach plums, which requires climbing windy sand dunes and combing through the jagged leaves of gnarled bushes to find the elusive, burgundy-colored fruit. Beach plums, which never make it to the grocery store, are growing increasingly hard to source from the wild. But those who find them are rewarded with a zesty, highly coveted jelly ingredient.

Beach plum jelly wasn't always so hard to find. Explorers have written about the presence of beach plums since 1524. Farmers cultivated the plant in the 1800s, and Ocean Spray even sold beach plum jelly back in the 1930s. But in recent years, coastal developments have taken over much of the beach plum's natural habitat. Some have taken to domesticating the plums in backyard gardens for the sole purpose of jelly-making, but purists say the garden variety is less flavorful than the wild one. Among those who still forage, the sites of known remaining bushes often become well-kept secrets, even within families.

How to try it

Delaware company Backyard Jams and Jellies makes a much-loved beach plum jelly. From late spring to early fall, the jams are sold at Delaware's Rehoboth, Milton, and Historic Lewes farmers' markets, and year-round in specialty stores listed on the company's website.

Tart like plums but bite-size like cherries, beach plums grow in sand dunes.

EVER-EVOLVING HEAT

FISH PEPPERS • MARYLAND

Fish peppers begin life a pale milky color, and then slowly transform into light then darker green, then orange with brown, then finally red, when the pepper is at its hottest.

The Caribbean pepper is believed to have arrived in North America around the 19th century. It was embraced by African Americans living in the Chesapeake Bay area, where it became a favored secret ingredient in the kitchens of crab and oyster

How to try it

The Seed Savers Exchange sells fish pepper seeds on its website, where it's listed as an "All-Time Favorite."

houses (giving the fish pepper its name). The young, pale-colored pepper melted discreetly into the white creamy sauces they used on fish, giving them an invisible kick that no one could name. The trick was passed down orally, rarely recorded in written recipes, which meant in the 20th century, when the pepper fell out of favor, its whispered existence nearly led to extinction.

In the 1940s, a Pennsylvania painter named Horace Pippin was treating his arthritis with an old folk remedy that required being stung by bees. To acquire the bees, he traded seeds with a beekeeper, and among those seeds was the forgotten fish pepper. The beekeeper, H. Ralph Weaver, passed the seeds down through his family and in 1995, his grandson made the fish pepper seed publicly available through the Seed Savers Exchange in Iowa.

Fish peppers taste a lot like fresh serranos—bright, crisp, decisively spicy—and can be used similarly. What makes them distinctive is their vibrant, ornamental appearance. Not only are the peppers on the plant perpetually in varying stages of color and ripeness, each leaf is marbled and flecked by a unique mix of green and white. No two leaves, and no two peppers, are quite the same, making the fish pepper especially suited for landscaped gardens.

Fish peppers ripen through several stages of colors and reach maximum heat when red.

A TINY EDIBLES COMPETITION

SMALL FOODS PARTY • MARYLAND

Baltimore locals have been shrinking wontons, crab cakes, banana splits, and other conventional-size dishes since 2006, when a group of artists began the tradition at a holiday party. Since then, their small-food obsession has morphed into an annual competition that now draws more than 500 people.

Participants of the Small Foods Party compete for everything from the Bad Idea award (where food is charmingly unappealing, like mini Tide Pods made with coconut gelée) to the International award (for food that originates outside the United States). The most innovative contestant takes home the Bright Idea award, while the chef with the best reproduction of a full meal claims the Blue Plate Special. Fingertip-size cupcakes and tiny sub sandwiches are among the past winners of the Golden Toothpick, which praises the most impressive proportional accuracy between full-size original and mini re-creation. The Yummo! award (honoring the party's decree, "Thou shalt not compromise taste for smallness") has gone to a Caesar salad atop a piece of fried parmesan.

To earn the grand prize, the tiny food must capture the "heart, mind, and stomachs of the people." One winning team performed as an assembly line of uniformed employees cranking out miniature "Crappy Meals," complete with a burger, fries, and lidded drink. In addition to becoming a small-food legend, the grand prize comes with a giant decorated can of mini corn and the chance to host the next year's showdown.

How to try it

The Small Foods Party is held at the American Visionary Art Museum. The event benefits Moveable Feast, an organization that brings nutritious food to Maryland people with life-threatening or chronic illnesses. Anyone can enter the competition, or simply attend, but no one should arrive hungry.

CONTROVERSIALLY KNOWN AS TAYLOR HAM

PORK ROLL • NEW JERSEY

Every morning, locals all over the Garden State start their day with the same sandwich: two eggs, American cheese, and pork roll—a processed meat that graces nearly every diner and deli menu. Pork roll is endemic to New Jersey and about as old school as it gets. In 1856, a state senator by the name of John Taylor started making the hefty roll of sliceable tube meat that exists somewhere on the spectrum between sausage, bologna, and Canadian bacon. He called it "Taylor's Prepared Ham," but was forced to change the name in 1906, when the Pure Food and Drug Act decreed that hams had to be actual hams.

Here begins a divisive New Jersey debate. People from the southern part of the state took to the name change. When Taylor renamed his product "John Taylor's Original Taylor Pork Roll," they went along with the changing times and began calling it pork roll. But up north, locals stuck with Taylor Ham—for more than a hundred years. The small state is still divided on terminology, and how someone refers to the porcine delicacy immediately gives away their New Jersey provenance and continues to be a source of friendly ire. But pork roll or Taylor ham, the way to enjoy it is not up for debate: slice the meat, cut slits in the sides to prevent curling in the pan, crisp it up, eat it for breakfast.

How to try it

Trenton, New Jersey, throws a Pork Roll Festival in May. Phillipsburg, New Jersey, throws a Pork Roll Palooza in October. For all months in between, check out any local bagel shop or deli.

THE GOLDEN AGE OF

In the early 20th century, newly industrialized America was eager for places to eat, and prefab, shippable diners were the perfect solution for entrepreneurs looking to fill the demand. Diners—designed to resemble train dining cars—were built in factories and transported, fully assembled, to their permanent locations around the country.

Starting in 1912, thousands of shiny metal restaurants were built and shipped from New Jersey. Although the diner manufacturing industry is all but gone today, some of New Jersey's original handiwork is still standing and operating across America.

WHITE MANNA, Hackensack, NJ. Opened in 1946, manufactured in 1939 by Paramount Diners of Oakland, NJ.

AGAWAM DINER, Rowley, MA. Opened in 1970, manufactured in 1954 by Fodero Dining Car Company of Newark and Bloomfield, NJ.

PEARL DINER, Manhattan, NY. Opened in the early 1960s, manufactured by Kullman Dining Car Company of Lebanon, NJ.

MICKEY'S DINING CAR, Saint Paul, MN. Opened in 1939, manufactured by Jerry O'Mahony Diner Company of Elizabeth, NJ.

NEW JERSEY DINERS

FRANK'S DINER, Kenosha, WI. Opened in 1926, manufactured by Jerry O'Mahony Diner Company of Elizabeth, NJ.

DAVIE'S CHUCK WAGON DINER, Lakewood, CO. Opened in 1957, manufactured by Mountain View Diners Company of Singac, NJ.

DAVIES' chuck wagon DINER

OPEN

PANCAKES
STEAKS
FRIED CHICKEN

The Lost Language of
NEW YORK SODA JERKS

Throughout the 1930s and 1940s, soda jerks across the country were known for a kind of esoteric slang. Behind the counter that was their stage, the soda jerks' responsibilities were manifold: breaking and draining eggs with one hand, carving chicken, remembering orders, pulling the correct spigots and spindles on the drugstore fountain, and, perhaps most important, juggling a beguiling linguistic shorthand for all the orders. Especially in New York City, where the density of candy stores, pharmacies, and customers kept soda jerks working at a quick-witted pace, the counter workers became a show in themselves.

An order of a simple float might yield a shout of "burn it and let it swim!" A more complex chocolate malted milk with chocolate ice cream: "Burn one all the way." If you nixed the ice cream and added an egg, your server would "twist it, choke it, and make it cackle." Coca-Cola flavored with cherry might be "shoot one in the red." Drinks without ice "held the hail." Big drinks were "stretched"; small ones were "short." But a term in one drugstore might not hold in another. In fact, most expressions didn't travel beyond one or two soda fountains, and there was a certain amount of pressure to keep mixing them up. A simple glass of milk might variously be called "cow juice," "bovine extract," or "canned cow," while water went by everything from "aqua pura" to "city cocktail" to the deeply unappetizing "Hudson River ale."

Alas, the era of razzle-dazzle soda jerks came to an end when decorum-minded owners started enforcing notepads and cracking down on shouting. While most of the slang and hijinks are forgotten, here are a few phrases from the heyday of the soda jerk.

In the world of soda jerks, you might start your day with a mug of murk and end it with a glob.

ADD ANOTHER: Coffee

ALL BLACK: Chocolate soda with chocolate ice cream

BABY: Glass of fresh milk

BLACK BOTTOM: Chocolate sundae with chocolate syrup

BLACK COW: Chocolate milk

C. O. COCKTAIL: Castor oil prepared in soda

CANARY ISLAND SPECIAL: Vanilla soda with chocolate cream

CHOC IN: Chocolate soda

CHOKER HOLES: Doughnuts

COFFEE AND: Cup of coffee and cake

COWCUMBER: Pickle

DRAW SOME MUD: Coffee

GIVE: Large glass of fresh milk

GLOB: Plain sundae

IN THE HAY: Strawberry milkshake

MAIDEN'S DELIGHT: Cherries

MUG OF MURK: Cup of coffee without cream

NINETY-FIVE: Customer walking out without paying

OH GEE: Orangeade

ONE ON THE CITY: Water

POP BOY: Soda man who doesn't know his business

RHINELANDER: Chocolate soda with vanilla ice cream

SALTWATER MAN: Ice-cream mixer

SCANDAL SOUP: Tea

YUM-YUM: Sugar

ORGANIC URBAN ROOFTOP FARMING

BROOKLYN GRANGE ROOFTOP • NEW YORK

Set against the Manhattan skyline is Brooklyn Grange, an expansive urban farm covering three rooftops and spanning a lush 5.6 acres (2.3 ha). The largest rooftop soil farm in the world, it produces almost 100,000 pounds (45,360 kg) of organic produce every year.

Started by a few New Yorkers, Brooklyn Grange was born in 2010 when a small team of workers craned 3,000 sacks of soil up seven stories and began laying down the farm over two weeks. The farm's foundation is comprised of a drainage layer and filter fabric, which protects the roof and acts like a giant sponge on rainy days, holding stormwater in the system and then draining it out slowly. Surprisingly, even while holding tens of thousands of gallons of stormwater, the farm weighs less than what the building's roof can hold. The farm's strategic positioning high above the road traffic also means less pollution: Heavy metal contaminants, which are denser than air, have a hard time reaching the vegetables.

Brooklyn Grange grows dozens of leafy greens and 40 varietals of tomatoes, as well as eggplants, peppers, turnips, beans, carrots, and herbs, which are sold at markets, via CSA membership, and used in restaurant kitchens around the city. They also operate an apiary, maintaining more than 30 honey-producing beehives.

In line with their mission of growing organic produce in a local, sustainable system, Brooklyn Grange doubles as an educational space in a city with little access to farming. Thousands of kids and adults come to the farm each year for workshops, and to bring home bundles of some seriously elevated veggies.

How to try it

The Brooklyn Grange holds a free open house on Saturdays, May through October. Private guided tours are available with advanced booking, as well as yoga classes, beekeeping workshops, and jam-making classes.

NEW YORK'S HIDDEN EATERIES

Secreted away in other establishments, some of New York City's tastiest spots are hard to find, open for limited hours, and known by multiple names. But for those who know where to find them, these hidden eateries offer a delicious portal to the world of the culinary cognoscenti.

NANO BILLIARD CAFÉ (185 E. 167TH STREET, BRONX): In the basement of a nondescript residential building is a fluorescent-lit pool hall, and in that pool hall is a lunch counter serving some of the city's best Dominican food. Before the pool players arrive at night, the mostly takeout spot slings home-style island classics like locrio de pollo (chicken and rice) and sancocho (meat and veggie soup) that people drive across state lines to eat.

5 DE MAYO FOOD MARKET (81–06 ROOSEVELT AVENUE, QUEENS): During the week, this market is a typical Roosevelt Avenue grocery store stocked with fruit and candy. But come during the weekend, head past the groceries, and you'll find a beloved taco stand with knockout lamb and goat barbacoa. Slow cooked for hours, the meat is folded into a fresh, warm tortilla and topped with onion, cilantro, and salsa verde.

STREECHA (33 EAST 7TH STREET, NEW YORK): Spot the Cyrillic sign and head downstairs into Streecha, a lace-curtained room with plastic tablecloths that serves top-notch, traditional Ukrainian food. The restaurant raises money for the nearby St. George's Ukrainian Catholic Church, and the cooks are all volunteers, which gives the place a homey, church basement feel.

GOVINDA'S VEGETARIAN LUNCH (305 SCHERMERHORN STREET, BROOKLYN): In the basement of a Hare Krishna temple is this meatless cafeteria serving a rotating assortment of (mostly) Indian food. The portions are large, chanting and hymns play from the speakers, and the clientele is businesspeople, bankers, bureaucrats, and monks.

MATRYOSHKA (88 FULTON STREET, NEW YORK): Descend into the Russian bathhouse in Manhattan's Financial District to find Matryoshka, the restaurant in this three-story underground spa. (Fittingly, matryoshka is the term for a Russian nesting doll.) Dine on pickle platters, beef tongue, pelmeni, borscht, and copious amounts of vodka—all made even more delightful by dining in a bathrobe.

TAOIST PURVEYORS OF MOCK MEATS

MAY WAH VEGETARIAN MARKET • NEW YORK

How to try it
May Wah is located at 213 Hester Street. It's open every day from 9:30 a.m. to 8 p.m.

One of the most unassuming landmarks in New York's Chinatown is a 25-year-old grocery store with a bright green awning. Inside, the shelves are crammed with chicken wings, pork belly, and spot prawns—all entirely animal-free. Although mock meats may seem like a modern phenomenon, they're actually a centuries-old tradition popularized by the Buddhist and Taoist principle of doing no harm to living things, and May Wah Vegetarian Market is a prime destination for impressively analogous meat substitutes.

In 1994, May Wah was started by two Taoist Taiwanese immigrants, Lee Mee Ng and her daughter Lily, who were homesick for mock meat. (In Taiwan, restaurants commonly offer mock meat versions of every dish they serve.) In the early years, the plant-based meat was hard to sell, but as vegetarianism grew increasingly popular, their store took off.

The Ngs work with a Taiwan-based manufacturing company called Chin Hsin Foods, which ensures the mock meat they're getting is as good as back home. Their chicken nuggets are made with soy protein and have chicken-like fibers when pulled apart. Their shark fin is made with plant-based gelatin. Their shrimp, made from the Japanese yam flower konjac, gets its fishy flavor from seaweed. Then there's jerky, ham, bacon, mutton, scallops, barbecue ribs, crab, and duck—all lovingly formed without harming a single animal.

LEGENDARY EEL SMOKEHOUSE

DELAWARE DELICACIES • NEW YORK

Ray Turner's smoked eels—which he catches in the Delaware River, smokes himself, and sells out of a wooden shack in the woods of Hancock, New York—are the stuff of local legend. Turner brines his eels in salt and dark honey before smoking them over applewood, resulting in a sweet and savory and hyper-local delicacy.

Getting these eels requires a pilgrimage: First follow the signs for "Delaware Delicacies Smoke House" on Route 17, then turn onto a dirt road, head past the quarry, and keep going until you hit the small store and smokehouse. Inside you'll find Ray with his long white beard presiding over his case of smoked goods, which includes not just eels but shrimp, trout, salmon, bacon, and Gouda.

How to try it

Delaware Delicacies is located at 420 Rhodes Road in Hancock. Eel season is in the fall and supplies are limited, so call ahead before venturing into the woods.

To find Ray Turner and his legendary smoked goods, follow the signs that say "EEL" nailed to trees along a dirt road.

A FOUNDING FATHER'S PARTY STARTER

BENJAMIN FRANKLIN'S MILK PUNCH • PENNSYLVANIA

How to try it

The good old internet hosts many contemporary spins on Benjamin Franklin's signature recipe. If your batch turns out clear rather than cloudy, you've done it right—the straining process really is clarifying.

Eighteenth-century England was rife with harsh liquors and devoid of refrigerators. Clarification solved both problems. In 1711, homemaker Mary Rockett recorded the earliest-known clarified milk punch recipe. Brandy was combined with lemon juice, sugar, and water, then mixed with a big glug of hot milk. After sitting for an hour, the mixture was strained through a flannel bag to produce a clear, silky-smooth, shelf-stable elixir that lasted for months, no refrigerator necessary.

Benjamin Franklin was a big clarified milk punch fan. He even had his own recipe, which he enclosed in a letter to the future governor of Massachusetts, James Bowdoin, in 1763. (He and the governor were pen pals for 40 years.) Franklin included in the note: "Herewith you have the Receipt you desired," implying this wasn't the first time the men had talked punch.

Ben Franklin's Milk Punch Recipe

Take 6 quarts of Brandy, and the Rinds of 44 Lemons pared very thin; Steep the Rinds in the Brandy 24 hours; then strain it off. Put to it 4 Quarts of Water, 4 large Nutmegs grated, 2 quarts of Lemon Juice, 2 pound of double refined Sugar. When the Sugar is dissolv'd, boil 3 Quarts of Milk and put to the rest hot as you take it off the Fire, and stir it about. Let it stand two Hours; then run it thro' a Jelly-bag till it is clear; then bottle it off.

The secret to clarified milk punch is the curdling, which makes it possible to strain out dairy solids through a cheesecloth or fine mesh until the beverage is clear. Since this can take hours, clarified milk punch can't be "made to order." But the process is cheap, requires little equipment, and makes milk punch essentially nonperishable. (When Charles Dickens died, they found milk punch in his cellar that had outlived him.)

THEMED FEASTS IN A 19TH-CENTURY UNDERGROUND BREWERY

BUBE'S BREWERY AND CATACOMBS · PENNSYLVANIA

How to try it
Bube's is located in the town of Mount Joy. An unbelievable lineup of events is posted on its website.

At least once a month, Bube's Brewery throws a pirate-themed dinner party in their 19th-century basement restaurant, called Catacombs, located 43 feet (13 m) underground. Actors in period costumes rub elbows with swashbuckling guests dining in candlelight, beside enormous wooden beer-aging barrels. On non-pirate-themed nights, Bube's Brewery looks like a cross between a Renaissance faire (which it becomes during monthly medieval festivals) and a Victorian haunted house (which it becomes during regular ghost tours).

This historic brewery was established in 1876 by a German immigrant named Alois Bube. At the time, Lancaster County, where Bube's is located, was known as the "Munich of America" for its thriving German beer scene. Capitalizing on the American love of lagers, Bube slowly built a beer institution, complete with a bar, the "catacombs," and an inn that featured the town's first flushing toilet. Today, Bube's still makes its own microbrews, which are brewed in what was once the icehouse.

AFRICAN AMERICAN HERITAGE CAFETERIA

SWEET HOME CAFÉ · WASHINGTON, DC

How to try it
Passes are required to enter the Smithsonian National Museum of African American History and Culture, where Sweet Home Café is located. While the dishes offered rotate, visitors recommend the Brunswick Stew and the Gospel Bird Family Platter.

In 19th-century New York City, African American restaurateur Thomas Downing ran an elite oyster bar known for its seafood specialties. While customers ate upstairs, Downing used the restaurant's basement to house people fleeing slavery, as a stop on the Underground Railroad. Today, you can order an oyster pan roast celebrating Downing at the Sweet Home Café, located inside the Smithsonian's National Museum of African American History and Culture.

Divided into four regions (the Agricultural South, the Creole Coast, the North States, and the Western Range), the cafeteria pays homage to the rich African, Indigenous American, Caribbean, Latin American, and European influences in African American cooking. From a Gullah take on Hoppin' John (a Southern New Year's staple) to Western-style pan-roasted rainbow trout with cornbread and mustard green stuffing, diners can sample dishes that demonstrate the breadth of African American cuisine.

The café's décor seeks to educate visitors about the importance of African American food, including the political struggle it has nourished: A photograph of the 1960 Greensboro Woolworth's Lunch Counter sit-in spans the length of the cafeteria, reminding diners of the people who fought to grant African Americans equal access to public spaces, like the one they're in.

RECLAIMING ROAD MEAT

ROADKILL COOK-OFF • WEST VIRGINIA

How to try it

The Roadkill Cook-Off is part of Pocahontas County's Autumn Harvest Festival, which usually takes place in September.

Since 1991, the 1,000 people who call Marlinton their home have been reclaiming the word *hillbilly*. The small town, which has suffered from poverty and scarce resources for decades, especially after the collapse of the coal industry, has amplified their redneck reputation to bring life and resources to the local economy. Each year, they set up shop in a big grassy field and welcome thousands of visitors, TV crews, and reporters to their town, all of them lured by the promise of eating roadkill.

Technically speaking, the featured meat does not have to be roadkill. The competition rules state that dishes must feature an animal "commonly found dead on the road," but they do not stipulate that it must have died there. Acceptable meats include groundhog, opossum, crow, snake, bear, and squirrel, and each is inspected before competition to ensure it's safe to eat. Not knowing the provenance of the meat, some say, also adds to the excitement of the day.

After the health inspection, it's time to cook. Following the spirit of the festival, many of the dishes have overtly redneck, tongue-in-cheek names. "Fender Fried Fawn Smothered in Vulture Vomit," for example, contains no vomit, but a reduction of apples, jalapeños, and onions. Other names, like "Ma, them hogs are runnin' wild in the pineapple!" are self-explanatory. Over the years, the competition has attracted rural cooks from all over America. In 2014, a team drove from California to prepare iguana tacos.

Festivalgoers pay $5 to run wild through the roadkill offerings, which are doled out in manageable two-ounce portions. Pots of bubbling turtle stew and plates of biscuits with squirrel gravy are classic offerings, but flavors can get international, too, with fried venison wontons and deer—and alligator—Solomon Gundy (a Jamaican paté). First-prize winners are awarded $1,200 by a panel of judges who "have been tested for cast-iron stomachs and have sworn under oath to have no vegetarian tendencies." Each year, the festival brings in tens of thousands of dollars for the town of Marlinton.

Cooking isn't the only title on offer at the festival. Each year, local girls compete in a beauty pageant for multiple age-specific crowns: Miss Roadkill, Miss Teen Roadkill, Miss Pre-Teen Roadkill, Little Miss Roadkill, and Tiny Miss Roadkill.

NEW ENGLAND

A FEMINIST VEGETARIAN CAFETERIA

BLOODROOT KITCHEN • CONNECTICUT

Inside one of America's last remaining feminist restaurants.

Founded by a small women's collective in 1977, Bloodroot Kitchen is one of America's last remaining eateries of the feminist restaurant movement. The cozy dining room has no wait staff, the walls are decorated with political posters, and there are plenty of discount books on offer. The space hearkens back to an earlier era, between the 1970s and early 1990s, when hundreds of feminist restaurants opened their doors. Often run by lesbian collectives, these spaces were a place for second-wave feminists to gather, relax, and organize.

At Bloodroot, like at many feminist restaurants, the self-service food is purely vegetarian. They offer a rotating menu of seasonal, often vegan, specials that include Thai vegetarian "chicken," chilled zucchini soup, and okra gumbo. There is also a popular chocolate dessert called the "devastation" cake made with sourdough, which you can enjoy beneath a bulletin board featuring slogans like "I'll be post-feminist in the post-patriarchy," and "The road to health is paved with good intestines."

How to try it

Bloodroot is run by lifelong feminists Selma Miriam and Noel Furie. The restaurant is located at 85 Ferris Street in Bridgeport.

SPECTACLE OF BONY FISH

SHAD BAKE • CONNECTICUT

A successful shad bake begins with the skillful use of a boning knife. A single filet contains about a thousand tiny bones, which must be removed before the filets are nailed to planks planted in a circle around hot coals. Angling the planks just right allows the shad to release excess oil, while the planks—which are usually hickory, oak, or cedar—impart smoky flavor and cook the shad in a way that doesn't require flipping. When the fish is ready, a grillmaster shouts "Board!"

How to try it

Although the shad is not as abundant as it used to be, it's still available in New England seafood markets from May through roughly mid-June. The town of Essex, Connecticut, throws a huge shad bake every year in late spring.

Shad strapped to their planks with bacon seatbelts.

which means it's time to remove the planks from the fire and feast.

This cooking method is hundreds of years old—at least—likely taught to colonial New Englanders by Indigenous Americans. Back then shad was so plentiful, with schools migrating each year from the North Atlantic to mating areas upriver, that prisoners revolted against being fed the bony fish every day. (One 19th-century story describes the shad as the devil's creation.)

In the late 1800s, the shad underwent a major rebranding. Appealing to the burgeoning middle class's interest in travel and Americana, marketers advertised the shad bake as a quintessential springtime event. Shad bakes took off across the Northeast, but the residents of Connecticut have been most vocal about claiming them as their own.

THE LUCRATIVE BUSINESS OF BABY EELS

ELVERS • MAINE

How to try it

Most American baby eels are raised and eaten in Japan, but some Maine restaurants have the local delicacy on their menu. Try Sammy's Deluxe or North Beacon Oyster, both in Rockland.

In 2011, a massive tsunami hit Japan, wiping out many eel farms. And, around the same time, Europe began tightening restrictions on eel exports. A gap opened in the lucrative international eel market, and importers turned to the United States.

In Maine, where teeny eels known as elvers wash up in rivers and streams, the sudden overseas need for eels has changed lives. The demand comes mostly from Asia, where elvers are farmed to adulthood and then sold into the Japanese food market. In 2018, a pound of the tiny, glassy eels fetched as much as $2,700 and the state allowed fishermen to harvest 9,688 pounds (4,394 kg). Apart from South Carolina, where the industry is small, Maine is the only US state that permits elver fishing. Government-restricted fishing permits have kept the eel population healthy, but the inflated price has ushered in a new wave of illegal eel traffickers.

Fishermen catch elvers at night, in quiet solitude, their nets cast into shallow fresh water. The already furtive technique made it fairly easy for gun-wielding poachers to come in and harvest illegally, cutting or stealing nets under nightfall, threatening legal fishermen, and selling their catch for cash on the elver black market.

An undercover federal investigation called Operation Broken Glass (after the glassy appearance of the elvers) led to the conviction of several eel bandits. Among them was Bill Sheldon, the so-called Grandfather of Eels, who was charged with seven counts of "conspiracy to smuggle eels." Sheldon was something of a celebrity in the Maine elver business. He played a central role in establishing the state's fishery and was considered a pioneer in the fledgling industry. (He even drove a truck with the license plate "EEL WGN.") In 2018, he pled guilty to buying 281 pounds (127 kg) of elvers valued at about $545,000 from states where the practice is illegal, then transporting them in his EEL WGN, and flying them to Asia.

International Food Crime

Cheese is the most stolen food in the world. According to a 2011 UK study, about 4 percent of the world's cheese gets lifted each year, which is reflected in the fromage heists of the last few decades: $875,000 worth of Parmigiano-Reggiano from Italy, 700 blocks of Saint-Nectaire from France, two prizewinning wheels of English cheddar, and dozens of loaded-up cheese trucks gone mysteriously missing. Cheese stealing may get a lot of attention, but there are so many more types of comestible crimes.

BAKED BEANS HEIST (WORCESTERSHIRE, ENGLAND): In 2013, the driver of a Heinz truck slept as thieves cut a hole in the curtain-walled vehicle and made off with 6,400 cans of baked beans with sausages worth about $10,000. A police spokesperson said they were "appealing for information, especially about anyone trying to sell large quantities of Heinz baked beans in suspicious circumstances," but the bean thieves were never caught.

WINE FRAUD (SILICON VALLEY, CALIFORNIA, USA): Rudy Kurniawan spent the early 2000s passing himself off as a Burgundy expert, repackaging bottles of red wine in his basement and then selling them as rare and expensive vintages to auction houses and wealthy wine buyers. He sold millions of dollars of forged wine before he was caught. In 2009, he was sued by billionaire art and wine collector William Koch, who'd bought Kurniawan's fake wine. Kurniawan was sentenced to ten years in a California prison and his personal wine collection was sold to help repay his debts.

AVOCADO KIDNAPPING (TANCITARO, MEXICO): The town of Tancitaro exports more than $1 million worth of avocados every day, a number that caught the attention of Mexican drug cartels. Gangs began kidnapping farmers, extorting landowners, and terrorizing those who refused to cooperate. Tancitaro became a site of violence and fear, until its citizens banded together to form an avocado police force. Since 2014, a team of trained officers in armored patrol trucks and bulletproof vests have been setting up checkpoints, patrolling farms, and generally protecting avocados and those who work with them. Half the force's funding comes from the government, and half from the avocado producers, who report that the new militia is keeping crime down.

TRUFFLE DOG SABOTAGE (ITALY & FRANCE): Hunting down Europe's elusive white truffle often requires the help of a dog, typically a pointer, hound, or setter trained to sniff out the expensive mushroom. In recent years, the truffle trade has become so cutthroat that truffle dogs have become the target of warring foragers. Dozens of dogs are sabotaged every year, taken from their homes or otherwise ensnared. In the Italian city of Celano, poisoned meatballs were hidden in bushes to eliminate dogs in prime truffle territory. These dogs are trained for multiple years, worth up to $9,000, and loved by their owners—their loss is not taken lightly, which means truffle season is also the time to see newspaper ads seeking missing pups and owners leading their dogs in circles, trying to lose anyone who might be following. (Miraculously, many missing truffle dogs turn back up when truffle season is over.)

AMISH CHARCUTERIE

CHARCUTERIE • MAINE

A decade ago, Matthew Secich was working in the kitchen of a Michelin-starred restaurant. That was before he left the high-stress world behind, converted to the Amish faith, and opened a small charcuterie shop in Unity, Maine.

Today, you'll find Secich at the end of a long road in the middle of a pine wood, beard down to his chest, hand-grinding meat to make sausages. In line with his faith, Secich's small shop is lit by oil lamps and heated by a wood stove. His meat is kept cool in a pine room stocked with 80 tons of ice that's hand-cut each winter after being harvested from a local lake. The low-tech kitchen produces high-quality charcuterie such as maple-tarragon kielbasa, smoked duck sausage, sweet bologna, and smoked cheddar—all marked by the finesse of an elite chef.

How to try it

Charcuterie is open only Wednesday, Friday, and Saturday, along Leelyn Road in Unity.

THE SITE OF A TERRIBLE MOLASSES ACCIDENT

THE GREAT MOLASSES FLOOD PLAQUE • MASSACHUSETTS

How to try it

The plaque is located at an entrance to the Harborwalk, at the intersection of Commercial Street and Copps Hill Terrace.

At 12:45 on the afternoon of January 15th, 1919, Boston Police patrolman Frank McManus shouted into his transmitter: "Send all available rescue vehicles and personnel immediately! There's a wave of molasses coming down Commercial Street!" A five-story-tall cylindrical metal tank, 90 feet (27 m) in diameter, had burst—and a two-story-tall wave containing 2.3 million gallons (8.7 million L) of molasses was surging in all directions.

The molasses spread across the city at an estimated 35 miles per hour. The tank itself was also deadly: It had torn into sharp projectiles, and metal bolts shot from its sides like bullets. As the wave and debris crashed down Commercial Street, buildings were smashed to bits or else floated away whole in the tide of

molasses. Electrical poles keeled over, exposing live wires. A steel elevated train support beam was torn to smithereens. Molasses covered everything. According to a *Boston Post* article, "Horses died like so many flies on sticky fly paper." And it wasn't just horses: The great Boston molasses flood killed 21 people.

After many years of litigation, the tank company was found culpable for the disaster and forced to pay settlement of $8 million in today's money. Cleanup required more than 87,000 man-hours, and the area was said to be sticky-feeling and sweet-smelling for years afterward.

Standing in Boston's North End, you'd never know a deadly molasses flood once destroyed a neighborhood—save for an easily missed plaque at the scene of the crime. The small green sign, while unremarkable, is worth seeking out if only to stand and contemplate how terrifying two stories of molasses moving at 35 miles per hour really is.

A Brief History of Presidential Cheese

The United States government has a centuries-long tradition of unloading tremendous amounts of cheese onto the American public. The practice of gifting, mismanaging, and partying with big cheese goes back to Thomas Jefferson—and although the meaning of cheese has evolved throughout the years, there has consistently been way too much.

THOMAS JEFFERSON: In July 1801, the residents of Cheshire, Massachusetts, milked every cow in town and made an enormous 1,200-pound (544-kg) wheel of cheese in support of presidential candidate Thomas Jefferson. Local pastor Elder John Leland, who led the cheesemaking in a giant cider press, conceived of the cheese as a way to praise Jefferson's support of religious and civil liberty. Leland insisted that "no federal cow" (owned by a federalist farmer) be allowed to contribute milk, and that only free people be allowed to make it "without the assistance of a single slave." On the hulking cheddar, he stamped the words "Rebellion to tyrants is obedience to God."

Too large for conventional transportation, the 4-foot-wide (1.2-m) cheese was pulled by Leland by sleigh to the Hudson River, where he and his cheese took a boat to Baltimore, then a horse-drawn wagon to Washington, DC. After a three-week, 500-mile (805-km) journey, Leland presented the cheese to President Jefferson on January 1, 1802. By then, much of America had heard about the celebrity cheese.

ANDREW JACKSON: Supporters of Andrew Jackson couldn't let their president be outshined by Jefferson's cheese. The task became competitive, and in 1835, dairy farmer Thomas S. Meacham crafted a 1,400-pound (635-kg) cheddar that was heavier and thicker than Jefferson's and wrapped in a belt inscribed with political slogans. Jackson's cheese was featured (with nine other cheeses) at a patriotic party in Oswego, New York, then went on a multicity publicity tour before landing at the White House.

Jackson, however, was less excited about his cheese and had no idea what to do with it. The hulking cheddar sat on display for nearly two years,

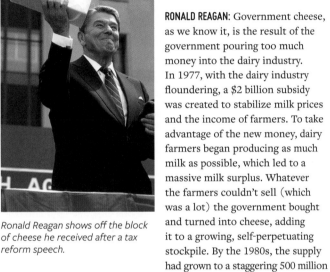

Ronald Reagan shows off the block of cheese he received after a tax reform speech.

but in 1837, his last year in office, he needed to get rid of it. During the final party of his presidency, Jackson invited the public to come and eat his cheese, which led to a greasy, smelly free-for-all that dismantled the 1,400 pounds in two hours. According to Jackson's successor, Martin Van Buren, the cheese room had to be aired out for many days, the curtains removed, and the walls painted.

RONALD REAGAN: Government cheese, as we know it, is the result of the government pouring too much money into the dairy industry. In 1977, with the dairy industry floundering, a $2 billion subsidy was created to stabilize milk prices and the income of farmers. To take advantage of the new money, dairy farmers began producing as much milk as possible, which led to a massive milk surplus. Whatever the farmers couldn't sell (which was a lot) the government bought and turned into cheese, adding it to a growing, self-perpetuating stockpile. By the 1980s, the supply had grown to a staggering 500 million (227 million kg) pounds of cheese, or 2 pounds of cheese for every American.

The government's bright yellow cheddar was distributed across the country to low-income citizens until the 1990s, when the dairy industry stabilized. Today, sentiments about government cheese are mixed. Some recall a moldy, inedible cheese and the shame of having to eat it. Others grew a fondness for it and insist the processed stuff made exceptional grilled cheese sandwiches and macaroni and cheese.

BARACK OBAMA: Big Block of Cheese Day was added to the presidential cheese canon by Barack Obama. Three years in a row (2014–2016), the Obama administration hosted an event inspired by Jackson's big cheese blowout. Big Block of Cheese Day, although less grotesque than Jackson's open house, was also a political event used to gather Capitol Hill VIPs and answer questions from the public. While the emphasis was more on policy than cheese, Obama served plenty of it, along with cheese-based puns. As stated on the White House website, "Excited? So are brie."

HUTS OF THE WHITE MOUNTAINS

MOUNTAIN HUT CROO • NEW HAMPSHIRE

How to try it

The huts are run by the Appalachian Mountain Club. While full service is available only during the summer, guests can use the kitchen facilities year-round.

Along New Hampshire's rugged White Mountains, which cover 87 miles (140 km) and contain the highest peak in the Northeast, are a string of eight outposts known as high mountain huts. These strategically placed lodges, modeled after huts in the Alps, allow hikers to sleep and refuel along their journey. From late May to mid-fall, a group of devoted staff called "croo" prepare 2,300 family-style meals for hikers.

While croo members are rarely professional chefs, a rich oral tradition ensures newbies learn tricks of the backcountry-cooking trade. Before the season starts, croos attend a five-day training, including six or so hours on cooking and baking. In May, helicopters airlift about 16,000 pounds (7,257 kg) of the heaviest supplies—including propane, flour, and canned goods—to each hut, after which deliveries are made by the croo. Twice a week, each of the roughly 50 staffers lugs trash and recycling out of the shelters and brings back 40 to 60 pounds (18 to 27 kg) of vegetables, frozen meat, butter, and cheese—all in a contraption made of wood, canvas, and leather called a packboard.

Today, the huts host 36–90 guests at capacity and are run by 5–11 croo members. Home-cooked meals are the main attraction, and hut binders display well-loved recipes: lentil soup, dijon mustard chicken, lasagna, garlic-cheddar bread, and vegan chocolate cake. To ensure hut-hopping backpackers eat varied meals along the way, each hut cooks a similar entrée on the same night of the week—stuffed shells on Sunday, beef on Monday, and so on.

According to croo members, hiking food in and trash out gets easier over the course of the summer. Many say the twice-a-week-supply sojourns put them in the best shape of their lives, providing a sense of strength and empowerment when the treks became enjoyable.

Greenleaf Hut, located near Mount Lafayette, is one of eight refueling outposts for White Mountains hikers.

FIRE POKER COCKTAIL TORCH

LOGGERHEAD • RHODE ISLAND

When British settlers in colonial America needed to boil cocktails, cauterize wounds, and ignite the occasional cannon, the loggerhead was their multi-tool of choice.

Fashioned by attaching a long iron rod to a short wooden handle, loggerheads were pole-shaped tools whose metal end was left to heat on an open flame. When red-hot, the loggerhead could melt solids and seal up flesh. Bartenders were big fans of the blistering rod, which helped them create hot and splashy cocktails. By plunging the heated metal into an earthenware pitcher or large pewter mug, they could caramelize, boil, and froth boozy concoctions into all kinds of steamy drinks. Before central heating, patrons warmed up with the help of hot beverages like toddies, hot punches, and the most popular colonial cocktail of all, the flip, made from frothed ale, rum, and sweetener.

In England, loggerheads were so ubiquitous that British people used the term as an insult, suggesting their target had a piece of iron for a head. The fights that arose after a night of many flips begot the idiom "at loggerheads," which means to be at odds with someone; on the pub circuit, the phrase came to imply a disagreement that escalated into physical violence. Some accounts of these bar brawls cite the dueling parties pulling the loggerheads from the fire and brandishing them against each other, which points to the clearest etymology of all.

How to try it

Loggerheads are no longer used, but fire pokers made from metal are still common household objects. Please enjoy responsibly.

THE OLDEST STILL-OPERATING TAVERN IN AMERICA

WHITE HORSE TAVERN • RHODE ISLAND

In 1673, a tavern opened in Newport with a sign depicting a white steed—the universal symbol of a public house (useful at a time when many were illiterate), and the image that would eventually give the establishment its official name.

William Mayes Jr., a notorious pirate, returned to Newport with pillaged bounty and inherited the tavern from his father in 1702. He ran the White Horse until the British pressured him to hand the reins to his sister and her husband. Pirate-run management reflected poorly on the establishment, which had become the official meeting place for Rhode Island politicians.

Until the 1730s, when the state built its Colony House, the White Horse hosted Rhode Island's General Assembly, Criminal Court, and City Council. Many say the business lunch began here, as politicians would charge their food and drink to the public treasury.

During the Revolutionary War, the British housed Hessian mercenaries in the building, forcing the owner, Walter Nichols, and his family out. When the war was over and the colonies won their independence, Nichols returned and refurbished his tavern.

How to try it

The White Horse Tavern is located at 26 Marlborough Street in Newport. The restaurant has a "business casual" dress code for dinner, when collared shirts for men are required.

The storied 17th-century White Horse Tavern was once owned by a pirate.

But the centuries of wear and tear took a toll on the White Horse. By 1954, the building was in desperate need of repair. The Preservation Society of Newport took on the job of meticulously restoring the building, and it reopened in 1957 when the work was complete. Today, the architecture remains faithful to the 17th century: Candles and oil lamps burn beneath the thick beams of the roof. During the winter, a fire burns in the massive hearth. The cuisine is still classic New England, the flag on display still has just 13 stars, and the tavern ghost is alive and well, lurking just to the right of the dining room fireplace.

COLONIAL SPORTS DRINK

SWITCHEL • VERMONT

How to try it

Vermont Switchel Company ships their immune-boosting elixir around the country. It's great on its own or mixed into cocktails. Recipes are also available online.

From the 1700s to the 1900s, it was common to see ceramic jars placed throughout fields—below the shade of trees or tucked alongside a stream—and filled with America's thirst-quenching, electrolyte-boosting sweetheart: switchel.

Made with ginger, apple cider vinegar, sweetener, and water, switchel had a flavor profile similar to lemonade—tangy, refreshing, and sweet. Farmers noted multiple health benefits to drinking the liquid, among them its ability to clear the throat and sinuses, provide energy, and fight off sickness. At the time, no one understood exactly how switchel worked, but science now points to the anti-inflammatory power of ginger, the potassium in molasses, and the microbial gut benefits of raw apple cider vinegar. Aside from the water, every ingredient in switchel contains potassium, which is an electrolyte—but electrolytes weren't understood until the late 19th century.

Beyond switchel's healthy properties, people really liked to drink it. The vinegar gave off the throat-warming heat of alcohol without any alcohol, which made it a favorite among temperance advocates. And while it tasted a good bit like lemonade, switchel required no citrus, which was much harder to procure than vinegar.

Latin America

MEXICO · CENTRAL AMERICA

THE CARIBBEAN ISLANDS · SOUTH AMERICA

MEXICO

MUSHROOM-FLAVORED CORN FUNGUS

HUITLACOCHE • MEXICO

How to try it

Fresh huitlacoche is available at markets in Mexico City, particularly the Central de Abastos. Throughout Mexico and beyond, it can be purchased canned or jarred in specialty markets.

When Aztec farmers found blue-black spores overtaking their corn, they didn't worry—they rejoiced! It was huitlacoche, corn infected by the pathogenic fungus *Ustilago maydis*, which bestows a rich, mushroom-like flavor, and makes an excellent quesadilla filling.

The name *huitlacoche* derives from the Aztec language, Nahuatl, and most believe it translates best to "sleeping excrescence" because the fungus grows around the kernels and impedes their growth. In the United States, farmers use a less poetic name: corn smut.

Although technically a plant disease, corn smut is a prized ingredient in Mexican cuisine, and an infected cob is worth significantly more than a regular one. The bulbous spores retain much of the corn's flavor, while contributing a nutty, mushroomy taste that makes it distinctly fungal. Sautéed with onions and chilies, the resulting inky mixture enriches everything from tacos to omelets.

Now a much-sought-after delicacy (some menus describe it as "Mexican truffles"), huitlacoche is a testament to the ingenuity of the Aztecs, who turned a scourge on their staple crop into a culinary blessing.

Baskets of the prized fungus at Mexico City's wholesale market.

LOVE POTION NUMBER DIE

TOLOACHE • MEXICO

Smoke a leaf of the nightshade *Datura innoxia*, and you might hallucinate. Drink a potion made from its seeds, and it's possible you'll fall in love. Steep a handful of the plant in hot liquid, and beware of death—a lethal dose is said to be about 5 ounces (150 g).

The perennial shrub, which produces a white, trumpet-like flower and prickly, bulbous fruit, has many names across the Americas. In Mexico, it's known as toloache, from the Nahuatl words for "bow the head" and "reverential." Elsewhere, the names are less affectionate: The Navajos call it ch'oxojilghei, or "crazy maker."

The plant is categorized as a "deliriant"—a hallucinogen that leads the mind away from the lucid world, triggering feelings of insanity and a loss of control over the physical self. For centuries, Mexican shamans have smoked cigars rolled with its leaves or eaten its seeds during divination rituals. In northwestern Mexico, the Tarahumara still prepare a ceremonial drink of sprouted corn and toloache to encourage visions.

In small quantities, toloache operates as a pain reliever. Ancient Aztecs wrote of a fever remedy based on a weak toloache infusion, while Uto-Aztecan oral histories describe midwives making a toloache brew to help ease childbirth pains. Modern practitioners of witchcraft (or *brujería* as it's known in Spanish) in Mexico make toloache love potion. Folklore suggests that mixing small doses into the food or tobacco of the person you desire will make them yours.

How to try it

Mercado de Sonora in Mexico City carries toloache products along with other powders, potions, and plants.

AUTO REPAIR SHOP TAQUERÍA

EL VILSITO • MEXICO

Visit El Vilsito during the day and you'll find mechanics working on cars. Stop by the humble garage after 8 p.m., and you'll find one of Mexico City's best taquerías.

Wielding giant knives, servers carve slices off hulking, spinning spits of al pastor—Mexico's beloved achiote-marinated pork. The juicy meat cylinder is formed by stacking thin slices of pork onto a vertical spit, a technique learned from Lebanese immigrants who brought shwarma to Mexico. The succulent, lightly charred meat falls into a warm tortilla, and is topped with a slice of pineapple (kept at the top of the rotisserie), and a sprinkling of onions, cilantro, salsa, and lime. Addictively sweet, savory, fatty, and acidic, there's a reason tacos al pastor are considered one of the most iconic dishes of the Mexican capital.

How to try it

Check El Vilsito's Facebook page for taco-serving hours. Don't show up outside those times unless you need to get your car repaired.

This rotating spit of al pastor is set up nightly in an auto body shop.

EGGS

The chicken egg is one of the most nutritious foods on the planet, packed with nearly every vitamin the human body requires. But not all eggs are created equal. Only a few varieties are more nutritionally potent than the hen's, and many are near nutritionless—which, incidentally, doesn't stop us from going to tremendous lengths to eat them.

Crocodile Eggs

Fiercely protected by their mothers, crocodile eggs are dangerous to harvest in the wild. The safest way to procure them is from crocodile farms in places like Southeast Asia, where the harvest is so abundant, locals hold crocodile-egg-eating contests. In Pattaya, on Thailand's southeast coast, the fastest person to eat ten hard-boiled crocodile eggs wins. The taste is described as strong, salty, and fishy.

Gull Eggs

Seagull eggs of the black-headed gull variety can be found only four to six weeks a year in the wetlands of England. A small group of licensed "eggers" have permission to forage for them, but the practice is highly regulated. Only one egg may be removed from each nest, and the nest locations are kept secret. After an egger removes an egg, they mark the remaining eggs with an X, so that the next egger will know to move along. When hard-boiled, the gull eggs' flavor is subtle but rich—rich being the key word here because a single gull's egg costs about $7.

Snail Eggs

These tiny, white, and glossy orbs are prized among European gourmands with a big egg budget. Snails, notorious for their leisurely pace, take two to three years to produce eggs. But Sicilian producers have found a way to make snails pump out eggs in about eight months using an accelerated maturing technique. The crunchy caviar has an earthy, woodsy taste often compared to baked mushrooms or asparagus, and sells for about $100 for 50 grams (roughly 2 tablespoons).

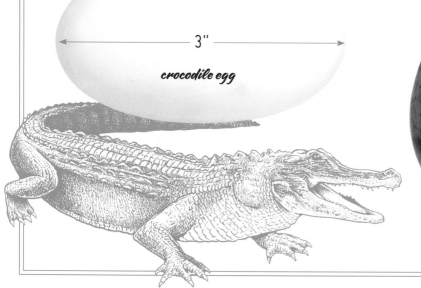

3"

crocodile egg

gull egg

Octopus Eggs

An octopus mother cares for her eggs for up to six grueling months. Nesting in dark underwater dens, typically found in the crevices of rocks, the mother hovers over her eggs, circulating them with fresh aerated water. During this brooding period, she usually does not leave the nest or eat, preferring to starve rather than abandon her young. Often, the mother dies when her job is done. Octopus eggs are sometimes found in Japanese sushi preparations, where the milky sacs are eaten raw. In nature they look like translucent teardrops, and as they mature, you can see the tiny octopus developing inside.

octopus eggs

Turtle Eggs

Eating the offspring of the endangered sea turtle is illegal in most of the world, but they're still considered a delicacy in many countries. In Nicaragua, where turtle-eating dates back to pre-Columbian times, turtle eggs are considered an aphrodisiac, and there remains a robust and largely unregulated black market trade. Under nightfall, poachers find nests in the sand and net up to 100 eggs with each sweep. For the unaccustomed palate, the soft shell and slimy, musty taste are reason enough to leave the eggs alone—but tradition keeps the practice alive.

Quail Eggs

For centuries, these mini eggs have been revered around the world for their extensive healing properties. In Chinese medicine, quail eggs are used to strengthen yin, the feminine, dark, and negative counterpart to yang. Yin can slow down the aging process, and so quail eggs are mixed into beauty products. They are also eaten to treat allergies, blood impurities, and skin conditions.

quail eggs

turtle egg

THE BARS SERVING GODLY ELIXIR

PULQUERÍAS • MEXICO

How to try it

Fresh pulque has a short shelf life, usually just a couple of days, so it rarely makes it out of Mexico except in canned form. In Mexico City, Las Duelistas is a small, beloved pulquería that's always sweaty and packed with a lively clientele. As is the case for many shops in the country, their pulque comes in an assortment of rotating flavors including mango, celery, and red wine.

Aztec goddess Mayahuel is often depicted with 400 breasts, each one pouring agave sap. According to ancient myth, the first agave plant sprouted at the site of Mayahuel's burial, and the sweet liquid is thought to be her divine blood.

Aguamiel ("honey water") is produced in the stalk of the agave. When the stalk is opened, the aguamiel can be scooped from the cavity like water from a well. Distill aguamiel, and you'll get tequila or mezcal. Ferment it, and within a couple of hours you'll get pulque, a thousand-year-old elixir that was once so sacred, it was held in reserve for priests, nobles, and a few of the sick and elderly and as the final treat for victims of ritual sacrifice. When Spanish Christian colonialists arrived in the 16th century, pulque fell out of favor because the colonists looked to eradicate local religions and customs.

Today, pulque is experiencing a revival. "Neo-pulquerías" are attracting a new, younger following, with some modern spins on the conventional brew (cookies-and-cream pulque, anyone?). In a pulquería, expect to drink a lot and to be judged by the size of your serving. The biggest, glasses, which hold 2 liters, are called macetas (flowerpots), followed by cañones (cannons), chivitos (little goats), catrinas (dandies), and tornillos (screws).

Sour, with a foamy, saliva-like texture, pulque's primary appeal is not its taste. The milky beverage has an ancient reputation for treating diabetes, stomach pains, and infertility. And while it is indeed alcoholic (2 to 8 percent ABV), drinkers describe a wide and eclectic array of sensations—from mysterious paralysis to chatty, blissful elation—that keep the pulquerías in brisk business.

A man draws "honey water" from the stalk of the agave.

SMOKED BOOZE WITH THE ESSENCE OF MEAT

MEZCAL DE PECHUGA • MEXICO

Traditional mezcal is made from the core of the agave plant, known as the piña. After roasting the piñas to give the drink its signature smoky essence, mezcaleros blend the piñas with fruits, nuts, and spices, then ferment and distill the mix three times. It's in this third round of distillation that mezcal de pechuga gets a special addition: a piece of raw chicken dangled over the top.

Suspended over the open clay or copper still, the chicken breast (pechuga means "breast" in Spanish) mingles with the vapors, and its meaty essence helps counterbalance the alcohol's bracing flavor. Some liquor historians believe that this tradition began as a way to mask the taste of subpar mezcal.

In Mexico, mezcal de pechuga is commonly consumed during special occasions, such as quinceañeras and weddings, but it's also gaining popularity in the United States, where it's stocked alongside bottles of more traditional, poultry-free mezcals.

Although the flavor of the chicken is subtle at best, the meat-dangling remains important. Some versions of mezcal de pechuga feature other types of meat, including rabbit, iguana, or Ibérico ham.

How to try it

Most mezcal is produced in Oaxaca. Head to the mezcal shop Mezcalillera, which doubles as a tasting room.

DESERT CAVIAR

ESCAMOLES • MEXICO

How to try it

Escamoles cannot be brought across the border, so interested parties must get to Mexico, where the eggs grace the menus of many restaurants. Try El Cardenal in Mexico City for upscale ant pupae tacos. Those looking for volume can go to the Mercado San Juan, where they sell the eggs by the kilo.

Ant pupae and larvae, an opulent treat in Mexico, resemble pine nuts, taste like butter, and have a texture akin to cottage cheese. To retain their delicate flavor, escamoles are often prepared simply, fried in butter with onion and chilies, then wrapped in corn tortillas.

This prized egg is produced by *Liometopum apiculatum*, or the velvety tree ant, but locals prefer a different name. *La hormiga pedorra* means "the farty ant," nicknamed after the sulfuric odor that wafts from their nests.

Escamoles are collected from the high plains desert of central Mexico, where the velvety tree ant tunnels its home among the roots of agave plants. Escamoleros, the people who track down these tiny eggs in the wild, are up against incredible demand, and although many carefully scrape away the tops of nests and use sieves to separate ants from their larvae, others are not so diligent, and the desert delight (which sells for up to $100 for 2.2 pounds/1 kg) is at risk of being overharvested.

Centuries before the larvae were trendy, before the Spanish arrived in what we now call Mexico, escamoles were favored among the Indigenous elite: Ancient menus tell us that Aztec emperors hosted elaborate banquets and feasted on this desert caviar.

Ant eggs are a delicate, buttery Mexican delicacy.

A SUMPTUOUS SHOWCASE OF CAKES

PASTELERÍA IDEAL • MEXICO

How to try it

Pastelería Ideal is located at Calle 16 de Septiembre 18, in Mexico City's Centro Histórico.

A wonderland of model cakes above Mexico City's iconic bakery.

On the second floor of the bakery institution Pastelería Ideal is a massive cake showroom featuring a dazzling array of custom confections that can be ordered downstairs at the shop. Towering multitiered cakes, advertised to weigh more than 200 pounds (90.7 kg), drip icicles of frosting from tiers that can reach 8 feet (2.4 m) in the air. Favorite cartoon heroes and movie princesses are represented in sugar, along with thousands of piped flowers and perfect fondant cutouts of everything from clowns to skulls. The cakes on display are for visual consumption only, so eat a snack at the bakery before taking the trip upstairs to wander among Supreme Cakedom.

SWEET-AND-SOUR CANDY PASTA

SALSAGHETI • MEXICO

How to try it

Taste the spicy tang of Salsagheti at corner stores in Mexico, or order up a bulk supply from online candy distributors.

Salsagheti, which combines the word *salsa* ("sauce" in both Spanish and Italian) with a misspelling of the latter half of the word *spaghetti*, might sound like a marinara-slathered Italian pasta dish, but it's actually a heap of spicy Mexican candy straws.

These tubular, sour watermelon–flavored gummies are coated in a refined mix of chili-tamarind powder and sugar crystals. A packet of tamarind sauce—the salsa—has a runny, gravy-like consistency. Squeeze the packet onto the 'gheti and enjoy a meal with almost no nutritional value.

✳✳✳ *Mexican Candy* ✳✳✳

The addictive union of sweet, salty, sour, and spicy is the hallmark of Mexico's whimsical world of candy. These confections sound like they sprang from the mind of a mad scientist with a sweet tooth: candy salsas, powdered candy that doubles as food seasoning, candy shaped like corn but flavored like strawberries. The surprising, explosive flavor combinations are made for the country's vibrant, chili-loving palate—and are like nothing else in the world.

SALSAGHETI

Squeezable sweet-and-sour tamarind gel

Pineapple suckers that foam like beer

Watermelon lollipops with a hard chili powder shell

Sweet-and-sour salted apricots showered in chili powder

Individual doses of powdered citrus and salt

Banana bubble gum with a liquid banana core

Cucumber meets chili for a spicy vegetal confection

Liquid spicy pickled fruit

Like Avocados?
Thank This Extinct Giant Sloth.

Mexico is the avocado capital of the world, with two central states (Michoacán and State of Mexico, aka the Avocado Belt) supplying nearly half of the global market. An Aztec symbol of love and fertility turned cosmopolitan salad ingredient, the trendy green fruit has been a hit since prehistoric times, when it got its first big break from an unwitting benefactor.

Though lestodons might sound like toothy, scaly dinosaurs, these Cenozoic-era creatures were sloths. They are the direct ancestors of the sloths still around today, but lestodons were enormous, putting the "mega" in "megafauna." Weighing from 2 to 4 tons, lestodons, along with other "ground sloths," roamed grassy plains in South America. Their diet consisted of grass and foliage and, occasionally, a more nutritious treat: the early avocado.

Giant sloths, along with megafauna such as gomphotheres and glyptodonts, feasted on whole avocados and spread their seeds over South America. These enormous creatures' digestive systems could process large seeds, and avocados

benefited. When pooped out, far from their parent trees, the seeds could sprout and grow without competition for water and sunlight. It was a good deal all around, and it likely resulted in avocados as we know them: fatty and large-pitted, all the better to attract huge sloths.

Enormous prehistoric sloths spread avocados by eating them and pooping out their seeds.

Near the end of the Pleistocene Ice Age (about 11,000 years ago), a fluctuating climate wiped out many megafauna. (Some survived, such as the much-bigger-than-you-think moose.)

The avocado might have survived only in a valley or two as a small, obscure fruit if a new propagator hadn't come along: us. Humans weren't swallowing the fruits whole, but they did plant them widely over South and Central America.

CINNAMON-FLAVORED BUGS

JUMILES • MEXICO

In the town of Taxco, the traditional way to eat jumiles is while they're alive. Harvested from their mountain homes, these ancient stinkbugs are commonly doused with lime, wrapped in tortillas, and consumed while the bug still has full capacity of its scuttling legs. The flavor is a medicinal blend of cinnamon and mint, and the smell is as pungent as the name "stinkbug" suggests.

Reports from the 1930s and 1940s describe Indigenous Mexicans using the insects to treat kidney, liver, and stomach ailments. They're also rumored to be aphrodisiacs.

Taxco holds an annual Jumil Day to honor the multipurpose bugs. It takes place on the Monday after the Day of the Deceased because many locals believe the insects are the reincarnation of their ancestors. It's not uncommon to hear locals ask, *Are you carrying family?* What they're really asking is if you have jumiles.

How to try it

You need to eat the bugs alive to experience their full mouth-numbing properties, but they're a tasty (and much tamer) experience when cooked. Jumiles are a favorite taco filling in Taxco, where you can buy them by the bagful at the local market.

THE 16TH-CENTURY HOT CHOCOLATE FROTHER

MOLINILLO • MEXICO

The molinillo is one of history's greatest unitaskers. Its one job: whipping hot chocolate into foamy perfection.

The wooden whisk's roots lie in colonization. When Spaniards arrived in Mexico in the 16th century, they didn't care for the local chocolate drink. Hernán Cortés and his conquistadores initially refused to drink it, and in 1590, a Jesuit writing about the sweet beverage compared its foamy consistency to feces.

But in recognition of chocolate's value as an Aztec status symbol, the Spanish kept it around and eventually developed a taste for it. Historians even suspect that the molinillo was a Spanish innovation because the Mesoamerican style of making the beverage was pouring molten chocolate from one pot to another.

Both functional and beautiful, the molinillo—often carved from a single piece of wood—has a long handle with a ball or square at the end with notched rings that speed up the agitation process. To use the molinillo, submerge the bulbous end into the liquid chocolate, press the handle between two palms, and twist back and forth until the drink is sufficiently foamy.

The cocoa-based confection, long considered an aphrodisiac, also influenced matters outside the kitchen. Legend goes that in some regions of Mexico, the key to finding a husband was a young woman's ability to impress with perfectly frothed hot chocolate.

How to try it

To make Mexican hot chocolate, melt semisweet chocolate into a pot of warm milk, add sugar, a cinnamon stick, a pinch of salt and cayenne, and twist away.

CENTRAL AMERICA

AN INTOXICATING CHRISTMAS TRADITION

BLACK FRUITCAKE • BELIZE

It's hard not to love a recipe that begins with a pound of butter, a pint of stout, and a quart of rum—which is why black fruitcake is the crown jewel of Belizean Christmas. In Belize, making Christmas fruitcake is (practically) mandatory. As is the inclusion of rum. Sure, some recipes say you can substitute grape juice for the hard stuff, but what kind of fruitcake would that be? Not a black fruitcake.

The origins of this particular cake date back to the 17th century, when English colonizers brought their sweet puddings to the Caribbean. Over the years, locals adapted the recipe to their own tastes, substituting rum for the English brandy and incorporating spices from the islands. The very best black fruitcakes start months, even a year, in advance. (A week, locals say, is the absolute minimum time needed to see a real transformation, but the longer the better.) A quart of rum is poured over a bounty of dried fruits such as raisins, currants, dates, and citrus peels. The fruit soaks in the rum along with some brown sugar throughout the summer and fall, expanding into juicy, potent morsels, while the rum thickens into a syrup.

The Belizean cake gets its black color from the pint of stout. The stout goes into a batter of flour, sugar, eggs, butter, allspice, and nutmeg. Then the soaked fruit is added. The rum syrup is reserved for pouring over the top of the baked and cooled cake.

Black fruitcake should be packed with fruit. It should have a dense, moist texture, and a rich, boozy taste. In Belize, where dried fruits are expensive, the gift of a fruitcake is a serious token of affection and respect. And with fruit soaking since summer, this is no last-minute gift.

How to try it

Black fruitcake isn't complete without a glass of rum popo, a creamy cocktail made with milk and eggs, because what goes better with rum than more rum? To the same effect: If the cake gets dry from sitting on the counter, locals suggest hitting it with a bit more rum.

THE CORN DRINK DANCE SONG

ATOL DE ELOTE • EL SALVADOR

Atol de elote is a warm, sweet, and corn-packed drink that's often so thick it's eaten with a spoon. The beverage is such a cultural institution, the band Los Flamers recorded a hit dance song called "Atol de elote." The chorus encourages listeners to dance three easy steps: Everybody should start by moving and getting low (moviendo agachadito), then moving the hips (moviendo las caderas), and moving the corn drink (moviendo el atol de elote). The corn drink is almost certainly a euphemism for butt. In the music video, dancers groove with the large wooden spoons traditionally used to stir atol de elote, while drums and horns sound euphorically around them.

Rich and silky, atol de elote gets its delightful texture from pulverizing fresh corn against a grinding stone. After mixing in milk, sugar, and spices such as cinnamon and vanilla, vendors heat the concoction in a giant pot until it's thickened, usually without the assistance of a dance track.

How to try it

Check out San Salvador's Mercado Central, where a piping-hot ladle of atol de elote sells for about a quarter. You can also make it at home in a blender.

LIME-CURED BULL'S TESTICLES

CEVICHE DE CRIADILLAS • GUATEMALA

Ceviche de criadillas, or bull testicle ceviche, can be just as tasty and refreshing as the seafood variety. Some say it tastes like a cross between two ceviche classics: tuna and octopus. After curing the testicles in citrus, a cook cuts up the testicles into slices or small chunks and tosses them with chopped onions, chilies, cilantro, and tomato. The spicy, tangy mixture is served cold or at room temperature. If you do acquire a taste for it, be careful about going nuts—Guatemalans say it's an aphrodisiac.

How to try it

Antigua, Guatemala, and Cajamarca, Peru, are known for ceviche de criadillas. Although some cevicherias stock fresh testicles, you may have to track down the raw materials yourself, from either a butcher or marketplace stall. Keep in mind that curing animal flesh with acid won't kill bacteria the way heat does, so make sure to use fresh, clean meat.

CHEESE AND CHARCUTERIE FOR THE DEAD

FIAMBRE • GUATEMALA

Every November 1, on All Saints' Day, Guatemalan families and friends unite at the grave sites of their loved ones to celebrate the lives of the departed. They tell stories, recite prayers, and adorn the grave with flowers and candles, and in the evening, the living share a meal—always making sure to leave food and drink behind for souls who have worked up an appetite.

Fiambre generally refers to cold cuts in Spanish, but in Guatemala, it's the signature dish of All Saints' Day. Made with an average of 50 ingredients, this giant colorful salad often includes shrimp, hard-boiled eggs, salami, cheese, pickles, pacaya flowers, sardines, and beef tongue. Families come together days in advance to purchase, pickle, grill, and dice, then make a cohesive dish by mixing and marinating everything in vinaigrette for at least a day.

Guatemalans pass down their own family recipes, and the massive salad is designed to give the deceased a smattering of options. Common variations include a vegetarian version, an unmixed style called divorciado (literally "divorced"), and rojo ("red") or blanco ("white")—renditions made with or without beets. Locals know it's tricky to surmise exactly what the dead are craving, so with fiambre, they give them an array of choices.

How to try it

Guatemalan fiambre is a homemade meal prepared only for All Saints' Day. In other Spanish-speaking countries, fiambre simply denotes cold food, such as platters of charcuterie and cheese.

A beautiful spread for snacking in the afterlife.

IT'S RAINING FISH

LLUVIA DE PESCES • HONDURAS

How to try it

The fish arrive with the first major rainfall, so those hoping to witness the phenomenon should arrive before May and prepare to be patient until July.

The residents of Yoro, a town in Honduras, have described the same annual phenomenon for more than a century: torrential rains, thunder and lightning, a biblical storm that keeps everyone indoors. After so many years, the locals know the drill well. They wait eagerly for the weather to clear, then go outside to collect their feast.

Every spring, the residents say, this blessed rain covers their town with hundreds of small silver fish—they writhe in the streets, so fresh they're still alive. And yet the closest body of water is the Atlantic Ocean, nearly 124 miles (200 km) away. Many believe the fish are a gift from God, and one popular theory credits 19th-century Catholic priest Father José Manuel Subirana, who prayed to God for sustenance to feed the town's hungry people, and at the end of his prayer, it rained fish.

Meteorologists offer a second opinion. They point to waterspouts, which have the capacity to pull small creatures, like sardines, from bodies of water and deposit them elsewhere. Another theory suggests there may be subterranean water beneath Yoro. Flash flooding could push fish to the surface and leave them stranded. But even experts admit it's pretty miraculous that these weather patterns could happen with such regularity.

As most residents believe the fish are a holy blessing, it's illegal to profit from the downpour, and the excess is distributed throughout the community during Yoro's annual festival.

The Original Food from Heaven?

According to the book of Exodus, after Moses led the Israelites out of slavery in Egypt, they endured two weeks in the desert before complaining of hunger. The Lord heard their murmurs and with the morning dew, manna appeared—"thin flakes like frost on the ground" (Exodus 16:14). The heavenly substance was "white like coriander seed and tasted like wafers made from honey" (Exodus 16:31) and would feed the Israelites for the 40 years they spent wandering the desert.

Some scientists believe that manna occurs naturally, then and now, in the Sinai Desert. The most popular explanation points to the tamarisk tree, a plant native to dry areas in Eurasia, which produces a sticky resin similar to wax that melts in the sun and is made mostly of sugar—just as the Bible describes. There is also an insect that feeds off the tamarisk tree's sap and secretes from its butt a sweet liquid called honeydew that loses its moisture quickly and turns into a sticky solid rich with carbohydrates that could, conceivably, be pounded into nourishing cakes as depicted in the book of Numbers. Many cultures eat honeydew, from Europe to the Middle East.

But this is no perfect science. Religious scholars believe there may have been as many as two million Jews in Moses's flock, a population that would require an ungodly amount of tamarisk trees and insect secretions to sustain. Additionally, the trees and their insect life choices produce the sweet stuff only seasonally, from May to July, while the manna in the Bible fell six days a week for 40 years.

A more scandalous theory cites Exodus 16:7, which reads, "and in the morning you will see the glory of the Lord because he has heard your grumbling against him." Several researchers who study the historical and societal impact of fungi believe manna may have come from a species of psychedelic mushroom. *Psilocybe cubensis* produces molecules that resemble frost and has been shown to incite spiritual and religious experiences. The scholars draw parallels between the mushroom's mind-altering effects (including heightened senses that, they argue, abetted the group's unlikely survival) and the Bible's warning that the Israelites would eat the manna and "see the glory of the Lord."

The Israelites Gathering Manna *by Ercole de' Roberti, ca. 1490s (National Gallery, London).*

THE CRAZY WOMAN'S SIGNATURE DISH

VIGORÓN ∘ NICARAGUA

Vigorón, the official dish of the city of Granada, Nicaragua, is a street food made with soft-boiled yucca, crispy fried chicharrón (pork skin), and curtido, a vinegar-and-chili-soaked salad of cabbage and a tangy local fruit called mimbro. The three crunchy, salty, sour layers are served on a banana leaf and always eaten with your hands.

The street snack was the invention of Maria Luisa Cisnero Lacayo, nicknamed La Loca ("the Crazy Woman"). In 1914, Lacayo was a vendor at the local baseball stadium and came up with the dish as a way to stand out from the typical offerings of boiled corn and sweet tamales. After seeing a poster for a health tonic called "Vigorón," she took the name for her game-day snack. A century later, her creation has become the most iconic food of her city. Locals say it's so addictive, you can't help but suck every last bit from your fingers.

How to try it
Granada may have lost La Loca, but it's found a worthy successor in La Pelona (the Bald Woman), who dishes out top-notch vigorón in the city's Municipal Market.

A DELICIOUS MONSTER

MONSTERA DELICIOSA • PANAMA

How to try it

Even when ripe, Monstera deliciosa still contains small amounts of oxalate and should be avoided by those who are sensitive to it. You may also notice some black specks in the fruit. These are edible but can irritate the mouth.

Monstera deliciosa should come with an instruction manual. Unripe fruits are chock-full of oxalate crystals, which, in oxalic acid form, is a substance strong enough to bleach wood and clean rust off metal. Those who make the mistake of biting into an unripe monstera experience severe throat and skin irritation. When ripe, however, this monster of a fruit is indeed delicious.

The fully ripe monstera offers a wonderful combination of strong tropical flavors like pineapple, coconut, and banana. When not eaten on its own, the fruit is most often prepared into jams or monstera-based desserts.

Unlocking that flavorful potential—and avoiding any painful toxicity—is all a matter of timing. To ripen the fruit, set it inside a jar or glass and cover it with a brown bag. In time, the green hexagonal scales that make up the outer skin will slowly fall off from one end to another. You can nudge the scales off gently with a finger, but should stop if you find yourself using force.

When the green scales fall off, the fruit is ripe.

A woman from the Emberá tribe, an Indigenous people of Panama, ceremonially decorated with jagua bodypaint.

THE NATURAL FRUIT INK

JAGUA TATTOOS • PANAMA

Centuries before anyone was peeling the plastic from stick-on temporary tattoos, isolated tribes across Central and South American jungles were making jet-black body art that would disappear within 20 days, using nothing but a fruit called jagua.

The unripe jagua produces a colorless juice that, when exposed to air, oxidizes and transforms from light brown to blue black to onyx. Applied to the surface of the skin, the fruit ink can create sharp, delicate tattoos that look every bit as real as the permanent kind. Among these remote tribes, painting the body still has countless functions, from looking fierce in battle to discerning one tribe from another to general beautification. The fruit also boasts medicinal properties, chiefly as an antibiotic, so applying the juice to the skin was considered a way to fend off parasites.

In modern tattoo culture, jagua is often mixed with henna to create a richer color, or as a way to test-drive a tattoo design before forever inking it to the body. Apart from its capacity to dye things profoundly black (not just skin but utensils, baskets, and fabric), jagua, of course, is an edible fruit. The fruit ranges in size from kiwi to grapefruit, and when ripe, it tastes like dried apple or quince. Those more excited by fruit than tattoos can opt for jagua sweets, wine, and syrup.

How to try it
Panama's Indigenous Emberá are among those who use jagua for tattoos. Some traditional Emberá villages, such as Ella Drua north of Panama City, welcome visitors and invite them to be tattooed.

FESTIVAL OF THE CHEESE CURL

FESTIVAL DEL ALMOJÁBANO CON QUESO • PANAMA

Variations of almojábano, or cheese bread, abound in Latin America, from fluffy baked buns to rice flour fritters. But only in Panama is there a four-day festival celebrating the snack, which in this country is shaped like an *S* and eaten all day long.

Technically, the festival celebrates almojábanos con queso, which in Panama means the national salty white cheese. Crumbled by hand, the cheese goes into a bright yellow dough made from milled corn, water, sugar, and salt. Hot from the fryer, the cheese should be supple when the crispy exterior is broken.

Every January or February, thousands of people flock to the tiny mountain town of Dolega to indulge in the traditional cheese curl, which is sold by dozens of vendors pumping out huge quantities of their unique family recipes. Over the years, the festival has incorporated a dynamic folklore component, with groups arriving from across the country to play Panamanian music, perform traditional dances, and ride in a parade with ox-pulled floats to the sound of tamborito, the country's vibrant percussion-filled, call-and-response song and dance.

The fritter is rolled by hand, first into a tube, then pinched in two places to make the customary curl, which mimics the shape of Panama.

How to try it

The closest airport to Dolega is in the city of David, 12 miles (19 km) away. A regional bus runs between the two towns, and the trip takes about 20 minutes.

THE CARIBBEAN ISLANDS

THE JEWEL OF ANTIGUA'S COAT OF ARMS

BLACK PINEAPPLE • ANTIGUA

How to try it

Roadside stalls selling Antigua black pineapples are sprinkled throughout the island, but for the best variety head south to an area called Old Road, also known as the fruit basket of Antigua.

Antigua's coat of arms is a gathering of the island's signature elements—the blue and white sea, two stately deer, bright red hibiscus, and the stars of their local produce. A yucca plant, the culinary staple of Antigua, stands parallel to a stalk of sugarcane, the historic cash crop. At the top, perched like a glistening crown, is Antigua's illustrious black pineapple, said to be the world's sweetest.

Brought to Antigua from South America by the Arawak people, the black pineapple has been cultivated on the island's southern coast for centuries. Black pineapples still grow on small farms, almost exclusively for local consumption.

Crisp in texture, low in acid, and high in sugar, black pineapples are delectable to the core, which is almost always eaten. Despite the name, the fruit is never black. The skin remains green, even when ripe, so picking the perfect orb relies heavily on smell and touch. Local farmers say the island's rich soil, moderate rainfall, and copious sunshine create an ideal growing climate that cannot be replicated anywhere else.

Fidel Castro's state-run ice-cream parlor can accommodate 1,000 people.

FIDEL CASTRO'S ICE-CREAM PARLOR

COPPELIA ∘ CUBA

Fidel Castro, insatiable dairy enthusiast, brought ice cream to his people with Coppelia, a sprawling, retro-modern helado complex. Commissioned in the 1960s by Castro himself, this grandiose ice-cream cathedral was erected on the site of an old hospital and designed to look like a UFO, with long concrete spokes radiating from the top of the structure and surrounded by a park that spans an entire city block. The enterprise was named after the favorite ballet of Celia Sánchez, Castro's secretary and close confidante, who was in charge of the project.

Determined to serve more ice-cream flavors than the parlors in the United States, Castro ordered 28 containers of ice cream from Howard Johnson's, then the largest American hotel and restaurant chain, and tasted every flavor they made. In those early days, Coppelia offered 26 ice-cream flavors and flavor combinations, with whimsical names such as Turquoise Special, Indian Canoe, and Chocolate Soldier. Today, patrons are lucky to find three flavors on offer.

Still, Coppelia continues to serve long lines of customers every day. Cubans eat ice cream in tremendous quantities, with amorous devotion. In the 1990s, when trade fluctuations meant the country had to decide between dairy resources for butter or ice cream, the people chose ice cream.

How to try it

Coppelia is located on Calle 23 in Havana's bustling Vedado district. The popular en salada is five scoops of ice cream and a sprinkling of cookies for about a quarter.

AN ILLEGAL TONIC TURNED CURE-ALL APHRODISIAC

MAMA JUANA • DOMINICAN REPUBLIC

How to try it

Available in most bars and markets in the Dominican Republic, Mama Juana can be tailored to what ails you. If it's virility you're after, ask for more mariscos, or "seafood," in the tonic (especially miembro de carey, or "turtle penis"). If you're trying to get pregnant, look for an ingredient called uña de gato, or "cat's claw."

The Taíno Indians—native to the island that is now home to the Dominican Republic—were remarkably resourceful. By the 15th century, they could remove cyanide from yucca, make balls out of natural rubber, and tap the medicinal potential of the abundant local flora. They brewed teas from barks and leaves to relieve everything from common colds to respiratory, circulatory, and digestive diseases. It wasn't until after 1492, when Christopher Columbus and his men landed on their island, that alcohol was added to the recipe, resulting in what is now known as Mama Juana.

Derived from the French term *Dame Jeanne*, which refers to a large squat bottle, Mama Juana is made by filling a jug with tree barks and herbs (think star anise, clove, basil, and agave), then adding rum, red wine, and honey. The taste of the liquor, which is woody and sweet, gets stronger with time and is sometimes compared to port wine, and other times to cough syrup.

In the 1950s, Mama Juana experienced a boost in popularity and reputation when a man named Jesus Rodriguez began selling the elixir as a medicinal tonic and aphrodisiac. It was a hit, and aspiring entrepreneurs jumped into the game, peddling all manner of potions and touting their alleged medicinal benefits. Rafael Trujillo, the country's president-turned-dictator, put a stop to the craze by declaring the sale of Mama Juana illegal unless dispensed by someone with a medical license. While this law put an end to the rogue vending, it also gave credence to the idea that Mama Juana was indeed medication.

Nowadays, Mama Juana is both legal and abundant. It's often referred to by Dominicans as the "baby maker" or El Para Palo, which translates to "The Stick Lifter." It's commonly made at home, and almost always consumed at room temperature as a shot. When the liquor is drained, simply add more rum and wine. The process, locals say, can be repeated for up to a decade.

A COLLABORATIVE BEACH DAY FEAST

OIL DOWN • GRENADA

Grenada's St. George market carries all the fresh produce for an oil down.

Grenadians love to lime, the island's expression for relaxing. Liming in cafés and along the marina is a favorite national pastime. When liming on the beach, it's only natural to bring a big pot, light a fire in the sand, and start an oil down.

Grenada's national dish is an all-day social endeavor. The enormous pot gets fired up early in the morning and slowly filled throughout the day. The women helm this operation, and although the dish is meant for a lazy beach day, the preparation requires some serious work. A ripe breadfruit must be chopped and soaked, along with green bananas, taro, and yams. Salt fish must be soaked and rinsed, leafy greens washed and chopped. Dumplings must be kneaded from flour and rolled into the customary shape of logs. Pig snouts and tails—a vestige from the sugarcane plantations, when these scraps were passed down from the plantation house—must be washed, broken down, and soaked.

Every cook has their own way of packing the pot, but a common method is meat and starchy stuff on the bottom, veggies in the middle, and fish and dumplings on top. Everything is boiled in coconut milk with spices such as turmeric, nutmeg, and ginger. The name *oil down* comes from the process of letting the ingredients soak up the coconut milk, until there's nothing left on the bottom but oil. The breadfruit and dumplings have a soft, spongy consistency that pairs well with the salty fish and leafy greens. It's customary for every guest to bring an ingredient to contribute, and so each creamy, steaming pot is uniquely enhanced by the people who will eat it.

How to try it
Thursday is Oil Down Day at the Coconut Beach restaurant in St. George's, where you can enjoy your meal with your feet in the sand.

A HISTORIC CARIBBEAN SOUP HOUSE

AN CHODYÈ LA • GUADELOUPE

How to try it

An Chodyè La is located at 59 Rue Gilbert de Chambertrand. The café is also known locally as "Kaz a Soup."

On a small Pointe-à-Pitre street is a café housed within a bright-turquoise building. Called An Chodyè La, it specializes in hearty, flavorful soups that tell a story about Guadeloupe—from its dark colonial past to the resilience of its people.

According to Jean-Claude Magnat, the restaurant's chef, his soups are deeply rooted in the island's history of slavery. Enslaved families were forced to survive on their masters' leftovers, which they boiled with water into soup. Over time, cooks infused their

own heritage flavors and techniques to make new recipes. Magnat's soups are re-creations of dishes originally made by his great-great-grandmother Lucille Deris. The turquoise building that contains his restaurant was once her home, which she purchased with money she earned from washing clothes.

The café's menu is conveyed verbally and features a rotation of soups such as traditional Caribbean lambi, oxtail soup, sea-snail soup, lobster bisque, and ouas-sous giraumon, a pumpkin soup with freshwater shrimp.

SPAGHETTI WITH HOT DOGS FOR BREAKFAST

ESPAGETI • HAITI

No one can explain exactly why Haitians eat spaghetti for breakfast, and yet it's a morning staple, ingrained in their cuisine as a national comfort food. There are two essentials to Haitian espageti: There must be processed tube meat (typically hot dogs, but Vienna sausage is also good), and there must be ketchup. It's a noodle dish that exists happily in a vacuum, with no reverence for Italy, so conventional pasta rules do not apply.

Americans, not Italians, were responsible for influencing the creation of this dish and the result is audaciously un-European. During the time when the United States invaded Haiti in 1915, they brought their processed foods. Dried spaghetti was introduced to the local diet alongside ketchup and salty, shelf-stable meats. Cross two oceans to another former US territory, the Philippines, and you'll find an entirely disparate cuisine that also loves hot dogs with their spaghetti—a dish they call spags.

For people pressed for time or on the go, Haitians have developed a workaround that still allows them to eat their espageti—or rather drink it. Vendors are happy to throw noodles and sauce into a blender and blitz until the meal can be pulled through a straw.

How to try it

Spicing the pasta is up to the whimsy of the chef, but a drizzle of ketchup over the top is de rigueur.

PEANUT BUTTER WITH SCOTCH BONNET PEPPERS

MAMBA • HAITI

When made by hand, mamba—a spicy peanut butter—starts with a giant cauldron over an open fire, often in a backyard. Locals roast the peanuts, keeping them moving against the hot cauldron walls, then pour them into a woven winnowing tray. The process of separating the peanuts from their shells is a practiced maneuver, a rhythmic tossing and catching, tossing and catching, until the peanuts are rendered shiny and skinless. The batch of nuts then takes a ride through a grinder, gets swirled with hot peppers like Scotch bonnets or habaneros, and is then ready to be spread onto its preferred partner, cassava crackers. The spice doesn't show itself right away. It creeps up at the end, cutting into the creamy richness.

Beyond the island's backyard production, Haiti boasts a few commercial labels, supplied by a budding peanut farming industry. Haitians abroad often complain that the peanut butters of other nations don't satisfy their cravings, so it's not uncommon to see suitcases leaving the island packed with jars of the spicy stuff.

How to try it

Brands Rebo and Compa Direct are 100 percent Haitian. The brand Manba is made from Haitian peanuts but is produced in Montreal. On the streets of Port-au-Prince, you can find street vendors selling mamba on cassava crackers.

PEANUT BUTTER

Fresh on the tree, ackee is chock-full of poison.

SAVORY DEATH-INDUCING FRUIT

ACKEE • JAMAICA

How to try it

Jamaica exports canned ackee around the world, but you're unlikely to find it fresh unless you're on the island. For best results, visit during the fruit-bearing season, which spans January to March, and June to August.

Ackee and salt fish, Jamaica's cherished national dish, is a combination of salted cod and a savory yellow fruit that contains so much poison, it's generally illegal to export when fresh. Still, Jamaicans find every excuse to remove the poison and dig in. The fruit contains hypoglycin A, a poison that, according to the FDA, can cause "vomiting with profound hypoglycemia, drowsiness, muscular exhaustion, prostration, and possibly coma and death." Boiling the ripe fruit leaches out the toxins and renders ackee safe to eat. Native to West Africa, the toxic fruit was brought to the island by slavers in the 1770s.

Jamaicans grow ackee in two varieties: the yellow-tinged, soft "butter ackee" and the cream-colored, hard "cheese ackee." Both types turn yellow when exposed to heat and have a mild taste many compare to hearts of palm or scrambled eggs, which makes them especially popular at breakfast time.

CRACK AN EGG, SEE THE FUTURE

EGG SETTING • JAMAICA

How to try it

Play it safe by cracking half a dozen eggs before going to bed; they can't all be caskets.

When the sun rises on Good Friday, many Jamaicans can be found looking into a glass of water, trying to divine their futures. Eggs, symbolic of new life, have always played a part in the Christian holiday, but in Jamaica, they're not just for painting and baskets. The much older, local tradition is to drop an egg white into a glass of water before Good Friday, then to study the form it takes when the sun comes up. An airplane or ship means there will be travel in the coming year, while a long dress foretells a marriage. Some islanders avoid the superstition altogether, warned off by tales of people seeing caskets and then dying shortly after.

Pantry Alternatives to Tarot Cards

Divining the future is all fun and games until someone gets arrested, which was surprisingly common in the psychic tea rooms of 1930s New York City. Fortune-tellers reading tea leaves for profit were busted by police sting operations. The women, serving a mostly female clientele, were accused by the *New York Times* in a 1931 editorial of causing "a wave of melancholia among women" because of their startling prophecies. But tea was just the beginning of the food prophecy racket: While the tea leaf readers were being chased, the onion oracles and the coconut clairvoyants were free to roam.

APPLES have been used to make love predictions for centuries: A 1714 English poem depicts a country maiden flinging an apple peel over her head and being thrilled by the "L" shape it forms because she's in love with a shepherd named Lubberkin. In Europe and the Middle East, the fruit has long been a mythological symbol of female fertility and youth. An apple peel thrown over a shoulder is still a common way to predict a lover's initial, but you can also recite the alphabet while peeling, stopping when the ribbon breaks from the fruit. Apple seeds come in handy when making more specific prophecies. If you're torn between lovers, assign them each a seed, then moisten the seeds and stick them to your face. The last seed standing is your true love.

COCONUTS are the best for answering yes/no questions. In Obeah fortune-telling—a West African divination practice—four pieces of coconut, with husk on one side and flesh on the other, are held in a diviner's hand. After a quick prayer over the question, the pieces are tossed like dice to the ground. All four pieces white side up is the strongest yes, while four dark sides is an absolute no, along with the implication that the asker needs some serious spiritual cleansing. An equal split means yes. Three whites is a maybe. Three darks is a no. In Yoruba culture, kola nuts were the original divining medium, but after the diaspora, coconuts replaced the hard-to-find nut, and the tropical fruit is now widely accepted as a suitable mouthpiece of the divine.

GASTROMANCY was a popular ancient Greek divination technique that involved listening to the gurgling of a human belly, believed to be voices of the dead who had taken up residence in the stomach. The keepers of these mystic bellies would interpret the voices and use them to communicate with the departed, in addition to predicting the future. This was a popular after-dinner activity, where even the marks on the outside of the belly were considered clues. Pythia, more widely known as the Oracle of Delphi, was one of the earliest prophets to use gastromancy and was known to communicate with Apollo through her stomach. During the Middle Ages, the practice was considered a form of witchcraft. By the 18th century, these belly prophets were revealed to be the world's first ventriloquists, simply manipulating their voices to project through their guts. With their spiritual credibility shot, they moved their act to the stage.

ONIONS, with their quick-growing sprouts, were the go-to veggie for divination in ancient Europe, Africa, and Siberia. To mine the depths of a person's soul, their name was inscribed onto an onion, then the onion was placed on an altar. Sprouting had a positive correlation: Depending on the question, a fast-sprouting onion could mean a person was happy, healthy, or suitable for marriage. In a German tradition, 12 pieces of onion, each representing a month of the year, are laid on a table and left out overnight with a grain of salt on each piece. In the morning, the onion pieces with the most liquid foretell the rainiest months.

How to try it

Irish moss can be found in cafés and bars. As of recently, there is also a canned version sold commercially as "Big Bamboo," in case anyone was unclear about the desired effect.

ROADSIDE APHRODISIAC SLINGERS

PUNCH MEN • JAMAICA

Imagine the texture of melted ice cream, add the briny flavor of algae, take a long, viscous gulp, and ask yourself: Are you feeling sexy? The men of Jamaica are saying yes.

Across the island, vendors called Punch Men sling liquid aphrodisiacs along the side of the road. Their erotic elixirs feature a red algae called Irish moss, touted for its abilities to moisturize skin, revitalize the mind, and, most notably, increase libido. To prepare the drink, the Punch Men wash the moss, then boil it, which releases an extract called carrageenan. A natural thickener—dairy producers often add it to yogurt—carrageenan provides the drink's signature gluey viscosity. Milk, vanilla, cinnamon, and nutmeg spice up the brew, which is left to cool before being dispensed to men (and some women) seeking a boost in the bedroom.

Native to Ireland, the red algae is packed with nutrition—10 percent protein and 15 percent mineral matter. During the Irish potato famine of the mid-1800s, the algae helped nourish the country's starving population. Irish immigrants to Jamaica brought their miracle moss, and it now grows on the island's rocks.

A PROCESSED, SPREADABLE EASTER CHEESE

TASTEE CHEESE • JAMAICA

How to try it

Tastee Cheese is easy to find in Jamaican stores, bakeries, and cafés. It's harder to find everywhere else, but it is sold in the US, in the UK, and on other Caribbean islands.

What does it take to make Jamaican Tastee Cheese? New Zealand cheddar cheese.

The dairy corporation Fonterra (formerly the New Zealand Dairy Board) grinds, pasteurizes, and cans their cheddar before shipping it off to Jamaica. Despite the involvement of around 10,500 Kiwi dairy farmers, Tastee Cheese is distinctly Jamaican—produced in flavors such as jerk (a Caribbean spice blend) and Solomon Gundy (a Jamaican pickled fish pâté).

Tastee Cheese is also an essential half of a classic Jamaican Easter food pairing, "Bun and Cheese." A Caribbean twist on the British hot cross bun, Tastee Cheese is spread inside a Jamaican spiced bun. Locals made a few tweaks to the recipe, shaping the dough into a loaf, swapping out honey for molasses, and adding dried fruit.

A CHICKEN TECHNIQUE PIRATED BY PIRATES

POULET BOUCANÉ • MARTINIQUE

During the 17th and 18th centuries, the island of Martinique was the site of relentless battles. The French, who arrived with ships of enslaved Africans, fought ruthlessly to displace the Indigenous Carib in order to grow sugarcane.

Pirates added to the violence, preying on European ships traveling to the island. It was off the coast of Martinique, in 1717, that the pirate Blackbeard commandeered a French slave ship, which became his infamous flagship the *Queen Anne's Revenge*.

How to try it

To find poulet boucané, look for smoke wafting off a hot barbecue. It's almost always served with sauce chien. Literally, "dog sauce," the parsley, chive, and chili blend gets its name from the French idiom *avoir du chien*, or "to have spunk."

Long before the French knew Martinique existed, the Indigenous islanders had honed a technique for smoking and preserving food, usually involving salt, wood, and fragrant plants. The invaders appropriated this method, and poulet boucané, or "buccaneer's chicken," was born.

After a long soak in onion, garlic, chili pepper, lime juice, thyme, and oil, a whole chicken is dried and placed in a smoker, which is often constructed from a metal drum cut in half lengthwise. Cooks place burning sugarcane at the bottom of the metal drum and chicken on a grate in the middle, then close the drum and let the smoke work its magic. The result is tender, zesty, and herbaceous chicken that can be taken on long and gruesome warring crusades, or eaten as a simple lunch.

THE CARIBBEAN'S ONLY PIZZA BOAT

PIZZA PI ∘ ST. THOMAS, US VIRGIN ISLANDS

One of the highest rated, most beloved restaurants in the US Virgin Islands has no official address and is best accessed by chartered boat, dinghy, or swimming. The floating pizzeria, called PiZZA Pi, is the Caribbean's only "food truck boat," specially fitted with a commercial kitchen that cranks out New York–style pizzas. The restaurant takes orders by boat radio, phone, or email, but collecting your pie is a little harder because the restaurant anchors about a mile off the shore of St. Thomas's Christmas Cove.

PiZZA Pi is the whimsical invention of Sasha Bouis, a MIT-educated mechanical engineer turned boat captain, and Tara Bouis, a teacher turned award-winning yacht chef. The American couple spent two years restoring an abandoned boat, adding a double-brick-lined pizza oven, hood ventilation, a water production system, and solar panels.

In 2018, Sasha and Tara sold their pizza boat to new owners Heather and Brian Samelson, another ex-pat couple whose daughter worked aboard the PiZZA Pi. Throughout the day, boats pull up to the floating pizzeria, tie up, and enjoy the freshly made pizza passed from the kitchen window. The restaurant also offers delivery via their dinghy, which doubles as a small dining area when the occasional swimmer arrives.

How to try it

PiZZA Pi moors off the shore of Christmas Cove, on the east end of St. Thomas. They are open every day from 11 a.m. to 6 p.m. Order ahead by calling +1 340 643 4674, or getting on marine radio VHF 16.

THE INTERNATIONAL ART OF

How to try it
La Casita Blanca, a homey San Juan institution located in a small white house, doles out pegao to those smart enough to request it.

STRATEGICALLY BURNED RICE

PEGAO • PUERTO RICO

In Puerto Rico, burning rice is an art.

Pegao means "stuck," as the rice is meant to stick to the bottom of a cast-aluminum pot called a caldero. According to Puerto Rican chef Jose Santaella, who dedicated an entire page of his cookbook *Cocina Tropical* to the crunchy layer, "the rice, the pot, the method, and the finishing are all crucial." The method involves cooking the rice until it's just done, then strategically raising the heat in the final few minutes to scorch the bottom of the pot. This finishing blast is tricky to get right because there's no way to see what's happening at the bottom. There's a fine line between rice that's chewy, nutty, and crunchy, and rice that's bitter and acrid. The technique takes practice, a developed sense of smell, and an intimate familiarity with pot and stove.

In Puerto Rico, there is etiquette to sharing a pot of rice. Diners should scoop a portion of the top, fluffy rice, then top the mound with a couple of scrapes of pegao. Ratios must be respected: To take more than a bite or two is considered rude.

guoba

nurungji soup

Burning Rice

Most every rice-eating culture has discovered the delectable magic of scorching their grains. Dominicans call it concon and make their rice in a seasoned aluminum pot. In Costa Rica, the term is a crunchy onomatopoeia: corroncho. In Colombia, cucayo is so sought after, there's a Barranquilla restaurant that specializes in crusty rice. A 1973 Peruvian song called "Arroz con Concolón" is still popular and sung widely today.

On the other side of the globe, burnt rice is just as tied to Asian culinary traditions. The Korean dish bibimbap is commonly served in a hot stone bowl called a dolsot that sears the rice at the table. In China, guoba is an all-purpose block of brittle rice that's a popular snack and starchy base for many dishes, a favorite being sweet-and-sour shrimp. Okoge is an important part of the traditional Japanese kaiseki meal, which is charred rice moistened with water, soup, or tea.

The Persians make scorched rice look glamorous: After the grains have formed a hard golden layer in the pot—called tahdig—it's overturned onto a plate so that it looks almost like a cake. The Iraqis break their layer into pieces to make sharing easier.

Then there's the international superstar paella, whose socarrat is cultivated carefully with a final blast of heat, creating a caramelized crust just before serving.

bibimbap

paella

okoge

tahdig

THE SECRET SAUCE OF CARIBBEAN COOKING

BROWNING • TRINIDAD AND TOBAGO

In Trinidad and Tobago, most dishes begin with something called browning, the little-known secret behind their cuisine's complex taste. While browning can be bought in a bottle, you'll rarely see one in a Caribbean kitchen, as it's simple to prepare.

Heat oil, add brown sugar, and allow it to—you guessed it—brown. When the sugar and oil have cooked for a few minutes and turned the color of coffee, Trini cooks can take the sauce in countless directions. Chunks of meat can be swirled in the sticky sauce to start a stew, or the browning can be added to cake batters for a distinctive toffee undertone. Simple but essential, browning is the elusive flavor note of Trinidad and Tobago's cuisine. The dark caramel flavor adds balance and depth to a cuisine that is typically spicy and intensely flavored.

The secret ingredient in rice and peas is often browning.

How to try it

Browning creates the base in popular recipes such as pelau (the country's rice-based dish), oxtail stew, rice and peas, and black cake. If you can't be bothered to caramelize sugar yourself, there are many commercial brands, such as Uncle Panks and Grace Browning, that will do it for you.

THE QUINTESSENTIAL TRINIDADIAN MEAL

RED SOLO, ROTI, AND DOUBLES • TRINIDAD AND TOBAGO

How to try it

Every local has their favorite spot, but try Amin's The Buss Up Shut King or Mona's Roti Shop, where you can watch them hand-making the flatbread. For doubles, use the Trinidad & Tobago Doubles Directory app to point you in the direction of more than 400 doubles shops. When ordering, keep in mind that doubles are always plural; even a single doubles is ordered as "one doubles."

Beginning in 1845, more than 100,000 Indians migrated to Trinidad to work as indentured laborers, and when their contracts ended, many chose to make the island their home. Indian flavors were absorbed readily into the local cuisine. Roti and doubles, two of the island's most iconic dishes, paired with a soda invented by the son of an indentured migrant, is often what homesick Trinis cite as the meal that transports them back to their island.

Roti, a Hindi word for bread, bends to a Caribbean sensibility in the style locals call "Buss Up Shut." Named for its resemblance to a tattered shirt, the roti is shredded on a griddle and then dipped in curry. "Dhalpuri" roti, the alternate style, is used like a pita, filled with a ground split pea mash. Then there's "doubles," two fried flatbreads called baras filled with curried chickpeas and a slew of fruit and hot pepper chutneys. These Indo-Trinidadian creations are acceptable fodder for breakfast, lunch, and dinner, and especially good for late nights and early Saturday mornings.

There is a correct accompaniment to roti and doubles. Locals call it Red Solo, a super-sweet soda made from the herbaceous sorrel plant, with a taste some compare to kiwi fruit or sour wild strawberries. For a truly Trinidadian experience, the Red Solo must be ice cold and served in a glass bottle.

JOSEPH CHARLES

(SERJAD MAKMADEEN, 1910–1965)

The story of Trinidad's beloved Red Solo soda begins with a young Indo-Caribbean boy named Serjad Makmadeen. The youngest of eight children, Makmadeen quit school at the age of ten to help support his family. As a teenager, he quickly became the top salesman at his local bakery. The young entrepreneur knew to spend money to make money, offering a free loaf of bread to anyone who bought 12 or more.

Years later, Makmadeen borrowed $250, combined it with his savings, and bought the small, hand-cranked soda factory down the road. With the help of his wife, he began cooking small batches of syrup and manually carbonating the soda. He started peddling his drinks to the customers on his bakery route, alongside his bread, with great success. At the same time, he sent letters off to soft drink producers in Britain, soliciting advice on how to make his budding business more efficient. All his letters went unanswered. On a hunch, Makmadeen wrote again, this time using the English pseudonym, Joseph Charles. Advice from England started coming in.

Business steadily ramped up, but the arrival of World War II brought a bottle shortage that threatened to

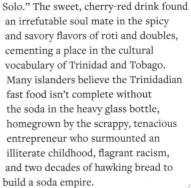

slow production. The newly christened Joseph Charles caught wind of a Montreal-based soda company going out of business and selling off its equipment. He bought their bottles sight unseen, and when they arrived in Trinidad branded with the name "Solo," alongside the image of a pilot and an airplane, Charles made yet another bold move. He commandeered the ready-made logo and gave the name to his bootstrapped soda. Two thousand miles (3,219 km) from Canada, under Charles's direction, the Solo label got a second life with a devoted island following.

By the time Charles died in 1965 and was succeeded by his sons, most every local knew the catchphrase "a roti and a Red Solo." The sweet, cherry-red drink found an irrefutable soul mate in the spicy and savory flavors of roti and doubles, cementing a place in the cultural vocabulary of Trinidad and Tobago. Many islanders believe the Trinidadian fast food isn't complete without the soda in the heavy glass bottle, homegrown by the scrappy, tenacious entrepreneur who surmounted an illiterate childhood, flagrant racism, and two decades of hawking bread to build a soda empire.

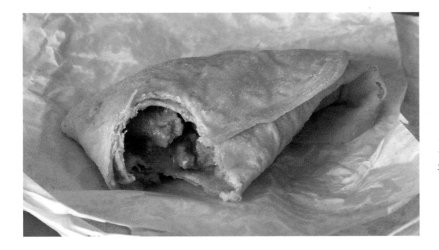

The chicken roti at Hott Shoppe in Port of Spain.

LOST CARGO OF THE HMS *BOUNTY*

BREADFRUIT • TRINIDAD AND TOBAGO

How to try it

Breadfruit salad, a dish that closely resembles American potato salad, is a popular restaurant side dish in Trinidad. Cheap in the Caribbean and expensive abroad, breadfruit is best produced locally.

In 1787, Captain William Bligh departed England for Tahiti with a single directive—collect breadfruit, known for its bread-like texture and potato-like taste. The Royal Society had selected the green fruit as the ideal cheap food for the thousands of enslaved Africans in the West Indies. Bligh's ship—the infamous HMS *Bounty*—spent ten grueling months at sea, followed by five months of collecting breadfruit in Tahiti. When the ship finally set sail for the West Indies, the commander's cabin was filled with 1,015 breadfruit plants.

Anyone familiar with the novel *Mutiny on the Bounty* knows things quickly fell apart from here. About 1,300 miles (2,092 km) west of Tahiti, the ship's crew rebelled against their captain. Often remembered as cruel and pompous, Bligh's personality is typically blamed for the uprising. But the men also missed Tahitian island life and were reportedly quite dehydrated, as Bligh was hoarding water for his breadfruits. Bligh and a handful of loyal men were set adrift in a tiny boat. The mutineers also took issue with their arrogant captain's treasured breadfruits, which were thrown overboard.

After reaching the island of Timor—3,600 miles (5,794 km) from where the crew cast off—Bligh made his way back to England. Undeterred, in 1791 he launched a second expedition to Tahiti, where he gathered breadfruit seedlings and successfully delivered them to the Caribbean. But in the end, no one liked breadfruit. The enslaved workers preferred bananas and plantains, and the breadfruit was fed mostly to pigs.

Breadfruit has since become a beloved staple starch across the islands, where it's treated much like a potato. Many of the trees that descended from Bligh's plants still stand in the Caribbean today. The next time you're eating on the island, there's a decent chance their progeny will end up on your plate.

SOUTH AMERICA

AN ENTIRE COW

VACA ENTERA • ARGENTINA

In Argentina, beef is a way of life, and a stroll down most any street will yield a parillero (a grill cook) hawking freshly barbecued steaks and other prime meaty bits. It makes sense that a country this passionate about beef would mastermind the vaca entera—a whole cow freshly splayed and suspended over an open fire.

Grilling an entire cow begins with a massive grilling rack. A dozen people heave the enormous cow into the apparatus, strap it in tight, and light four wood fires in the corners of the pit beneath. The first half of the 24-hour process is all about controlling the fire. Grill masters typically won't even touch the cow until the second half, when they must use brute strength to manually rotate the grilling cage like a rotisserie. With scalding fat dripping from the flesh, a blazing fire, and searing metal grates, it's a job that requires concentration, strength, and finesse.

The shopping list for vaca entera is brief: a butterflied cow and a pound (0.45 kg) of salt. A gallon of chimichurri, the Argentinian green herb sauce, is nice but not entirely necessary. The nonedible supplies are far more involved: two cords of wood—a stack of logs 16 feet wide, 4 feet high, and 4 feet deep (4.9 x 1.2 x 1.2 m); a pulley system set in concrete; a two-sided truss; and a 9-foot (3 m) sheet of corrugated metal to tent the cow like a massive piece of foil. Lastly, and arguably most tactically difficult, vaca entera requires a dozen loyal and robust insomniacs willing to wait out the night while fending off packs of wild foxes and coddling a raging, tempestuous fire, all for the love of beef.

How to try it

Los Talas del Entrerriano, in northwest Buenos Aires, is a locally beloved rustic steakhouse where you can watch whole cows being grilled as you await your meal.

THE WORLD'S ONLY BAR MADE FROM GLACIAL ICE

GLACIOBAR • ARGENTINA

The Argentine city of El Calafate is the gateway to Los Glaciares National Park, a trekking and climbing hot spot that contains an incredible array of glaciers, including the 121-square-mile Perito Moreno. For those looking to learn more about glaciers, there is Glaciarium, a center with multimedia exhibitions explaining how ice is formed and how glaciers move and shape their surroundings. If all this sounds a little too serious, Glaciarium is also home to Glaciobar, the world's only bar built entirely from glacial ice.

The Glaciobar is so cold, you can only enter after donning the capes, gloves, and boots provided. Inside, everything is made of ice, including the seats, tables, and glasses. Even with proper attire, you can only stay for 20 minutes—just long enough for a cocktail on the frozen couch.

How to try it

Entrance to the Glaciarium is 480 Argentine pesos ($11 US). It's an additional 300 pesos ($7) to enter the Glaciobar, which includes a drink and warm clothing rental. (RP11, Z9405 El Calafate, Santa Cruz, Argentina)

VOLCANIC ROCK SOUP

K'ALAPURKA • BOLIVIA

How to try it

From Potosi's city center, take a $1 taxi over to Doña Eugenia, a k'alapurka institution serving bubbling crocks of the breakfast soup to the town's locals. A bowl typically costs around 35 bolivianos ($5) and should be paired with a dark and malty morning beer.

The city of Potosí is home to Cerro Rico, or "Rich Mountain," which once produced 80 percent of the world's silver—a fortune that, between the 16th and 18th centuries, bankrolled the Spanish Empire. That bounty came at an enormous cost to human life. Hundreds of thousands of miners, predominantly conscripted native Peruvians and enslaved Africans, perished in the treacherous, disease-ridden mines. A bowl of k'alapurka, or volcano soup, was often what they ate for breakfast before descending into uncertain doom.

Hearty and blistering hot, this soup is a cauldron of comfort. An earthen bowl is brought to the table and a scorching volcanic rock is dropped, tableside, into the yellow corn-flour broth, creating a steaming ripple and violent bubbles that appear in the stone's wake. Long before Cerro Rico was the world's source of silver, the mountain was a volcano, and the rocks in k'alapurka are chips off that ancient block.

K'alapurka is considered by many visitors to be one of Bolivia's tastiest dishes. It packs sweetness and spice, with chili pepper, oregano, ají sauce, and aromatic chachacoma leaves. Potatoes, vegetables, and a savory meat—often beef jerky or fried pork—soften the spices and add heft to the meal. Perfectly paired with 13,000 feet (3,962 m) of rugged elevation, harsh winds, and frigid temperatures, k'alapurka is a dish that bears a dark history and happens to be delicious.

SLOW DINING ON THE ISLAND OF THE SUN

LAS VELAS • BOLIVIA

On the streets of Isla del Sol, a small island suspended in the middle of Lake Titicaca, there is no motorized traffic: Everything moves at the pace of your feet. To get to the restaurant Las Velas ("The Candles"), located at the top of a rocky peak, you must hike 30 minutes from the southern pier, uphill through

A llama on Isla del Sol, overlooking Lake Titicaca.

a eucalyptus forest. Just when you think you might be lost, a stunning view of the water will open before you, and you will have arrived.

Located in a thatched-roof cottage and run entirely by Chef Pablo and his wife, Las Velas has no electricity. During the day, Pablo cooks using natural light, and at night, he lights candles and sometimes straps on a headlight. The signature dish is quinoa and baked trout, pulled straight from the lake below. Pablo uses a wood oven and cooks alone. He makes everything from scratch and to order, so be prepared to hang out for a couple of hours, if not three. There are Bolivian wine and decks of cards to keep you entertained, but the view is more than enough: Blue during the day and inky silver at night, it's easy to see why Lake Titicaca is the setting of the Incan creation myth, which says the Sun God was born on this island, followed by the first Incas.

How to try it

Las Velas is open daily from 9 a.m. to 10:30 p.m., but keep in mind these hours are subject to island time. Although most people make the trek by foot, it's possible to rent a donkey.

THE WORLD'S FIRST FREEZE-DRIED FOOD

CHUÑOS • BOLIVIA

Freeze-drying, the food preservation technique famously used by NASA, was purportedly invented in a Parisian laboratory in 1906. But mention that fact around the Andean highland and prepare to be corrected, because in these parts, people have been freeze-drying potatoes for millennia.

Chuños, as the preserved tubers are called, start off as freshly harvested potatoes. Farmers leave them outside in freezing mountain temperatures for several nights until they are frosted over. During the warmer daytime hours, farmers trample the potatoes underfoot, flattening them and pushing out as much liquid as possible.

The routine continues for several days, stomping during the daytime and refreezing at night, before the chuños are ready to be fully dehydrated. If left out in the sun, they become chuños negros, or black chuños. If washed and protected from sun exposure while drying outside, they're known as chuños blancos, or white chuños.

Farmers freeze-dry potatoes, naturally, at extreme elevation.

Chuños can be stored for years without degrading. They are a blessing in the harsh Andean climate, where the tubers are often rehydrated in soups or pulverized into flour and used in baked goods. This ultra-stable spud was conceived as a cunning way to feed many people during periods of drought and scarcity. In the pre-Columbian era, centuries before spacemen required portable meals, Incan armies marched into battle on chuños, the world's first freeze-dried food.

How to try it

Although produced in June and July, when the day and night temperatures are most extreme, the preserved tubers are available at markets and restaurants year-round. Try them as the traditional accompaniment to sajta, a Bolivian chicken stew, or in black potato soup.

◆ ◆ ◆ ◆ ◆ ◆ ◆ ◆ ◆ ◆ ◆ ◆ ◆ **REGION OF WONDER** ◆ ◆ ◆ ◆ ◆ ◆ ◆ ◆ ◆ ◆ ◆ ◆

La Paz

Flying into the city of La Paz is an experience you're not likely to forget. Perched in the Andes and set against a towering range of snowcapped mountains, La Paz is the highest capital city in the world, with the highest international airport. Brick buildings cling to the sides of cliffs, descending down into a basin. The weather is nicer down below, which is where you'll find the technicolor markets, street vendors, and untold restaurants that take most visitors by surprise. Here's the best of La Paz:

Salteñas are sold all over Bolivia, but in La Paz they're the traditional midmorning snack. A cross between an empanada and a soup dumpling, the half-moon pastry contains a meat-and-potato filling seasoned with olives and raisins, and a lot of sauce. For clean handling, take a bite out of the top and sip out the sauce first.

Sanduíche de chola is the city's signature sandwich, made with slow-cooked, crispy-skinned pork topped with pickled onions and spicy

chili sauce. They're named after the Indigenous Aymara women (cholitas) who sell them, and the best of these vendors have been selling the same sandwich, from the same spot, for half a century. The bread, a light crunchy roll called marraqueta, is also a La Paz specialty.

Seafood is abundant in La Paz, as Lake Titicaca is about 50 miles (80.5 km) north. Unlike in other cities, here salteñas come in shrimp and

fish varieties, and ceviche is fresh and abundant. Look for ispi, a small lake fish, which is fried and eaten whole.

Llajwa de mani, the unsung national peanut sauce, deserves a lot more attention considering the peanut originated in ancient Bolivia. The thick, spicy, and garlicky sauce tops the ubiquitous street food anticuchos—a skewer of grilled beef heart that makes a good entry point into offal.

BRAZIL'S WINE CHURCH

CAPELA NOSSA SENHORA DAS NEVES • BRAZIL

At the heart of Brazil's winemaking region is a chapel called the Capela Nossa Senhora das Neves, or the Chapel of Our Lady of the Snow, a small and unassuming historic building constructed out of wine.

Brazil's Vale de Vinhedos (Valley of Vineyards) was settled in the late 1800s by Italian immigrants, who began growing grapes and making wine as they had in Italy. In 1904, 20 local families began work on Nossa Senhora das Neves, but a terrible drought struck and halted their progress. With water scarce, the community decided to tap their stores of wine. Each family donated 300 liters, which was kneaded with clay and wheat straw to make mortar, and the chapel was completed in 1907.

The chapel's appearance is also a nod to its unusual building material, from the exterior paint accents (a wine-red) to the altar made of wine barrels. These days, the wine church no longer holds services and is undergoing a restoration, but visitors are very much welcome.

How to try it

The wine church is located in the southern town of Bento Gonçalves, which is considered a center of winemaking and Italian immigration to Brazil.

When a drought halted construction of this church, residents made mortar out of wine.

CACAO'S TANGY COUSIN

CUPUAÇU • BRAZIL

Overshadowed by its hyped-up chocolate-making cousin, cacao, cupuaçu has some tricks of its own. When ripe, the large, oblong fruit has a dreamy, tropical smell before it even leaves the tree: a mix of pineapple, chocolate, and, some say, bubble gum. Beneath its hard brown exterior, the taste is even more complex. People have compared it to pears, bananas, coconuts, and chocolate.

Cupuaçu can perform some of cacao's tricks, too. Rich in fatty acids, cupuaçu butter (pressed from the seeds of the fruit) has a similar consistency to cocoa butter. Slathered on hair, lips, and skin, cupuaçu works as a natural moisturizer, sunscreen, and anti-inflammatory. Studies show the antioxidant-packed fruit helps the immune system and lowers blood pressure when ingested.

Recently, the easy-to-grow jungle fruit is attracting new attention as a serious contender to displace Brazil's reigning "superfruit," the acai. Scientists have found that pound for pound, cupuaçu outmatches the trendy berry in antioxidants, vitamins, and affordability.

How to try it

Outside the Amazon jungle, cupuaçu can be found on the internet's Amazon in whole fruit, capsules, powders, drinks, and butter.

THE COFFEE VERSION
OF THE NEW YORK STOCK EXCHANGE

BOLSA OFFICIAL DE CAFÉ • BRAZIL

How to try it

The port city of Santos is 43 miles (70 km) south of São Paulo and easily accessible by plane, bus, and car.

n the early 20th century, coffee was Brazil's main export, and Bolsa Official de Café (Portuguese for the "official coffee exchange") was where the money was made.

Built in 1922, this opulent building was where the captains of the industry haggled over the price of coffee. To take part in these discussions, merchants had to buy a chair, which could cost as much as a house. Until the trading floor closed in the 1960s, it was the financial epicenter of Brazil.

The wealth generated by coffee is evident in the palace's grandeur. The building is topped with a 130-foot-tall clock tower, while Ceres, goddess of agriculture, and Mercury, god of commerce, look out from either side of the entrance. Inside, the opulence continues with a massive stained glass ceiling, marble floors, and a jacaranda wood table in the traders' room.

Food Currencies

Bringing Home the Bacon, Making the Cheddar, Raking in the Clams

n 2014, a Russian farmer named Mikhail Shlyapnikov petitioned to create, print, and use a currency of his own invention, called kolions, which would be pegged to the price of potatoes. Each kolion would be worth 10 kilograms (22 lbs) of potatoes and would be used to trade for goods within his rural farming community. In his town, where access to rubles was extremely limited, a potato-pegged currency would insulate against external economic turmoil. Although a Moscow court ruled against Shlyapikov and eventually declared his kolions illegal, history favors the farmer's ingenuity. For centuries, food has doubled as a popular and effective currency, selected for its inherent value, relative stability, and ability to keep people alive when markets tank.

CHOCOLATE
During the reign of the Aztecs in Mesoamerica, cacao was considered a spiritual, even mystical substance. The Mayans, who had been growing it for hundreds of years, traded the beans with the newly arrived Aztecs, who in turn developed an obsession with cacao, conquered the Mayans, and took over their beans. The Aztecs couldn't get enough: They demanded taxes in the form of cacao and pegged the price of goods to their magical crop. In the 1500s, a turkey hen was worth 200 cacao beans, while one of its eggs went for three beans.

PEPPERCORNS
During the Roman Empire, pepper was considered a precious commodity, so valuable it was stockpiled in the treasury. By the time the Roman Empire fell, the city's invaders—including Attila the Hun—demanded the city's ransoms not in gold, but in pepper.

The building now houses the Coffee Museum, which names Francisco de Melo Palheta as the man who brought coffee to Brazil. Palheta, a Portuguese lieutenant colonel in the Brazilian army, was sent to French Guiana in 1727 under the guise of settling a land dispute between the French and Dutch colonies. His real mission was to bring back a coffee plant. The French governor refused to share the lucrative crop. As the 300-year-old story goes, Palheta seduced the governor's wife, and on his last evening in Guiana, she gifted him a bouquet of flowers with cuttings of a coffee plant.

This building was once exclusively open to wealthy coffee tycoons.

PARMESAN CHEESE

It's not easy to get a loan in Italy, but if you happen to have a massive spare wheel of Parmigiano-Reggiano, your chances just got a lot higher. Italy's Credito Emiliano, a regional bank locally known as Credem, has been accepting wheels of cheese as collateral for loans since 1953. At last count, it has 360,000 wheels in its possession, stacked 20 shelves high. Credem charges between 2 and 3 percent interest on the loans, depending on the quality of the cheese, plus a fee for maintaining the cheese vault, where they care for the wheels as the cheese makers would, lovingly cleaning and rotating their investment.

AFRICAN POTATO MASHER

In the area now known as Cameroon, the Bafia people used rare and heavy iron potato mashers called ensubas, which weighed around 11 pounds, to bring muscle to a serious financial transaction. In the 19th century, a Bafian wife would cost about 30 potato mashers.

TEA BRICKS

Compressed bricks of tea were the preferred currency in parts of Asia for more than a thousand years, from the 9th to the 20th century. Tea leaves, ground or whole, were compacted into various sizes, using herbs to add flavor and occasionally animal manure to hold them together. A value was stamped on the brick, which corresponded with the quality of the mixture. In Tibet, the price of horses and swords was set in tea bricks. In China, taxes could be paid to the emperor in tea.

A traditionally dressed woman from Bahia stuffs an acarajé.

THE FLUFFIEST BEAN FRITTERS IN BAHIA

ACARAJÉ DA CIRA • BRAZIL

How to try it

Acarajé da Cira is located on Largo da Mariquita, a small square in the neighborhood of Rio Vermelho. The shrimp are meant to be eaten whole, so don't let the locals catch you peeling them.

The first stop for many visitors to Salvador is the restaurant Acarajé da Cira, the holy grail of Brazilian bean fritters.

It's not an easy trek: The 5-mile (8 km) trip south of the city will take half an hour on a local bus. But once there, you will be greeted by women called baianas, dressed in traditional skirts and headdresses, presiding over an elaborate series of silver pots in the open air.

You, like the rest of the hungry crowd, are here for the acarajé, a bean fritter made from black-eyed peas and stuffed with a variety of tidbits from those silver pots. To make the bean batter, the baianas individually peel each black-eyed pea, which helps give the fritter its fluffy, cloud-like consistency. The batter is fried in dendê palm oil. Cira's trademark is that the oil is used only once, so the fritters will never be tainted by less-than-perfect oil. Hot from the fryer, the acarajé is split open and stuffed with a fresh tomato salad, a spicy coconut and peanut paste called vatapá, and whole, unpeeled shrimp.

Originally from West Africa, acarajé was brought to Brazil with the Atlantic slave trade. When slavery was abolished in the late 19th century, acarajé was a vital source of income for the newly freed Africans. The baianas have since become a cultural touchstone. Between 1993 and 1994, the back of the short-lived 50,000 cruzeiro real note displayed a baiana assembling an acarajé, which may or may not be as delicious as the ones at Cira's.

Other Enticing Bean Fritters

INDIA

Mangodae, made with mung beans ground with ginger, green chilies, cumin, and garam masala

MYANMAR

Baya kyaw, made by blending yellow split peas, onion, cilantro, turmeric, and garlic

TURKEY

Fasulye mucveri, made with fresh green beans, scallions, and dill in an egg-and-flour batter

STUFFED GOAT'S STOMACH

BUCHADA DE BODE • BRAZIL

Northeast Brazil is goat country, so it makes sense that one of the region's traditional dishes focuses on making the most of every last bit of the bode, the Portuguese word for "goat." Buchada, whose name comes from *bucho*, or "stomach," can be made out of any animal stomach, but goat is the most common in the Brazilian states of Pernambuco and Ceará.

The overall concept will sound familiar to anyone who's ever tried haggis: The stomach is stuffed with whatever entrails or organs are on hand (blood, intestines, liver, lungs), seasoned, and then sewn up and cooked. Restaurants will often serve buchada inside a larger stew. When plated as a main dish, the distinctive pattern of the stomach lining is clearly visible.

Buchada doesn't have many fans outside Brazil, but inside the country, especially in the northeast, it's not uncommon for politicians running for office to feel they must publicly consume one to prove they can relate to everyday people.

How to try it
Bode do Nô restaurant in Recife serves its buchada as a whole, intact stomach.

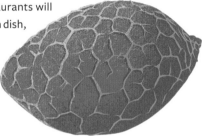

AIR-BREATHING MONSTER FISH

PAICHE • BRAZIL

Chuck a line into the Amazon River and you might pull out a convulsing, prehistoric leviathan twice the length of an adult human.

The paiche, also known as arapaima or pirarucu, is one of the largest freshwater fish in the world. Fully grown, it can reach up to 15 feet (4.6 m) from tip to tail. Weightwise, paiche can reach anywhere from 200 to 400 pounds (90.7 to 181 kg).

This fish has been around for so long it's considered a living fossil, dating back to the Miocene epoch (5.3 million to 23 million years ago).

This prehistoric relic has some strange traits, including the need to surface for air. In addition to gills, the fish has a lung-like organ. The ability to breathe air is helpful in the oxygen-deprived waters of the Amazon basin but leaves the paiche vulnerable. When the fish surfaces, it often sucks in air with a loud, distinctive gulp that local fishermen can identify from some distance away, making the paiche easy to catch. Amazonian fishermen have long prized the fish for its large size and tasty meat, netting or spearing the fish in such large numbers that its future was in doubt by the beginning of the 21st century.

Conservation efforts and an increase in farmed paiche have ensured that this ancient fish will not disappear anytime soon. And that's a great thing for Amazonian cuisine, as paiche is a delectable and meaty fish, with a firm fillet that stays succulent in most preparations, whether roasted, grilled, or steamed. It's also a fantastic fish for ceviche.

How to try it
You can find fresh paiche at the Mercado Municipal in Manaus.

Paiche is considered a living fossil.

Delicious Diaspora

JAPANESE IN BRAZIL

In 1908, the first boat of Japanese immigrants arrived in Brazil to work in the expanding coffee industry. Japan's feudal system had recently collapsed, leaving many rural citizens hungry and desperate for work. Seven hundred and eighty-one Japanese workers, mostly farmers, came over on the first boat from Kobe to São Paulo. By the 1990s, more than 200,000 of their countrymen had followed.

For nearly 50 years, life was hard for the Japanese in Brazil. Ostracized from Brazilian society, they lived in enclaves on meager wages, treated as a cheap source of labor. But the Japanese strengthened the Brazilian farming industry and eventually earned a reputation as skilled agriculturists. In the 1970s, as Japan rose to economic power, Japanese Brazilians gained newfound prestige, wealth, and respect. Today, Brazil is home to 1.5 million people of Japanese descent, the largest population outside of Japan.

Collaboration and intermarriage between the nations has led to a culture uniquely its own. Brazilian jujitsu, where strength meets cleverness, is a joint endeavor. In Japanese Brazilian homes, sticky short-grain rice is eaten alongside feijoada, the Brazilian bean stew, and sushi can be made with churrasco instead of fish. But Japanese Brazilian cuisine is not just the typical mash-up of a dish from one culture fused with a dish from another: It's a blending of lifestyles, techniques, and preferences.

Japanese rodízio is Japanese cuisine served in the popular Brazilian steakhouse style (rodízio) that includes an all-you-can-eat buffet. In Japan, buffets are a rare spectacle, but in Brazil almost every barbecue-meat-slinging restaurant has one. The Japanese style means sushi and sashimi, along with tempura, gyoza, and yakisoba, in unlimited quantities until you say stop.

Temakerias are fast-casual sushi restaurants making elaborate hand rolls (temaki). While the concept, in theory, is Japanese, the execution is definitively Brazilian. Mangoes and kiwis are common additions to hand rolls, which are astoundingly huge. In Japan, a hand roll is just a few bites; in Brazil, it's more like a meal. A popular Brazilian variety is deep-fried temaki, filled with cream cheese and salmon.

Pastéis are the omnipresent street snacks of Brazil, made of paper-thin dough filled with meat, fish, or cheese, then deep-fried. Like an empanada but lighter and crispier, the pastéis is believed to be an invention of Japanese migrants, who riffed on the Chinese recipe for fried wontons.

Sakerinhas are caipirinhas—Brazil's national cocktail—made with sake instead of cachaça.

Persimmon, Fuji apples, and ponkan oranges are among the fruits developed by early Japanese farmers. The introduction of new fruit as well as sustainable farming practices changed the Brazilian diet and brought more fresh produce to the table, laying the groundwork for the extensive fruit industry of today.

Cashew apples

Cashew nut

THE APPLE JUICE OF BRAZIL

SUCO DE CAJU • BRAZIL

The beloved, buttery cashew grows from a false fruit called a cashew apple, which often goes to waste once the nut is harvested. Recently, industrial drink producers such as PepsiCo have been devising ways to transform this cashew by-product into something delicious, drinkable, and lucrative. The Brazilians, one of the top producers of cashews, have been doing exactly that for years.

Cashew apple juice, known locally as suco de caju, is a popular Brazilian beverage that can be bought ubiquitously, from supermarket shelves to roadside stalls. The liquid is sour and bright, with hints of raw green pepper and subtle citrus. Often sold in concentrated form, cashew apple juice has become a mainstay at large gatherings and birthday parties and reminds many Brazilians of childhood.

How to try it

A few cashew juices are bottled and sold internationally, most notably the Brazilian brand Maguary. You can press your own, but beware that the apples are highly perishable and must be processed within 24 hours of falling from the tree.

BEER MADE FROM FOG

ATRAPANIEBLA • CHILE

The Atacama Desert, in the northern reaches of Chile, is the world's driest non-polar desert, with less than 0.004 inch (0.102 mm) of rain each year. In coastal communities such as Peña Blanca, the main source of fresh water comes in the form of thick cloud banks, known as camanchaca, that roll inland off the Pacific Ocean.

Set up along hillsides in prime fog areas, fog-catching nets capture the condensation. Droplets drip down the nets into piping that sends the water to barrels and reservoirs. The project, which began in the 1950s, has been a huge success, revolutionizing modern desert water collection. It also gave two local brewers an idea.

How to try it

Bars and restaurants in Chile's Coquimbo region serve Atrapaniebla beer in bottles and on tap.

Brothers Miguel and Marco Carcuro started the Atrapaniebla brewery, which produces the world's first beer made from fog water. Atrapaniebla ("fog catcher" in Spanish) currently produces 24,000 liters each year that are distributed around Chile. The Carcuro brothers say that the water from the camanchaca gives their beers a wholly unique taste, and that the fresh purity of the fog water adds clarity and depth that's unrivaled by other brews. The taste, drinkers say, is crisp and refreshing with just the slightest hint of atmospheric salt.

Shape-Shifting Strawberries

ANTIFREEZE STRAWBERRIES

Much speculation surrounds the creation of this fishy frankenberry, which began as an attempt to give the soft, fragile fruit a longer shelf life during the winter months. To do this, scientists in Thailand injected the seeds of the garden variety red strawberry with a gene found naturally in arctic flounder: antifreeze. The antifreeze gene—discovered and isolated in the late 1960s—increases tolerance to cold while mitigating damage caused by freezing. Addressing public concern, experts assure that the gene does not make its subjects taste like fish. While further experimentation is still required before antifreeze strawberries hit the market (the gene is being tested on everything from frozen foods to therapy for hypothermia), the future looks promising for winter produce.

SEA STRAWBERRIES

This crab-claw-shaped fruit grows along the saltwater coasts of California, Mexico, and Chile, where it hides in grassy tufts sprouting from black rocks and sand. While *Carpobrotus aequilaterus* is not technically a strawberry, it earned the name "sea strawberry" because it tastes just like one, albeit very salty. The claws are filled with a sugary red goop that resembles the inside of a soft fig and is extremely perishable. The fruit is ripe for just two to three weeks a year, after which it turns to mush.

PINEBERRIES

Strawberries that taste like pineapples may seem like genetically modified fruit. But pineberries are simply strawberries that have been slowly and selectively bred for their appearance and taste. Due to their tiny size (smaller than an inch) and low yields, pineberries are both expensive to buy and not especially profitable to grow. For a few weeks each summer, you might find them at American farmers' markets or high-end grocery stores, but pineberries are unlikely to be mass distributed anytime soon.

Pineberries have been bred to taste like pineapples.

THE MOTHER OF ALL STRAWBERRIES

PURÉN WHITE STRAWBERRY • CHILE

How to try it
Get to Purén during the summer harvest and find a local market, where the berries will be sold directly by the small collective of farmers.

The DNA of the pale, lightly floral Chilean strawberry exists in every supermarket in the United States, most of Europe, and anywhere large red strawberries are sold. The modern strawberry, or garden strawberry, is a hybrid of two species. Growing side by side in an 18th-century French garden, a strawberry from Virginia bred with a strawberry from the Chilean mountain town of Purén, and voilà, the contemporary variety was born.

The Chilean berry was originally prized for its impressive size, but its colorless appearance and delicate flavor are now its most distinctive traits. The pigment is what gives red strawberries their signature tartness, and so Chile's berries are light on acid and their taste is surprisingly floral—almost like eating strawberry perfume.

Fewer than 30 farmers work the strawberry fields in the small town of Purén, where the berries grow on steep, terraced hillsides facing the sea. Without any mechanized equipment, the farmers till 14 hectares (34.6 acres) of clay terrain and harvest strawberries by hand during the short two-month season.

White strawberries have a light, floral flavor.

BLUE EGG HENS

ARAUCANA • CHILE

Every now and then, chicken farmers will find an anomaly in the coop: nestled among regular white and brown eggs, a bright blue orb. There's no predicting when or how often a chicken's eggs will come out looking like Easter, which is what makes the Araucana chicken so special. The domesticated Chilean breed lays a dazzling aquamarine egg every single time.

No one knows exactly where Araucana chickens originated, as their history was undocumented until the Spanish observed them in the early 20th century. Some believe they are a serendipitous hybrid of native Chilean birds, while others credit foreign influence. Araucanas are a rumpless chicken, meaning they lack a last vertebra and have no tails, which points to Asian chickens as their ancestors—specifically the Balinese breed carried to Chile by Dutch traders. But Balinese chickens don't produce blue eggs, and so theories of their heritage remain roundly debated among poultry historians.

In order to lay these enchanted eggs, Araucanas require one thing: the outdoors. The chickens can't survive in industrial chicken farms, and so the shell's blue hue has unwittingly become an indicator of a happy chicken with a free-range life.

How to try it

Araucanas have been bred with many other chicken varieties, whose blue-egg-laying offspring now live throughout the world. Before eating, enjoy the aesthetic as much as you can because the taste is exactly like a normal egg.

The Araucana chicken lays Easter eggs.

A STONY SEA CREATURE WITH A GORY INTERIOR

PIURE • CHILE

Anyone swimming by this unassuming rock-like sea creature might not give it a second glance. But slice into its bumpy carapace and you'll find little orifices filled with swollen masses of tomato-red flesh, oozing clear blood.

Chilean fishermen harvest and sell the creature, known as piure, to local vendors, who remove the vibrant innards and hang the fresh or dehydrated meat from strings. Locals compare the taste to sea urchin but are quick to add that piure's

How to try it

Piure live off the coast of both Chile and Peru but are primarily eaten in Chile. Santiago's Mercado Central is sure to carry it. In Valparaíso, try the Caleta Portales ("Fisherman Cove"), where the local catch is brought each day.

flavor is less delicate. Packed with iron, titanium, and shockingly high levels of the rare element vanadium, it has a metallic taste with a bitter or soapy quality.

Along the coast, locals enjoy fresh piure in ceviche with onion, coriander, and lemon juice. They also slice and boil it for a rice-and-salad pairing or incorporate it into a traditional seafood stew called paila marina.

Piure belongs to the class of immobile, invertebrate filter feeders known as "sea squirts," all of which are hermaphrodites. Born male, piure becomes a hermaphrodite at puberty and can reproduce, alone or with others, by shooting out eggs and sperm that then mingle together in a cloud.

Perhaps the creature's versatile sexual abilities are why piure has also been touted as an aphrodisiac.

THE WORLD'S OLDEST CLAMBAKE

CURANTO • CHILE

How to try it

Chile's spring and summer (dry season) is the only time to take part in a traditional curanto feast. For those just wanting to eat it, head to Dalcahue and look behind the local crafts market for the food stalls being run by a team of grandmothers.

On a Chilean archipelago of lush islands called Chiloé, archaeologists discovered a 6,000-year-old cooking pit. It contained skeletal remains of nutrias, sea lions, birds, fish, and whales, along with shells from scallops, snails, abalone, mussels, and clams. These were the vestiges of an early curanto, one of the most ancient recipes still prepared today.

The word *curanto* means "hot rock" or "stony ground," and it begins with a 3-foot (1-m) hole lined with stones that have been heated in a bonfire. After the rocks, ingredients go in, and while the components vary from century to century, pit to pit, it's typically an assortment of shellfish, smoked meat, chicken, longaniza (sausage), and potatoes.

The last ingredient is where the curanto really shines. Chilotés are masters of the potato, cultivating hundreds of varieties on their islands. A proper curanto showcases the bounty and variety of these tubers with chapaleles (potato pancakes), milcaos (potato dumplings), and whole steam-roasted potatoes.

After loading ingredients into the cavity, the cook covers the hole with wild rhubarb leaves, damp sacks, and packed dirt. As the shellfish cook, the shells open and release juices that sizzle on the hot rocks and help steam the rest of the food, while also imparting a distinct smoky flavor. The formidable feast emerges several hours later, slicked in briny juices and meaty oils, offering a delicious glimpse into a more primal past.

A FRESH BLOOD GELATIN SNACK

ÑACHI • CHILE

Making ñachi means moving fast. As soon as butchers slaughter the animal (typically a pig, lamb, or goat), they immediately collect the hot blood and mix it with lemon juice, salt, cilantro, and smoked pepper. After a setting period, the blood coagulates with the lemon's acid and forms a solid jelly. Chileans typically cut the jelly into cubes and serve it with bread, but ñachi can also be eaten while still soup-like.

The word *ñachi* means "blood" in Mapudungun, an Indigenous Chilean language. Ñachi is a dish of Chile's Mapuche people that is now enjoyed countrywide. Blood has long been consumed in the region for its nutritional value, but experts caution that eating raw blood comes with a pathogen risk. For the initiated, a glass of wine or chicha (a spit-fermented drink) is the stomach sterilization method of choice.

How to try it

To find ñachi, head out to Chile's countryside. Blood in small doses is typically safe to ingest, but don't overindulge. Too much blood can cause hemochromatosis, an iron buildup that leads to liver, lung, and nervous system disorders.

BRIGHT YELLOW CHICKENS

GALLINAS CAMPESINAS • COLOMBIA

An hour north of Bogotá is the town of Ubaté, so renowned for its dairy industry that an imposing metal cow statue presides high above the main traffic circle. Visitors to Ubaté are typically drawn to the row of small specialty cheese shops. Others skip the cheese, heading straight for the gallinas campesinas and stuffed chicken necks.

On the outside, the most striking detail about gallinas campesinas is their color: The chickens are a bright, unnatural yellow. Looking at them, stacked on top of each other and lit beneath a heat lamp, you can't tell that each of these birds died an expectant mother, their necks swiftly broken when their eggs reached the embryo stage. They are a regional dish found only in Ubaté and are prized for their soft, luscious texture. The birds are slowly braised over a charcoal stove with aromatics and spices such as onions, thyme, and bay leaves. Right before being served, the whole bird is split down the middle, exposing the eggs and the tender flesh. The best-tasting eggs are very young. They're mostly yolk, have no shell, and make for decadent chicken broth–infused bites. Stuffed hen necks, or gallinas rellenas, are often found nearby: A chicken's head, severed from the base of the neck, is stuffed with a mixture of potatoes, rice, peas, and chicken blood. Sewn shut, the chicken-head sausage is roasted over an open flame. The flavor is so rich and earthy, the small portion is plenty for a single sitting.

How to try it

The Ubaté town square is surrounded by food stalls, one of which is La Chata, where you'll find the town's favorite chickens and stuffed chicken necks.

THE DISAPPEARING HOT SAUCE

AJÍ NEGRO • COLOMBIA

How to try it

Ají negro is in danger of disappearing from Amazonian communities. Colombian chefs, however, have taken an interest in the preservation of traditional recipes, and ají negro is making appearances on the menus of high-end restaurants like El Panóptico in Bogotá.

South American cooking is teeming with recipes that find a way around the poisonous nature of cassava, the starchy tuber that fills out the diet of nearly half a billion people. Ají negro, a hot sauce that requires several days to detoxify, is one example of such ingenuity.

Traditionally a product of northwest Amazonia, ají negro begins with cassava that's been peeled, washed, diced, and left to soak in a stream for several days.

The smoked chicken with cassava and ají negro at Bogotá restaurant El Panóptico.

A hollowed-out tree is the customary vessel for the next step, which involves pounding the cassava in the giant arboreal mortar until it becomes a pulp. Transferred to a woven sack, the pulp undergoes hours of twisting to extract the juice, which is then filtered to remove the starch and simmered for half a day until it becomes dark and thick. Only then can cooks use the starchless juice to make the hot sauce.

Recipes vary significantly between ethnic groups. Along with hot peppers, the sauce can include fish, meat, ants, vegetables, flowers, and seeds.

EASTER SOUP TOPPED WITH A BUFFET

FANESCA • ECUADOR

How to try it

When spring rolls around, Ecuadorian restaurants start competing for the brisk fanesca business, and the establishment that serves the best bowl is a source of infinite debate. In Quito, Casa Gangotena serves the general manager's great-grandmother's recipe in an upscale setting; a few blocks away, El Criollo is a family-run favorite. In Cuenca, the kiosks in El Centro market are a good place to sample a variety of bowls.

The ingredient list for fanesca, Ecuador's Easter potage, sounds more like an elaborate buffet spread than a recipe for soup—the garnishes alone (fried plantains, hard-boiled eggs, peppers, mini empanadas, and fresh cheese) cover all five food groups. It's no wonder this Holy Week indulgence takes two days to prepare.

Fanesca's thick base begins with salt cod cooked in milk and thickened with pumpkin seeds or peanuts. Then chefs add a dozen different beans, vegetables, and grains—one, some say, for each of Jesus's twelve apostles (Jesus himself is represented by the cod). Each fanesca maker has a unique veggie-and-legume lineup, but popular choices include peas, pumpkin, lupini beans, and hominy. When the soup's finished, it's time to add the garnishes, which float on the surface of the dense, sunset-colored soup.

Why the onslaught of ingredients? One story traces the tradition to the pre-Columbian Andes, where people celebrated a bountiful harvest by throwing the abundance into a single soup.

While fanesca is especially popular for lunch on Good Friday, Ecuadorians feast on the soup throughout Lent and Holy Week. After all, the memory has to last for the rest of the year.

Fanseca is the official Good Friday lunch of Ecuador.

INTELLIGENT DREAMING

GUAYUSA • ECUADOR

t's just before sunrise in the Ecuadorian rain forest. Members of the Kichwa community boil leaves from the guayusa (pronounced "gwai-yoo-sa") tree in a large metal pot. When the brew is ready, they sit around the fire, sip the tea, and discuss their dreams.

This is how the Indigenous tribe begins each day. They believe that guayusa facilitates dream interpretation, which is essential to decision-making in the community. One Kichwa legend tells of twins who went in search of a plant that would teach them how to dream. After they fell asleep, they dreamed of meeting their ancestors, who gifted them guayusa leaves. When they awoke, they were still clutching the plants in their hands. The Kichwa believe that dreams show a glimpse of the future, and they use their nocturnal visions to guide how they approach the day's work, especially hunting.

How to try it

Tips for lucid dreaming include reading fiction before bed, setting random alarms throughout the night, and waking up with your eyes closed. Guayusa may be the easiest entry point, available from tea distributors online.

The slightly bitter, caffeine-and-antioxidant-packed tea is now a popular natural stimulant. It's earned the nickname "the night watchman" for the calm wakefulness it provides, which allows for a second application: lucid dreaming. Those in the practice of cogent dreaming tap into the subconscious mind, effectively allowing them awareness in the realm of sleep. Some lucid dreamers claim guayusa guides them into a shallow sleep while still keeping them sharp enough to participate in their dreams.

SPIT-FERMENTED LIQUOR

MASATO • PERU

How to try it

Traditional, spit-made drinks can carry hepatitis B, but if you're brave and immunized, some small shops in Peru still carry it.

Masato, an ancient Amazonian drink made from boiled yuca, starts its fermentation process in the mouths of village women. They chew the tuber, which mixes with enzymes in their saliva that break the starch down into sugar, then spit the mash into a pitcher, where it ferments, over several days, into a fruity, sour-tasting drink with enormous nutritional value.

Their husbands, who typically skip lunch, rely on this carb-heavy, lightly alcoholic brew to power them through their workday. It's essential to their diet and livelihood, and so the ancient spit drink has become a kind of bargaining chip for the village wives, who dispense their masato strategically, depending on whether they are rewarding or punishing.

On its own, masato has a tart, almost vinegary taste, but it's often infused with warm spices such as cloves or cinnamon, then mixed with fresh fruit, which gives the drink a more refreshing, cocktail-like quality. Refusing a glass of masato is considered deeply offensive, so if you enter the jungle and find a circle of women munching on yuca, be prepared to partake in this intimate ritual.

FESTIVAL OF THE BABY BREAD

FESTIVAL DEL PAN WAWA • PERU

How to try it

The Festival of the Baby Bread is held annually, around the Day of the Dead, in Cusco's Plaza Túpac Amaru.

On the Day of the Dead, Peruvians believe the souls of their loved ones visit the Earth. To welcome them, they prepare pan wawa, bread baked into the shape of a swaddled baby. The loaves were originally presented as gifts at the tombs of children, but now the bread is enjoyed by all ages, both living and dead.

At Cusco's annual Festival of the Baby Bread, a titanic toddler is constructed by some of the city's best bakers. In 2012, 22 bakers joined forces in an attempt to set the record for the largest ever made: They built a pan wawa 72 feet long and 26 feet wide (22 x 8 m).

How the Colombian Government Killed Spit-Fermented Drinks

Outside the Amazon, South American spit-fermented libations go by the name chicha.

Colombian chicha had been ritually consumed by the pre-Columbian Muisca people since 3000 BCE. When the Spanish colonists arrived in 1499, the mouth-made brew grew popular among the working classes. By the 19th century, Bogotá alone had more than 800 chicherías—bars dedicated to the cheap brew—whose primary clientele were artisans, farmers, and those whose schedules didn't adhere to typical work hours. Patrons came to socialize over dice and cards, eat a meal, buy groceries, or slip into a room to sleep. Chicherías were deeply communal, with one large bowl of chicha generally passed among tablemates.

Between the years 1910 and 1920, Colombians were suffering from extreme poverty, and Colombian politicians found a scapegoat in chicha. Chicherías came under fire as hotbeds of public disorder and the sole impediment to Colombia's rise as an industrialized economy. The bulk of Colombia's poor were Indigenous people, who were considered a drag on progress. Chicha—with its ancient heritage, association with unstructured days, and production method of chewing and spitting—made a convenient symbol for the country's problems.

But chicherías, inextricable from the daily lives of the lower classes, were too popular to eradicate neatly. The government needed more muscle, so they turned to German immigrant Leo Kopp and his new beer operation, Bavaria Brewery. Founded in 1889, Bavaria Brewery quickly established dominance in the Colombian beer market, positioning itself as the spiritual opposite of chicha and chicherías. The brewery buildings were industrial and modern, production was efficient, and the beer was served in individual, sterilized glass bottles. To the Colombian government, Bavaria Brewery represented European progress—a model they badly wanted to emulate.

For thousands of years, chicha has been brewed over an open fire.

Colombia's bourgeoisie latched on to Bavaria, but most Colombians didn't have cash to burn on beer. Chicherías remained everywhere, but the Colombian government did not relent. Prominent doctors, likely at the behest of politicians, visited poor neighborhoods, pronouncing the drink "unhygienic" and a hazard to the country's well-being. They even invented an illness—"chichism"—which purportedly made its sufferers insane. (Many modern, unbribed doctors agree that chicha's alcohol content and freshness would render most versions safe to drink.)

Bavaria doubled down on the government's efforts, giving its beer shameless names such as "No Mas Chicha," "Consum Bier," and "Hygienic," alongside images of robust, healthy-looking ladies and children happily drinking beer. Meanwhile, the government launched an aggressive propaganda campaign. "Chicha begets crime," read one political poster, along with a filthy hand clutching a bloody knife. "The jails are filled with people who drink chicha," read another, which featured a nun weeping over a man peering out from behind bars. The government also hiked taxes and enacted strict, arbitrary rules for chicherías. Unable to comply, establishments shuttered or moved underground.

With chicha already on life support, the plug was abruptly pulled on April 9, 1948, when Jorge Eliécer Gaitán, a liberal presidential candidate, was murdered on a Bogotá street. Gaitán was widely regarded by the working class as the country's populist savior, and his death set off a ten-year period of brutal unrest known now simply as La Violencia.

While bloody riots swept through the city, President Ospina Pérez signed a law declaring that all fermented beverages had to be industrially produced in individual glass containers—a de facto ban on the centuries-old tradition.

THE SALT PANS OF MARAS

SALINAS DE MARAS • PERU

Perched 3,000 feet (914 m) high in the Andes, the salt in this intricate network of ponds once belonged to the sea. Twenty-five million years ago, the mountains began their rise, pushing the seabed up and locking stores of salt into the rocks.

Salinas de Maras, as the mines are known locally, were built by the Chanapata people (200–900 CE), who once ruled the entire Cusco valley. Over the centuries, nearly 5,000 ponds have been added to the mines, etched into terraces that descend the mountain like a patchwork of steps.

The salty abundance, which floods the ponds from above, is carried by a natural spring, warm and viscous with minerals. Each pool is tended by sight and feel. A keeper opens a notch in the side of the pool's wall, letting in the stream, then closes the notch when it's adequately full. Evaporation does the rest. When the pool is crusted a bright white, the salt crystals are ready to be scraped up with wooden batons and left to dry in baskets.

Like its popular counterpart from the Himalayas, salt from Maras is rich in minerals, which lends it a faint pink hue. Producers allege that it is also healthier, packed with minerals such as magnesium and calcium.

Any member of the community is eligible to own a salt pool, and this inclusive policy has turned the mines into a place where locals gather and work together, all while peppering their incomes with . . . salt.

How to try it

Maras is located about 25 miles (40 km) north of Cusco. While it's a common stop on Sacred Valley big bus tours, you can get there on a colectivo (local bus) headed to Urubamba. At the colectivo station on Avenida Grau in Cusco, tell the driver you're getting off in Maras. Once there, hire a taxi to take you the last ten minutes to the salt mines.

This terraced salt mine contains nearly 5,000 ponds.

BIG-ASS ANTS

SIQUI SAPA • PERU

Large as a cockroach and curvy as a pinup, the siqui sapa (literally "big butt" in the Quechua language) are coveted by gourmands around the world—but they're not easy to procure.

The big-butt ants that make for good eating are dominated by the females. They live up to 20 feet (6 m) underground and are protected by a rigid caste system. Worker ants build the anthill; soldier ants defend it. The princesses, as the females are known, are tasked solely with reproduction. After mating with prince ants in a ritual called chamuscada, a term that refers to passion, the males die and the princesses fly off to each start a new anthill where they'll become queen.

The mating season, October to November, is the only time to harvest siqui sapa. If hunters can move swiftly enough to get past the soldier ants that attack with bites that draw blood, they will be rewarded with females that fetch $15 a pound (0.45 kg) during peak season and up to $40 when supplies are scarce.

In South America, the bugs are soaked in salted water, roasted, and eaten like peanuts. At first, the flavor is reminiscent of pork rinds, but it quickly evolves into something earthier and more bitter. They are sometimes compared to caviar, which seems an unlikely match until you realize their "butts" are so well endowed because they're swollen with eggs.

How to try it

You can find big-butt ants in markets in the Amazon region of Peru. Vendors in the main square in the city of Tarapoto sell small bags of the ants for just a few soles.

ICE-CREAM BEAN

INGA EDULIS • PERU

Money may not grow on trees, but in tropical swaths of Central and South America, you can find king-size candy bars dropping from tree branches.

A foot-long confection produced by inga trees, ice-cream beans are actually legumes. Split open the pod and you'll find seeds wrapped in white fluff that looks like cotton candy and tastes like vanilla ice cream. Eat the fluff, spit out the seed, and within a year it's likely a new tree will stand where you were snacking.

As far as vending machines go, inga trees are generous. They grow with velocity and ease up to 60 feet (18 m) and are commonly used as shade for other crops. Farmers have found pods that hold an impressive 6 feet (2 m) of fluff.

In countries such as Peru, Ecuador, and Colombia, locals eat ice-cream beans raw, as do monkeys, birds, and other animals that enjoy the treat. But only humans can roast the otherwise inedible seeds as a snack and mix ice-cream beans into chocolate, coffee, or cream.

How to try it

Pick up some inga edulis at Mercado N° 1 de Surquillo in Lima, a market full of fruit vendors. Or, if you're feeling ambitious, you can purchase a starter plant online for $100.

WE WERE EATING HERE FIRST
The Inca Empire

The Incas (1438–1533 CE) developed the most sophisticated food supply chain in pre-Columbian history, feeding millions of subjects across steep, mountainous terrain that ran along the western coast of South America. Here's how they did it.

TERRACED FARMING

The Andes mountain range lay at the heart of the Inca Empire. The largely vegetarian, agriculture-focused kingdom had to adapt to a multitude of extreme climates. They cut flat terraces into the Andes, working from the valley upward, and built stone retaining walls around each field, which absorbed the sun's heat during the day and released it at night, keeping crops from freezing at high elevation.

LABOR FORCE

The Incas built cisterns and irrigation systems that collected rainwater and melting glacial ice, to carry it through the fields and down the mountains. Their plots were fertilized with guano (seabird poop), so prized that anyone caught killing a guano-producing bird was sentenced to death.

The Incas' three staple crops were potatoes, corn, and quinoa, each developed for resiliency at specific elevations ranging from sea level to 14,000 feet (4,267 m). Between these elevations, farmers traded crops with one another and also grew a rotating variety of produce to hedge their bets against failure each season.

QULLQAS (COLLCAS)

The Incas prioritized food security and deliberately grew excess crops, to store in tens of thousands of qullqas, or storehouses.

Qullqas were built near every city, farm, and crop-producing estate. For the best ventilation, qullqas were mostly built on the sides of hills, where wind would keep the temperature cool and the moisture low. Channels below the buildings acted as drainage canals, whisking away moisture and minimizing rot. Fresh crops could last up to two years; freeze-dried products lasted four.

Circular qullqas stored corn and rectangular qullqas stored potatoes. Both crops were held in ceramic pots to deter rodents. Often a layer of herbs, straw, or gravel was laid as the storehouse's foundation, which allowed air to circulate and kept worms out.

Inventory of the qullqas was kept by state officials using a quipu, an accounting device of colored strings and knots.

THE ROYAL HIGHWAY

The Incan road system included two major north-south roads with many offshoots, extending 25,000 miles (40,234 km), known as the Royal Highway. Ordinary civilians were not allowed to use the road—it was only for the transportation of goods. Most everything was carried by herds of llamas and alpacas, whose nimble feet could handle steep mountainous terrain.

LABOR FORCE

Chaski (or chasqui) were the most skilled messengers of the Inca Empire. Chosen as boys, the chaski trained in speed and endurance, running at grueling altitudes, which helped strengthen their lungs and splay their feet. The chaskis transported important messages and perishable foods, such as fish and fruit, between cities as fast as possible using a relay system. They ran at top speed between refueling stations called tampus, where they would blow on a conch shell trumpet to alert the next runner who would sprint to receive the package and run the next leg. If the emperor in Cusco had a desire for fresh seafood, it could be run from the coast, 250 miles (402 km) away, in about two days.

THE INCAN ROAD SYSTEM included two major north-south roads with many offshoots, extending 25,000 miles (40,234 km), together called the Royal Highway.

INCAN ROAD

QULLQAS

TERRACED FARMING

Panama City

San Cristobal

Medellin

Cali

Bogota

COLOMBIA

Quito

ECUADOR

Guayaquil

Tumbes

Sechura

Cajamarca

Cruzeiro do Sul

PERU

Jauja

Lima

Cusco

Riberalt

Vilcas Huaman

Chala

La Paz

Arequipa

B

Iquique

San Pedro de Atacama

CHILE

Copiapo

Santiago

Mendoza

Concepcion

Instead of bread and wine, Jesus and his disciples ate guinea pig and chicha.

A RODENT STARS IN CATHOLIC CONVERSION ART

GUINEA PIG LAST SUPPER • PERU

How to try it

The Cusco Cathedral is located in the Plaza de Armas in the center of town. Entrance costs 25 soles (about $8) and includes an audio guide.

Da Vinci's *Last Supper* displayed a classic menu of unleavened bread and wine—but in the Cusco Cathedral, guinea pig is the centerpiece.

The Last Supper, as painted by Marcos Zapata, in 1753, is an obvious standout among the massive collection of art and archaeological relics housed in the basilica. Lying paws-up on a golden serving tray, the cooked guinea pig sits right in front of Jesus. Instead of wine on the table, the disciples are drinking chicha, the local Peruvian libation.

It's surprising that this painting was tolerated by the Catholic Church, especially during the time of the Inquisition, but Zapata was a big deal in his day—as were guinea pigs. It is possible church officials felt that the painting, featuring two hometown heroes, could be pardoned as a populist conversion technique. Whatever the reasoning, his painting was hung in the newly built Cusco Cathedral.

Today, cuy, as Peruvians call the domesticated rodent, is typically reserved for festivals and holidays, when the guinea pig is baked, fried, or spit-roasted. Before the arrival of cattle, eating cuy was synonymous with eating meat, and the practice is still going strong. Peruvians consume 65 million guinea pigs a year, and the furry critters have become something of a cultural icon.

Mitterand's Last Supper

A last meal is a final, impossible attempt at pleasure and comfort before being swept away by certain death. It demands a deep scrutiny of desires, and the underlying question: What and how much should a person consume when there is literally no tomorrow?

In December 1995, former French president François Mitterrand knew he was about to die. He had been battling prostate cancer for years, a fact that he and his doctors hid for the majority of his presidency. When faced with the reality and urgency of his condition, Mitterrand chose to hold a feast for 30 people on New Year's Eve. He was so weak, he had to be carried to his chair where he began the voracious but anguished consumption of three dozen Marennes oysters, foie gras, crusty bread, capon (a castrated rooster bred for fatness), and enough wine to keep him occupied for four hours. The grand finale came as a surprise—not for Mitterrand, but for his guests. A man appeared holding a tray of tiny songbirds

called ortolans, a dish that was once a rite of passage for macabre gourmands and was now illegal (and prohibitively expensive) to consume in France.

The pale brown, palm-size birds are caught in southwest France and kept in pitch dark, which disorients them and compels the birds to gorge themselves until their tiny bodies stretch like balloons (Roman emperors used to blind them to achieve the same effect). The swollen creatures are then drowned in Armagnac, a French brandy that acts as a marinade, roasted for exactly eight minutes, then plucked.

While not all of Mitterrand's guests consented to eat an ortolan, some did. The modest way to consume the bird is with a cloth over your head, shielding the shameful act from view. The bird goes feet first into the diner's mouth, the head is bitten off, and the ortolan is consumed whole: a sodden mouthful of tiny bones and guts and liquor. On this night, Mitterrand ate two. He passed away eight days later.

THE LENT-APPROVED AQUATIC RODENT

CAPYBARA • VENEZUELA

In the 18th century, local clergy in Venezuela wrote to the Vatican with a special request. They had discovered a local animal that lived in water, had webbed feet, and resembled a fish. With Lent and Holy Week approaching, they asked the Vatican to grant the animal the status of fish, so they might eat it during the meat-free religious holiday. By letter, the Catholic Church agreed, and the capybara—the largest living rodent in the world—became the favorite "fish" of Venezuelan Lent.

Locals quickly developed a taste for the giant aquatic rodent. The demand grew to a fever pitch, and illegal poaching threatened to wipe out the population. With the help of government regulation and speedy reproduction, capybaras are no longer endangered, but there is still a robust black market trade. Capybara is considered an essential holiday extravagance, and Venezuelans happily shell out twice the amount they pay for beef.

The flavor, locals say, is more fish than meat because capybaras survive mostly on aquatic grasses. Capybara is almost always dried, salted, and shredded. The prepared "fish" goes into everything from soup to casseroles to empanadas.

How to try it

Venezuela's national dish is pabellón criollo: shredded beef, rice, black beans, and fried plantains. During Lent, capybara often replaces the beef. In Caracas, try traditional Venezuelan restaurants such as La Cocina de Francy and La Gorda.

Glorious Lent Cheating

I n 1522, Zurich pastor Ulrich Zwingli was arrested for attending a sausage dinner during the Lenten fast. To be clear, the pastor had not actually eaten any sausage—simply witnessing the act was crime enough.

Zwingli defended his behavior by citing the Bible, which never actually prohibits meat during Lent. Meat fasting was a 4th-century invention of the Catholic Church, a tradition with a long and elaborate history of loopholes, fishy interpretations, and freewheeling bishops. Here are some Catholic Church–sanctioned meat alternatives that keep the faithful from being arrested or shamed.

MOCK EGG
In the Middle Ages, all animal products including dairy were forbidden during Lent. On these days, chefs had to get creative, channeling the power of almonds to bind pastry, thicken sauces, and make an eerie approximation of a hard-boiled egg. A 1430 recipe book instructed chefs to fill an empty chicken's egg with a mixture of almond-milk-based jelly and a crunchy almond center, dyed yellow with saffron and ginger. By most accounts they were nearly inedible.

DOLPHINS
The medieval German word for dolphin is merswin, or "pig of the ocean." The term was likely a way to excuse the fact that dolphins are warm-blooded, like God himself, and therefore probably prohibited on

days of meat abstinence. But they came from the sea, so for a while, they were Lent-approved. Dolphin sausages were a trendy choice year-round for posh British families, as were dolphin roasts.

BARNACLE GEESE
This black-and-white goose, which breeds above the arctic circle and migrates to Europe for the winter, confused bird-watchers of the 13th century, who never saw a nest. Unaware of seasonal migration, they hatched a theory that the geese were born not from eggs but from barnacles that fell into the ocean off driftwood or rocks. And a goose that hatched in the ocean? Well, that was definitely a fish.

ALLIGATOR
In New Orleans, where alligator is a popular protein, the Catholic

community hoped they could still enjoy their gator sausage, gumbo, and jambalaya during the Lenten fast. To be sure, in 2010 a parishioner wrote to the archbishop of New Orleans, who assured them: "God has created a magnificent creature that is important to the state of Louisiana, and it is considered seafood."

BEAVER
When the Europeans arrived in North America, two of their primary objectives were to collect as many beaver pelts as possible and to convert the local population to Catholicism. The locals liked to eat the beaver meat, which was convenient for the Europeans, who only cared for the skin. In a colonialist two-for-one, the 17th-century bishop of Quebec granted Lent keepers permission to eat

the semiaquatic rodent, hereby a fish, to make the religious holiday more accommodating to new converts. Some modern-day Missourians still eat beaver as a meat substitute.

CORNED BEEF
In Ireland and Irish-heavy parts of America, when Saint Patrick's Day falls during Lent, certain exceptions must be made. The traditional meal of corned beef is difficult to reclassify, as cows spend so little time in the ocean. But a benevolent God, many countrymen argue, would never dream of keeping the Irish from their national celebration meal, and the archbishop of Ireland agrees. Depending on how the calendar falls, sometimes beef is allowed during the meatless fast.

Antarctica

When explorer Ernest Shackleton's crew ventured across Antarctica in the early 1900s, they dined on old army biscuits soaked with seawater and meat-and-fat energy bars (page 246). Today, an Antarctic researcher can tuck into seared scallops with black pudding at the British Rothera Research Station, snag some nagashi somen (page 133) at Japan's Shōwa Station, or grab a Crown Royal cocktail at the American Amundsen-Scott South Pole Station.

With approximately 4,400 summer residents and 1,100 winter residents, representing 31 countries and spread across 40 active permanent research stations, Antarctica is an increasingly busy place. And for the researchers scattered across the continent, from geologists at India's Maitri Station to ecologists at Italy's Zucchelli Station, food is a point of pride—and a way to break the monotony of life at an icebound research facility.

Because most stations get their entire supply of "freshies" only once a year (supplemented by a few occasional greenhouse veggies), creative and careful supply management is a must for Antarctic chefs. For example, by using the age-old technique of oiling the shells of fresh eggs, creating a protective barrier to contamination, chefs can make their precious supply last all year.

Lucky stations are quite close to one another, just a brisk walk away. At the Chilean Villa Las Estrellas base and craving Chinese food? Throw on a parka and dash over to China's Great Wall Station for the best peppery chicken on the continent.

BASE STATION *Cuisine*

1 ZUCCHELLI STATION • ITALY

At Zucchelli Station, time is measured not in weeks, but in pizzas. Antarctica is a land without day or night, so the passage of time becomes difficult to track. But at Zucchelli, you know it's Saturday when it's pizza day. So don't be surprised when a researcher tells you they've been stationed at Zucchelli for "seven pizzas."

2 MCMURDO STATION'S SOUTHERN EXPOSURE BAR • UNITED STATES

For the best party on Antarctica, join the people who keep McMurdo Station running at Southern Exposure. A bar with an interior indistinguishable from that of a Wisconsin dive, this watering hole is a mixing pot of carpenters, ice tractor drivers, and scientists who need a drink after a long, cold day. Smoking is allowed here, since stepping outside for a cigarette isn't recommended.

3 GREAT WALL STATION • CHINA

The Chinese Great Wall Station has a reputation for incredible food, so much so that researchers from other stations will gear up and venture out across the ice just to eat there. Just a short walk (less than a mile!) or snowmobile ride from the Argentinian, Brazilian, Chilean, Polish, Russian, South Korean, Uruguayan, and other Chinese stations, the Great Wall outpost has something no other station can boast: a team of culinary professors and students who have been returning for years to cook for the researchers posted there—and a hydroponic greenhouse that provides the Chinese chefs with fresh vegetables

China's Great Wall Station boasts a hydroponic greenhouse.

long after the other stations have run out.

4 CONCORDIA STATION EUROPEAN UNION

Run by Italian and French agencies, Concordia Station has a serious culinary reputation to uphold. While its researchers are testing Martian travel conditions, its chef is busy making foie gras, Yorkshire

pudding, and chicken Parmesan, all served with a side of French wine. To become the chef at Concordia Station, candidates enter a lottery. Incredible chefs from around the world apply, and the winner gets the chance to go work day and night, with limited ingredients, in the most remote place on the planet. Of course, few other chefs can claim that Lonely Planet called

Concordia Station

their food the best cuisine on an entire continent.

5 SHŌWA STATION • JAPAN

At the Japanese Shōwa Station, the meal marking the end of an expedition is often held outdoors. What better meal to serve than nagashi somen, or cold noodles served in flowing water? Normally plucked with chopsticks as they flow by in a bamboo water slide, in Antarctica the noodles are served flowing through a channel cut right into the ice. Picture an Olympic luge track, only with noodles in place of athletes. It wasn't the only inventive food served at Shōwa Station. Akuma no onigiri, or "devil's rice balls," a mixture of edible algae, fried tempura batter, and rice, was invented by the station's chef before becoming a popular convenience store snack back in Japan.

6 VILLA LAS ESTRELLAS • CHILE

One of the stations built closest to the tip of South America, Villa Las Estrellas is part research station, part military base, and part town. It's the largest of two civilian settlements on Antarctica and home to most of the very few children who live on the continent. Like most other kids, the 21 youngsters who live with their families at Villa Las Estrellas go to school, play games, and enjoy the kid-friendly meals of mashed potatoes, chicken, and Fanta soda that the chef offers up.

7 DAVIS STATION • AUSTRALIA

Each person at Australia's Davis Station is allocated more than a pound of Vegemite per year. It may be just a tad more than is needed; visiting researchers often leave with an extra jar of the thick, salty, dark brown spread in their luggage.

8 ROTHERA RESEARCH STATION UNITED KINGDOM

On Saturday evenings, white tablecloths and candles elevate the normally mundane dining room at Rothera Research Station. Wine, bread baskets, and cheese plates are part of the impressive food offered by the chef. Dinner can stretch up to 12 courses and includes dishes such as seared scallops with black pudding and apple. As the kitchen pantry starts to thin out over the year, the chef haggles with other stations, trading British staples for a broader range of ingredients, such as antelope meat from the South Africans or peanut butter from the Americans.

9 HENRYK ARCTOWSKI STATION POLAND

Arctowski Station prides itself on serving a traditional Polish Easter breakfast, complete with a pot of schmaltz (rendered chicken fat), bread, cold cuts, plates of sausages (including wurst-like links and blood sausages), head cheese, mustard, and borscht and featuring the exchange of elaborately decorated pisanka eggs.

10 MAITRI STATION • INDIA

Maitri's 24/7 convenience store, well stocked with sweet and salty snacks (including namkeen, papads, and other goodies from famous Indian snack manufacturer Haldiram), means researchers can satisfy their cravings at any hour of the day. No money is required—it's all on the house.

11 JANG BOGO STATION SOUTH KOREA

The brand-new Jang Bogo Station came with hot-plate stations ready to serve up piping-hot Korean pork and BBQ prawns. International researchers with a high tolerance for spicy food preferred.

12 VERNADSKY STATION · UKRAINE

Originally the British Faraday Station, this research base was taken over by Ukraine in 1996. The Ukrainians renamed it Vernadsky (in honor of one of that country's most distinguished scientists), redecorated the station's bar, and made three-dollar vodka the signature drink.

ACKNOWLEDGMENTS

Bringing this book to life required incredible orchestration of teamwork and wizardry. Luckily, we were blessed with a highly skilled team of magicians at Workman Publishing, who helped us transform a concept about wonder and food into a big, beautiful book. Thank you to Suzie Bolotin, Maisie Tivnan, Janet Vicario, and Dan Reynolds for their unwavering support, enthusiasm, and wisdom. For introducing this book to the world, we are thankful to the inimitable marketing team of Rebecca Carlisle, Chloe Puton, and Moira Kerrigan. Many thanks as well to the keen eyes and creative minds of Amanda Hong, Kate Karol, Barbara Peragine, Claire McKean, Anne Kerman, Sophia Reith, Aaron Clendening, Doug Wolff, Sun Robinson-Smith, Analucia Zepeda, Eric Wiley, Alan Berry Rhys, and Rachel Krohn.

Gastro Obscura is the creation of countless talented and curious people, many of whom we get to call colleagues. Thank you to Alex Mayyasi, Sam O'Brien, Anne Ewbank, and Rachel Rummel, whose fingerprints are on every page of this book. To the unflappable Marc Haeringer, who kept this project on a years-long tightrope: You are the unsung hero of all Atlas Obscura books.

We are grateful to everyone at Atlas Obscura who tracked down a remarkable food and contributed to this book: Reina Gattuso, Leigh Chavez Bush, Rohini Chaki, Abbey Perreault, Luke Fater, Natasha Frost, Kerry Wolfe, Eric Grundhauser, Meg Neal, Cara Giaimo, Matt Taub, Paula Mejia, Josh Foer, Samir Patel, Sarah Laskow, Vittoria Traverso, Ike Allen, Michael Inscoe, Abi Inman, Samantha Chong, Larissa Hayden, Michael Harshman, Anika Burgess, David Plotz, Ella Morton, Tyler Cole, Tao Tao Holmes, and Sommer Mathis. To Lisa Gross, Alexa Harrison, and Kit Sudol: Thank you for being Gastro Obscura's champions.

Most important, this book would not be possible without the writers, users, and contributors who make Atlas Obscura the treasure trove it is. We are inspired each day by what you find and share with us.

CECILY: Dylan, your magnetic energy, creativity, and genuine sense of wonder has left a huge stamp on my brain and heart: Thank you for being our inexhaustible buoy. Marc, thank you for keeping me sane and fed, for supporting me when I needed it most, and for being simply the best; know that I will forever think of this book as our child. Alex, thank you for your tenacious vision and care, your steady hand, and your emergency supply of squid ink. Thank you to Sam for the heroic guidance, to Rachel for throwing me perfect sentences like alley-oops, and to Anne, who pulls astonishing things from the internet like no one I've ever met. Thank you also to Ella for showing me the way. Finally, thank you, Read, for patiently listening to all my obscure food knowledge for the last two years and remaining married to me.

DYLAN: Like *Atlas Obscura* that came before it, this book is the product of many people. First and foremost the users and contributors of Atlas Obscura and Gastro Obscura: It is your unending curiosity that inspires us to keep exploring the world. To Reina Gattuso, Leigh Chavez Bush, Rohini Chaki, Abbey Perreault, Luke Fater, Natasha Frost, Paula Mejia, and many more, you are all immensely talented writers and editors, and you have shared culinary wonders with us that I could scarcely have imagined. We wouldn't have been able to serve this dish without Rachel Rummel, Annie Ewbank, Sam O'Brien, and Alex Mayyasi—you are all head chefs of this restaurant, and your dedication to making *Gastro Obscura* into something great shines through this book. Sommer Mathis and Lisa Gross, thank you both for your sage advice and for help guiding this project. Josh Foer, none of this would exist without you. Marc Haeringer, you are everyone's rock. To everyone at Workman: Susan, Dan, Maisie, Rebecca, Janet, thank you for taking a chance on us in the first place and for doing it again with *Gastro*. Saving the best for last: Cecily, you bring joy, delight, and brilliance to all that you do, and this book is the epitome of that generous spirit. I count myself extremely lucky to have my name on a book next to yours.

Thank you to the following writers who wrote entries for *Gastro Obscura*: Tatiana Harkiolakis, Susan van Allen, James Rudd, Susie Armitage, Jared Rydelek, Awanthi Vardaraj, Sarah Corsa, James Jeffrey, Shannon Thomson, Elphas Ngugi, Amanda Leigh Lichtenstein, Ximena Larkin, Tony Dunnell, Zoe Baillageon, Leah Feiger, Richard Collett, Mariellen Ward, Tiffany Ammerman, Jennifer Walker, Jennifer Nalewicki, Megan Iacobini de Fazio, Faith Roswell, Jacob Wallace, and Karissa Chen.

We are grateful to our entire community of users, in particular: AaronNetsky, Max Cortesi, mjespuiva, sarahcorsa, Rob, trevorxtravesty, Rachel, giraffe1541, capemarsh, jessemiers, Annetta Black, lewblank, cnkollbocker, Dr Alan P Newman, hovpl, Dampo, hrnick, Tawsam, moroccanzest, ewayte, meganjamer, canuck, Gastropod, hfritzmartinez, CPilgrim, Megan8777, GizzysMama, Leslie McIntyre, Michelle Enemark, e1savage, rebeccaclara, Dana Stabenow, and Chris Kudrich.

The following stories were first published on Gastro Obscura's website, then adapted for the book. We are immensely grateful to these talented writers.

EUROPE:
- "The Club Devoted to Celebrating Great Britain's Great Puddings" by Lottie Gross
- "How a Special Diet Kept the Knights Templar Fighting Fit" by Natasha Frost
- "The Worst Freelance Gig in History Was Being the Village Sin Eater" by Natalie Zarrelli
- "Inside the World's Only Sourdough Library" by Anne Ewbank

- "Remembering When Runners Drank Champagne as an Energy Drink" by Katherine Alex Beaven
- "The Strange History of Royals Testing Food for Poison with Unicorn Horn" by Anne Ewbank
- One of Florence's Wine Windows Is Open Once More" by Lisa Harvey
- "Gladiator Diets Were Carb-Heavy, Fattening, and Mostly Vegetarian" by Ryleigh Nucilli
- "The Ancient Walled Gardens Designed to Nurture a Single Citrus Tree" by Kristan Lawson
- "When the Soviet Union Paid Pepsi in Warships" by Anne Ewbank
- "Why the World's Greatest Toasts Happen in Georgia" by Pesha Magid
- "The Brief, Wondrous, High-Flying Era of Zeppelin Dining" by Natasha Frost
- "On Restaurant Day in Helsinki, Anyone Can Open an Eatery, Anywhere" by Karen Burshtein
- "A Banana Grows in Iceland" by Kasper Friis

ASIA:
- "America's Pistachio Industry Came from a Single Seed" by Anne Ewbank
- "How Bootleg Fast Food Conquered Iran" by Sarra Sedghi
- "The Prickly Symbolism of Cactus Fruit in Israel and Palestine" by Miriam Berger
- "For Thousands of Years, People Have Been Obsessed with Fat-Tailed Sheep" by Anne Ewbank
- "The Festival Where Millions of Women Prepare a Feast for a Goddess" by Jessica Gingrich
- "How Mumbai's Dabbawalas Deliver 200,000 Homemade Meals a Day" by Akanksha Singh
- "The Restaurant Reconstructing Recipes That Died with the Ottoman Empire" by Jen Rose Smith
- "The Chinese City Famous for Eggs with Two Yolks" by Anne Ewbank
- "The Mandatory Canteens of Communist China" by Hunter Lu
- "At Sea on Taiwan's Last Fire-Fishing Boats" by Leslie Nguyen-Okwu
- "The Special Stew at the Heart of Sumo Wrestling" by Natasha Frost
- "The Hidden History of the Nutmeg Island That Was Traded for Manhattan" by Mark Hay
- "How Building Churches out of Egg Whites Transformed Filipino Desserts" by Richard Collett

AFRICA:
- "The Egyptian Egg Ovens Considered More Wondrous Than the Pyramids" by Vittoria Traverso
- "In 1930s Tunisia, French Doctors Feared a 'Tea Craze' Would Destroy Society" by Nina Studer
- "The Language Used Only by Lake Kivu's Fishermen" by Leah Feiger
- "To Revive This Royal Music, Ugandans Had to Grow New Instruments" by Natalia Jidovanu

OCEANIA:
- "After Decades of Being Ignored, a Nut from 20-Pound Pine Cones Is Back on Australian Menus" by Laura Kiniry

- "The Curious Case of August Engelhardt, Leader of a Coconut-Obsessed Cult" by Zoë Bernard
- "Australia's Growing Camel Meat Trade Reveals a Hidden History of Early Muslim Migrants" by Reina Gattuso
- "A Japanese Sculptor's Tribute to Wild Rice Covers an Australian Floodplain" by Selena Hoy
- "When the Māori First Settled New Zealand, They Hunted Flightless, 500-Pound Birds" by Anne Ewbank
- "The Livestock Living at the End of the World" by Abbey Perreault

CANADA:
- "The Canadian Towns That Icelanders Visit for a Taste of Their Past" by Karen Burshtein
- "Meet the 81-Year-Old Greek-Canadian Inventor of the Hawaiian Pizza" by Dan Nosowitz

USA:
- "Remembering 'Brownie Mary,' San Francisco's Marijuana Pioneer" by Anne Ewbank
- "Indigenous Cuisine Is Being Served in the Back of a Berkeley Bookstore" by Richard Foss
- "How Alaska's Roadkill Gets a Second Life as Dinner" by Mark Hay
- "Americans Have Planted So Much Corn That It's Changing the Weather" by Eric J. Wallace
- "When Eating Crow Was an American Food Trend" by Anne Ewbank
- "The Burmese Restaurant at the Heart of 'Chindianapolis'" by Mar Nwe Aye and Charlotte Chadwick
- "America's First Butter Sculptor Was an Artist and a Celebrity" by Cara Giaimo
- "How a Tiny Wisconsin Island Became the World's Biggest Consumer of Bitters" by Leigh Kunkel
- "The Mysterious Bounty of Mobile Bay's Midnight Jubilees" by Anna Marlis Burgard
- "The Underground Kitchen That Funded the Civil Rights Movement" by Jessica Gingrich
- "Competitive Eating Was Even More Gluttonous and Disgusting in the 17th Century" by Eric Grundhauser
- "Drink Up at the Home-Museum Displaying over 10,000 Beer Steins" by Eric J. Wallace
- "The Family That's Sold New York Mock Meats for Decades" by Priya Krishna
- "The Lost Lingo of New York City's Soda Jerks" by Natasha Frost
- "The Scholar Mapping America's Forgotten Feminist Restaurants" by Reina Gattuso
- "The 'Croos' That Haul 50-Pound Packs to Feed Hungry Hikers" by Courtney Hollands

LATIN AMERICA
- "Like Avocados? Thank This Giant Extinct Sloth" by Anne Ewbank
- "Inside a Brazilian Chapel Made out of Wine" by Danielle Bauter
- "How a Brewer and the Government Killed Colombia's Ancestral Drink" by Lauren Evans

COVER CREDITS

Front Cover Credits (In Clockwise Order): (Pigeon Houses) mauritius images GmbH/Alamy Images; (Donut) Elena Milenova/Alamy Images; (Filipina Dancer) Mariano Sayno/Moment/Getty Images; (Black-headed Gull) Nature Photographers Ltd/Alamy Images; (Bird Pie) WHAT.DONNA.LIKES/Atlas Obscura; (Australian Emu) Anan Kaewkhammul/Alamy Images; (Bunya Pine Cone) downunder/Alamy Images; (The Ghan Passenger Train) MMphotos/Alamy Images; (Steaks with Pitchfork) Layne Kennedy/Corbis NX/Getty Images; (Goldfish Candy "Amezaiku") Ayumi H/Shutterstock.

Back Cover Credits (In Clockwise Order): (Honey) RTimages/Alamy Images; (Yakut Woman) Tatiana Gasich/Shutterstock; (Dhow Boat) Robert Harding/Alamy Images; (Breakfast Sandwich) Aaron Bastin/Alamy Stock Photo; (Ukadiche Modak) RBB/Moment/Getty Images; (Antique Print) Antiqua Print Gallery/Alamy Images; (Horse Rider) ZUMA Press, Inc./Alamy Images; (Bottle Cap) Jpbarrass at English Wikipedia/Public domain.

EUROPE

AGE fotostock america, Inc: Picture-Alliance/dpa p. 79 (right). **Alamy:** Mauricio Abreu p. 32 (top); ACORN 1 p. 23 (top); agefotostock 76 (top); Agencja Fotograficzna Caro p. 48 (bottom); ams images p. 42 (top); Yi Ci Ang p. 52 (top); Arco Images GmbH p. 67 (bottom right and top); Chronicle p. 66 (bottom left); COMPAGNON Bruno/SAGAPHOTO.COM p. 72; Contraband Collection p. 21 (top); Guy Corbishley p. 61 (left); Luis Dafos p. 50 (top); Design Pics Inc p. 74 (top); Bertie Ditch p. 16 (top); Anton Eine p. 45; David R. Frazier Photolibrary, Inc. p. 44 (bottom); Nick Gammon p. 16 (bottom); Clive Helm p. 20; L A Heusinkveld p. 35; imageBROKER pp. 25, 57 (bottom); INTERFOTO p. 56 (bottom left & bottom right); ITAR-TASS News Agency p. 62 (top); Andrey Khrobostov p. 58 (bottom); Dorling Kindersley p. 55 (bottom); kpzfoto p. 46 (top); Josef Kubes p. 46 (bottom); Andrew Lockie p. 2; Lordprice Collection p. 3 (top left & top middle); Marcin Marszal p. 52 (bottom); Steven McAuley p. 13 (top); David L. Moore—ISL p. 75 (top); Jeff Morgan 11 p. 40 (bottom left); Niday Picture Library p. 39 (bottom); Nordicphotos pp. 66–67 (background); OlegMit p. 63; PA Images p. 15 (top); Panther Media GmbH p. 22 (bottom); Massimo Parisi p. 41 (top middle); Amir Paz p. 65 (bottom); Photononstop p. 21 (bottom); PicoCreek p. 69; Pictorial Press Ltd pp. 3 (top right), 11 (bottom); Picture Partners pp. 76 (bottom), 80 (middle right); Graham Prentice p. 8; Prisma by Dukas Presseagentur GmbH p. 5; Kay Roxby p. 14; Russell p. 6 (bottom left); Neil Setchfield p. 9; Dmytro Synelnychenko p. 67 (bottom left); The Advertising Archives p. 41 (bottom left); Marc Tielemans p. 1; Trinity Mirror/Mirrorpix p. 19; Lillian Tveit p. 79 (left); unknown 56–57 (background); Martin Williams p. 10 (top left); Naci Yavuz (fogbird) p. 66 (top); Michael Zech p. 71; ZUMA Press, Inc. pp. 27 (bottom), 74 (bottom); Yurii Zushchyk p. 61 (right). **Can Stock Photo:** Olga Berlet p. 22 (top); drstokvektor p. 57 (top); santi0103 p. 28. **Dreamstime:** Lenutaidi p. 54 (top); Aleksandra Suzi p. 68 (top). **Getty Images:** Franco Banfi/WaterFrame

p. 31; Bettmann/Contributor p. 48 (top); coldsnowstorm/iStock p. 53 (bottom left); Denis Doyle/Getty Images News p. 44 (top); Denis Doyle/Stringer p. 18; Alexander Farnsworth/iStock p. 75 (bottom left); Katie Garrod/AWL Images p. 53 (top); Dorling Kindersley p. 56 (top); Peter Lewis/Stone p. 7; Xurxo Lobato/Getty Images News p. 43; Pronina_Marina/iStock p. 53 (bottom right); New York Daily News Archive/Contributor p. 24; Stefano Oppo/Cultura Exclusive/Publisher Mix p. 29; photovs/iStock p. 51; Yelena Strokin/Moment Open p. 59; SVF2/Universal Images Group p. 55 (top); vandervelden/iStock Unreleased p. 66 (bottom right); Alvaro German Vilela p. 32 (bottom); Horacio Villalobos/Corbis News p. 40 (bottom right); Peter Williams p. 6 (bottom right). **Shutterstock.com:** Ismael Silva Alves p. 38 (top); Anna_Andre p. 47; bonchan p. 38 (bottom); Bruno Tatiana Chekryzhova p. 41 (bottom right); Formatoriginal p. 39 (top); Tatiana Gasich p. 60 (bottom); Toni Genes p. 40 (bottom right above); Dimitris Legakis p. 80 (bottom); Hanna Loban p. 62 (bottom); Natalia Mylova p. 37; nelen p. 49; Korea Panda p. 75 (middle); ronstik p. 57 (middle).

Wikimedia Commons: The following images are used under a Creative Commons Attribution CC BY-SA 4.0 License (https://csreativecommons.org/licenses/by-sa/4.0/deed.en) and belong to the following Wikimedia Commons users: Cholbon p. 60 (top); Raimond Spekking p. 68 (bottom); Sergei Frolov p 54 (bottom). The following image is used under a Creative Commons Attribution CC BY-SA 3.0 (https://creativecommons.org/licenses/by-sa/3.0/deed.en) and belongs to the following Wikimedia Commons user: Holger Ellgaard p. 78. **Public Domain:** pp. 13 (bottom), 23 (bottom).

Courtesy of Atlas Obscura Contributors:
Jennifer Adhya p. 42 (bottom); Anja Bbarte Telin, Produktionskollektivet p. 80 (top right); HaliPuu p. 69 (top); Capemarsh p. 4; Deutsches Zusatzstoff Museum p. 80 (middle left); Finnmark Sauna/finnmarksauna.com p. 65 (top); Lisa Harvey p. 27 (top left and top right); Frank Schuiling p. 36 (top and bottom); Jesse Miers/Jessemiers p. 10 (top right); Andrea Fernández @lvfoodgasm p. 75 (bottom right); Emiliano Ruprah p. 30; Karl De Smedt p. 17 (bottom); Starkenberger p. 17 (top); Trinenp23 p. 64.

ASIA

Adobe Stock: milosk50 p. 99. **Alamy:** agefotostock p.158 (top); Kiekowski Anton/Hemis Fr. p. 161; Burhan Ay p. 110; Walter Bibikow/Danita Delimont Creative p. 95 (top right); Frank Bienewald pp. 102–103 (spread); Nattanai Chimjanon p. 148; Chronicle p. 137 (bottom); Robert Cicchetti p. 154; Zaneta Cichawa p. 115; Iconic Cornwall p. 125 (top); Samantha Crimmin p. 127; Dar1930/Panther Media GmbH p. 157 (bottom); Michele Falzone/Jon Arnold Images Ltd p. 93; Oleg Fedotov p. 84 (top); Guenter Fischer/Alamy Stock Photo p. 95 (top left); Fotosearch/Unlisted Images Inc. p. 131 (bottom); Stephen Frost p. 121 (top); Biswarup Ganguly p. 90 (top right); Rania Hamed p. 91 (top); Hemis pp. 113, 125 (bottom); Historic Collection p. 162 (bottom); Historical image collection by Bildagentur-online p. 87 (bottom); Jim Hubatka p. 101 (top); Janny2 p. 91 (bottom); Peter

Group Editorial pp. 332 (top right), 333 (waitress); Dirck Halstead/The LIFE Images Collection p. 345; Historical Picture Archive/Corbis Historical p. 290 (bottom); Phil Huber/Sports Illustrated p. 314; Layne Kennedy/Corbis NX p. 294 (bottom); Kohjiro Kinno/Sports Illustrated p. 317; Robert Landau/Corbis Historical p. 298; John Preito/Denver Post p. 333 (b/w); Joe Raedle/Hulton Archive p. 283; George Rinhart/Corbis Historical p. 308; Chip Somodevilla/Staff p. 303 (bottom); The Washington Post p. 320 (bottom); University of Southern California/ Corbis Historical p. 327. **Shutterstock.com:** Stephen Albi p. 306; Dan4Earth p. 272 (top left); Keith Homan p. 325 (top) Purplexsu p. 282; tishomir p. 268. **The Pocahontas County Chamber of Commerce:** The Pocahontas County Chamber of Commerce p. 340 (top).

Wikimedia Commons: The following images are used under a Creative Commons Attribution CC BY 2.0 (https://creativecommons.org/licenses/by/2.0/deed.en) and belong to the following Wikimedia Commons users: CGP Grey p. 297; Diçdoco p. 322 (bottom); K. Shuyler p. 275 (middle). **Public Domain:** Boston Public Library p. 344 (bottom).

Courtesy of Atlas Obscura Contributors: Patrick Lehnherr p. 312 (bottom); Auntie_Nadine p. 278 (top); Big Cedar Lodge p. 307; makam-'ham/Cafe Ohlone p. 270 (top); Chin Brothers LLC p. 300; Michael Clifton Tran@cliftontran_ p. 342 (top); Spencer Darr/ spencerdarr.com p. 284 (bottom); Dani Bittner p. 280; Jennifer Souers Chevraux p. 284 (top); Door County Visitor Bureau p. 310 (bottom right); Downstream Casino Resort p. 296 (top); Jon Hauge p. 311; Rick Heineman and Washington Island History p. 310 (top); Farrell Parker, D.C.-based artist p. 337 (bottom left); Mike Mehlhorn p. 344 (top); WhiskeyBristles p. 282 (inset); Pam Jarrin p. 341; Scott Sommerdorf/San Francisco Chronicle/Polaris p. 269; Stephanie Eng p. 337 (bottom right); Teakwoods p. 339.

LATIN AMERICA
AGE fotostock america, Inc: Eric Lafforgue p. 365; Helene Rogers/Art Directors & Trips Photo p. 374 (top). **Alamy:** 19th era 2 p. 353 (middle right); AGB Photo Library p. 349; Album p. 354; Antiqua Print Gallery p. 389 (bottom); Jennika Argent p. 384 (top); Lee Avison p. 361 (top); Suzanne Bosman p. 380; Marc Bruxelle p. 375 (top); Olena Danileiko p. 386 (bottom right); dbimages p. 379 (bottom); Adam Eastland p. 367 (bottom); Foto Arena LTDA p. 385 (bottom); Tim Gainey p. 392; Nicholas Gill p. 396; Vladislav Gudovskiy p. 363 (bottom); Hemis p. 364 (bottom); Andrii Hrytsenko p. 353 (bottom left); Tommy Huynh p. 367 (top left); Iconotec p. 369 (top); Idea studio pp. 402–403 (Background and inset); JG Photography p. 359 (top); Jesse Kraft p. 403 (top); Jason Langley p. 400; Y.Levy p. 404; Lordprice Collection p. 367 (top right); Tatsiana Mastabai p. 364 (top); Anamaria Mejia p. 401 (top); Cathyrose Melloan p. 356; Raquel Mogado p. 376 (bottom left); Carlos Mora p. 399; MsFong/ Stockimo p. 382; National Geographic Image Collection p. 402 (top); Nature Photographers Ltd p. 352 (bottom right); olneystudio p. 359 (bottom); Panther Media GmbH p. 387 (middle left); Pulsar Imagens p. 387 (top);

Ievgen Radchenko p. 381 (top); Simon Reddy p. 378; Ewart Rennalls p. 372 (top); Ed Rooney p. 358 (top); Andriy Sarymsakov p. 387 (bottom right); Wei Seah p. 363 (bottom); Neil Setchfield p. 355; Anton Starikov p. 371 (top); Kyoko Uchida p. 377 (bottom right); Wisnu Haryo Yudhanto p. 377 (top). **Can Stock Photo:** anatolir p. 371 (bottom); buriy p. 372 (bottom); Danler p. 366 (top); ican pp. 376–377 (background); nebojsa78 p. 395; stargatechris p. 371 (pepper). **Dreamstime:** Adolfolazo p. 361 (bottom); Jaboticaba Fotos p. 390 (middle). **Getty Images:** bonchan/iStock p. 393 (top); John Bulmer/Popperfoto p. 383; dexph119_066 p. 376 (middle); Donyanedomam/iStock p. 368; GI15702993/ iStock p. 377 (bottom left); Hermsdorf/iStock p. 366 (bottom); jmillard37/iStock p. 401 (bottom); George Kalaouzis/Moment p. 384 (bottom); Dorling Kindersley p. 377 (middle); MCT/Tribune News Service p. 350; Luiz Henrique Mendes/iStock p. 390 (bottom right); Eiichi Onodera/Emi Kimata p. 376 (top); Layla Pujol/500px p. 397 (top); Jaime Razuri/AFP p. 398 (bottom); rchphoto/iStock p. 403 (middle) Alex Robinson/AWL Images p. 388; Danilo Saltarelli/iStock p. 390 (bottom left); ToprakBeyBetmen/iStock p. 393 (bottom); ullstein bild Dtl. P. 394 (bottom); Iara Venanzi/DigitalVision p. 386 (bottom left). **Shutterstock.com:** 365FOOD p. 376 (bottom right); Larisa Blinova p. 394 (top); Chai Chaiyo p. 353 (bottom right); FINNARIO p. 371 (top); Erika Kirkpatrick p. 353 (top left); Re Metau p. 369 (bottom); MicroOne p. 360 (top); Moriz p. 352 (bottom left); photomaster p. 405 (top); Pictures_for_You p. 352(top); pixpenart p. 353 (bottom middle); rukxstockphoto p. 352 (bottom middle); Anny Ta p. 391 (top).

Wikimedia Commons: The following image is used under a Creative Commons Attribution CC BY-SA 2.0 License (https://creativecommons.org/licenses/by-sa/2.0/) and belongs to the following Wikimedia Commons user: penelope_134 p.381 (bottom). The following image is used under a Creative Commons Attribution CC BY-SA 4.0 License (https://csreativecommons.org/licenses /by-sa/4.0/deed.en) and belongs to the following Wikimedia Commons user: Koen Adams p. 401. **Public Domain**: gallerix.ru p. 363 (top).

Courtesy of Atlas Obscura Contributors: Andrew Reilly p. 375 (bottom); Danielle Bauter p. 385 (top); brunomichauxvignes p. 370 (top and bottom); Tony Dunnell p. 398 (top); Samantha O'Brien p. 351; Tastee Cheese p. 374 (bottom).

ANTARCTICA
Alamy: Imaginechina Limited p. 408 (top); Terence Mendoza pp. 410–411 (spread); Niebrugge Images p. 407; B.O'Kane p. 410 (inset); David Parker p. 409; Science History Images p. 408 (bottom); Graeme Snow pp. 408–409 (background).

Wikimedia Commons: The following images are used under a Creative Commons Attribution CC BY-SA 4.0. (https://creativecommons.org/licenses/by-sa/4.0) and belongs to the following Wikimedia Commons user: Σρτ p. 409.

INDEX

ABOUT THE AUTHORS

CECILY WONG is a writer for Atlas Obscura and the author of two novels. Her debut, *Diamond Head*, was a Barnes and Noble Discover Great New Writers Selection, received an *Elle* Readers' Prize, and was voted a best debut of the 2015 Brooklyn Book Festival. Her second novel, *Kaleidoscope*, will be published in 2022. Her work has appeared in the *Wall Street Journal*, the *LA Review of Books*, *Self* magazine, Bustle, Atlas Obscura, and elsewhere. She lives in Portland, Oregon, with her husband and daughter.

DYLAN THURAS is the cofounder and creative director of Atlas Obscura. Coauthor of the #1 *New York Times* bestseller *Atlas Obscura: An Explorer's Guide to the World's Hidden Wonders* and the *New York Times* bestselling kids' book *An Explorer's Guide for the World's Most Adventurous Kid*, he is also the host of the *Atlas Obscura* podcast. He lives in New York State's Hudson Valley with his family. Visit him online at @dylanthuras.

ABOUT GASTRO OBSCURA

Gastro Obscura's mission is to inspire wonder and curiosity about the world through food and drink. Launched in 2017 as part of the travel and media company Atlas Obscura, our articles, videos, recipes, and global guide to places to eat and drink, as well as the experiences and trips we run around the world, allow readers, travelers, and curious people to explore what food and drink reveal about the places where they're made and the people who make them.

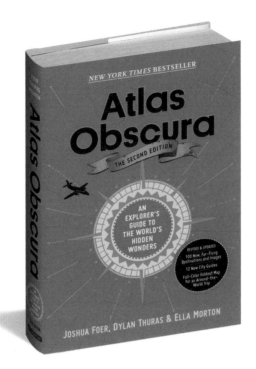

"A wanderlust-whetting cabinet of curiosities."

—*The New York Times*

The #1 bestselling travel book that changes the way we think about the world, expanding our sense of how strange and marvelous it really is. With its compelling descriptions, hundreds of photographs, surprising charts, maps for every region of the world, and city guides, *Atlas Obscura* is a book that you can open anywhere and be instantly transported.

Let your curiosity be your compass.

Available wherever books are sold, or visit workman.com